TREASURES OF
Alberta

Emerald Lake, Yoho National Park
Photo by James Koole

by William Faubion
and Mark S. Zurba

a part of the Morgan & Chase Treasure Series
www.treasuresof.com

MORGAN & CHASE PUBLISHING INC.

THE TREASURE SERIES

Morgan & Chase Publishing, Inc.
531 Parsons Drive, Medford, Oregon 97501
(888) 557-9328
www.treasuresof.com

Printed and bound by Taylor Specialty Books–Dallas TX
First edition 2007
ISBN: 978-1-933989-24-2

I gratefully acknowledge the contributions
of the many people involved in the writing and production of this book.
Their tireless dedication to this endeavour has been inspirational.
–Damon Neal, *Publisher*

The Morgan & Chase Publishing Home Team

Operations Department:
 V.P. of Operations–Cindy Tilley Faubion
 Travel Writer Liaison–Anne Boydston
 Shipping & Receiving–Virginia Arias
 Human Resources Coordinator–Heather Allen
 Customer Service Relations–Marie Manson, Elizabeth Taylor, Vikki West
 IT Engineer–Ray Ackerman
 Receptionist–Samara Sharp

Production Department:
 Office Manager–Sue Buda
 Editor/Writer–Robyn Sutherland
 House Writer–Prairie Smallwood
 Proof Editor–Clarice Rodriguez
 Photo Coordinator–Wendy L. Gay
 Photo Editor–Mary Murdock
 Graphic Design Team–C.S. Rowan, Jesse Gifford, Tamara Cornett, Jacob Kristof

Administrative Department:
 CFO–Emily Wilkie
 Accounting Assistants–David Grundvig, Tiffany Myers
 Website Designer–Molly Bermea
 Website Software Developer–Ben Ford

Contributing Writers:
 Mary Beth Lee, Ronald Seniuk, Catherine Wright, Darryn Young, Dusty Alexander,
 Jeanie Erwin, Karuna Glomb, Kate Zdrojewski, Louis F. Pierotti, Marek Alday,
 Mary Knepp, Maya Moore, Patricia Smith, Paul Hadella, Sandy McLain, Sarah Brown,
 Timothy Smith, Todd Wels, Tamara Cornett

Special Recognition to:
 Casey Faubion, April Higginbotham, Gregory Scott, Megan Glomb, Eric Molinsky, Gene Mitts

We dedicate this book to the magnificent geography and cultural diversity of the province, and most of all to the people who call Alberta home.

Foreword

Welcome to *Treasures of Alberta*. This book is a resource that can guide you to some of the best places in Alberta, one of Canada's prairie provinces. Alberta is one of two land-locked provinces, and directly to its south is the U.S. state of Montana. Western Alberta is well known for its milder temperatures mainly due to the surrounding mountains and winter Chinook winds.

While home to the world-famous Calgary Stampede, better known as the greatest outdoor show on earth, and international sporting events such as the Olympic Games, Calgary is also known for grain production, ranching, and dairy farming. While considering which popular activities you wish to pursue, remember Alberta is a well-known photographer's paradise. Whether you choose to visit the expanse of Banff National Park or see the exciting streets of Edmonton, this province has everything to make your visit complete.

From the beginning of this project we were blessed to see incredible works of art and explore communities that were so much more than just a place to visit. Whether you are a world traveller or you have spent your entire life in Alberta, you will find people and places in this book that will both inspire and interest you. The idea for the Treasure Series of books was created over 20 years ago by entrepreneurs who were both raised in family-owned businesses. Today they oversee overall book quality and help maintain the high selection standards for the Treasures who are featured within the Treasure Series books.

In preparing the *Treasures of Alberta* we talked to literally thousands of business people about their products, their services and their vision. We reveled in the beauty of Jasper National Park and the incredible views along the Icefields Parkway. We visited historic Bonnyville and watched buffalo and Bighorn sheep make their way across the Rocky Mountain areas. We tried local dishes throughout the province and were shown incredible art work in Lethbridge. You are holding the result of our efforts in your hands. *Treasures of Alberta* is a 417-page compilation of the best places Alberta has to eat, shop, play, explore, learn and relax. We had the privilege of seeing all the people and places this book is about. All you have to do now is to enjoy the result of our efforts.

—Cindy Tilley Faubion

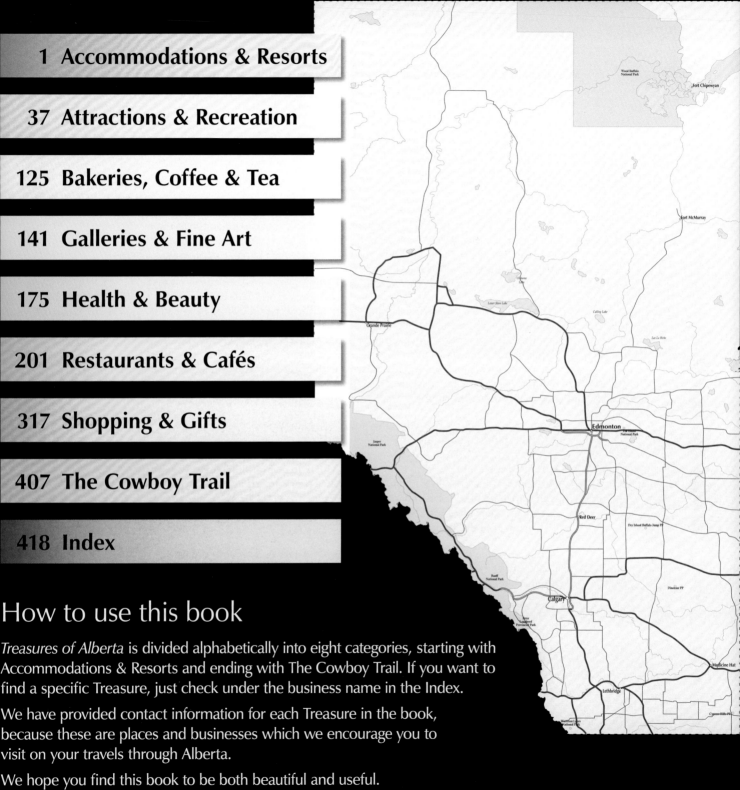

How to use this book

Treasures of Alberta is divided alphabetically into eight categories, starting with Accommodations & Resorts and ending with The Cowboy Trail. If you want to find a specific Treasure, just check under the business name in the Index.

We have provided contact information for each Treasure in the book, because these are places and businesses which we encourage you to visit on your travels through Alberta.

We hope you find this book to be both beautiful and useful.

Accommodations & Resorts

Mount Robson Inn

Being in the glorious Canadian Rockies makes some people think of romance, some of adventure. The Mount Robson Inn in Jasper National Park offers a wide range of room styles to accommodate any type of holiday. You'll love the spectacular view of the south and east valleys from the plush Patricia Suite, your room when you choose the Honeymoon Package. The suite comes with a king-size bed and features a separate sitting room with fireplace and Jacuzzi. Bring your chair right up to the window as you pop the cork on your complimentary bottle of champagne and nibble the goodies in your gift basket. The Romance Jasper package offers the same benefits with a stay in the Sunwapta Suite, featuring a Jacuzzi and deluxe bathroom with heated floors and a body massage shower. The adventure seeker will love our two outdoor whirlpools as well as free storage for mountain bikes, skis and snowboards. Families will feel at home in the family suite, with its separate kids bedrooms featuring bunk bends, a large screen television and gaming console. Mount Robson Inn has been family-owned and operated since 1973. A Jasper landmark, it offers first class amenities and rooms which are continually updated and renovated to meet its customer's ever-changing needs. The on-site Mount Robson Steakhouse serves breakfast and dinner. Come to Jasper for romance or adventure and let the Mount Robson Inn provide your fantasy vacation.

902 Connaught Drive, Jasper AB
(780) 852-3327 or (800) 587-3327
www.mountrobsoninn.com

A Banff Boutique Inn

Travelers looking for a peaceful, luxurious place to enjoy Banff will find A Banff Boutique Inn's Pensión Tannenhof an absolute delight. *Pensión Tannenhof* translates as "lodge in the pine trees," which is entirely appropriate, given the beautiful mountain and forest views available in every room at this inn. The beautiful, rustic, English-style mansion was built in 1942 as a single-family dwelling. Lee and Becky O'Donnel have owned the home since 2006. Guests here have all the privacy and luxury of a hotel, combined with the warmth of a home. Each of Pensión Tannenhof's 10 rooms has its own unique ambiance. Hosting up to 30 guests at a time, the inn is an ideal location to hold weddings, receptions and other special events. Pensión Tannenhof is a prime location for taking advantage of everything the Rocky Mountains have to offer, from cross country skiing to hiking and mountain biking. The inn is just minutes away from the Cascade Gardens and other Banff attractions. If you're looking for a cozy place to stay or hold a special event in the Rockies, visit A Banff Boutique Inn's Pensión Tannenhof.

121 Cave Avenue, Banff AB
(403) 762-4636
www.banffboutiqueinn.com

Hotel Arts

True to its name, the chic new Hotel Arts presents a decidedly avant-garde image to complement the growing sophistication of Calgary's Midtown. Located just steps from the city center, the hotel balances a contemporary urban feel with four-star luxuries. Its rigorously designed interior is decked in contemporary art pieces, from the flatware to the ceiling. A brainchild of visionary developer John Torode, Hotel Arts is managed by Calgary native Mark Wilson. The hotel's 12 floors of luxury rooms include several specialty suite options. The Luxury Suites include a sitting area with a pull-out sofa, plasma television, wet bar and marble bathroom. Luxury Jacuzzi Suites incorporate a spacious Italian Carrera marble washroom with a 52-jet two-person Jacuzzi. The Pool Suites feature spacious baths with two-person spa rain and steam showers as well as private balconies overlooking the pool. The pool, spruced up with oversized planters, has been featured in photo shoots and movies. On the poolside patio, the hotel's Raw Bar serves drinks and Pacific Rim-inspired seafood dishes in a cabana-style setting. The indoor Saint Germain is an award winning French bistro. Hotel Arts courts business conventions and special events with specialized services and event spaces. In 2008, the hotel will unveil the new Arts Complex, featuring a three-story retail and office complex and a 6,000-square-foot ballroom. To join the wave of the Calgary future, book your stay at Hotel Arts.

119 12 Avenue SW, Calgary AB (403) 266-4611 *www.hotelarts.ca*

The Athabasca Hotel

In 1928, the road between Edmonton and Jasper was finally complete. A three-story brick hotel on the corner of Patricia and Miette Streets in Jasper brought its own autos to the railway station to pick up guests and whisk them away to unexpected luxury in this pioneer town. Today, the site is home to the renovated Athabasca Hotel, a luxurious boutique hotel with 60 guest rooms that feature high ceilings, heritage mouldings and richly coloured bedspreads and coverings. The classic antique furniture includes brass beds. Executive suites come with big-screen televisions, kitchenettes and balconies. The hotel, affectionately called the Atha-B for several decades by tourists and locals, has attracted many celebrities, including Marilyn Monroe, who stayed at the Atha-B during the making of *River of No Return*. Today's guests dine in the O'Shea's dining room and take in their favourite sporting event on plasma televisions in O'Shea's lounge. If you feel like kicking up your heels, you will find either DJ-driven or live music at the Atha-B nightclub. The trophy room features billiards beneath mounted wildlife heads from 1910. The Atha-B, a haven of nostalgic charm and modern amenities, is just minutes away from calm lakes, wild rapids, ice walks, skiing, snowboarding and hiking. You can expect stellar service from the long-term staff. They are knowledgeable about the area and can give advise on activities for one person or a large group of people. Revel in Jasper's pioneer past at the Athabasca Hotel.

510 Patricia Street, Jasper AB
(780) 852-3386 or (877) 542-8422
www.athabascahotel.com

The Inn and Spa at Heartwood

In the heart of the Canadian Badlands, the Inn and Spa at Heartwood is more than simply a place to stay; the non-smoking, pet friendly Heartwood is a place for rest and rejuvenation. This Inn is a heritage structure over 90 years old that has been beautifully refurbished by new owners Patrice and Zeke Wolf. Their appreciation of fine art is evident as the entire Inn has a gallery atmosphere with original artwork throughout. Zeke is known for his gourmet breakfasts and tantalizing cuisine at catered events. The warmth from the main floor fireplace entices one to linger awhile in cozy, comfortable surroundings. Well appointed guest rooms are air-conditioned and most have oversized jetted tubs and fireplaces. The Inn property also includes a Hideaway Cottage and the Chancel Guest House that sleeps six and is ideal for spa parties. The Inn also has a meeting room with wireless Internet and can accommodate up to 30 people. The Spa at Heartwood is on the upper level of the Inn. Immerse yourself in the pleasures of the Spa's aesthetic services—manicures, pedicures, therapeutic soaks, invigorating exfoliations, wraps and the signature facials. Feel your stress melting away under the expert touch of their registered massage therapists. As they say, the Inn and Spa at Heartwood is not simply a place to stay. Make spa treatments a part of your next corporate retreat. Your staff will love you.

320 N Railway Avenue E, Drumheller AB
(403) 823-6495 or (888) 823-6495
www.innsatheartwood.com

Deer Valley Bed & Breakfast

When you close your eyes and picture your dream home, what do you see? If it's a home in the woods, then you'll love staying at the Deer Valley Bed & Breakfast. Since 2002, owners Rob and Alana have been welcoming dreamers into their log and cedar residence nestled in the trees. Their gift for hospitality in addition to beautiful lodgings and a tranquil setting have earned the Deer Valley Bed & Breakfast a four-star rating from the Alberta Hotel & Lodging Association. Whether guests stay in one of the two rooms or the private cottage, they feel perfectly at ease in the fluffy robes and slippers provided here. Couples seeking a romantic honeymoon or anniversary getaway find just the warm and pampering experience they are looking for here, beginning with the ultra-therapy spa bath in their room. Fitness packages, another specialty, take advantage of Alana's skills as a certified personal trainer. She is happy to show any guest how to use the treadmill and strength equipment and to consult with him or her regarding fitness and nutrition goals. In the morning lodgers wake to a selection of scrumptious breakfast choices served at their leisure. Make Deer Valley Bed & Breakfast your choice for a dreamy four-star experience in the woods. It is wheelchair accessible and located on a private acreage five minutes from town and one hour from Calgary or Red Deer.

215 6 Avenue NE, Sundre AB
(403) 638-3448
www.deervalleyalberta.com

Calgary Westways Bed & Breakfast

At Calgary Westways Bed & Breakfast, such amenities as hair dryers, cable television and high-speed Internet will remind you of a top hotel, but the intimacy and ambience are definitely that of a refined home. Guests are treated to luxurious robes and mattresses while lodging in spacious rooms that come with jetted tubs and gas fireplaces. The 1912 Edwardian home is a charmer with such original features as built-in glass cabinets and box beam ceilings. Persian carpets adorn the hardwood floors. Guests enjoy hearty breakfasts on fine bone china and cut crystal. You can walk to city centre from this stylish neighbourhood that offers shops, restaurants and crafts stores. Since the inn is close to the Saddledome, your hosts Jonathon Lloyd and Graham McKay offer Calgary Flames hockey specials here. They offer a romance package, too, which includes a five-course meal. You can order a Rolls Royce to pick you up. If you are driving your own vehicle, you can park for free. Your hosts also provide free coffee, tea and bottled water in a pantry area equipped with a fridge and microwave. You can count on high standards of cleanliness at Calgary Westways, the only Calgary bed and breakfast inspected and approved by AAA, Canada Select and Western Canada Bed & Breakfast Innkeepers Association. Visit Calgary Westways Bed & Breakfast expecting excellence and leave looking forward to your next visit.

216–25 Avenue SW, Calgary AB
(403) 229-1758 or (866) 846-7038
www.westways.ab.ca

Treutler's Resort Bed & Breakfast

Treutler's Resort Bed & Breakfast is Banff's only five-star bed-and-breakfast. This Mediterranean-style villa provides spectacular views, plus lovely antique furnishings, an indoor pool and spacious rooms. Owners Ossi and Freya Treutler, world travellers themselves, excel in the art of making you feel at home. A stay at this bed and breakfast is a truly luxurious and romantic experience. As you enter, the crystal chandelier, curved wooden staircase and Oriental rugs over polished wood flooring are just the beginning. The magnificent dining room is appointed with European antique furniture, wood flooring and artful accessories. A delicious full breakfast is served daily. Children are welcome at this inn. The large guest rooms are elegant and comfortable. Once you've settled in, take a dip in the glassed-in sunroom pool, which

offers breathtaking year-round views of Banff National Park. Freya and Ossi are happy to help you discover Banff. You're just minutes away from skiing, fishing and hiking. Browse the many shops, go antiquing or just see the sights. Golfing and biking are other popular activities. Freya and Ossi revel in the opportunity to keep in touch with their guests. A visit to Treutler's Resort Bed and Breakfast is a magical experience you won't soon forget.

608 Wolf Street, Banff AB
(403) 762-3798 or (403) 762-4652
www.treutlersresortbb.ca

The Wee Scottish Inn

There is nothing wee about the view from the backyard of The Wee Scottish Inn. The mountains loom in all their glory, and when the sky fills with stars at night, the feeling is magnificent. The

Wee Scottish Inn offers just one suite with a queen bed, futon, sitting area and kitchenette. Guests receive a voucher for breakfast at the nearby Bear's Paw Bakery, where they can choose from fresh muffins and pastries or the popular breakfast sandwich while experiencing a little bit of the community. People return again and again to The Wee Scottish Inn whenever their travels take them through Jasper. They enjoy being the only guests on the premises and all the privileges that this entails, including a private entrance and bath. The bright, spacious suite at main level becomes as familiar to them as a second home. Enjoy total privacy in which to count the stars at The Wee Scottish Inn.

1101 Patricia Crescent, Jasper AB
(780) 852-8309 or (780) 852-3747
www.bbcanada.com/theweescottishinn

The Fairmont Hotel Macdonald

When you step through the doors into the historic Fairmont Hotel Macdonald, you are no longer merely a traveler or tourist. You are royalty, and your reign has just begun. Enjoy one of the special packages and let the Fairmont take care of the details. This beautiful French chateau has been part of the Edmonton cityscape since 1915 and overlooks the North Saskatchewan River valley. There are 199 beautifully appointed guestrooms on eight floors, each elegantly decorated and equipped with state-of–the-art amenities such as high-speed Internet. Guests also have access to the Macdonald Health Club, a full-service fitness facility. Get a great workout on the resistance and cardio equipment, or swim in the 40-foot saline pool then relax in the sauna. Enjoy everything from fine dining to family meals or afternoon tea at the hotel's restaurant, the Harvest Room. You will enjoy the house-made soups, delicious entrées and superb service. The Fairmont is the perfect choice if you are planning a meeting, conference, wedding or any special event. The hotel offers a wide range of function rooms, from elegant and high tech board rooms to magnificent ball rooms in which every detail has been thoughtfully considered. Make plans to visit the Fairmont Hotel Macdonald and experience luxury and service that few can match.

10065-100 Street, Edmonton AB
(780) 424-5181
www.fairmont.com/macdonald

Varscona Hotel on Whyte

The Varscona Hotel on Whyte combines the amenities of a world-class hotel with the care and comfort of a cozy bed-and-breakfast. Located in the Old Strathcona district of Edmonton, the hotel offers 89 guest rooms and suites to choose from with something for every kind of traveler. Business travelers will delight in the executive suites, outfitted with high-speed Internet access and other amenities. Comfort is foremost here, with luxury mattresses, plush robes, and a morning paper delivered each morning. Continental breakfast and an evening wine and cheese hour are also complimentary. Under the hotel roof, you'll find a gourmet espresso bar and an old fashioned Irish pub. Murrieta's Bar and Grill makes a succulent swordfish entrée. The Varscona and all its facilities are 100 percent smoke-free. If you're looking for a place to hold a meeting, the hotel offers six meeting rooms fully outfitted with both creature comforts and the latest technology. The Varscona can even cater meals for all of your associates. The banquet room is an ideal place to hold a wedding or other event. The Varscona is conveniently located near a variety of Edmonton attractions, including the University of Alberta. If you're looking for excellent accommodations in Edmonton, come to the Varscona Hotel on Whyte.

8208-106 Street, Edmonton AB
(780) 434-6111
www.varscona.com

Mount Royal Hotel

The Mount Royal Hotel is located in the heart of downtown Banff, though some would go further and say that it is the heart of downtown. Since 1908, the Mount Royal has stood on the corner of Banff Avenue and Caribou Street. The original red brick structure boasted 60 guest rooms beneath its turreted lead roof. The spacious dining room, billiard room and cocktail lounge were welcome sights to weary CP Rail travelers. They were also the last trappings of civilization that adventurers enjoyed before setting off on guided backcountry treks in the Canadian Rockies. Today, the hotel still fills with visitors drawn to the area by the natural beauty of Banff National Park. Its 135 guest rooms are fitted with all the modern amenities. Three suites—the Brewster, Pinnacle and Presidential—offer deluxe accommodations. For refreshment, there's a Tony Roma's restaurant and the Buffalo Paddock Lounge and Pub. Relax in the sauna or enjoy a soak in the whirlpool between sightseeing in and around Banff. Special events are in store for 2008, when the hotel celebrates its 100th birthday. Make your stay in Banff extra special by choosing the Mount Royal Hotel.

138 Banff Avenue, Banff AB (877) 442-2623
www.mountroyalhotel.com

Hotel Selkirk

In the early part of the 20th century, the Hotel Selkirk, now located in Fort Edmonton Park, was Edmonton's number one society spot, a place to see and be seen in every sense of the word. The historic hotel was destroyed by a tragic fire in 1962, but has since been marvelously rebuilt to incorporate a sleek combination of old world elegance and modern comforts. Hotel Selkirk is a seasonal hotel, open May through September, which offers 30 handsomely restored guest rooms and suites. Each is tastefully decorated with antiques and reproduction pieces. Modern amenities include wireless Internet, in-room temperature control and private bathrooms. Johnson's Café, in the hotel, features an elegant 1920s motif, an exemplary wait staff and an array of delectable entrées. Hotel Selkirk's Mahogany Room, once known as Canada's longest bar, has been masterfully designed with sumptuous architectural details and a rich décor that closely replicates the bar's original, pre-fire look. This is an ideal place to unwind in the evening with friends while enjoying a sampling from the exclusive wine list or sipping some of the bar's exceptional spirits. In addition to offering excellent accommodations, the hotel serves as a gathering place and events hall for community activities, such as weddings and holiday galas. Sign your name to the guest book and leave your mark in the annals of history at Hotel Selkirk, where the fusion of past and present will yield wonderful memories in the future.

1920s Street, Fort Edmonton Park, Edmonton AB (780) 496-7227 or (877) 496-7227 *www.hotelselkirk.com*

Banff Caribou Lodge and Spa

If you were to close your eyes and imagine the quintessential mountain lodge, wouldn't it have snow-capped peaks in the background? Wouldn't its architecture blend with the environment, relying on balance, rather than boldness, for its beauty? In fact, chances are that it would look a lot like the Banff Caribou Lodge. Even if you weren't staying in one of its 195 rooms, you would want to walk around the outside of this spectacular building and take pictures from many vantage points. The fact that you were a guest will become a source of pride for many years to come when you open your photo album and tell everyone about your Banff vacation. Hand-hewn logs accent the lobby. With a warm, crackling fire dancing in the massive fieldstone fireplace, the mood is absolutely enchanting. Choose between a standard or superior room, or go deluxe in a loft suite or Jacuzzi suite. All rooms feature high-speed Internet access, the Mountain Feather Beds and down duvets. Facilities include a heated underground parkade and an exercise room with a 35-person jetted hot pool and steam room. The on-site restaurant is the Keg Steakhouse & Bar. The lodge's Red Earth Spa offers a full menu of services, including body treatments, Vichy rain showers and facials. Downtown shops and restaurants are accessible via a pleasant 10-minute walk or by the complimentary evening shuttle service. For a picture-perfect stay in the Canadian Rockies, choose the Banff Caribou Lodge.

521 Banff Avenue, Banff AB
(403) 762-5887
www.banffcariboulodge.com

Chickadee Pines B&B

With spectacular views of the Three Sisters Mountains and the Bow Valley, the Chickadee Pines B&B is a sublime location for your next getaway. Owners Stan and Kathleen Niemiec created the lush gardens on the grounds from scratch, garnering both the Best Garden and Best Garden Feature awards in Canmore's 2006 *Communities in Bloom* competition. The two guest rooms and the two-bedroom suite are just as inviting as the gardens. They are decorated in warm earth and peach tones, with Scandinavian-style wood furnishings. Beds sport down duvets. Each room has a private bathroom. A guest lounge is furnished with Oriental rugs, comfy couches and plenty of pillows, and is well equipped for entertainment with satellite television, wireless Internet access, DVD and CD players, as well as books, games and trail maps of the area. Next to the lounge is a kitchenette, with a refrigerator, microwave, coffee maker, kettle and toaster. You can step out on a private covered patio where you can relax and savour views of the garden and the magnificent Canadian Rockies. Each morning, a delicious Continental breakfast is served, which you may enjoy in the dining room or in your quarters, as you prefer. A short walk brings you to Canmore's downtown specialty shops, galleries and restaurants. Put the Chickadee Pines B&B on your itinerary for a fabulous vacation.

9 Grotto Place, Canmore AB
(403) 609-9464 or (403) 763-3036
www.chickadeepines.ca

Union Bank Inn

Renaissance and rebirth aptly describe the Union Bank Inn, a modern Renaissance inn that offers incomparable luxury and gracious hospitality reminiscent of Europe's finest hotels. This historic 1911 Union Bank of Canada was the original occupancy of the splendid building that had its architectural rebirth in 1997. The stylish boutique hotel of today features 34 rooms and suites in two wings. Each room is handsomely furnished with an elegantly understated décor and comes with a variety of pampering touches, such as fireplaces, goosedown bedding and fleece robes. Additional complimentary services include in-room Internet access, an evening guest tray with a glass of wine, cheese plate and home-baked cookie, plus a full a la carte breakfast served each morning. Union Bank Inn can easily support corporate and private events, including retreats, weddings and awards ceremonies. The inn features several especially pleasing rooms for such occasions, including the Devonshire for boardroom meetings and the Giverny Ballroom on the upper level, perfect for receptions or large dinners. The hotel's Madison Grill, which also features the modern renaissance architecture found throughout the inn, offers a superior culinary experience provided by an award-winning Chef. Give new life to your next vacation with a stay at the Union Bank Inn.

10053 Jasper Avenue, Edmonton AB
(780) 423-3600
www.unionbankinn.com

Whistler's Inn

People come from all over the world to ski, hike and explore the ice fields at Jasper National Park. Centrally located within walking distance of all shops, attractions and mountain activities, Whistler's Inn offers a welcoming base for those excursions with homey comforts that only a boutique hotel can provide. The inn is one of the few locally-owned hotels in the town of Jasper. It was built in the 1930s, when the new railway first made Jasper a desirable vacation spot, and it was originally known as the Pyramid Hotel. Bruno Ritter and a local group of three business men partnered to reopen the hotel as Whistler's Inn in 1992. Renovated in 2000, it offers 64 spacious rooms decorated in warm colors and wood accents, many with breathtaking views of the surrounding Rockies. The *pièce de resistánce* is the two rooftop hot tubs with a view, and a steam room, an ideal way to end a day in the mountains. The Inn offers one restaurant accessed through the lobby and another one behind the hotel, two gift shops on the premises and the charming Whistle Stop Pub, where you'll find eight varieties of ale on tap. The inn is also home to the Den, Jasper's wildlife museum, which features local wildlife realistically displayed in life-like habitats. You'll find displays of each of the four regions of the province: mountain, prairie, aspen parkland and northern forest. Get close to grazing elk and caribou, cougars, black bears and cubs as you soak up the mountain ambience at Whistler's Inn.

105 Miette Avenue, Jasper AB (780) 852-3361 *www.whistlersinn.com*

Amethyst Lodge

A jewel in the heart of Jasper, the Amethyst Lodge is a warm and inviting retreat just a short walk from shopping, theatre, rail-bus station, the historical museum and the aquatic centre. In short, you'll find endless activities just outside your door. The lodge has 97 spacious and comfortable rooms and suites. Most rooms have balconies or patios that provide spectacular mountain views. You will enjoy a dip in one of the two outdoor hot tubs while taking in the amazing scenery around you. Enjoy excellent cuisine at Anthony's Restaurant, which features Mediterranean cuisine and local specialties that include Alberta steaks. You will also find chicken entrées and pastas along with your favourite comfort foods such as hamburgers and salads. Additionally, light snacks and dinner are available in the Mountain View Lounge. The lodge is also an ideal place for conventions, banquets and weddings. The Forest Room easily accommodates up to 200 people. The Amethyst Dining Room combines an elegant setting with professional service for smaller events. If you are planning an executive reception or other more intimate event, consider the Andrew and Signal suites. The catering service offers a wide range of menu selections, with breakfast lunch and dinner options, and staff can assist in all you your meeting needs. Visit the Amethyst Lodge and find everything you need for a fun and relaxing time.

200 Connaught Drive, Jasper AB
(780) 852-3394
www.mpljasper.com/hotels/amethyst_lodge

Lobstick Lodge

Nearly 200 years ago, pioneers in the Canadian Rockies marked trails and rendezvous points by cutting all but the top branches off trees. They called these markers lobsticks. Today, true to its name, the three-diamond Lobstick Lodge serves as a pleasant landmark and gathering place for travelers. Nestled below the pine forests of the Pyramid Bench, it offers 139 spacious rooms with two queen or king beds and a mini refrigerator. Kitchen suites add a separate kitchen and living room, a double sofa bed and dinnerware for six. Swim a few laps in the indoor pool or enjoy a relaxing soak in any of the three outdoor and two indoor hot tubs. Other facilities include a sauna, steam room and laundry room. The home-style Rocky Mountain cuisine at the lodge's Country Inn restaurant caters to families or anyone with a hearty appetite. A magnificent stone fireplace and outdoor patio are main draws at the Skyline Lounge, a Jasper favorite. The Lobstick Lodge is located four miles from Pyramid Lakes and Jasper Tramway, six miles from Jasper Park Golf Course and nine miles from Maligne Canyon. Pull off the trail and enjoy some rest, relaxation and Rocky Mountain dining at the Lobstick Lodge.

94 Geikie Street, Jasper AB
(780) 852-4431
www.mpljasper.com/hotels/lobstick_lodge

Marmot Lodge

Located on Jasper's main street and tucked into the evergreens of Jasper National Park, Marmot Lodge a popular nature retreat with skiers and tourists of the magnificent Canadian Rockies. The lodge is on the route of the ski bus that goes up to Marmot Basin as well as just a minute's drive to downtown Jasper. The attractive rooms and suites offer kitchen combinations to accommodate families and groups. Some include gas fireplaces and Jacuzzi tubs, while all guests enjoy a heated indoor pool, hot tub and sauna. After a day on the trails or the slopes, come home to the hotel's award-winning Embers Steakhouse. Consistently rated as one of Jasper's best places to dine, it features AAA Alberta beef, lamb chops and grilled seafood. Select something from the outstanding wine list while enjoying a view of the Rockies that will make you swoon. The Fireside Lounge offers cocktails and appetizers in an intimate fireside venue. For great value in a great location, try the Marmot Lodge.

86 Connaught Drive, Jasper AB
(780) 852-4471
www.mpljasper.com/hotels/marmot_lodge

Pocahontas Cabins

Situated at the base of the Miette Hot Springs Road on the Yellowhead Highway 16, just five minutes from the east gate of Jasper National Park, Pocahontas Cabins awaits the adventurer. Located outside the hustle and bustle of Jasper town, it is in an area that affords the peace and tranquility you deserve on your vacation. A marsh nearby is favored by migrating waterfowl both common and exotic. Where there's a marsh, you are sure to find moose, deer and elk, as well as an occasional mountain goat and black bear. Relax in one of the 42 well-appointed cabins or 15 cedar log motel units in a resort style setting. Recent renovations include 13 brand new cabins with gas fireplaces and kitchenettes that include microwave ovens. The site offers a souvenir shop, grocery and camping store, barbecue area, casual dining at Poco's Café and more. A large heated pool and a hot tub are a nice way to relax after your day in the outdoors. If you want to escape the ordinary, visit Pocahontas Cabins for your next vacation.

Yellowhead Highway (Highway 16), Jasper AB
(780) 866-3732 or (800) 843-3372
www.mpljasper.com/hotels/pocahontas_cabins

Pyramid Riding Stables

Nestled in the foothills of Pyramid Mountain just five minutes north of Jasper, Pyramid Riding Stables offers travelers the extraordinary opportunity to explore the scenic Rocky Mountains on horseback. You'll join qualified guides on circular trails through mountains, valleys and lakeshores on tours that last between an hour and a full day. A short trip takes you to the top of a bluff for a magnificent view of the Athabasca River Valley where three mountain ranges meet. Wildlife enthusiasts enjoy the two-hour excursion to Cottonwood Creek, home of beaver dams, waterfowl and abundant woodland life. A day trip through the scenic area of Cabin Lake includes a picnic lunch. Pyramid Riding Stables also provides an unforgettable way to see the town of Jasper. Just hail the open-air carriage and step aboard for a romantic ride through the streets. The Dine & Ride package offers a carriage or wagon ride around town between dinner at Embers Steakhouse and dessert at the Fireside Lounge, both located at Marmot Lodge (10 or more). Let horses lead you through the wonders of the Jasper region with a ride from Pyramid Riding Stables.

200 Connaught Drive, Jasper AB
(780) 852-RIDE (7433)
www.mpljasper.com/jasper/pyramid_riding

Ski Marmot Basin

Discover a winter paradise that not only takes your breath away but inspires lasting memories, a place where dry champagne powder falls from the heavens and views extend into infinity. Tucked away in Jasper National Park is the beautiful Marmot Basin ski area. Marmot Basin is home to 1,675 acres of skiing and snowboarding terrain, split evenly between beginner, intermediate and expert, making this mountain perfect for any level of skier or snowboarder. A laid back, uncrowded atmosphere is just one of the many reasons skiers and snowboarders return to Marmot Basin season after season. With no cues in the lift lines, skiers have lots of room to breathe and more time to enjoy the 3,000 vertical feet of skiing terrain. The resort is easy to navigate and allows the freedom to explore the mountain and discover, at your own pace, which runs to call your own. A total of 84 marked trails fill the mountain's three separate reaches, all of which afford spectacular views of the Canadian Rockies' vistas. Answer the call of the wild. Break free from the flock and ski Marmot Basin.

Marmot Basin, Jasper AB
(780) 852-3816 or (866) 952-3816
www.skiingjasper.com

Photo by D'Arcy Norman

Banff Inn

A true mountain beauty opened in the summer of 1993. In the years since, the Banff Inn has welcomed many guests from around the globe. Located within Banff National Park yet only minutes from downtown restaurants, shopping and nightlife, Banff Inn is ideal spot for your Canadian Rockies vacation. All rooms have individually controlled heating and air-conditioning, and most have balconies so that guests can enjoy the splendour of the Canadian Rockies from the comfort of their rooms. The rooms are modern and spacious, with colours that evoke warmth. Bi-level loft units are available with two beds on ground level and one upstairs. The beautiful honeymoon suites have fireplaces and whirlpools. A continental breakfast is served daily with fresh fruit, bagels, cereal, juices, tea and hot coffee. The centrally located sauna, eucalyptus steam room and large Jacuzzi whirlpool are great places to unwind after a day of sightseeing, skiing, hiking or other recreation. In the evening, you can relax in front of the fireplace in the smoke-free lounge with two large plasma televisions. The Banff Inn even has a newly renovated spa called the Uptown Spa that offers a wide range of services—hot stone massage, aromatherapy, wraps, facials, manicures and pedicures. For your next getaway, let the Banff Inn spoil you.

501 Banff Avenue, Banff AB (403) 762-8844 or (800) 667-1464 *www.banffinn.com*

Thea's House

This elegant boutique-style bed-and-breakfast inn is only a short walk from downtown Banff, yet it takes its guests far away in terms of restful comfort. This striking log and stone structure was designed with your comfort and privacy in mind, being that the guest accommodations are completely separate from the main residence of your hosts, Greg and Jami Christou. The second-floor guest rooms are luxurious and spacious, with dramatic vaulted ceilings, antique and custom-made furnishings as well as exquisite artwork. Each room features a king-size bed with goose down duvet and pillows, gas fireplace, sitting area, ensuite bathroom with jetted tub and a walkout balcony with stunning mountain views. Other standard amenities include an entertainment unit with cable television, DVD player and stereo, plus slippers and bathrobes. Guests are also provided with tea and coffee service, local calls, high-speed wireless Internet, fitness center passes and the use of mountain bikes, which are all complimentary. Breakfast service consists of a continental breakfast buffet, along with a different hot entrée provided each day. After breakfast you can retire to the guest lounge to relax, read the paper or plan your day while gazing out at Mount Norquay through the 25-foot floor-to-ceiling windows. Thea's House offers its guests the perfect home-away-from-home for which to enjoy the beauty of the Canadian Rockies.

138 Otter Street, Banff AB
(403) 762-2499
www.theashouse.com

La Bohème Restaurant and Suite Bed & Breakfast

Spend a night in Gay Paree without ever leaving Edmonton. La Bohème Restaurant and Suite Bed & Breakfast whisks you away to the world's most romantic city to dine and dance to your heart's content. Established in 1982, La Bohème restaurant is nestled on the first floor of the historic 1912 Gibbard Block building. Architect Ernest Morehouse captured the essence of Paris that guests still relish today. You'll marvel at the original Edwardian pressed-tin ceiling. Intimate dining awaits you amid the European furnishings and sophisticated ambience. La Bohème serves classic French cuisine with elegance and panache. Choose from an ala carte menu or the table d'hote, a five-course meal that changes weekly. There are also special menus for groups. You can host a party in one of five individually decorated rooms. The oak Wine Cellar offers wine tasting and seats up to 18 people; the Tango Salon sports sassy plum-colored walls with vintage tango photographs and an open dance floor. Above the restaurant, eight elegantly appointed bedroom suites welcome guests who want to stay a little longer. Before retiring, top off the perfect evening with a stroll along the scenic North Saskatchewan river, only two blocks away. Enjoy a romantic evening at La Bohème Restaurant and Suite Bed & Breakfast.

6427 112 Avenue, Edmonton AB (780) 474-5693
www.laboheme.ca

Bear Hill Lodge

Quietly nestled at the edge of the forest, Bear Hill Lodge offers accommodations to suit the tastes and inclinations of any visitor. You can choose among 39 accommodations that include rooms, cottages, and distinctive log cabins, from roomy modern suites that offer space for family gatherings to the smaller Forest Cottages that provide a romantic alternative for two. The Heritage Log Cabins are typical of Canadian Rockies cabin construction during the early 1900s, yet they have all the modern conveniences. All accommodations feature cozy duvets on comfortable beds and full baths with showers. A healthy breakfast buffet to start your day is included in the room rate for the Forest Cottages and for a nominal sum otherwise. Since 1985, Bear Hill Lodge has been owned and operated by Paul Butler and his parents, Wally and Joyce Butler, and they carry the family spirit into their services. Bear Hill Lodge is family oriented and family friendly. You'll find many picnic tables on the property where you can enjoy the fresh air, scenery or a barbecue. A spa in a beautiful glass-walled solarium is centrally located at the main lodge and can be used any time, rain or shine. It is the perfect place to soak after an activity-filled day in the Rockies. If you are seeking the solitude of nature or the exhilaration and adventure of the mountains, you will appreciate the ambience, comfort and convenience of Bear Hill Lodge.

100 Bonnhomme Street, Jasper AB
(780) 852-3209
www.bearhilllodge.com

Service Plus Inns and Suites

Service Plus Inns & Suites offers more than just a place to sleep. A well-equipped exercise room overlooks an exceptional indoor water park with a waterslide and pool. The rooms offer such amenities as free high-speed Internet, free local calls and a 27-inch cable television with Pay Per View movies available. When you are ready for sleep, choose the room that best fits your needs. Styles include Jacuzzi suites, business suites and family suites with a special room for kids that includes bunk beds. The newly upgraded breakfast bar offers comfortable seating, a microwave and complimentary continental breakfast. Next door, you can dine on southwestern cuisine at the Mohave Grill. For a sweet snack, Tim Hortons Donuts is open 24 hours a day. On Wednesdays, there is an evening social in the inn. Service Plus is an ideal place for meetings with business facilities filled with natural light and Michigan arm chairs. The inn will expertly cater functions of two to 70 people. Take a break from your travels and relax at Service Plus Inns and Suites.

6853 66 Street, Red Deer AB
(403) 342-4445
www.serviceplusinns.com

Stanford Inn

A convenient work desk with data ports for Internet access is standard in each room at the Stanford Inn, a hotel designed for the business traveler. The 62 tastefully appointed executive suites come with a convertible lounging sofa and 27-inch cable television. The luxurious, deep bathtub is perfect for relaxing tense muscles after a big meeting. Ask about the corporate rate plans. Conference and event facilities can accommodate up to 200 people. To keep pace with your busy life, the hotel provides an exercise room and laundry facilities on every floor as well as daily dry cleaning service. All work and no play can leave you feeling grumpy, so the Stanford Inn features a lounge where you can enjoy your favorite beverage while shooting pool or taking in the game on one of the large screen televisions. Delmonico's restaurant offers daily breakfast, lunch and dinner specials. Located near the heart of the downtown Red Deer business core and major recreational facilities, the Stanford Inn makes luxury affordable. Check in and see for yourself.

4707 50 (Ross) Street, Red Deer AB (403) 347-5551 or (877) 347-5551 *www.reddeerstanfordhotel.com*

Lucasia Ranch Vacations

Experience the romance of the traditional western lifestyle at Lucasia Ranch Vacations, a historic, family-owned and operated ranch in the picturesque Porcupine Hills of Southwestern Alberta. Whether you'd like to try on the cowboy vocation or just relax at the authentic 19th century homestead, Lucasia Ranch can accommodate you. Stay in one of two guest rooms in the ranch house, with charming western décor throughout and home-cooked meals. The Lucas family serves ranch-raised beef and fresh garden produce (in season) and a hearty western-style breakfast. For a more rustic experience, you may prefer the refurbished 1900s log bunkhouse. A second, recently built log cabin offers two bedrooms and private baths. Vacation packages allow guests to choose from a range of activities at the ranch. You can participate in cattle drives, branding days and seasonal round-ups. The Lucas family offers basic training in team roping, using a dummy for practice. You can explore the 4,000 acres of rolling, natural grassland on horseback or on foot. Herds of elk and deer mingle with Texas Longhorns, crossbreed cattle and Percherons, Appaloosa and Quarter horses on the ranch. The hills are abundant with wildlife and birds while a crystal-clear spring flows through the yard into a pond that is home to ducks and geese. Back at the homestead, a crackling campfire, generous deck and a friendly game of horseshoes await. Guests interested in the naturalist side of things will be interested to know that the ranch supports four different ecosystems. The Lucas family looks forward to sharing its legends, history and culture with you at Lucasia Ranch Vacations.

Claresholm AB (403) 625-2295 or (877) 477-2624 *www.lucasiaranch.com*

Chateau Suites at Sylvan Lake

Whether you are planning a day, a week or a month at Sylvan Lake, you'll settle in quickly at Chateau Suites at Sylvan Lake, where 61 one- and two-bedroom guest suites offer lakefront luxury. A two-bedroom suite comes with two full bathrooms, a walk-in closet and separate living room with a gas fireplace. You'll enjoy sitting on your private patio and using your gas barbecue with views of the lake. A full-sized kitchen contains all necessary appliances and dishes. You say your family can't agree about television shows? Chateau Suites has read your mind, providing two televisions and a DVD player. No need to waste precious vacation time looking for laundry facilities when you will have one right in your room. The five-floor hotel offers a commanding location on the popular lake with Wild Rapids Waterslide Park right next door. The hotel's main level features the Bayshore Market and the Bayview Café. Sylvan Lake is a four-season destination, located just 15 minutes from Red Deer and 90 minutes from Calgary or Edmonton. Beyond ample water sports, the area offers a half dozen golf courses. You can strike up a game of beach volleyball, stroll past the only lighthouse between the West Coast and Winnipeg or visit quaint shops in downtown Sylvan Lake and Hewlett Park Landing. Winter opens possibilities for skating or cross-country skiing as well as ice fishing and snowmobiling. Families appreciate the Santa Claus parade in early December and Winterfest in February. Enjoy the activity of your choice, then come home to Chateau Suites at Sylvan Lake.

#1-5100 Lakeshore Drive, Sylvan Lake AB
(403) 887-6699
www.chateausuites.ca

Fairmont Palliser

The Fairmont Palliser spares no expense when it comes to luxury. This elegant historical landmark offers some of Calgary's most visually stunning accommodations. Along with a gracious doorman, the classic Edwardian architecture and softly lit exterior welcome you into the exquisite lobby. With beautifully detailed handmade rugs, sparkling candelabras and elegant marble pillars and floors throughout, the hotel is reminiscent of a palace. Each of the 405 guest rooms are luxuriously decorated and offer all the modern amenities, such as high speed Internet access and in-room movies. If you're seeking the ultimate in elegance, stay in one of the rooms on the exclusive Fairmont Gold floor, which offers concierge services as well as private check-in and check-out. Enjoy the private bar and lounge and the exclusive morning delivery of coffee, juice and a newspaper. The Fairmont also offers a health club, and a pool area with a 12-person whirlpool, swimming pool and steam room. Have a sumptuous dinner from the skilled culinary team that caters to your preferences, whether you dine in your room or in one of the elegant restaurants. For the ultimate convenience in meetings, the Fairmont is connected by Skywalk to the Telus Convention Centre, the Calgary Tower and the Glenbow Museum. Calgary is a spectacular city to visit anytime of year. With a thriving arts community, the downtown scene and the famous Calgary Stampede, Calgary's most elegant hotel welcomes visitors lured back year after year by the hotel's impeccable service and hospitality. When you visit Calgary, treat yourself to white-glove service and exceptional accommodations at the Fairmont Palliser.

133 9th Avenue SW, Calgary AB
(403) 262-1234
www.fairmont.com/palliser

Stonehouse Chalet

You will have no trouble finding the Stonehouse Chalet, even if your directions should fly out the window of your car. Just ask for it by its popular name—the Stonehouse—and anyone in Sylvan Lake can point you to it. One of the town's most famous buildings, this guest house was built in 1913 by Auguste Loquet, who had come directly from France. You will marvel at the stone masonry while envying the patience of anyone who could put each piece in the right place to make perfect matches on the entire front of the building. One of the house's architectural curiosities is the upstairs door, which opens to the outside with no railing or exit stairwell. You may think it was left unfinished, but actually the door allowed for the upstairs carpets to be shaken out without requiring someone to lug them through the house. Stonehouse Chalet has been completely renovated on the inside with modern amenities to accommodate guest parties. The large lot offers plenty of room for entertaining. The chalet is located just minutes from the beach and within walking distance of all the town's most popular attractions. Experience the charm of a truly original home at the Stonehouse Chalet.

4916 48 Avenue, Sylvan Lake AB
(403) 887-3000

McCracken Country Inn & Tea House

Whatever you may need for relaxation, you'll find it at McCracken Country Inn & Tea House. Each of the nine guest rooms uses antiques and country décor to provide an old-fashioned setting. One bedroom on the main floor has a separate entrance with wheelchair access. The upstairs rooms offer full baths and cable television. You can reserve one of two suites with a whirlpool tub. All guests enjoy a Continental breakfast in the tea house. When you are not out enjoying the mountain environment around Hinton, you can snuggle up by a corner fireplace in the parlour with a book, a puzzle or game from the shelves. The tea house serves flavoured teas, specialty coffees and freshly made pies and scones. Lunch comes with a house-made soup. The inn is near an 18-hole golf course and trails for hiking, biking and cross-country skiing. Fay and Kyle McCracken opened the inn in 2001 and ran it with the help of their daughter Gerri. Recently, Fay and Kyle moved to Clearwater B.C. to operate a bed-and-breakfast while Gerri manages the inn. For a cozy retreat full of country charm, visit McCracken Country Inn & Tea House.

146 Brookhart Street, Hinton AB
(780) 865-5662 or (888) 865-5662
www.mccrackencountryinn.com

Cat's Meow Bed & Breakfast

Be as active or lazy as you like at the Cat's Meow Bed & Breakfast. This alpine inn, nestled in the historic town of Canmore, sits about five minutes from downtown. Enticing breakfast smells lure you out of the bed in the morning. Eggs and omelettes, sizzling Canadian bacon, cinnamon buns and muffins baked fresh daily and seasonal fresh fruit decorate the dining room table. Top off your delicious meal with a cup of piping hot coffee or herbal tea. You can visit the recreation room, which sports a pool table. Curl up with a good book or tackle some outdoor fun. The

Rocky Mountains offer exceptional cross-country and downhill skiing. The surrounding beauty invites you to hike, bike or play a few rounds of golf. You have a choice of two rooms, one with twin beds. Both rooms have private baths. Owners Tara and John Breurkens pride themselves on superb hospitality and an exceptional knowledge of the area. Be sure to check the window ledges and sofas at the Cat's Meow Bed & Breakfast for the two additional hosts who await your arrival—C'mere and Simon, felines in residence.

221 Cougar Point Road, Canmore AB
(403) 678-4051
www.bbcanada.com/1502.html

Alpine Village

A stay at Jasper National Park calls for the combination of rustic charm and tasteful appointments you will find in 42 log cabins at Alpine Village, which has a three-diamond rating from AAA. You are just two miles from the village of Jasper on 11 acres of pine woodland. From a 16-foot hot pool, you have panoramic views of the Athabasca River and the towering backdrop of Mt. Edith Cavell. Rooms come in various configurations that suit everyone from honeymooners to families. You are sure to adore the log ceilings of the family cabins and the convenience and comfort of kitchens, private decks with barbecues and wood-burning fireplaces. You can soak in an outdoor hot tub and watch wildlife saunter by your cabin during a season that runs from May 1 to mid-October. Whether you stay in a new cabin or one of the 60-year-old heritage rooms, you'll discover historic character throughout. Clean, modern features are set off by pine, slate and fieldstone. From this home base, guests take off to explore such attractions as the Jasper Tramway, Maligne Lake and the Columbia Icefields. The Alpine Village staff can get you on your way to whitewater rafting, golfing, hiking, fishing or shopping. Many visitors return each year to refresh their spirits. Your hosts are Rena and Chris Allin, who have owned the resort for 21 years. Live mountain life to the fullest with a visit to Alpine Village.

Highway 93A North, Jasper AB
(780) 852-3285
www.alpinevillagejasper.com

The Rimrock Resort Hotel

The Rimrock Resort Hotel is nestled at the base of Sulphur Mountain, a short walk from the world-renowned Banff Upper Hot Springs and next to Banff Gondola. This pristine mountain setting provides unsurpassed views of Mt. Rundle and the Bow Valley from an elevation of 5,000 feet. The hotel is a four-diamond designate, casual yet elegant—you'll experience unrivaled service and accommodations. Guest rooms are large. All have cable television, in-room movies and video games, an on-command media centre, mini-bar and Aveda beauty products. Other standard amenities include two telephones, data ports and high-speed wireless Internet access. The resort's Eden dining room is one of just two five-diamond-rated restaurants in Alberta and one of eight in all of Canada. *Wine Spectator* has awarded Eden its Best of Award of Excellence. The Primrose dining room offers international and regional cuisine in a comfortable setting that welcomes everyone. The Larkspur is the very grand and comfortable lobby lounge, and Divas, the martini jazz lounge, often features live entertainment. The Rimrock's fitness centre provides a squash court, indoor pool and whirlpool. The full-service Rimrock Spa offers an extended menu of spa treatments, including facials, body treatments, hand and foot care and massages. The hotel offers 16 conference rooms. A complimentary bus shuttle takes you to downtown Banff. The Rimrock Resort Hotel is truly a resort like no other.

300 Mountain Avenue, Banff AB (403) 762-3356 or (800) 661-1587 www.rimrockresort.com

Westridge Country Inn

Nestled in the heart of the Canadian Rockies, only a five-minute drive from Banff National Park, Westridge Country Inn is in a tranquil, scenic world of its own. The Inn offers the comfort of an Old West mountain getaway with an authentic European flair. The Tillmann family, which founded the lodging and runs it today, has been in the hotel business for five generations. They brought both their experience and their antique European furnishings from Germany to Alberta. The Inn prides itself on being a home away from home and providing the perfect mountain experience for its guests. A tasty complimentary breakfast is served in the spacious rustic breakfast room daily. With extras such as in-room fireplaces, Jacuzzis and family suites, the Inn offers coziness with style. It also provides stunning views of the Three Sisters mountain peaks. Guests often relax on their balconies or patios as they absorb the breathtaking panoramic views and enjoy the fresh mountain air. Ready to conquer the mountains with a full-day hike? Do you just want to take a scenic drive? The friendly staff members know the surrounding areas inside and out, and they will help you plan your perfect day or week. If you're looking for a homey, low-key mountain getaway, come to the Westridge Country Inn.

1719 Bow Valley Trail, Canmore AB
(403) 678-5221
www.westridgecountryinn.com

Jasper House Bungalows

John Forabosco was a young Italian immigrant when he helped build the original 28 units of Jasper House Bungalows in 1956. In 1977, he and his wife, Josie, purchased the cedar log bungalows and doubled the number of guest units. They also expanded the dining room, where you just might gaze out on elk, deer or other wildlife as you enjoy the breakfast buffet. Jasper House and the surrounding Jasper National Park are named after Jasper Hawes, who operated a Northwest company trading post in the area in 1817. The resort sits on 3.7 acres amidst some of the grandest wilderness in the Rocky Mountain range. It is open May 1 to mid-October and features 56 modern rooms in several styles. You will find standard rooms and suites with compact kitchens. In a separate building, an executive suite comes with a whirlpool tub and electric fireplace. Your fellow guests are likely to be an assorted gathering of Canadian, American and European tourists drawn by the wild beauty of the park and the secluded setting under the shelter of Whistlers Mountain. A nearby trail along the Athabasca River makes an ideal path for an after-dinner walk. Dinners at Jasper House have a broad appeal, with such choices as chicken pot pie, Wiener schnitzel and medallions of beef in red wine sauce. Two of the seven Forabosco children, Vera and Tina, manage the business today. They can help you make the most of your stay in the park and direct you to area attractions. For comfortable living in a wild setting, plan a visit to Jasper House Bungalows.

612 Connaught Drive, Jasper AB
(780) 852-4535
www.jasperhouse.com

Metterra Hotel on Whyte

Business travellers are well served at the Metterra Hotel, a swanky boutique hotel in Edmonton's hip and historic Old Strathcona district. The Metterra is contemporary throughout with just the right touches of warmth. You will find a state-of-the-art business centre and hospitality rooms along with a fitness centre, in-room high-speed Internet with Wi-Fi access and valet parking. Guests enjoy 98 spacious rooms with a trendy environment that mixes a modern Western style with Eastern art, including Indonesian pieces that add a touch of funk. The minimalist features are softened by the warmth of dark maple woodwork, the strategic use of stone and such extras as fireplaces and recliners. You can begin your workday with the morning newspaper and a complimentary Continental breakfast. Relax at the day's end with wine tasting and cheese. It's just steps from a sleek lobby featuring striking artwork and a two-story stone wall and waterfall to the hot spots of Old Strathcona, where theatre, restaurants, pubs and shops promise sparkling urban entertainment. You'll be five minutes from downtown or the University of Alberta, and a short walk from the spectacular North Saskatchewan River valley. Look forward to your next business venture with a visit to Metterra Hotel on Whyte or its sister hotel, Varsona Hotel on Whyte.

10454 - 82nd Avenue (Whyte Avenue), Edmonton AB
(780) 465-8150 or (866) 465-8150
www.metterra.com

Bärgnäscht Bed & Breakfast

Swiss natives Silvia Albrecht and Fritz Schüpbach opened their original Bärgnäscht Bed & Breakfast at the foot of the Three Sisters Mountain in Canmore, Alberta—hence the name, which means *mountain nest* in a Swiss dialect. In 2009, this dynamic duo will unveil the newest incarnation of their bed-and-breakfast in Osoyoos, a Californiaesque oasis in British Columbia. Visit their website to keep up-to-date on the progress of the adobe house being built after their own design. Like many houses in the area, it will feature such classic Southern Mexican features as rounded doorways and an inside open courtyard. Its three suites will each have their own outdoor patio overlooking 25 acres of Ponderosa pines and prairie grass. Almost like complete apartments, they will include living rooms and kitchenettes but still benefit from Silvia's famous European breakfast spread. She'll take full advantage of the mild climate to offer fresh local fruits in addition to exotic cheeses and cold cuts—never the same assortment two days in the week. Nellie the cat and her two newest sidekicks will follow Silvia and Fritz to Osoyoos. This talented husband-wife-cat team has been making loyal fans with their hospitality since 1995. Come see their newest Bärgnäscht Bed & Breakfast in Osoyoos in 2009.

1175 Highway 3 E, Osoyoos BC
www.telusplanet.net/public/baerg

Canadian Artisans Bed & Breakfast

Owners Valerie and Robert Knowlden have created a little piece of heaven called Canadian Artisans Bed & Breakfast. Surrounded by peace and tranquility, this luxury Rocky Mountain retreat is perfect for your romantic mountain honeymoon, anniversary or any other occasion. The bed and breakfast offers a choice of two suites, the Treehouse or the Foresthouse. Both suites feature comfortable furnishings and décor. Best of all, eight full-length windows in each suite bring nature's beauty to you. The Treehouse offers a double steam shower, and the Foresthouse has a double whirlpool tub right beside your bed. Dine in complete privacy overlooking the

yard, where a fire pit adds romance to the night. You'll enjoy the chattering squirrels, the songs of the ravens, the wind in the trees and the presence of the river nearby. Cuddle up beside your private cozy gas fireplace in this inviting retreat or take a three-minute walk to downtown Canmore, where fine restaurants, quaint boutiques and art galleries welcome you. The Knowldens built and decorated this charming vacation spot themselves, employing their combined knowledge of architecture and fine arts. They created every detail, from stained glass to hidden dragons. Breathe deeply and rest well. Your time at the Canadian Artisans Bed & Breakfast will soothe your spirit and invigorate you.

1016 9 Avenue, Canmore AB
(403) 678-4138
www.canadianartisans.ca

The Lady MacDonald Country Inn

As you approach the Lady MacDonald Country Inn, you're struck by the comfortable, traditional feel of this two-storey dormered home that's set against the backdrop of the breathtaking Canadian Rockies. Upon entering, you'll know you've chosen a good place to stay. The warm tones of the hardwood flooring complement the massive stone fireplace in the solarium dining room. Seating is restaurant style. Tables are set in the French manner, with Provençal tablecloths atop white linen. Each morning, you are treated to a sumptuous homemade breakfast to get your day off to a good start. The 12 guest rooms are individually decorated and all are lovely. All have fireplaces, full en-suite bathrooms and are equipped with cable television. Some of the rooms feature feather beds, canopy beds and Jacuzzi tubs. The inn also offers a honeymoon suite, loft rooms with dormer windows, and a two-bedroom suite ideal

for a family or group. Owners Tammy Freeman and Peter Eggmann are experts on the Canmore area and are happy to share their knowledge with you. They can guide you in the right direction to local hiking trails and scenic drives. When in Canmore, pamper yourself at the Lady MacDonald Inn, where you'll come as a guest and leave as a friend.

1201 Bow Valley Trail, Canmore AB
(403) 678-3665 or (800) 567-3919
www.ladymacdonald.com

Attractions & Recreation

Bragg Creek

FEEL THE GENTLE POWER OF BEAUTY ™

It's Monday morning, 6:30 am, and its time to get ready for work—but not before your morning jog. As you lace up your runners, the spring dawn sky turns a shocking shade of red as the sun creeps up in the east, casting its pink glow on the snow-capped peaks of the majestic Rocky Mountains to the west. Taking your first stride, you greedily inhale the crisp clean country air, lightly infused with the exhilarating aroma of the surrounding pine, spruce and aspen forest. After traversing the quiet but physically challenging country roads for the next half hour, you return home feeling energized and mentally prepared for a productive day at your office in Calgary, one of the world's most vibrant economic centers and only a 40-kilometre commute from your expansive country acreage in beautiful Bragg Creek. Popularly known as the Gateway to Kananaskis, the tiny unincorporated hamlet of Bragg Creek is situated amidst the foothills of the Rocky Mountains, bordering one of the most stunning protected landscapes in the world.

Truly a recreational paradise, Kananaskis country boasts hundreds of kilometers of scenic trails for hiking, cycling, horseback riding, cross-country skiing and off-roading. If it's a more relaxed experience you're seeking, you could pack a picnic lunch for the family and commune with nature at nearby Elbow Falls, a powerfully beautiful natural spectacle where the Elbow River collides with the rugged and rocky slopes of the mountains. Then again, perhaps a quiet meditative day of fishing would be more to your tastes, or a contemplative paddle in your canoe around Allen Bill or Forgetmenot Pond. The recreational opportunities are truly endless in this 4,000-square-kilometer natural playground. When Bragg Creek is your home, this pristine and virtually untouched recreational paradise is, quite literally, in your own backyard.

While it successfully maintains its comfortable and intimate country feel, the small hamlet of Bragg Creek is able to provide most services and comforts to suit the modern lifestyle. In addition to medical, dental and emergency services, Bragg Creek boasts a community center and association offering many locally-based programs, as well as a volunteer-run performing arts group that provides Bragg Creekers with the opportunity to enjoy professional entertainment in their own community. There is a local school, a spa, a physiotherapy clinic and a thriving senior's association offering many exciting social opportunities. Between the local supermarkets, impressive art galleries, charming clothing boutiques and fantastic little gift shops, most shopping needs are easily met. Bragg Creek also offers a truly impressive selection of fine-dining opportunities, from Bavarian to Italian to a splendid Asian-western fusion, as well as a number of family-style restaurants. It is home to a vibrant collection of artists and artisans, many of whom are willing to instruct neighbors who wish to explore their artistic side. Bragg Creek is an ideal community in which to raise your children. Few places on earth are able to offer such pristine natural beauty combined with a healthy and culturally rich lifestyle, all within half an hour of a major urban centre and at affordable prices.

It's rare to find such a small, vibrant and spectacularly beautiful community so close to one of the fastest growing economic centers in the world. Land costs are still attractive, but Bragg Creek's extraordinary combination of spectacular mountains, crystal-clear mountain streams, Kananaskis Country and proximity to Calgary set the stage for unparalleled growth in property values. Bragg Creek offers affordable resort-style living, as well as the opportunity for serious returns on investment. It's true—you can have your cake and eat it too. The next time you pass through Bragg Creek, remember that you are passing through one of the most important areas in Alberta, a community that marries one of the most vibrant economic centers of the world with the pristine, natural beauty of Kananaskis. It invites you to enjoy a more relaxed and healthier lifestyle, while you also make what could be the investment of your life. Dwayne Zaba of Royal LePage Benchmark in Bragg Creek has trademarked a phrase that he believes describes Bragg Creek and its surrounding area: Feel the Gentle Power of Beauty.™ Visit Bragg Creek to discover how that phrase so aptly describes the little piece of paradise Bragg Creekers call home. You can contact Royal LePage Benchmark at its office, its web site or by phone.

6–27 Balsam Avenue, Bragg Creek AB
(403) 949-3400
www.braggcreekrealestate.ca

Photos courtesy of the Gateway Gazette

Town of Black Diamond

The landscape is no longer studded with derricks as it was during the oil boom from 1914 to 1947, but the history of Black Diamond is still a visible presence. The buildings along Main Street are restored to look as they did during the boom, and the Turner Valley Gas Plant, a national historic site, interprets the role that petroleum production played in the economic development of the area. Before the discovery of oil, coal mining and ranching were the major industries. Bar-U Ranch National Historic Site has been a part of Western Canada's ranching history for more than 100 years. Its original ranch buildings now serve as a working museum, featuring videos and demonstrations. Black Diamond is located in the foothills of the Rocky Mountains, 52 kilometers southwest of Calgary at the junction of Highways 7 and 22. This charming town is just as exciting today as it was in the past. The abundance of galleries is evidence of a thriving artistic community. Enjoy a meal in one of the town's many restaurants. Accommodations include the Turner Valley Hotel and the 10-room Black Diamond Hotel, in addition to several bed-and-breakfasts and nearby campgrounds. For a pleasurable day trip from Calgary or a relaxing and history-filled stopover along the Cowboy Trail, consider spending some time in the town of Black Diamond.

301 Centre Avenue W, Black Diamond AB
(403) 933-4348
www.town.blackdiamond.ab.ca

Calgary Stampede

There is nothing in the world like the Calgary Stampede. From its humble beginnings as an agricultural fair in 1886 it has earned its reputation as The Greatest Outdoor Show on Earth through more than 100 years of celebrating the unmistakably timeless heritage and values of the Canadian west.

The appeal of the Calgary Stampede may stem from the mythology of cowboys and the settlement of the western half of North America but today's Calgary Stampede represents much more than mythology.

It's a volunteer-supported, not-for-profit community organization. A visit to the Calgary Stampede and Stampede Park offers an authentic experience characterized by western hospitality, commitment to community, integrity and pride of place, 365 days a year. Year-round facilities host more than 1,300 events per year, and agricultural programs bring together rural and urban communities.

At the heart of the organization is The Stampede - the ten day celebration every July which is famous around the world. Each year, over a million visitors come from across North America and around the world as well as from Calgary and Alberta to experience the heart-stopping action of one of the world's roughest and richest Rodeos … the awesome power of the world's top Chuckwagon Races … the spectacular theatrical presentation known as the Evening Grandstand Show … world-class agricultural activities … and adrenalin-pumping rides at North America's largest mobile midway. In the Indian Village, a cornerstone of the Stampede since 1912, visitors step back in time to share in authentic Plains Indians' cultural practices. Western Showcase embraces western culture through its world-class art displays.

The Calgary Stampede is proud to be the community's cradle of western heritage and traditions, helping to preserve the unique identity and soul of Calgary.

Information: (403) 261-0101 or (800) 661-1260
Tickets: (403) 269-9822 or (800) 661-1767
www.calgarystampede.com

TELUS World of Science-Edmonton

TELUS World of Science-Edmonton, a broad-based and interactive science centre, is operated by the Edmonton Space & Science Foundation, a non-profit organization. Since 1984, TELUS World of Science has been an integral part of Edmonton's skyline when famous Canadian architect Douglas Cardinal's unique design became reality in the form of what was then called the Edmonton Space Sciences Centre. Located in beautiful Coronation Park, the original building housed western Canada's first IMAX® theatre and Canada's largest Planetarium. In 2001, to fulfill the Edmonton Space & Science Foundation's vision of creating a world-class science centre, the building underwent a significant expansion, designed by local architect Donna Clare of Cohos Evamy. From the moment you step into the soaring lobby of the new building, a world of incredible learning, fun, and excitement comes at you in wave upon wonderful wave: five permanent exhibit galleries, one feature gallery, an IMAX theatre, a science demonstration stage, the Margaret Zeidler Star Theatre and a myriad of on-floor activities, factoids and events.

TELUS World of Science, which is very much in tune with its public's thirst for knowledge, maintains a strong focus on offering an ongoing Community Speaker series and its flagship program *Brightest Minds*. Under the umbrella of *Brightest Minds*, TELUS World of Science has hosted world-renowned scientists and explorers such as Dr. Mark Plotkin, one of the world's leading ethnobotanists; Dr. Zahi Hawass, Secretary of the Supreme Council of Antiquities for Egypt; Colonel Mike Mullane, a highly-regarded NASA Astronaut; Jean-Michel Cousteau, a world leading ocean explorer; and Dr. Richard Leakey, the world's most famous paleo-anthropologist and an environmental activist.

For a cool place to visit and to learn in a fun and engaging way, TELUS World of Science is it.

TELUS WORLD
of SCIENCE
edmonton

Visit TELUS World of Science—Edmonton, the place with something for everyone who has an inquisitive mind. Stimulate your senses in the themed exhibit and feature galleries exploring the vast frontiers of the amazing world of science. See what the human body looks like in a larger-than-life 3D version in the Body Fantastic. Find out how your body really works and how your brain interprets the world around us. Space Place is the ultimate outer space experience right here on earth. Join a space team exploring life on other planets for an out-of-this-world experience.

The Greens' House lets you explore their backyard to learn more about yours. From environment and weather to alternate energy sources, you'll find it all in their living and breathing backyard. Pretend you're a CSI detective when you explore the crime scene in Mystery Avenue. Collect your clues and analyze your findings in the forensic lab to figure out whodunit. For the little ones, there is no better place than Discoveryland where curiosity will easily lead to fun and discovery with Waterworks; a giant-sized piano keyboard for little feet to step on and create their own tune; Potter's Corner and much more.

Whether you delve into the interactive galleries, immerse yourself in the ultimate IMAX experience, participate in science demonstration stage activities, take in a night of stargazing at the Observatory or browse in their amazing Gift Shop, you will discover your inner scientist and have a blast doing it. Visit TELUS World of Science for a memorable family outing.

TELUS WORLD
of SCIENCE
edmonton

IMAX is a registered trademark of IMAX Corporation.

Calaway Park

Experience an adrenaline rush as you suddenly see the world upside down, take in a foot tapping stage show, or just enjoy time with your family as you share a meal at Calaway Park. The park opened in 1982 and now boasts 33 family thrill rides, 25 dining locations and 24 games of skill, all on 160 acres of land in the foothills of the majestic Canadian Rockies. The focus at Calaway is on the family, and the friendly staff members receive extensive training on how to make your visit a special one. The folks at the park tell customers Your Smile is Our Mission, and you are sure to be grinning as you zip around the corkscrew rollercoaster or try out one of four new rides in 2007, including a 12 meter drop ride. While you are at the park, be sure to check out Calaway Live, one of the stage shows included in the price of admission. Adults and kids alike get a kick out of the high energy productions, which provide plenty of music and humor. When you are ready to eat you have many options to choose from, including burgers, pizza, subs and hot dogs. Also, for the family-member with a sweet tooth, check out the candy shop for fudge, candy apples and all sorts of goodies. The park includes an on-site campground with full RV hook-ups, so you can easily extend the fun another day. Calaway packs a lot of fun into its season, which runs from May through October. Be sure to check the website for days and hours of operation before you go. Find excitement, entertainment and great food in a family-oriented atmosphere at Calaway Park.

245033 Range Road 33, Calgary AB
(403) 240-3822
www.calawaypark.com

Warner Guiding & Outfitting

Imagine a leisurely horse or wagon ride along the winding path of a river as you make your way to the site of your picnic breakfast. Or perhaps an evening jaunt is more your style, with a cookout of barbecued steak, baked beans and potatoes at the end. At Warner Guiding & Outfitting, Ron Warner and his team of riders offer guided outings like these that get folks out and about in the wonderful Canadian Rockies. Ron has been in love with the Rockies since the moment he pulled his pickup into town in 1962. He started guiding not long after. From one-hour jaunts along the Bow and Spray Rivers to six-day expeditions into bear and wolf country, the Warner team has a horseback vacation for you. Rough in a tent or cozy up in a mountain lodge at night. To meet the wilderness without staying overnight, consider the Explorer Day Ride. You'll begin at Sulphur Mountain, with its breathtaking views of Mt. Rundle and the Spray River. Enjoy a lunch of steak cooked over an open fire. The return trip passes along the base of Mt. Rundle by Bow Falls. Saddle up with Warner Guiding & Outfitting. Some of the most gorgeous mountain wilderness in the world awaits you.

132 Banff Avenue, Banff AB
(403) 762-4551 or (800) 661-8352
www.horseback.com

Home on the Range Adventure Tours

If you're looking to enjoy the rustic splendor of the West and its people, you'll feel right at home on a Home on the Range Adventure Tour. Since it opened more than five years ago, this Calgary enterprise has been helping travelers discover the beauty of Alberta. The business, owned by Joseph Macdonald and Fletcher O'Grady, came about as a result of an idea hatched around a campfire. The idea—as simple and ingenious as most ideas born around a good fire—was that knowledgeable locals could better present the province to tourists than simply letting them discover attractions by accident. Home on the Range offers a variety of tours that highlight the authentic Western experience. You can spend a day in the Rockies, with their snow-capped peaks and waterfalls, or try the 13-day Cowboys, Castles and the Coast trip that takes in rodeos, powwows and trail rides from Calgary to Vancouver. No matter which tour you book, you're guaranteed to get a firsthand look at the people and places that define Western Canada. If you want to hold a wedding amid the majestic beauty of the Rockies, several options are available, including an authentic Native American wedding ceremony. Home on the Range also offers corporate retreat and team-building activities. Home on the Range Adventure Tours invites you to explore the natural and cultural wonders of Western Canada.

Unit #4, 2nd floor, 4101–19 Street NE, Calgary AB
(403) 229-9090 or (866) 760-8334
www.homeontherange.ca

Vulcan Tourism & Trek Station

The fate of your Starship crew rests in your hands as you prepare to confront alien invaders. The thrill of playing captain in the virtual reality game called Vulcan Space Adventure awaits you at Vulcan Tourism & Trek Station, a destination for science fiction fans which doubles as the official tourist information centre for Vulcan County. The building was designed to resemble a space station and to honour the town of Vulcan's association with *Star Trek* and Mr. Spock's fictitious home planet. Trekkies converge upon the small prairie town for the Vulcan Spock Days/Galaxyfest convention, held the second weekend in June. The annual event features costume contests, celebrity appearances and Star Trek vendor tables. Contrary to popular belief, the town was not named after Spock's home planet. In 1910, a surveyor for the Canadian Pacific Railway dubbed the town Vulcan in honour of the Roman god of fire. The railroad carried Vulcan's wheat to market. Vulcan's relationship with *Star Trek* dates to the earliest days of the original television series, and by now the community declares its love wherever you look, beginning with the replica starship standing sentinel at the entrance to town. Space murals adorn several of the local businesses, while at the space-themed waterpark, folks douse their friends with blasts of water from the space cannons and dodge the showers spouting from the starship. Brush off that Starfleet suit hanging in your closet and make your way to the town of Vulcan for some intergalactic fun.

115 Centre Street E, Vulcan AB
(403) 485-2994
www.vulcantourism.com

Head-Smashed-In Buffalo Jump

The hunting history and culture of Canada's Plains Indians are on display for travellers from around the world to see at Head-Smashed-In Buffalo Jump. One of the oldest and best-preserved communal bison hunting sites in North America, Head-Smashed-In Buffalo Jump was declared a World Heritage Site by the United Nations in 1981, placing it alongside such famed sites as the Taj Mahal in India, the Pyramids of Egypt and Britain's Stonehenge. The site gains its name from a legend in which a young brave watched from below as his people drove a herd of bison over the cliffs during an unusually good hunt. As the bodies piled up, the boy became trapped and was discovered with his skull crushed by the weight of the carcasses. Archaeological evidence shows that the native peoples hunted at this site for nearly 6,000 years. The layers of animal bones, tools and other items stretch down some 11 metres deep into the soil. At Head-Smashed-In Buffalo Jump, you'll learn all about hunting techniques, which required complicated planning to herd the bison over cliffs. Programs for children compare modern tools with the early equivalents, and look at teepee construction and other aspects of native culture. Each education program features a guided tour of the interpretive centre, which include the cliff-top trail and buffalo culture displays. A variety of special events are held throughout the year, including opportunities to camp in Blackfoot teepees and a June celebration of National Aboriginal Day, which celebrates First Nations' contributions to Canadian society. Come on a hunt through history at Head-Smashed-In Buffalo Jump.

Highway 785, Fort MacLeod AB (403) 553-2731 *www.head-smashed-in.com*

Head-Smashed-In
Buffalo Jump

UNESCO
World Heritage Site

Alberta

Rothney Astrophysical Observatory

Everyone has marveled at the night sky, but have you marveled at it from a state-of-the-art research facility? You can, at University of Calgary's Rothney Astrophysical Observatory. This institution is dedicated to expanding knowledge of the universe and educating, exciting and inspiring people. The observatory houses one of the three largest telescopes in Canada as well as the only telescope that continually scans the sky for asteroids. As an educational establishment, you would expect informative tours and an awesome interpretive centre and you will not be disappointed. There are 2,200 square feet of ultra-modern classroom space and interactive educational displays that are continually updated to be current with events. The University can arrange private tours of ten or more and tailor them to the needs of your group. You can take students on an intellectual adventure and show them real life applications of classroom science concepts. The meeting space is also available to groups seeking a unique venue that is wheelchair accessible and has ample parking. Rothney hosts open house nights that offer star watching from the observation deck, check their website for open house dates and information. Come find your place in the universe at Rothney Astrophysical Observatory.

2.4 km S of the Highway 22x/Highway 22 interchange, Calgary AB
(403) 931-2366
www.phas.ucalgary.ca/rao

Old Strathcona

Old Strathcona is surely one of Canada's coolest neighborhoods. The turn-of-the-century historical district is home to a cornucopia of restaurants, shops and community celebrations. Old Strathcona is south of the North Saskatchewan River, across from central Edmonton, near the University of Alberta. More than 400 merchants are located along Whyte Avenue (82 Avenue), the hub of the district. Hungry? Close to a hundred coffee houses, cafes, restaurants and other places to eat present a cross-section of cuisines: German, Italian, Thai, Vietnamese or Greek, just to name a few. On Whyte Avenue and tucked into side streets, you'll find everything from trendsetting fashions to folk guitars. The Strathcona Hotel, built in 1891, is Edmonton's oldest. Other places to stay include boutique hotels and the guest rooms provided by Hostelling International.

Within two square blocks, eight thriving theatre companies perform out of four venues. If you're thirsty, Whyte Avenue pubs and clubs collectively provide about 10,000 seats. After dark, DJs and live performers entertain at the pubs and clubs. Country, jazz, blues, rock and salsa overflow into the streets. Old Strathcona hosts Edmonton's Fringe Theatre Festival, International Film Festival, the Art Walk Festival and Marketplace and the Silly Summer Parade. A bustling Farmers' Market on Saturdays brings a touch of the farm to the heart of the city year-round.

Strathcona, incorporated as a town in 1899, was named after Lord Strathcona (born Donald Smith), a major figure in Canadian history. Old-Fashioned trolley rides over the High Level bridge are offered throughout the summer months. Part of the popularity of Whyte Avenue is due to its brick buildings. In 1902, the town passed a bylaw that required building with brick to prevent fires. Much of the current brick stock was erected during a 1910 to 1912 boom. Old Strathcona is one of very few areas left in Canada with a first-generation building stock. The Old Strathcona Business Association invites you to visit one of Canada's premiere playgrounds.

#6 10436-81 Avenue, Edmonton AB
(780) 437-4182

Heritage Park Historical Village

For over 43 years, Heritage Park has been bringing the past to life with this picturesque living historical village. See the Old West come alive when you stroll through the bustling town square. With a number of old-fashioned shops and buildings, such as the blacksmith shop, bakery, school and church, this railway prairie town functions just as it would have in its original days. One of the most enticing sights is the original Canadian Pacific Railway steam locomotive. When you see it chugging down the tracks, you will be swept back in time. The newest addition to the park is the Aboriginal Encampment, complete with a fur trading fort, Native American tipis and mission house. Take a walk towards the banks of the pristine Glenmore Reservoir and get your tickets for a ride on the *S.S. Moyie*, a beautiful paddleboat with two spacious decks. If you really want to take advantage of what Heritage Park offers, the special events and seasonal happenings are a must see. Kids will enjoy the various day camps and activities offered at the park, in which they are provided with costumes and hands-on fun, educational activities. Have your wedding here and take a romantic ride in a horse-drawn carriage. Animal lovers will enjoy the ranching area, where they can experience agricultural history first-hand. Take a trip to Heritage Park Historical Village for a true celebration of western heritage.

1900 Heritage Drive SW, Calgary AB
(403) 268-8500
www.HeritagePark.ca

Greidanus Honey Mill

Tucked away just outside the town of High River is a 22 acre farm where some of the finest unprocessed honey can be found year-round. The Greidanus Honey Mill is run by Sidney Greidanus and his son, Henrik Greidanus. They offer unprocessed and unfiltered honey in jars and pails, raw beeswax and a variety of beeswax candles. The honey at Greidanus Honey Mill is collected by their bees from Alberta clover and canola and is very mild, making it perfect as a sweetener for coffee or tea and delicious in your favorite baking and canning recipes. The Greidanus Honey Mill offers school tours and tours to travellers. It also serves many locals. With more than 4,000 hives, the Greidanus Honey Mill is one of the largest beekeeping operations in Alberta, producing over a million pounds of unpasteurized clover honey each year. Much of this honey is exported to countries such as the United States and Germany. The Greidanus Honey Mill sells honey online and sells its products at farmers' markets. The Greidanus family left a dairy farm in Holland in the early 1970s. They settled in Alberta and began working in the honey industry. Henrik, a second-generation beekeeper, considers beekeeping a win-win situation. He gets to collect the honey and farmers get their crops pollinated. Much of the hive's success revolves around the queen bee, whose job it is to lay eggs. It is very difficult to obtain a large number of queen bees locally, so the Greidanus Honey Mill imports queen bees from as far away as Australia and Hawaii. Taste the goodness of natural unprocessed honey at Greidanus Honey Mill, a healthy way to satisfy your sweet tooth.

12 Avenue S (6 km W of town), High River AB
(403) 652-7647
www.honeymill.ca

Sylvan Cruises

You have heard of frequent flyers, but around Sylvan Lake there are scores of people who could call themselves frequent floaters. They are the ones who find any occasion to take a spin around the lake on a tour boat operated by Sylvan Cruises. Owner and captain Cynthia Leigh sees familiar faces every time she welcomes guests aboard the Miss Mermaid, a paddlewheel vessel, and the Zoo Cruise, a 40-passenger pontoon boat. Couples have been married on these boats, families have celebrated grandma's 90th birthday and revelers have danced to the beat at such theme parties as Mardi Gras Night and '70s Night. Dinner cruises combining a three-hour jaunt with either a light meal or buffet are popular. Since 1993, locals have stood side by side on the deck with guests from around the world, feeling that magical moment out on the water when the sun is setting and the loons are calling. If you are simply seeking a fun and relaxing way to experience the beauty of Sylvan Lake, a one-hour trip will satisfy your needs. Family and adult excursions leave throughout the day. Reserve a space on Miss Mermaid or the Zoo Cruise to begin logging your frequent floater miles.

4916–48 Avenue, Sylvan Lake AB
(403) 887-3000
www.sylvancruises.ca

Evergreen Golf Centre

Evergreen Golf Centre offers the best of both worlds with its combination of sheltered, heated stalls and simulated greens and the par three natural grass and championship features. It is possible to play throughout the year in 34 heated stalls with contoured target greens, sand traps and a water hazard that provides a close approximation to real golf. The par three has natural grass greens and tee boxes, and holes that vary in length from 65 to 310 yards. For casual fun, the Mini Putt course is built over 22,000 square feet with a coal mine theme, including reproductions of the number-eight mine headworks and water tower, with features such as water falls, multiple streams and ponds throughout. The clubhouse has a licensed tee line and snack bar with seating for 40, an outdoor patio and a convenient meeting room. The pro shop is fully stocked and provides a test drive center, custom club fitting services to improve your game and a repair shop. Their go-kart track appeals to all levels of interest with its multi-layout circuit and top quality electronic kart control and timing systems. Evergreen hosts junior camps for young players to offer them the necessary tools and skills that lead to a lifetime enjoyment of the game. Evergreen Golf Centre was named one of the Top Ten New Ranges in North America in 1998 and the Lethbridge Chamber of Commerce Business of the Year in 1999. Whether you're learning the game or honing your acquired skills, you'll enjoy your time at Evergreen Golf Centre.

5225–24 Avenue S, Lethbridge AB
(403) 329-4500
www.evergreengolfcentre.com

Snowy Owl Sled Dog Tours

Celebrating its 24th anniversary this year, Snowy Owl Sled Dog Tours is a company rich in family history. The Arsenault family and their staff members aim to give their guests the most educational and comprehensive sled dog adventure available. Every tour represents authentic Canadian culture and tradition. Snuggle into cozy sleds with beautiful blankets. Trips vary from two to eight hours, all of which include stunning scenic mountain views as you sled on an extensive network of trails throughout the Spray Lakes. Drive a team of gorgeous, friendly Canadian Huskies yourself or relax while your instructor takes control. Growing up surrounded by pristine mountain landscapes in the Canadian backcountry, owner Connie Arsenault learned essential survival skills from her father, a local park ranger. Connie had been dog sledding for only a few years when she met Charles, her future husband and business partner. They shared a passion for sled dogs and the wilderness, and in 1983, they opened Snowy Owl Sled Dog Tours, laying the foundation for the Arsenault family legacy. That same year, Connie co-founded the Alberta International Sled Dog Classic of Canmore. Charles passed on in 2006, but the couple's two children, Carlin and Jereme, have since stepped up to help lead the family business. Give Snowy Owl Sled Dog Tours a call and experience a new twist on Canadian tradition.

104-602 Bow Valley Trail, Canmore AB
(403) 678-4369
www.snowyowltours.com

McKenzie Meadows Golf Club

The picturesque course at McKenzie Meadows Golf Club suits any skill level. The club also gives you all the extras that make it easy to spend the entire day at the club, including top-notch instruction. The course rewards golfers with remarkable views of both the mountains and the city skyline from a variety of vistas. Seven lakes throughout the course make for scenic challenges. With four tee boxes at every hole, beginners and experts alike can enjoy the course. McKenzie Meadows boasts a first-class Golf Academy that improves the games of more than 500 clients each year. Take a private lesson tailored to your needs, or join with friends for semi-private instruction. Children get a head start on the game with the Junior Academy, available for kids ages eight and up. After the game, stop by the bar and grill in the clubhouse for delicious meals, a full bar and three plasma televisions. The pro shop carries the best in equipment and apparel from brands such as Ping and Callaway. If you are organizing a golf tournament, McKenzie Meadows makes it a breeze, with tournament packages that include catering, a separate facility for large groups and attention to every detail that makes your event a success. Scott Orban is director of operations for the public course, which is bordered by the Bow River and Fish Creek Provincial Park. Visit the McKenzie Meadows Golf Club for the best in golfing, lessons and dining.

17215 McKenzie Meadows Drive SE, Calgary AB
(403) 257-BALL (2255)
www.mckenziemeadows.com

Helen Upperton and Heather Moyse, Canadian bobsleigh team

Amber Petersen, freestyle skier

International guests receive instruction on the bobsleigh ride open to the public

Olympic calibre 22-foot half-pipe
Photo by Nick Foy

North America's fastest zipline, Skyline at the Park
Photo by Dave Buston Photography, courtesy CODA

The ski hill, in summer, becomes a mountain bike park
Photo by Dave Buston Photography, courtesy CODA

Catching air at Canada Olympic Park

Jumps and stunts on the ski hill in summer

A carpet lift takes skiers and snowboarders to a beginners' run

Photos by Dave Buston Photography, courtesy CODA (this page)

Canada Olympic Park

Located at the gateway to the fabulous Rocky Mountains, Canada Olympic Park is just 15 minutes west of downtown Calgary. Perhaps the most visible legacy of the 1988 Olympic Winter Games, the venue is not only a popular recreation facility, but also a must-see tourist destination. As the hub facility for the nation's proposed first Centre of Sport Excellence, Canada Olympic Park also serves as a multi-purpose competition and training area for development and high-performance athletes that are all looking for their place on the podium in Vancouver 2010 and beyond.

More than 292,000 skiers and snowboarders hit the slopes during the winter months with lessons available for both children and adults of all ability levels. The Park features a world-unique 22-foot half-pipe which replicates the 2010 Olympic venue, and a freestyle aerials and moguls site, built to international standards. The ski jump tower is the highest viewpoint in Calgary and now serves as the launch pad for the exciting Skyline at the Park, North America's fastest zipline ride. Visitors can also take an adrenaline-pumping ride down the same track used by the Jamaican Bobsleigh Team immortalized in the movie *Cool Runnings*—at speeds of up to 120 kilometres per hour. Learn how the bobsleigh and luge athletes train with a visit to the Ice House, the world's only indoor refrigerated building used for start training.

As the days get longer, the fun continues with plenty of summer activities as well. Mountain bike trails criss-cross the ski hill, mini-golf, climbing walls and Eurobungee all keep you busy. Visit the Frank King Olympic Visitors Centre and the Slopestyle retail store for the latest in summer and winter soft goods, and enjoy dinner at the Paskapoo Restaurant and Lounge. The Olympic Hall of Fame and Museum offers the largest collection of Olympic memorabilia in North America, including 23 Olympic torches. Holdings date back to the 1936 Berlin Games. Come to Canada Olympic Park, where you can discover the glories of the Olympics.

88 Canada Olympic Road SW, Calgary AB
(403) 247-5452
www.canadaolympicpark.ca

Reptile World

Boa constrictor Brittany loves to give hugs and Fred the 600-pound American alligator has a healthy appetite. These are just two of the more than 200 animals you will find at Reptile World. This conservation-oriented reptile house opened its doors in Drumheller in 1989 and moved to its current location in 2004. Owner Dave Bethel has been fascinated with reptiles since his childhood in England. Dave, head keeper Shawn Fraser and the rest of the Reptile World staff are dedicated to educating the public about this largely misunderstood class of creatures, many of which are threatened with extinction. Reptile World practises what is literally a hands-on approach. Guests can handle Brittany, who was born at the facility in 1994. You'll also find cobras and pythons, black mambas and Gila monsters. The enclosures that hold the animals resemble their natural environments. If you are looking for creatures with a big bite, check out Fred the alligator or his distant relatives of the crocodile family. In addition to presenting guests with thrilling and educational experiences, Reptile World is dedicated to preservation, and it has many captive reproduction efforts underway. Slither on in to Reptile World for a hands-on experience with some of nature's most fascinating creatures.

95–3 Avenue E, Drumheller AB
(403) 823-8623
www.reptileworld.net

Jubilations Dinner Theatre

It's well known that hilarity aids digestion, which makes Jubilations Dinner Theatre the ideal mix of food and entertainment. Jubilations serves a four-course dinner complimented by spoofs of popular television shows and movies. Expect to become part of the action along with waiters and bartenders who dress in character for the show. Jubilations produces five shows each year in two theatres with Randy Apostle as artistic director of WOW Productions. The company has been going strong in Edmonton for nine years, where Georgina Theissen is owner. Riley Fitzpatrick owns the five-year-old Calgary theatre. Expect live vocals of familiar country rock and easy listening songs, professional sets and lots of laughter with your meal. In 2007, WOW combined moments from Jerry Seinfeld with contemporary tunes and Monty Python with Beatles classics for some imaginative musical comedy. Dinner unfolds in a leisurely manner with soup and salad following the first act. Your entrée comes just before the second act. Another break offers a choice of two desserts and a celebration of any birthdays or anniversaries in the audience with singing and a small gift. A third act completes the dramatic festivities. Enjoy old-fashioned dinner theatre with up-to-date wit at Jubilations Dinner Theatre.

1002 37 Street SW, Calgary AB
(403) 249-7799
8882 170 Street, Edmonton AB
(780) 484-2424 or (877) 214-2424
www.jubilations.ca

Spruce Meadows: The Venue

Within the city limits of Calgary yet nestled among the foothills of Western Canada, Spruce Meadows offers 175 hectares of stunning country scenery, and nearly 52,000 square feet of elegant and flexible space for corporate events, meetings, weddings, special events or magical theme parties. In addition to Spruce Meadows' reputation as an internationally renowned venue for the sport of show jumping, it's also known as a gathering place for families to spend quiet time together and a spot for social functions of all kinds. Adorned with beautiful displays of flowers, hedges, berms, spruce trees and aspen groves, the grounds of Spruce Meadows really shine. A stroll reveals a trout pond, singular and fanciful statuary, and dedicated park and open spaces. Indoors, the Spruce Meadows Congress Hall offers 12,000 square feet of sophisticated meeting space that can be set up to suit your specific needs. The British House's Georgian Room boasts an intimate atmosphere and 3,600 square feet of space. The Equi-Plex's flexibility and 36,000 square feet can host everything from equestrian events to conferences uniting professionals from all over the world. Spruce Meadows boasts an annual attendance of more than 400,000, and it's no wonder why: its beautiful grounds, superior venues and staggering size make it unmatched in the world. Spruce Meadows is a welcoming, tranquil getaway from the hustle and bustle of urban living. For a getaway experience that can be anything you want it to be, plan an escape to Spruce Meadows.

18011 Spruce Meadows Way SW, Calgary AB
(403) 974-4227

Spruce Meadows: The Sport

Recognized as number one in the world for the sport of show jumping by the Fédération Equestre Internationale (FEI) for four years in a row, Spruce Meadows is an unparalleled venue for sportsmanship and an international destination for fans of equestrian sports. Spruce Meadows is home to national and international tournaments nearly year-round. Beginning in February with the indoor February Classic and stretching through November with the Pony Classic, there's always something going on. Over Spruce Meadow's rich history, the family behind it all, the Southerns, have watched attendance at the tournaments grow into the tens of thousands; the prize money grow to six figures and athletes become household names. They have seen media coverage grow to reach 740 million homes via satellite television. Spruce Meadows is familiar to horse lovers in Europe, the Middle East, Asia and South America. Spruce Meadows is also an innovator in the world of show jumping. It created the Riders' Cup, a match play competition that has gained success and acceptance since its inception in 1999. Athletes from all over the world compete in Spruce Meadows' tournaments: In 2004 alone, athletes came from 20 countries. It's no wonder that, in addition to garnering FEI recognition, international athletes have voted to give Spruce Meadows the coveted Eric Wauters Award for best venue. Spruce Meadows provides excitement for everyone from enthusiastic fans to curious show goers. You'll fondly remember a trip to Spruce Meadows for a lifetime.

18011 Spruce Meadows Way SW, Calgary AB
(403) 974-4227
www.sprucemeadows.com

Spruce Meadows: Complimentary Activities

In addition to the indoor and outdoor tournaments that draw excited crowds, the meandering paths and breathtaking scenery, the charming architecture and awe-inspiring amenities, Spruce Meadows offers a number of year-round activities that complement and enrich the Spruce Meadows experience. At each tournament, the International Plaza is transformed into an international festival, country fair or historical village. Exhibits entice, enchant and entertain, adding to the excitement and thrill of the show jumping itself. You'll find equine themed art exhibits and booths offering locally made arts and crafts. The whole family can enjoy a variety of fun activities. Each moment at Spruce Meadows is sure to be filled with wonder. Every exhibit is free with the price of admission. Christmas is one of the most magical times of year at Spruce Meadows, and visitors will find the Congress Hall and British House decked in wonderfully ornate Christmas trimmings. The grounds are transformed into a winter wonderland that will bedazzle the whole family. The dedicated and friendly staff is currently developing an international children's village that will feature Christmas classics from around the world. It will be unveiled in an upcoming Christmas season. For a taste of the international, the Canadian and the beautiful, pay a visit to Spruce Meadows.

18011 Spruce Meadows Way SW, Calgary AB
(403) 974-4227
www.sprucemeadows.com

Spruce Meadows: The Horses

Not only does Spruce Meadows host the world's most talented riders and most competitive and legendary horses, you can actually buy a horse as well. All Spruce Meadows horses have been trained and ridden by Spruce Meadows' experienced professional staff. All have approved progeny and bloodlines. At Spruce Meadows, each horse is matched with its potential owner personally, and the staff asks that all prospective buyers visit the grounds. This gives potential buyers the opportunity to meet and interact with the horses and to choose a horse that is right for them. With a full range of stabling accommodations and a full-time staff dedicated to caring for and training each animal, buyers know that Spruce Meadows horses are well-treated, superior equine companions. Spruce Meadows specializes in Hanoverian horses, known for their dominance in show jumping. The enterprise also offers a breeding program that provides horse breeders all over the world with the genes that create champions. All Spruce Meadows' stallions are approved by the Verband Hannoverscher Warmblutzuchter e.V., the Canadian Warmblood Horse Breeders Association and the Canadian Sport Horse Association. Spruce Meadows is the place to look for a champion-quality horse that will serve you well for years to come.

18011 Spruce Meadows Way SW, Calgary AB
(403) 974-4227
www.sprucemeadows.com

Marge and Ron Southern

Spruce Meadows: The History

The first tournament at Spruce Meadows took place in 1976. In those days, sporting events were typically only televised locally, but television broadcast capabilities have been present at Spruce Meadows since the start. It's innovation of this kind that has made Spruce Meadows what it is today. From the beginning, Spruce Meadows has embodied the Southern family's dream of combining good friendship, good commerce and good sport. Spruce Meadows pioneered many trends now taken for granted in equestrian sport, such as sponsor-funded prize money. Most extraordinarily, however, Spruce Meadows has from the outset remained accessible to people from all walks of life. With affordable entry fees and a wide range of activities, people from all over can enjoy Spruce Meadows. Over the decades, the staff has grown from seven to 87 full-time employees, the prizes offered have grown to six figures, the facilities have expanded to include venues for corporate hosting and hospitality, and the series of tournaments have expanded to more than 14 national and international events. The Southern family has carefully invested in Spruce Meadows' future, adding a media centre in 1987, an on-site television production and editing suite in 1994, an industrial kitchen in 1997, the Re/Max Family Center and Superstore Playground in 2004 and two more beautiful parks in 2005 and 2006. With meticulously sculpted grounds and attentively considered expansion, it's no wonder that Spruce Meadows has an international reputation, and will continue to build upon that reputation in the years to come.

18011 Spruce Meadows Way SW, Calgary AB
(403) 974-4227

Spruce Meadows: The Sponsors

Spruce Meadows offers nearly unlimited opportunities for sponsors great and small. From individual donations to taking on financial responsibility for an entire sponsor-funded prize, fans and corporations alike all have a place among the sponsors. Volunteers are the mainstay of Spruce Meadows. The Pegasus Club currently consists of over 500 people who help during tournament time with a variety of tasks. Major sponsors know that Spruce Meadows has a media footprint through television that reaches more than 400 million households in more than 100 countries. Needless to say, sponsorship doesn't go unnoticed. In addition, Spruce Meadows Television, an award-winning division of Spruce Meadows, has established network and distribution agreements and can offer preferred rates and terms that it can pass along to sponsors. Spruce Meadows Television creates and implements a variety of programs annually, including corporate and education programs and campaigns for clients ranging from corporations to government agencies. Sponsors can choose from a host of worthy causes, including the Spruce Meadows' Legacy Fund, established with the goal of ensuring Spruce Meadows growth and financial security for future generations. Additionally, sponsors may choose to support a specific tournament or event. Whether your choice to become a sponsor is a ringing endorsement for your company, or a contribution according to your means, an investment in Spruce Meadows is an investment in the future.

18011 Spruce Meadows Way SW, Calgary AB
(403) 974-4227
www.sprucemeadows.com

Town of Okotoks

One of Alberta's finest recreation areas, Okotoks is nestled in the pristine Sheep River Valley in the heart of the Alberta Foothills. The front range of the Rocky Mountains borders the town on the west, while closer to home, rivers, meadows and forests offer fishing, tubing and hiking. To the north, Calgary lies within 20 kilometers. Natural beauty and city conveniences set the scene for what has become one of Alberta's thriving artist communities. Visitors will find local art works on display at the Station, a good place to start in Okotoks. This former railway station now houses the town's visitor centre as well as cultural programs and art exhibits. You'll find art inspired by the landscapes and wildlife of the region as well as abstract and avant-garde styles. A gift shop at the centre carries locally-crafted cards, jewellery and glass art. While at the Station, pick up a walking tour guide of Okotoks's 34 historic buildings, including remnants of the Lineham lumber mill that was the mainstay of the town's early economy. The Okotoks Heritage House houses the town's historical museum. Don't miss this charming getaway destination, the Town of Okotoks.

49 N Railway Avenue, Okotoks AB
(Heritage House) (403) 938-8969
53 N Railway Avenue, Okotoks AB
(Station Cultural Centre) (403) 938-3204
www.okotoks.ca

Weekend Warriors Paintball

Brothers Mike and Pat Radford found an outlet for their interest in military strategy when they launched Weekend Warriors Paintball in 1987 with their sister Kim. The all-year facility, located between Didsbury and Olds, offers a 15,000-square-foot indoor arena with a dust-proof surface, a pro shop and 35 acres of outdoor playing fields that feature such props as school buses and airplanes. Creating a one-of-a-kind fantasy scenario for a group is one of Mike and Pat's favourite activities and requires advanced planning. You can dream up your own game or choose

Roman gladiator or Rambo themes. As connoisseurs of paintball, Mike and Pat specialize in practices for tournament play and hosted the 2007 field for the MR Paintball Series, the largest tournament in western Canada. The game has entertained groups of men, women and children between the ages of 10 and 72 and attracts organized groups and gatherings of friends. One staging area includes barbecue grills, picnic tables and a playground for the little ones. You can leave the field intact, thanks to complimentary camouflage wear, protective face gear and body armor. The staff stays close to assure everyone has fun and that the equipment works properly. Get you adrenalin pumping at Weekend Warrior Paintball.

Rural Route #2, Olds AB
(403) 556-2132 or (866) 556-2132
www.weekendwarriors.ab.ca

Mountain View Taxidermy

The scene is wild at Mountain View Taxidermy, where Povl and Bibianne Munksgaard practice the art of making mounted animals appear very much alive. On a typical day in the showroom, a cougar bares its fangs to an intruder that has entered its territory, while a pair of ducks takes

flight from a bird of prey. A black bear balances on its hind legs as it catches a scent on the breeze. Since 1987, wildlife enthusiasts Povl and Bibianne have mounted just about every wild mammal and bird that can be hunted or found in Alberta, including elk, bobcat and owls. They are renowned around the world for their artful way of recreating nature in its most natural form. Their work fills the exhibits at the Chester Mjolness Wildlife Museum in Sundre. Hunters can bring their catch, accompanied by licenses and permits, to Povl and Bibianne for mounting. If you're not a hunter but are thinking that a mount would look good in your den, Mountain View Taxidermy is a great place to shop for one. To see taxidermy treated as an art, go to Mountain View Taxidermy.

6312 46 Street, Olds AB
(403) 556-6644
www.mountainviewtaxidermy.com

Photo by Pocketwiley

The Saskatoon Farm

Why just reminisce about the good old days when you can visit them? The Saskatoon Farm is a place where things are done the old fashioned way, on site and by hand to assure the highest quality and standards. Come to the garden centre to find an excellent selection of Saskatoon bushes and other prairie-hardy fruit-bearing trees and shrubs. There's also a wide selection of perennials, annuals and beautiful hanging baskets, as well as landscaping items. Your visit need not stop there, however. The Saskatoon Farm also has a fabulous café and gift shop. The café offers wholesome daily specials such as meatloaf or homemade pizza. Indulge yourself in some famous Saskatoon pie by the slice or homemade soup and sandwiches. Make time to enjoy the recently expanded gift shop which features many interesting gift ideas such as fountains, copperware, custom gift baskets and furniture. It's like shopping at a boutique with farm prices. The farm also offers a selection of berry jams, toppings and pie fillings all from its own kitchen. The u-pick Saskatoon season starts in late July and is a fun adventure. You may even catch a glimpse of the herd of buffalo while you are enjoying the river and orchard views. Come to the Saskatoon Farm for a wonderful and relaxing time.

338 Avenue, DeWinton AB
(403) 938-6245 or (800) 463-2113
www.saskatoonfarm.com

The Canadian Badlands Passion Play

Putting on the Canadian Badlands Passion Play is the main mission of the Canadian Badlands Passion Play Society. Its members, volunteers and employees work tirelessly on the project. The play, which takes place annually in July, is set in a natural, outdoor amphitheatre chosen for superior acoustic qualities and a landscape that resembles the ancient Holy Land. Each year the script is revised and loyal fans come back to see each new production. Despite the ever-changing script and a rotating roster of professional actors and volunteers, the play follows as accurately as possible the life, death and resurrection of Jesus Christ as related in the Gospels. A choir of hundreds provides live musical accompaniment. Each of the 2,500 stadium seats boasts a superb view of the stage and every performance is a powerful event. Many theatergoers have described the experience as deeply spiritual. Attractions Canada has called it Alberta's top cultural attraction. During other times of the year the society uses the amphitheatre for other cultural events, such as a performing arts summer school, a Christmas concert and a Beethoven in the Badlands concert series. The site also serves as a year-round interpretive centre, enriching the community with cultural resources and knowledge. Come see the Canadian Badlands Passion Play, Canada's largest dramatization of the life of Christ in a panoramic setting that matches the sweeping arc of the story.

605 17 Street SW, Drumheller AB
(403) 823-2001
www.canadianpassionplay.com

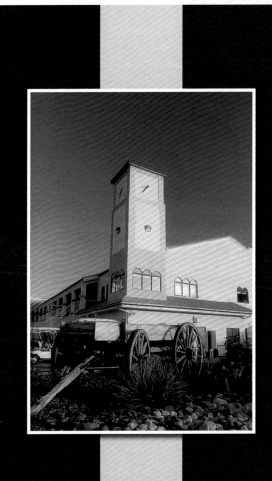

Paradise Canyon Golf Resort

Paradise Canyon Golf Resort is one of the top 100 courses in Canada and rated the number one golf course in Southern Alberta. This RCI Points affiliated resort boasts gold crown status, attracting visitors from all over the world. The course is a lush oasis tucked deep within a canyon beside the hills and cliffs and the river. It has a clubhouse, driving range, on-site accommodations and a full resort including fine dining with an outdoor terrace. Enjoy the pool with a slide, hot tub, health club, tennis courts, driving range and putting green. Some visitors never want to leave, and purchase one of the arts and crafts-style homes on nearby Canyon Crest to stay near the course. For out of town visitors, there are studio and one and two bedroom suites available in the Golf Villas. All villas are within walking distance of the Arizona-style clubhouse, with full kitchens, televisions and fireplaces, and can be booked alone or with a golf package. The golf course offers exciting challenges, prompting more than one serious golfer to claim that it provides an unrivaled golf resort experience, and has a seven-month season. A professional staff provides private and group lessons to get you on top of your game in a teaching facility with grass and artificial teeing areas, putting greens and practice bunkers. The city of Lethbridge recognized Paradise Canyon as the 2004 Business of the Year for its hospitality, evident throughout the resort. The course was also the host of the 2008 Canadian Amateur game. Challenge your game in an unusually stunning setting at Paradise Canyon Golf Resort.

185 Canyon Boulevard W, Lethbridge AB
(403) 381-GOLF (4653) or
877 707-GOLF (4653)
www.playinparadise.com

Dinosaur Trail Golf & Country Club

Dinosaur Trail Golf & Country Club offers players a variety of scenery and challenges, making golfers feel as though they have experienced two different courses in one. On the front nine, enjoy a beautiful mature course. The back nine is a challenging example of target golf, full of dramatic vistas and breathtaking views of the Drumheller Valley badlands. The course first opened in 1965, with nine tree-lined holes along a peaceful river. The back nine opened in 1996. Golf professional Phil McCluskey says the second half of the course is one if the purest forms of target golf you will ever play. Tee off at the tenth hole with a 100-foot drop on either side of the fairway. As you tackle the twelfth hole, the green stands as an island in the distance, far below you. Walking through the 78 acres dotted with coulees and hoodoos, you can find nearly as many fossils as stray golf balls. Dinosaur Trail offers a full-service pro shop, driving range and lessons for all skill levels. A fully licenced clubhouse seats 85, and with a view of the first tee and the ninth green, it makes an ideal venue for any special event. Phil and the rest of the team at Dinosaur Trail strive to offer only the highest quality services and amenities, while keeping prices affordable. Come play a round at the Dinosaur Trail Golf & Country Club and experience the challenges, excitement and natural beauty of a magnificent course.

N Dinosaur Trail, Drumheller AB
(403) 823-5622
www.dinosaurtrailgolf.com

Bar U Ranch
National Historic Site

Between rolling foothills and the Rocky Mountains lies the Bar U Ranch
National Historic Site of Canada. Established in 1882, it is one of Canada's
first and most enduring corporate ranches. Set aside plenty of time to
wander the 148 hectares of living history that commemorate ranching in
Canada. Climb aboard the wagon and feel the power of the Percheron
horses as they take you on a tour through the site. Immerse yourself in
stories of ranching pioneers—fortunes made and lost, cattle killing winters
and massive roundups. You may want to plan your visits around one of the
special events that are hosted throughout the season. There's a Polo Day
that's not to be missed and an Old Time Ranch Rodeo in which working
cowboys from many of Alberta's top ranches compete. Experience western
hospitality when you enjoy an authentic and delicious meal at the Bar U
Café and visit the western Gift Shop featuring items by local artists and
craftspeople. Come to the Bar U Ranch, a site that honours the important
role of ranching in Canada's history. You can be sure of a memorable day.

Highway #22, 13 km S of Longview AB
(403) 395-3044 or (888) 773-8888
www.pc.gc.ca

Hinton Golf Club

Playing golf at the Hinton Golf Club places you in the heavily forested foothills of the Rocky Mountains on terrain that is both challenging and inspirational. The first nine holes of the course were carved out of the forest in 1962, and the second nine followed in 1993. The course is known for its many secluded holes and several remarkable mountain views, including the view looking back from the third hole and the dramatic backdrop as you contemplate the narrow fairway of the signature 11th hole. Ample challenge and a bountiful dose of serenity make this course well worth the drive no matter where your journey began. Whatever your caliber of play, you will find something to shoot for on the course that hosted the 2003 Clarica Alberta Men's Amateur Championship. The course runs from 5,433 to 6,729 yards. The semi-private club attracts new members regularly. You'll find a full-sized driving range and a well-stocked pro shop featuring top products. The two resident pros offer lessons and club fittings. The clubhouse dining room and lounge give you a satisfying excuse to linger and replay your game in the company of friends. Get off the beaten path and go to the Hinton Golf Club, known to locals as the enchanted forest.

725 Gregg Avenue, Hinton AB
(780) 865-2904 or (866) 666-2904
www.hintongolfclub.com

Lakeside Go-Karts & Mini-Golf

Lakeside Go-Karts & Mini-Golf is a clean, safe and friendly environment that serves one great purpose: it provides fun times for everyone. Owned by the Ellerby family, Lakeside Go-Karts has installed the best outdoor go-kart track in the area and hired a knowledgeable staff to assist visitors. Events such as birthdays, corporate outings or family get-togethers can be twice as fun with all of the options available, including kiddie cars, bumper cars, adult and double-seater go-karts and a challenging 18-hole mini-golf course to truly test your skills. After taking on

the curves and hairpins on the track, walk over to the concession stand and choose from a selection of hot dogs, nachos, corn dogs, soda pop and all the standard concession stand fare you would expect to find. Tim and Melody Ellerby take great care in the safety, maintenance and presentation of their grounds, and are grateful for the family and friends who have been so supportive over the years. Lakeside Go-Karts & Mini-Golf offers entertainment for all ages, so choose your activity and be prepared to smile.

5324 Lakeshore Drive, Sylvan Lake AB
(403) 887-3190
www.lakesidegokarts.ca

Sylvan Lake Paintball

Adrenaline rush season runs May through October in Sylvan Lake. That's when Sylvan Lake Paintball is open, where fans of this rapidly growing sport can test their tactics and mettle while pushing their physical limits to the max. The four-acre grounds are smattered with trees, natural bunkers and high grass areas. For a different kind of challenge, try stationary speed ball or inflatable speed ball on the course called the Money Field. Sylvan Lake Paintball books groups as well as individuals, and in fact, many business companies are discovering the team-building benefits of paintball, a sport that requires responsible communication among teammates.

Experienced referees and gun techs are on site to keep the game clean, if such a word can apply. The pro shop carries Tippman 98 semi-automatic rifles and other top-of-the-line rental equipment, including coveralls and face shields. Owner Branden Majeau, who loves the thrill of the game, left a management position in the paintball business to found Sylvan Lake Paintball. He hasn't raised his prices since opening in 2003. Take aim and open fire at his challenging and exciting paintball course.

17 Westwood Court, Sylvan Lake AB
(403) 887-4487

The World's Largest Dinosaur

More than 26 metres (86 feet) tall and weighing in at more than 65 tonnes (145,000 pounds), it truly is the World's Largest Dinosaur—and you'll delight in climbing right into its mouth. This attraction had its start in 1979, when a band of Drumheller businessfolk conceived of the idea of a giant dinosaur for the downtown. The idea gained strength in the 1990s, when local boosters learned of a five-storey interior-accessible pike fish at Wisconsin's Fishing Hall of Fame. The Wisconsin artifact demonstrated that it would be possible to create a fearsome dinosaur in the same manner. Construction began on-site in late 1999, while the dinosaur's skin was manufactured in China. In October 2000, the dinosaur opened to rave reviews. The creature is about four times the size of a real *Tyrannosaurus rex*. The skin alone covers more than 750 square metres. Guests can enter the dinosaur at the base and climb 106 stairs into the dinosaur's mouth, where they are treated to a spectacular view of Drumheller and the beautiful Canadian Badlands. The World's Largest Dinosaur has won awards from Travel Alberta and Attractions Canada. Want a keepsake of your time in the dinosaur's fierce jaws? Check out the Gift Shop and Tourist Information Centre, where you can find clothing, toys, fossils and giftware, and also learn about the Drumheller region's other attractions. Come and experience the best view of Drumheller from inside the mouth of the World's Largest Dinosaur.

60-1 Avenue W, Drumheller AB
(866) 823-8100
www.worldslargestdinosaur.com
www.traveldrumheller.com

Hotel Selkirk

In the early part of the 20th century, the Hotel Selkirk, now located in Fort Edmonton Park, was Edmonton's number one society spot, a place to see and be seen in every sense of the word. The historic hotel was destroyed by a tragic fire in 1962, but has since been marvelously rebuilt to incorporate a sleek combination of old world elegance and modern comforts. Hotel Selkirk is a seasonal hotel, open May through September, which offers 30 handsomely restored guest rooms and suites. Each is tastefully decorated with antiques and reproduction pieces. Modern amenities include wireless Internet, in-room temperature control and private bathrooms. Johnson's Café, in the hotel, features an elegant 1920s motif, an exemplary wait staff and an array of delectable entrées. Hotel Selkirk's Mahogany Room, once known as Canada's longest bar, has been masterfully designed with sumptuous architectural details and a rich décor that closely replicates the bar's original, pre-fire look. This is an ideal place to unwind in the evening with friends while enjoying a sampling from the exclusive wine list or sipping some of the bar's exceptional spirits. In addition to offering excellent accommodations, the hotel serves as a gathering place and events hall for community activities, such as weddings and holiday galas. Sign your name to the guest book and leave your mark in the annals of history at Hotel Selkirk, where the fusion of past and present will yield wonderful memories in the future.

1920s Street, Fort Edmonton Park, Edmonton AB (780) 496-7227 or (877) 496-7227 *www.hotelselkirk.com*

Rutherford House Provincial Historic Site

Rutherford House Provincial Historic Site is the vividly restored home of Alberta's first Premier, Alexander Cameron Rutherford, and his family. It is now a designated provincial historic site and living museum. The Rutherford's took possession of their new home overlooking the North Saskatchewan River in February of 1911, and quickly became known for their gracious hospitality as they hosted events for friends, family and the area's political and social elite. The family's hospitable traditions continued until 1940 when Mattie, Alexander's wife, died at the age of 74. Alexander sadly joined his wife a year later, but the Rutherford's convivial legacy lives on in the home he so dearly loved. Rutherford House was opened as a provincial historic site in 1973 and today welcomes more than 15,000 guests each year who come from across Canada and the globe to explore this historical *grand dame*. The house has been completely restored to reflect how it would have looked at the start of the First World War. The gleam of highly polished silver, the teasing scent of warm scones and costumed interpreters are just a few of the nearly magical, yet remarkably simple things that send you whirling back to a bygone era of afternoon teas and Irving Berlin. You can also get a taste of the past in the Arbour Restaurant, which serves vintage recipes. Then wander over to the gift shop for keepsakes that recall the end of an era. Enjoy a glimpse of the past with a visit to Rutherford House today.

11153 Saskatchewan Drive, Edmonton AB
(780) 427-3995
www.tprc.alberta.ca/rh

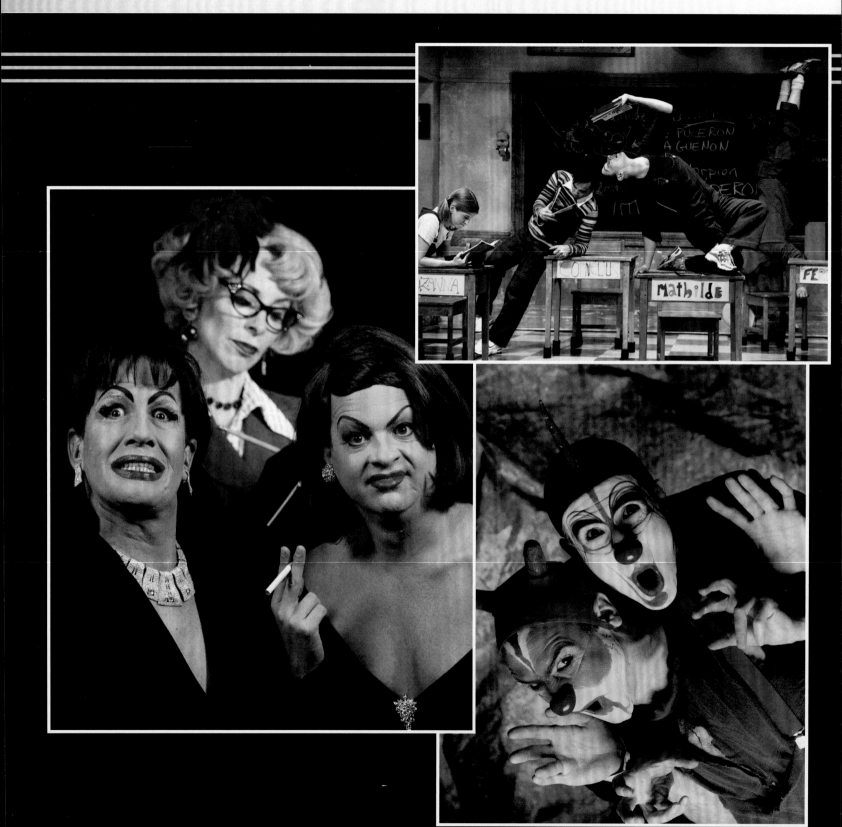

The Edmonton International Fringe Theatre Festival

An annual event since 1982, the Edmonton International Fringe Theatre Festival is at the forefront of edgy theatre in Canada. Edmonton's answer to the Edinburgh Fringe Festival drew 45 theatre groups in its first year and has steadily grown since, averaging 150 groups in recent years. Some 70,000-plus audience members flock to the festival each year, making it second only to the original in size. That doesn't count the nearly half-a-million folks just there for the carnival atmosphere. With everything theatre is capable of imagining, this festival has something for everyone. Clowns and street performers entertain passers-by at the outdoor festival. The Bring Your Own Venue tradition stages performances outside of traditional theatres, in such venues as local homes, garages and churches. Those looking to laugh will find both intentional and unintentional camp. You'll even find productions by award-winning playwrights such as Kenneth Brown of *Life After Hockey* fame, who got his start here. All acts are admitted by lottery in order to avoid any kind of censorship. For theatre with the spirit of invention, don't miss the Edmonton International Fringe Theatre Festival.

10330–84 Avenue, Edmonton AB
(780) 448-9000
www.fringetheatreadventures.ca

Lakewood Golf Resort

For nearly 40 years, Lakewood Golf Resort has been a golfer's delight for recreational golfers. The nine-hole course in Sylvan Lake is looking better than ever thanks to a 2004 makeover in which all the holes were remodeled to bring the course up-to-date. Owner Darcy Carruthers says the end result is a course with more variety, offering challenges for both novice and experienced golfers. You'll delight in the beautiful scenery, with well-manicured greens and full, tall trees. Some things have remained happily familiar at Lakewood, such as the friendly help you'll get at the pro shop from Butch Bouchard and Ken Greggain, both of whom have been here more than 20 years. The resort offers lessons, a practice range and putting green to help improve your game. Members can participate in several leagues at the resort. Groups looking to hold a tournament can rent the facilities at the resort. The Lakewood Concession offers snacks and light meals. If you're looking for great golf, beautiful scenery and friendly faces, come to Lakewood Golf Resort.

Highway 20 N, Sylvan Lake AB
(403) 887-2477
www.lakewoodgolfresort.ca

Telephone Historical Centre

The Telephone Historical Centre is a museum to phone home about. Located in the Prince of Wales Armouries in Edmonton, the Telephone Historical Centre is the brain child of a group of ED TEL retirees who were looking to preserve the history of the telephone in Edmonton. Beginning with the importation of two telephones into Alberta by Alexander Taylor in 1884, the museum's exhibits trace this history to the present day, showing how advances in technology have completely changed the telephone industry. You'll see the earliest systems featured here, with manual switching and bell-shaped microphones that doubled as both mouth- and earpiece.

Trace the advances to the digital age through the touchable, interactive exhibits. Children will be delighted to have a conversation with Xeldon, the museum's talking robot. In addition, the museum offers a variety of outreach and educational programs for students and groups. A gift shop offers collectibles, books and souvenirs. Dial into an enjoyable visit with the history of the telephone in Edmonton at the Telephone Historical Centre.

10440 108 Avenue, Edmonton AB
(780) 433-1010
www.telephonehistoricalcentre.com

The Bridges at Claresholm Golf Course

If you're looking for a course that will challenge your golf game and please your senses, you'll find the Bridges at Claresholm Golf Course to be a delight. The Bridges was originally built as a nine-hole public course in 1978, but recently received a complete makeover with nine new holes and a new clubhouse. The course has a par 5 with a double dog leg. Twelve of the 18 holes feature water hazards, and one of the man-made lakes is so full of goldfish that the water itself seems to have a golden hue. The new nine was created by renowned designer Les Furber, who sought to make them challenging enough for seasoned golfers while also being accessible to

newcomers. The golf course has a fully stocked pro shop, along with a driving range to practice your swing. The new clubhouse features a comfortable restaurant and a beautiful wood deck overlooking the putting green and 18th hole where you can enjoy your food and drink. The course prides itself on reasonable rates, with specials during the week. The course is owned by the Town of Claresholm but run by its members. Swing on by the Bridges at Claresholm Golf Course for a round.

349 39 Avenue W, Claresholm AB
(403) 625-3500
www.bridgesgolfatclaresholm.com

Muttart Conservatory

With more than 700 species of plants from around the world on colourful display, Muttart Conservatory offers a vision of Eden in Edmonton. The conservatory officially opened its doors in 1976. Architect Peter Hemingway designed the conservatory as four pyramids, each providing a particular climate for a particular class of plants. The Temperate Pyramid features a lush forest of deciduous and evergreen plants, many of which wouldn't survive an Alberta winter outdoors. The Tropical Pyramid is a jungle paradise, with plants from Central and South America as well as Southeast Asia and Australia and a waterfall at the centre. Cactus lovers will thrill to the variety of dry-weather plants in the Arid Pyramid. Mother Nature puts on her finest in the Show Pyramid, with flowering displays that reflect the brightest and most beautiful colours of the season. You can also stroll through the outdoor trial beds and enjoy a picnic in the outdoor arboretum. A gift shop will help you find the perfect souvenir of your trip through this floral fantasy. It's also a beautiful location for weddings and other occasions. Visit Muttart Conservatory for a vision of nature's beauty from around the world.

9626-96A Street, Edmonton AB
(780) 496-8735
www.edmonton.ca/muttart

Valley Zoo

Since 1959, the Valley Zoo has been a paradise for lovers of wildlife. Located in the west end of Edmonton, the zoo is home to more than 100 exotic, endangered and native species. Among familiars like porcupines, rabbits and ponies, you'll see spider monkeys, Bactrian camels and meerkats year round at the zoo. Endangered species include elephants and Siberian tigers. A member of the Species Survival Plan, the Valley Zoo recognizes the special needs of endangered animals and works to preserve the future of the species as well as of its own animals. Through the Adopt an Animal program, citizens can sponsor their favorite residents of the zoo. Guides are always on hand to answer questions about the animals. The staff produces a variety of educational programs and activities for kids of all ages. Enjoy a delicious meal at the lunch bar and find the perfect keepsake at the gift shop. During the summer, paddle boat and pony rides are available. See wildlife from across the globe up-close and personal at the Valley Zoo.

Buena Vista Road and 134 Street, Edmonton AB (780) 496-8787
www.edmonton.ca/valleyzoo

CELEBRATE THE TIMES OF OUR LIVES!

Fort Edmonton Park

Fort Edmonton Park offers visitors a chance to take a step back in time and experience what life was like in several important eras in Edmonton's history. On 64 hectares of parkland, Fort Edmonton Park is Canada's largest living history park. Costumed staff and volunteers guide visitors on a trek through time. The journey begins at a reconstruction of Fort Edmonton, where during the latter half of the 19th century the Hudson's Bay Company had their headquarters. There the men built boats for their summer's journey to Hudson Bay, where they would send to England the furs they had acquired in trades with the Aboriginals. Your next stop on the tour is about four decades later on 1885 Street, where you'll experience the height of the horse and buggy era. Take a stagecoach ride and stop by Kelly's Saloon for something cool to quench your thirst. On 1905 Street, you'll see the town at the turn of the 20th century, with streetcars and a steam train. Proceeding to 1920 Street, you'll experience Edmonton during the roaring '20s. Stop for a treat at Bill's Confectionery or even stay the night at the full service, 1920s-style Hotel Selkirk. Experience Edmonton through the decades at Fort Edmonton Park.

Intersection of Fox Drive and Whitemud Drive, Edmonton AB
(780) 496-8787
www.edmonton.ca/fort

Kane's Motor Cycle Shop Ltd.

When horses were the main mode of transportation, riding high in the saddle with the wind in their hair gave riders an adventure and an intimacy with nature that was hard to beat. That experience became even more exciting when powerful choppers took to the open road. Kane's Motor Cycle Shop supports the journey. Kane's sells everything related to the motorcycling lifestyle, from clothing and necessities to collectibles. Check out the gleaming new bikes, request a part or get a high-performance tune-up from the factory trained technicians. Owner Mick Cawthorn was originally hired by the late Robert Kane Sr. as a mechanic when Cawthorn bet Kane that he could repair an unfixable bike. He did. A legend was born and Cawthorn has been with the business ever since, eventually purchasing it from Kane. This year, Kane's celebrates 50 years of business with a blowout celebration of fun and friends. The celebrations bring diverse people from all over the world together, united by the love of the ride with a contagious positive energy, ready and willing to enjoy the food, camaraderie and street parties. Cawthorn holds an NHRA Top Fuel bike license and plans to continue racing with the team. He sums up the appeal of biking in one resonating sentence: "The whole thing is we just want to have fun." Kane's serves as a nexus for motorcycle events, charities and groups in and around Calgary. Take the time to sign up for the Harley Owners Group® (H.O.G.®) and you'll meet traveling companions who share your passion for the open road. Your travels will take you to pristine lakes, glacier-capped mountains and prairie fields. There is still no better way to enjoy the beauty of Alberta than to rent or saddle up on a Harley® from Kane's Harley-Davidson® in Calgary.

914 11 Street SE, Calgary AB (403) 269-8577
www.kanesharleydavidson.com

Jasper Tramway

The high life begins at the Jasper Tramway. Built in 1964 to accommodate hikers to the alpine zone atop Whistlers Mountain, the aerial tramway now transports over 125,000 people annually from April through October. The Jasper Tramway is the longest and highest tramway tour in Canada. It provides visitors with spectacular views of six mountain ranges, glacial fed lakes, the town of Jasper below and Alberta's longest river, the Athabasca. You begin at an elevation of 1,304 metres above sea level at the lower station. You won't need to wait long, so be sure to allow enough time to browse through the gift shop or have a leisurely hot or cold drink on the patio. Once aboard the enclosed tram cabin, which accommodates up to 30 guests, you'll have a smooth seven minute ride with unbelievable views. The cabin operator and tour guide describe the sights, the history of the area, points of interest and wildlife, as well as answering any questions. The upper station, at an elevation of 2,277 meters, has its own high-altitude gift shop from the lower station. Get your Altitude Junkie t-shirt or that perfect gift for friends and family. Enjoy a hike or a walk on the boardwalk in a setting like no other. After the adventure whips up your appetite, you can find something to satisfy it at the Treeline Restaurant. You'll enjoy stunning views from its glass enclosed seating area while you dine in a cozy cafeteria-style setting. For a trip all will cherish and a true Alpine experience, take the Jasper Tramway and let your heart soar.

Whistler Mountain Road, Jasper AB
(780) 852-3093 or (866) 850-TRAM (8726)
www.jaspertramway.com

Friends of Jasper National Park

If you're on quest to explore the natural and cultural heritage of Jasper National Park, you'll probably meet Friends of Jasper National Park and its many volunteers. People from around the world offer their time and expertise to the organization, which funds research, performs park improvement projects, publishes park-related materials and offers interpretive programs. Interested in watching birds, taking a hike beneath the full moon or participating in a historical guided tour? The Friends make events like these happen. They also post interpretive signs, manage restoration projects and publish a brochure for walkers. Friends of Jasper National Park relies on charitable donations and grants as well as memberships and merchandise sales. Its gift shop is located in Jasper's Information Centre and features note cards, books, maps and outdoor clothing. In 2007, the organization put out a special line of products in celebration of the park's centennial year. Each year the Friends invite visitors to put on their hiking shoes and join the Jasper Institute for environmental instruction in the wildest setting in the Canadian Rockies. The 25-year-old nonprofit organization enhances the park's core programs but does not replace them. Members act as independent advocates with the common goal of protecting and preserving this precious mountain landscape. Take an inside look at the history and natural forces at work in Jasper National Park with help from Friends of Jasper National Park.

415 Connaught Drive, Jasper AB
(780) 852-4767
www.friendsofjasper.com

Freewheel Cycle

Whether you are an amateur or expert, when you walk into Freewheel Cycle you'll be well on your way to being the rider you want to be. Owner Wendy Hall and her partners Steve Stanko, Gunner Ireland and Dave MacDowell are there to help you realize the possibilities. The shop offers a wide range of equipment, including a variety of mountain bikes, snow boards, skis, clothes and more. You will find awesome gear from Dakine, Specialized, Sugoi, as well as Quicksilver and others. The goods range from street wear and tech wear to parts and accessories. You'll find dozens of brands. Freewheel Cycle is fully stocked so you can be fully stoked. The shop also organizes and sponsors local events and stays involved in the community. Kids love Freeskool, a young riders club that teaches techniques and safe trail practices. From your basic tune-up to a complete overhaul, put your wheels in the capable hands of the service department. Think you have a problem that's impossible to fix? From the chunkiest clunkers to the sharpest new rides, the repairfolk have seen it all. Freewheel Cycle also has a complete rental department, with bikes to meet every need and skill level, from full-suspension mountain bikes to 21-speed town cruisers. Whatever type of riding you do, come in to Freewheel cycle and let the friendly and knowledgeable staff help you experience the outdoors the way you want to.

618 Patricia Street, Jasper AB (780) 852-3898 *www.freewheeljasper.com*

Sundre Pioneer Village Museum

A giant crocodile and hippo, antique machinery, a ranger station, and even an old-fashioned taxicab from last century—you'll find all of these at the Sundre Pioneer Village Museum. It took decades to acquire all the artifacts on display. Operated by the Sundre & District Historical Society, the museum captures the history of the area through the eyes of its early pioneers. Visitors see an on-site blacksmith, a bona-fide early 20th century settler's home and displays of hand-made tools and equipment. The Society has moved several historic buildings onto the site and reconstructed them. A barn is set up with stalls, mangers and antique equipment. The Bergen School, built in 1908, is complete with original desks and books. Also on-site are the 1913 Pioneer Cabin, the Ferryman's House from the Garrington Ferry Crossing and the old James River Ranger Station. Immediately next to the Pioneer Village Museum is the recently opened Wildlife Museum, home of *Chester Mjolsness' World of Wildlife*. The Wildlife Museum showcases a variety of big game animals from all corners of the earth. They are set against beautiful murals depicting their natural habitats. In all, the museum has more than 150 animal mounts. Over the years, Chester Mjolsness, a local huntsman, has collected the majority of the animals on display. The museum teaches visitors that hunters are conservationists and do much to enhance the habitats of animals. Come to the Sundre Pioneer Village Museum, where you're sure to take away new information about early Canadian life.

211-1 Avenue SW, Sundre AB
(403) 638-3233
www.museum.sundre.com

Rosebud Theatre

Photo by Morris Ertman

The community of Rosebud doesn't even have a gas station, but it does have Western Canada's largest rural theatre. With fewer than 100 full-time residents, Rosebud is a vibrant arts community that draws more than 40,000 visitors a year, with Rosebud Theatre squarely at the centre. The theatre has its origins in the early 1980s, when Rosebud School of the Arts (then just a high school) put on its first play, which expanded into a full season of live theatre by 1988. Now a professional theatre with student apprentices, Rosebud Theatre productions take the stage at the town's historic Opera House, which has undergone extensive renovation, and at the Studio Stage, a multi-use black-box theatre. Patrons to Rosebud Theatre enjoy a pre-show dinner at the Mercantile Dining Room, formerly the general store. In keeping with its mission to provide top quality programs, Rosebud Theatre plays range from comedy and drama to musicals. *Travel Alberta* has awarded Rosebud Theatre the prestigious Alberta Pride award for catching the essence of the Alberta experience. Come to Rosebud Theatre for a theatre experience that could change the way you view the world.

102 Railway Avenue, Rosebud AB
(403) 677-2350 or (800) 267-7553
www.rosebudtheatre.com

Atlas Coal Mine

In 1911, about 50 people lived in the entire Red Deer River Valley. By the late 1920s, the population had jumped to more than 10,000. The reason was a coal boom, which brought hardy souls to work in the 139 mines that suddenly cropped up all over the valley. Atlas Coal Mine, now a National Historic Site, employed about 150 workers, many of them immigrants, for around five dollars a day. Atlas Coal Mine is the most complete remaining coal mine in Canada. Visitors can attend guided tours of the facility. You can ride on the mine locomotive

or walk at your own pace along the interpretive trail, past mine machines and ghostly outbuildings. The mine preserves the last wooden tipple in North America—a building for loading coal into boxcars. Discover what conditions were like inside the tunnels and learn what the men did to pass the time when they weren't working. Journey back to the era of the great coal boom at the Atlas Coal Mine, rapidly becoming one of the most popular historical sites in Alberta.

110 Century Drive, East Coulee AB
(403) 822-2220
www.atlascoalmine.ab.ca

Aero Space Museum

The Aero Space Museum of Calgary, established in 1975, shares the love and thrill of flight with people of all ages. The museum's collection of civil and military aircraft is a living history documenting Canadian achievements in aviation and space. Learn the history of trailblazers who dreamt of flight and discover the pioneers who adapted aircraft for trade and recreation. Be inspired by the heroes who fought for Canada from the skies, and the adventurers who set their sights on outer space. The museum hosts several special events throughout the year and

rents the museum hangar and classrooms for private events. The gift shop boasts a large selection of aviation books, prints and memorabilia. Hands-on activities, flight simulators, on-going restoration projects and exhibits, including a gallery room featuring the works of renowned Canadian wildlife and aviation artist Randy Fehr, provide something for everyone at the Aero Space Museum.

4629 McCall Way NE, Calgary AB
(403) 250-3752
www.asmac.ab.ca

Casino Calgary

Casino Calgary is a grand entertainment palace of 52,000 square feet, featuring 728 slots and 30 game tables and a 24-hour poker room. As much as size and game counts matter to General Manager Phil Bates, however, he spends most of his working hours striving to ensure Casino Calgary remains the premier facility in the city. From the handsome woodwork and paintings to the bronze statues that contribute to the Western theme, this treasure has a distinct and memorable ambience. Phil leads his staff in seeing that everything stays respectable and that patrons are comfortable. Seventeen of the gaming tables are devoted to blackjack with the rest hosting baccarat, roulette, craps, Pai Gow and other exciting games of chance. Away from the gaming action, Casino Calgary features a full-service dining room, lounges and an entertainment bar with live music and sports on the big screens. Casino Calgary is located just off the Trans Canada Highway and is near the airport with many hotels in the area. Although travellers find it easily accessible, the majority of patrons are locals, who appreciate the rich, comfortable atmosphere. They also recognize that the casino generates revenue for community charities and organizations. The action starts early in the morning and goes into the wee hours of the night at Casino Calgary, and you're invited to become a part of it.

1420 Meridian Road NE, Calgary AB
(403) 248-9467
www.casinoabs.com

Ukrainian Museum of Canada

It might be hard to believe that the Ukrainian population of Canada only began to arrive in the 20th century. At the Ukrainian Museum of Canada of the Ukrainian Women's Association of Canada in Alberta, visitors can rediscover the still vibrant history and culture of this population. The Ukrainian Museum of Canada has its roots in Saskatoon, where the Ukrainian Women's Association first established it in 1936. The Alberta branch opened in Edmonton in 1944, owing to the large Ukrainian influence in the region. In fact, it is attached to St. John's Ukrainian Orthodox Cathedral. The museum displays art, clothing and other historical artifacts dating back to the very first Ukrainian immigrants, Ivan Pylypiw and Wasyl Eleniak, who arrived in Canada in 1891. You'll see regional folk costumes and costumed dolls, wedding headdresses, sculptures and religious icons, as well as farm equipment and household items. The museum also hosts several antique shows with local collectors and appraisers who can offer advice on how to care properly for historical pieces. The museum is open seasonally from May to October, but tourists can visit by appointment in the off-season. Explore the roots of the Ukrainian Canadian at the Ukrainian Museum of Canada of the Ukrainian Women's Association of Canada, Alberta Branch.

10611 110 Avenue NW, Edmonton AB
(780) 425-9692
www.umc.sk.ca

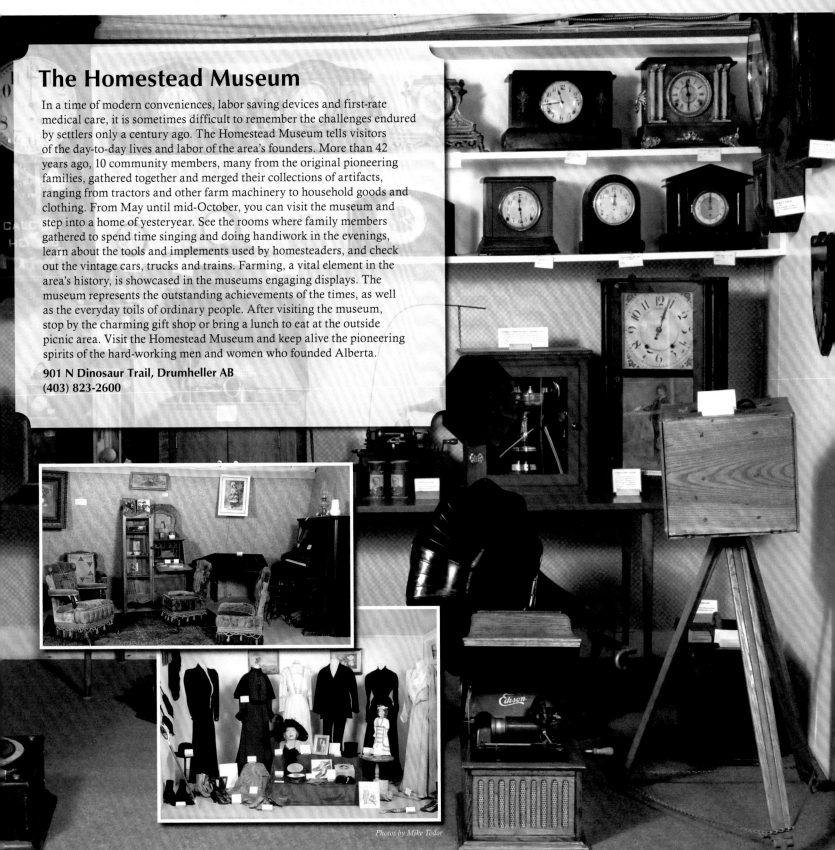

The Homestead Museum

In a time of modern conveniences, labor saving devices and first-rate medical care, it is sometimes difficult to remember the challenges endured by settlers only a century ago. The Homestead Museum tells visitors of the day-to-day lives and labor of the area's founders. More than 42 years ago, 10 community members, many from the original pioneering families, gathered together and merged their collections of artifacts, ranging from tractors and other farm machinery to household goods and clothing. From May until mid-October, you can visit the museum and step into a home of yesteryear. See the rooms where family members gathered to spend time singing and doing handiwork in the evenings, learn about the tools and implements used by homesteaders, and check out the vintage cars, trucks and trains. Farming, a vital element in the area's history, is showcased in the museums engaging displays. The museum represents the outstanding achievements of the times, as well as the everyday toils of ordinary people. After visiting the museum, stop by the charming gift shop or bring a lunch to eat at the outside picnic area. Visit the Homestead Museum and keep alive the pioneering spirits of the hard-working men and women who founded Alberta.

901 N Dinosaur Trail, Drumheller AB
(403) 823-2600

Photos by Mike Todor

Canmore Caverns

Spelunkers, eco-tourists and adventure-seekers can explore caves beneath Grotto Mountain with the help of Canmore Caverns tours. Head guide Eli Brager and his team lead year-round natural history tours of the Rat's Nest Cave, a million year-old cave system. This exiting tour starts with a 30-minute hike up a forested mountain trail overlooking the Bow River before descending into Rat's Nest, an undeveloped cave with no artificial lights, boardwalks or handrails. The four-kilometre-long cave is replete with glacial deposits, pools of sparkling water and calcite formations. Guides point out animal fossils dating back 7,000 years and human artifacts that are 3,000 years old. Canmore Caverns owner Charles Yonge, originally from England, discovered caving at the University of Surrey, where he was studying physics. He came to Canada for graduate study, transferred to University of Calgary and settled in Canmore. Yonge received a Provincial Science grant to start the caving business in 1986, but he still stays active in the scientific community. He was drawn to cave science in part because it unites fields such as physics, chemistry and biology. For a tour that's both educational and challenging, take a trip to Canmore Caverns and let your caving adventure begin.

1009 Larch Place, Canmore AB
(877) 317-1178
www.canadianrockies.net/wildcavetours

Turner Valley Golf & Country Club

Turner Valley Golf & Country Club has a colourful history dating back to the 1930s, when sand greens were the standard and an old bunkhouse served as the clubhouse. Today the course, which started as a nine-hole course for executives on land donated by Royalite Oil Company, features 18 holes with four sets of tees and speedy, well maintained greens. The course is just 30 minutes from Calgary on rolling terrain with the Rocky Mountains and Sheep River as a backdrop. You'll be sure to remember the signature 10th hole, a par-3, 170-yard beauty with a 70-foot drop and swirling winds that warrant careful club selection. Steve Moe, the president of Alberta's PGA, has been the pro at Turner Valley for 13 years and sets a high standard for his professional staff. The club offers clinics and personalized lessons to improve your swing and

a pro shop featuring major brands. The club continues to improve and recently purchased 72 new golf carts. In 2000, the clubhouse underwent a 5,000-square-foot renovation. The inviting space includes a lounge that seats more than 60 people with another 40 on the deck and a banquet room with room for 130. Take your golf game to the inspiring 178-acre Turner Valley Golf & Country Club.

700 Imperial Drive, Turner Valley AB
(403) 933-4721
www.turnervalleygolf.com

The Firefighters Museum

Calgary firefighters started collecting artifacts in the 1960s and the collection has grown to 35 pieces of wheeled apparatus, numerous pieces of firefighting equipment and memorabilia, as well as photographs of fires, firefighters, sporting events and early Calgary. The oldest piece of apparatus on display is a 1890s Ronald Steam Fire Engine, while the youngest apparatus is a 1973 Super Pump. Exhibits illustrate the development of extinguishers, the evolution of nozzles and the little known Corps of Canadian Fire Fighters for Great Britain. Visitors can see the evolution of firefighting from hand-drawn to horse-drawn, from steam-powered to diesel, from buckets to super pump and from canvas coat to Kevlar bunker gear. Take the time to meet Maggie, a 1929 Magirus Aerial, and hear stories about Silverbell, the last Calgary Fire Department truck to arrive with a bell. The Museum is open Thursday to Monday from

May to October, with off-season tours by appointment. Most of the trucks have been retired from the Calgary Fire Department, with a few rigs that started service in the Royal Canadian Air Force, Swift Current Saskatchewan, Dumont, New Jersey, and Benton County, Washington. The museum staff looks forward to greeting you at the Firefighters Museum.

4124 11 Street SE, Calgary AB
(403) 246-3322
www.firefightersmuseum.org

Oh Canada Eh? Dinner Show

Meet singing Mounties, jolly lumberjacks and Avonlea's own Anne of Green Gables while savouring bite after bite of a five-course meal at Oh Canada Eh?—a dinner show unlike anything you've ever seen. The original Oh Canada Eh? began more than 15 years ago in Niagara Falls, Ontario and the hilarious musical revue has been evolving ever since. Audiences are delighted night after night from May to October with the antics of actors, both on stage and off. Unlike most dinner show experiences, Oh Canada Eh? offers a unique interaction, as the performers also serve the guests their five course, family-style meal while the show carries on around them. The rugged wilderness-inspired design of the log cabin theatre has a character of its own, providing the perfect atmosphere for an evening of fun and entertainment. The professional actors have been cast from all over this great country and bring you the greatest talent and a most entertaining night of laughs, dinner and characters found anywhere in the Canadian Rockies. Discover it for yourself, and see Canada at its best, eh?

125 Kananaskis Way, Canmore AB
(403) 609-0004
www.ohcanadaeh.com

GlobalFest

Every August, GlobalFest explodes into a two-week celebration in the downtown core and on the lush grounds of Calgary's Elliston Park. With a sparkling lake and a natural amphitheatre, this is the perfect place to watch a multitude of events. Showcasing cultural diversity with cultural artisans, musicians and performers in a festival setting, GlobalFest has everything from first-rate heritage exhibits to dancing, ethnic food and five nights of international pyromusical fireworks presentations. GlobalFest's OneWorld Festival features over 12 different cultural pavilions. Experience the heritage of countries such as India, the Caribbean, and Africa. Let the colourful costumes of an ancient Mexican culture captivate your eyes and let the enchanting rhythms of Middle-Eastern music drift you to a far off oasis. In addition to being one of the biggest and most celebrated venues in Calgary, GlobalFest is a not-for-profit festival with a mission to bring together diverse communities, to bring issues of human rights and environmental responsibility to light. Calgary's downtown hosts GlobalFest's noon-hour Human Rights Forum and Global FilmFest. Events begin with the Human Rights Forum, where you can sit in on discussions and hear special guests talk about various human rights issues, such as immigration and racism. In the second week, enjoy GlobalFest's noon-hour film festival featuring themed diversity films. Beginning Friday evening of the first week, the sky lights up with thousands of fireworks effects choreographed to music in the International Fireworks Competition. Your fireworks experience is mirrored in Elliston Lake, doubling your viewing pleasure. Make this exciting cultural adventure your next destination and join with thousands to celebrate the diverse world around us.

285, 2323 32 Avenue NE, Calgary AB
(403) 569-9679 or (866) 666-8308
www.globalfest.ca

The Fossil Shop Inc.

The Fossil Shop invites customers to peer millions of years into the past with fascinating displays of fossils and minerals. Since 1986, the dedicated team have stocked an amazing series of finds from around the world. Whether you have a beginning interest in fossils or are a serious collector, the Fossil Shop has something to pique your interest. See the complete skeleton of a cave bear or a beautiful spiral shell of an ammonite. The shop carries dinosaur, mammal, insect, sea life and plant fossils as well as minerals. Each fossil has a unique story of how it is a clue to the past. As you examine a fossilized bone complete with bite marks, it is easy to let your imagination wander to all the possibilities of how the creature died. The Fossil Shop also carries a variety of gift items, including educational books, t-shirts and miniature model dinosaurs. For the fossil lover who has everything, consider a dinosaur bone belt buckle or pair of trilobite earrings. The store serves collectors from around the globe and ships items worldwide. Visit the Fossil Shop—come touch the past.

61 Bridge Street, Drumheller AB
(403) 823-6774
www.thefossilshop.com

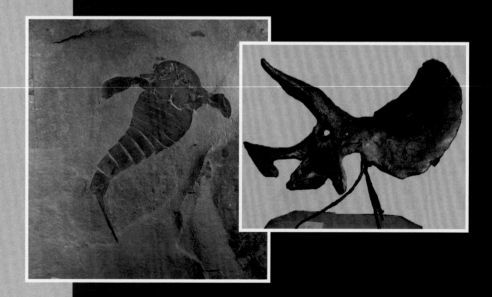

Sylvan Lake Golf & Country Club

Sylvan Lake is a resort town built around a main attraction—the lake. There are many things to do and places to go in the area, but one of the best is the Sylvan Lake Golf & Country Club. The clubhouse is an impressive 8000 square feet, with part of the space occupied by fine dining in the Eagle's Nest Dining Room, or for more casual fare, Birdie's Lounge and Bogie's Restaurant. Duffer's Den can accommodate groups of up to 100 in a neighborhood-style pub environment. Larger groups may opt for the 19th Hole Club House, a secluded and modern facility located off of the 15th green and suitable for parties of up to 225 people. There is a campsite around the 19th Hole Clubhouse for overnighters. The Pro Shop serves a dual purpose: the professionally trained staff books tee times and answers questions while the shop provides all the equipment, attire and golf accessories you'll need on the course, ranging from custom clubs and divot tools to headwear and clothing. Over the years, the owners have continued to reconstruct and improve the course. Excellent tournament facilities and some of the finest banquet facilities in Western Canada make Sylvan Lake Golf & Country Club an ideal place for events such as weddings, private parties and group and tournament play. Enjoy a full hospitality experience in a beautiful setting when you tee up at Sylvan Lake Golf & Country Club.

5331 Lakeshore Drive, Sylva Lake AB
(403) 887-6695
www.sylvanlakegolf.com

The Military Museums

The Military Museums is a compendium of seven museums integrated within one facility to display the Canadian Forces' history and heritage from the beginning to present day. The Military Museums is an institution designed to remember all those who contributed to Canada's liberty, to preserve and display the collections and artifacts that have been entrusted and to provide an educational opportunity for the public with emphasis on youth. You will learn about the Canadian Navy, the Lord Strathcona Horse (Royal Canadian), the Kings Own Calgary Regiment, the Princess Patricia's Canadian Light Infantry, the Calgary Highlanders, the Canadian Air Force and the connection of the Canadian Forces with the province of Alberta and the city of Calgary. Each gallery incorporates all medians of display, story telling and teaching. See an original Victoria Cross, walk through a World War I bunker system, view a life size World War II battle scene from above or at ground level, learn about the single handed charge of John Pattison, V.C., on a machine gun nest, engage in the interactive discovery centre as a key decision maker, look through a submarine periscope, view the rotating displays in the temporary display gallery or the art gallery, or just sit, relax and read and learn in the Library archive area. There is something for all at The Military Museums. The Military Museums is situated on 13 acres and encompasses 190,000 square feet of display area. The Military Museums is proudly supported by the Calgary Military Museums Society, the Naval Museum of Alberta Society, and the Air Force Museum Society of Alberta along with numerous friends. The Museums' Director, on behalf of all staff, volunteers and friends, invites you to visit and to learn more about the museums and Canada's military history and heritage.

4520 Crowchild Trail SW, Calgary AB
(403) 974-2851
www.museumoftheregiments.ca

Sun Dog Tour Company

The folks at Sun Dog Tour Company defy the notion that you can't be everywhere at once. On a typical day, they are all over the Canadian Rockies, providing private transfers, charters and sightseeing tours between Calgary, Edmonton, Jasper, Lake Louise, Fernie and Banff. In their backyard are places of natural beauty as spectacular as any on the planet, and they love helping people see as much of it as possible. They run day trips to the Columbia Icefields and shuttle guests to the Jasper Tramway. They take tourists to the dock for a Maligne Valley boat trip and to the depot for a popular half-day train trip from Jasper to Harvey and back. Do you specifically want to see wildlife? Sun Dog can bring you to where the creatures roam. Owner Paul Hardy leads a team of drivers and guides who live, work and play in the Rockies. Their love and enthusiasm for their surroundings is infectious. Summer is their busy season, but that doesn't mean that they hibernate in winter. They would rather take visitors snowmobiling and dog sledding. Spend an unforgettable afternoon in the Rockies with the Sun Dog Tour Company, or let its staff of vacation planners design a longer itinerary for you.

414 Connaught Drive, Jasper AB
(780) 852-4056 or (888)-SUNDOG1 (786-3641)
www.sundogtours.com

Photos by Edward Ross

The Calgary Tower

Over 190 m high (626 ft) and located in the heart of downtown Calgary, the Calgary Tower is the symbol of civic pride and is the World's Highest Tourism Tower... above sea level that is. The Observation Deck itself stands at an amazing 1240 m (4066 ft) above sea level. For the 1988 Winter Olympics, a natural gas burning cauldron was installed at the peak of the tower, creating the World's Largest Olympic Torch. The flame is still lit today for special occasions, as well as city and provincial events. As the elevator doors open on the Observation Deck, visitors are greeted by an awe-inspiring 360 degree panoramic view from the city streets to the mountain peaks, more than 150 km away. Just steps from the elevator doors is the Glass Floor Experience. At 11 m (36 ft) long and 1 m (4½ ft) wide, visitors are able to get a whole new perspective on Calgary, virtually stepping out over the bustling streets below.

After the thrill of the glass floor, head on into the revolving Panorama Dining Room, a one-of-a-kind dining experience in Calgary's most unique setting. As does the landscape, the menus change with the seasons to showcase the best of Canada's wealth of ingredients. Take a piece of the experience home—the Spirit of Calgary Boutique has selections of Calgary Tower memorabilia; one-of-a-kind and unique collectibles. Conveniently located at the base of the Tower is an Information and Retail Super Centre. If you are looking for where to stay or what not to miss in Calgary, this centre has all the information you need to plan the next adventure!

101–9 Avenue SW, Calgary AB
(403) 266-7171
www.calgarytower.com

124 Street & Area Business Association

The merchants of the 124 Street business district banded together in 1988 with the purpose of stimulating growth in their immediate area. The newly formed 124 Street Business Association worked diligently with the City of Edmonton to accomplish its goals. Over the years, streetscaping and infrastructure were markedly improved, benefiting the businesses locating or expanding within the 124 Street area. Today, the association works on behalf of the 350 business owners who populate the 124 Street area. A mosaic of specialty shops, professional services, fine restaurants and bistros and the Gallery Walk, featuring some of the best art in Edmonton, have transformed the area into a high-end haven of shopping, dining and culture for visitors and residents alike. The tree-lined street is a pleasing combination of style and convenience, with decorative street lights and cobbled sidewalks. Historic homes and commercial buildings have been carefully preserved, and the merchants exhibit old-fashioned quality and personal service. Guided walks of the original west end are available for the curious, and the environmentally-conscious Provincial Museum of Alberta is located in a nearby park just west of downtown. The 124 Street Business Association invites you to enjoy the fruits of its labour in the beautifully revitalized 124 Street business district.

201, 10706-124 Street, Edmonton AB
(780) 413-6503
www.124stbrz.com

Lacombe Corn Maze

The Lacombe Corn Maze is 15 acres of sculpted fun. Each year the path in the maze is cut to represent a different Alberta historical event. Past shapes include the Alberta emblem to commemorate the centennial and the Battle of Alberta to represent the rivalry between Edmonton and Calgary. Puzzles and riddles will guide you out of the maze, that is, if you can answer them correctly. From the end of July to the middle of October, corn stalks reaching heights of up to ten feet form the path walls. If walking the maze doesn't entice you, riding a pedal cart through it might be more your style. It usually takes one or two hours to explore the maze, but there are many other activities to occupy the rest of your visit. There is a concession stand on-site, fire pits for marshmallow roasting and a barrel train. Enjoy feeding friendly farm animals and going on a goat walk. The site is also the location of the Jumping Pillow, a large inflatable cushion to bounce on. Mini-mazes and a large slide cater to the younger set. The Lacombe Corn Maze won the Best Tourism Business of the Year at the Red Hat Awards in 2005. You can thank Linda and Ed Kraay, as well as Reuben and Rachel, Jesse Kraay and Dan Horneman for this country attraction. Get your interactive passport and start your adventure at Lacombe Corn Maze, where getting lost means having fun.

Site 6 Box 9 RR1, Lacombe AB
(403) 782-4653
www.lacombecornmaze.com
www.edmontoncornmaze.ca

The Royal Tyrrell Museum

The Royal Tyrrell Museum celebrates the spectacular diversity of life on Earth, from the tiniest grain of pollen to the mightiest dinosaur. The world-renowned museum and research facility is situated in the rugged Alberta badlands in Midland Provincial Park, six kilometres west of Drumheller. The badlands not only offer a spectacular view, they also hold some of the richest deposits of dinosaur fossils in the world. Canada's only museum devoted exclusively to palaeontology (the study of plant and animal life based on the fossil record) offers something for everyone. Hundreds of thousands of people each year are captivated by one of the world's largest collections of dinosaur skeletons, most of which have been discovered in the Canadian Badlands. Dynamic displays that spark curiosity, dispel myths and encourage life-long learning are just a part of the Royal Tyrrell Museum experience. During the summer months, visitors can also participate in education and interpretation programs that help them understand how the past and present are related. Individuals and families alike can learn about the wonders of the badlands during a guided hike, create a cast of a real fossil or try their hand at digging in a quarry. The Royal Tyrrell Museum holds appeal for all ages and provides a rare opportunity to discover the fascinating history of life on planet Earth.

Highway 838 Midland Provincial Park, Drumheller AB
(888) 440-4240 or 310-0000, then (403) 823-7707 (toll free in Alberta)
www.tyrrellmusuem.com

Chasmosauri

Lougheed House

Lougheed House breathes history to a degree that few other Calgary buildings can match. Sen. James Lougheed and his wife, Isabella, moved into the house in 1892 when Calgary had fewer than 4,000 inhabitants. Then called Beaulieu, the house became the centre of Calgary's social scene as the Lougheeds welcomed oil millionaires, politicians and entertainers into their home. George V knighted Sir James in 1916, making him the only Albertan ever to receive the honour. Today, metro Calgary's population exceeds one million, and the Lougheed House Conservation Society has restored this heritage site to all its former glory. One of the finest pleasures of a visit to the house is a stroll through the formal Beaulieu Gardens. The Lougheeds were leaders in gardening, often winning Horticultural Society first prizes. The gardens today are historically accurate. Isabella's Restaurant, on the main floor of the mansion, is fast becoming one of Calgary's top lunch spots. Isabella's also serves a popular Saturday and Sunday brunch. Any day, you can enjoy beef stew, *coq au vin*, elk meatloaf and other dishes carefully prepared with local ingredients. Treasures Gift Shop offers merchandise that reflects the era of the house, including chinaware, jewellery and teddy bears. Lougheed House is well suited to weddings and corporate functions and can accommodate private gatherings of up to 120 people. Come visit elegant Lougheed House, where the past lives on.

707–13 Avenue SW, Calgary AB
(403) 244-6333
www.lougheedhouse.com

Galt
Museum & Archives

The Galt Museum & Archives is a meeting place featuring displays of a regional history centered on the local aboriginal inhabitants and the colonization spurred by the coal mines. As a focal point for the community, the Galt does an excellent job of keeping history vibrantly accessible through hands-on exhibits, programs and events that capture the interest of visitors of any age. Collections of artifacts and archival documents representative of the southwestern Alberta region carry out this mission. The Discovery Hall has a permanent exhibit gallery as well as two or three temporary exhibitions each year. One of the key features is the Kainai (Blood Tribe) Arbour. The exhibit includes a computer kiosk with access to a website, which is the result of an ingenious project that forged ties between the past and the present. Modern technology was used to pass down the rich tradition of the Kainai people's time-honored relationship with indigenous plants and their healing properties. It began as a school project. Students in the fourth grade were taken out in the field to learn about local plants and their uses for healing. With the help of the Galileo Educational Network, they interviewed elders, took photos of plants and assembled a website. It did not end there, when they reached the sixth grade two years later, they mentored students in the third grade, giving new life to the traditions of the past and sustaining ancient knowledge and culture. Galt Museum & Archives has become a museum that aids in preserving a living history for the benefit of all visitors.

502–1 Street S (5 Avenue S & Scenic Drive), Lethbridge AB
(403) 320-GALT (4258) or (866) 320-3898
www.galtmuseum.com

Elbow River Casino

The 80,000 square foot Elbow River Casino is a stunning ultra-modern structure with two levels of heated and secure underground parking. It boasts more than 600 slot machines, a 24-hour poker room and game rooms for smokers and nonsmokers. A signature feature of the casino is a progressive slot carousel of 15 machines surrounding a new car. Someone can hit the jackpot while playing the maximum bet and drive the car home. Patrons enjoy live entertainment and dancing in the Jester's Court, featuring Ron Casat on piano. Feature acts join Ron on the stage regularly. The casino hosts special celebrations on holidays. Don't be surprised to find eight lions dancing on the Chinese New Year or a gentleman distributing free roses to the ladies on Valentines Day. Free coffee, tea and fountain drinks circulate throughout the casino, while a full dinner menu is available in the Jester's Court. Casual dining is available at the Jesters Deli and the Sports Lounge. The Elbow River Casino promotes responsible gambling in partnership with the Alberta Gaming and Liquor Commission. Enjoy diverse, responsible gambling, free refreshments and entertainment at the Elbow River Casino. Private rooms are available for banquets, meetings, fun money or poker nights.

218 18 Avenue SE, Calgary AB
(403) 289-8880
www.elbowrivercasino.com

September Springs Ranch

On a Highway 507 hilltop, immediately west of Pincher Creek, September Springs Ranch spreads out over 80 acres and offers visitors a plethora of choices at Unique Art Antique and exquisite meals or an elaborate Devonshire cream tea at Memories Café & Tea Room. Discover special alpine gardens, an old ski lodge and Blackfoot teepee. The magnificent panoramic view of Pincher Creek extends from Old Chief, Castle and Crowsnest Mountains to Livingstone Ridge and the Porcupine Hills. The Ranch is well-known for the thousands of colorful irises that bloom each year. The Ranch is owned by Sheran Carter, widow of Maurice (Mo) Carter, the famous race car driver, politician, broadcaster and GM dealer. Like Maurice, Sheran is a vibrant personality with many interests. A retired international commercial real estate broker, she hosts an Iris Festival, market fairs and health and wellness seminars in the summer. Among the many items of art, fashion, jewellery and antiques that she collects and sells, there are unusual finds, such as a magic dress that can be worn over 30 different ways. It comes in a spate of colors and will fit any size. Antique collecting is Sheran's passion. She has done it for so many years, her experienced eyes have amassed a fortune in quality merchandise. Enjoy your time browsing among the many treasures at Unique Art Antique. Take your camera into the gardens or on a nature walk and then stop for a gourmet experience at Memories Café & Tea Room. The charm of September Springs Ranch is sure to bring you back often.

Highway 507 (3 km W of Pincher Creek), Pincher Creek AB
(403) 627-2706 or (877) 6UNIQUE (686-4783)
www.uniqueartantique.com/
SeptemberSpringsRanch.htm

Edge Control

Everyone knows where to get the edge in Jasper. Since 1978, customers have come to Edge Control for high-quality, professional overnight ski repairs and tune-ups. The shop offers ski rental packages for adults and children as well as clothing and accessories by Spyder, Volkl, Head and more. Boot fitting has also become a shop specialty using Superfeet. Make sure you check out Edge Control for all of your hiking gear. It offers a full line of under and outer gear, boots, backpacks, travel clothing and accessories. Owner Blair Timmins has worked for the Parks Board Service and is quite knowledgeable about the area and its trails for skiing and hiking. In the beginning, Blair and Terry Harris started what they called the world's smallest ski shop in the Astoria Hotel. The shop occupied little more than a storage area. The shop has grown tremendously since its humble beginnings, but you still find Blair in the shop daily, providing the same excellence in workmanship. Whether you are on your way to the slopes, or gearing up to hike the trails, be sure to stop in at Edge Control for all of your needs.

626 Connaught Drive, Jasper AB
(888) 242-3343

Alberta Aviation Museum

Three words sum up the Alberta Aviation Museum—adventure, excitement and romance. Historically, Edmonton has been aviation's gateway to the Canadian North. The museum, established in 1991, preserves this history and educates the public about it. The museum has a program for 6th grade students that teaches both the history of aviation and the aerodynamics of aircraft. More than 84,000 square feet of displays let you journey through aviation history, from the days of wood and fabric through to today's jet age. The 34 interactive exhibits are divided between civil and military aviation. You can see the 1916 Curtis Special, which delivered the first airmail to Western Canada. Also on display is a DeHavilland Mosquito, one of only six

Photo by Ceasol

in the world. More than 30 aircraft are on display. The museum is staffed by volunteers who restore aircraft from all eras of aviation history. The gift shop has model kits, clothing, prints and videos. In September, the museum hosts a Battle of Britain Parade that commemorates history's most important aerial battle, one in which many young Canadians participated. Come see the silver wings at the Alberta Aviation Museum.

11410 Kingsway Avenue, Edmonton AB
(780) 451-1175
www.albertaaviationmuseum.com

Museum of the Highwood

What was it like to live as a pioneer 100 years ago? Museum of the Highwood captures the spirit of the Wild West era, focusing on the Highwood River Basin, now known for its ranching and oil industries. Both an interpretive center and research facility, the museum sits in what was once a Canadian Pacific Railroad Station, a well-restored sandstone building originally built in 1893. The station was moved piece by piece to its current location in 1911, and has housed the museum for the last 40 years. Stepping into the museum, you'll find a surprisingly interactive experience, with creative displays of photographs, archival documents and artifacts from the old West, and a family discovery room, which offers hands-on learning for all ages. The gift shop sells reproductions of old time toys, books about the area and other souvenirs. Museum of the Highwood also hosts the Historic Homes Tour, showcasing seven of High River's oldest homes, which date as far back as the late 1800s. In these modern times of cell phones and computers, it's

hard to imagine the pioneering life as it really was. Museum of the Highwood can help you recreate those times in a fun and interactive way.

406 1 Street SW, High River AB
(403) 652-7156

Bakeries, Coffee & Tea

Byblos Bakery

While working as supermarket bakers back in the 1970s, the Daklala brothers had an insight. The future of pita, a staple of their native Lebanese diet, seemed very bright, if they could introduce it as a healthful and novel alternative to bread. Acting upon their dream to get pita into every household in Calgary, they founded Byblos Bakery. At first a modest operation that produced about 500 pitas a day, the business grew rapidly and now uses state-of-the-art equipment from Germany to supply some 15,000 pitas a day to Calgary supermarkets and restaurants. The Daklala brothers remember those early days fondly when they brought their goods straight to the people, offering free samples of pita stuffed with cold cuts and peanut butter at area grocery stores. Once pita bread caught on with the public, they added bagels and tortillas to the Byblos lineup and later baklava. Demand for the dessert morsel took all of them by surprise. To keep everyone in Calgary supplied with its goods, Byblos Bakery now operates around the clock and employs a staff of 140. In 1983, Byblos Bakery began giving back to the community that embraced its products by establishing For Pita's Sake, a program that encourages nutritious and healthy food choices in the elementary schools. The Daklala brothers, Calgary's pita pioneers, invite you to try something from Byblos Bakery soon.

2479–23 Street NE, Calgary AB
(866) 229-2567
www.byblosbakery.com

Java Jamboree

Les and Ottilia Jaworski opened Java Jamboree in 2002, and have since drawn quite a crowd of followers who pass through to get their daily dose of artfully presented coffee. Your sensory experience doesn't begin with the first sip. It starts, instead, the moment you receive your cup and find that the barista, an artist in an apron, has created a foamy work of slurp-able art right atop your beverage. Latte Art, which has become very popular throughout Canada and the United States, consists of imaginative designs drawn in the milk foam produced when the drink is made. Artists deftly form hearts, *fleurs de lis,* apples and other images while serving up a steady line of cappuccinos, espressos and lattes. The Jaworski's dream was to bring the sensuous coffee drinks of Italy to Alberta. To do so they began by searching for the perfect coffee blends, which they found at a trade show in Seattle. Blended from specially selected beans, Java Jamboree's signature coffee exudes a rich, perfectly brewed flavor that is highly prized by professional cuppers everywhere. Become a patron of the arts, while indulging in your coffee passions with a stop at Java Jamboree.

9-312 5 Avenue, West Cochrane AL
(403) 932-6240

Black Diamond Bakery & Coffee Shop

Imagine the aroma of fresh-baked pastries. Black Diamond Bakery & Coffee Shop, a local favorite for more than 20 years, specializes in Danish pastry (also called Vienna bread), a layered pastry with almond, cream and spice filling, topped with hazelnuts and sugar. The shop also sells a variety of hearty, fresh baked breads including four kinds of Danish rye, the shop's own Trail of the Cowboys Sourdough, Italian, whole grain and flax. For something light try the Nordic-style breakfast buns, the *Birkis* or *Rundstikker*, or choose from five kinds of cinnamon rolls. For lunch, Black Diamond Bakery serves sandwiches, chili and two kinds of soup daily. Owner and head baker George Nielsen trained in his native Denmark. He bakes everything from scratch, and many of the recipes are his own creation. He strives to keep up with changes in the baking industry while maintaining the traditional quality he values. Says Nielsen, "You have to have passion and knowledge to create." Nielsen also bakes traditional Danish wedding, birthday and anniversary cakes made from pure almond paste. Party trays are available, and can contain sandwiches, pastries or fruit. Whatever your taste, Black Diamond Bakery & Coffee Shop will hit the spot.

119 Centre Avenue W, Black Diamond AB
(403) 933-4503
www.thecowboytrail.com/bdbakery.html

Rustic Sourdough Bakery

A family tradition born in Switzerland, Rustic Sourdough Bakery has been making life in Calgary more wholesome for 40 years. Jos and Verena Rehli, like most of the bakers who work for them, originate from Europe and have lifetimes of experience in the trade of artisan sourdough production. Their legion of devoted customers includes people who take their bread very seriously. If you, too, regard a freshly baked loaf as a miraculous gift from nature, you will be absolutely spellbound as you gaze at the perfect ryes, multi-grains and San Francisco sourdoughs on display in the cases here. The bakers use the same sour starter for many years, refreshing it daily. They never add chemicals to imitate a sour note as large commercial bakeries do. All breads are 100 percent natural, and they are scaled, rounded and shaped by hand. Jos, a pastry chef in addition to a master baker, provides customers with an exquisite selection of sweet goods daily. You can also buy something to put with your bread, thanks to a deli on the premises, which features a wide variety of cheeses, meats and imported gourmet foods. Verena grew up in the hotel and restaurant trade and she brings her visionary and creative skills to the deli side of the business. Good food, good fun and warm personal service are the priorities. Enjoy masterful bread from a legendary Calgary business at Rustic Sourdough Bakery.

1305 17 Avenue SW, Calgary AB
(403) 245-2113

Carlson's on Macleod

Carlson's on Macleod is a cappuccino bar, art gallery and venue for special events. In the near future it will also offer fine wines and live music. After completing extensive renovations to this historic building, owners Brenda and Don Carlson opened for business on December 1, 2006. Original artwork adorns the walls and beautiful antiques offer interesting conversation pieces. Many of the materials that were used to renovate and decorate the building have been salvaged from the scrap heap or reclaimed from somewhere. The bar and structural columns are made from reclaimed fir timbers that were once used by the British Government to build aircraft hangers. Granite steps from the Clairsholm Post Office were used to build the fireplace and some of the maple flooring is from an old apartment building in Lethbridge. Pieces of an old iron bridge have been used to decorate the bar. If you are looking for character, you will most definitely find it here. This building has a story to tell and the Brenda and Don are happy to share it with you. The inviting atmosphere makes Carlson's a popular venue for group gatherings and you can rent the space for special occasions. Carlson's offers full catering services for all of your special event needs. Stop by for a cup of coffee in a setting so inviting that you might want to be late to work.

129 3 Avenue SW, High River AB
(403) 601-4707

Evelyn's Coffee Bar & Catering

The aroma of freshly baked goods and hot, brewing coffee are the first of many delights for the senses at Evelyn's Coffee Bar & Catering. Everything at this Banff café is made fresh daily—as it has been for 15 years. Owner Wout Pauw fell in love with the Canadian Rockies on his first visit back in 1978. After a brief return to his native Holland, he brought his wife, Marini, and son, Jimmy, back to Canada, where they have made their home and living ever since. It's a family business at Evelyn's, with Marini handling the cooking and Jimmy and his siblings, Tom, Robin and Sarah, helping out. Your taste buds will delight in the variety of freshly made goods at Evelyn's, ranging from pies of all flavours to chewy cookies, scones and muffins. If you're looking for a fresh and fast lunch, try some of the delicious homemade soups and sandwiches offered here. Evelyn's also caters special events. All 25 varieties of Evelyn's coffee are roasted in Calgary, ensuring a fresh taste. Wout estimates that at least 50 percent of his customers are local. Wout and Marini give back to their community by supporting local sports teams and the community centre. Let the Pauw family support your family and community with fresh and delicious coffee and treats at Evelyn's Coffee Bar & Catering. Now with three locations to serve you: Evelyn's, Evelyn's Too and Evelyn's Again.

201 Banff Avenue, Banff AB (403) 762-0352

Natur'el Tea Room

The Natur`el Tea Room is a quaint tea house that offers a relaxing spot to escape the hustle and bustle, enjoy a lovely cup of tea and lunch and do a bit of shopping. With more than 60 of the world's finest teas and tea blends, you'll find a flavor to love, served in an elegant china tea cup. Most are organically grown. A delicious selection of soups, sandwiches and organic baked goods are offered for lunch. Once you are refreshed and relaxed, check out the intriguing collection of artistic wares. Browse the shop's dozens of tea pots, including glass, ceramic and hand-thrown clay tea pots, plus sleek stainless steel designs and even cast-iron pots. You'll find an enticing selection of tea tins, decorated with heritage photos, packaged right at the shop. The Natur`el Tea Room also stocks a carefully chosen selection of handmade one-of-a-kind silver jewellery, the work of local Canadian artists. The walls showcase lovely patchwork-style art made of pieces of vintage Japanese kimonos. Other gift items include locally produced honey, jams and tea-infused jellies. Chocolate lovers rejoice in the tea-infused chocolate goodies. The shop's bath line is also tea-infused. Unusual handbags and quality candles round out your choices. For a healthy and uplifting experience, indulge yourself with a visit to the Natur`el Tea Room.

103 Banff Avenue, Banff AB
(403) 760-2511
www.naturelifestyle.com

Bear's Paw Bakery

Few can savour the aroma of baked goods traveling on the crisp mountain air without stopping by to discover the source—European style pastries, tortes, cakes and artisan breads at Bear's Paw Bakery. The Jasper bakery is a popular place for sipping espresso, feasting on fresh baked goods and visiting with neighbours. Bear's Paw first opened in 1997. It became so popular following its 2002 purchase by Stewart Laing and his partner Kim Stark that a new location called the Other Paw is opening soon. Stewart's cinnamon rolls have the power to take over your senses, unless you've already fallen under the spell of his raspberry white chocolate scone. You might want to travel with his trail cookies in your knapsack or devour such hearty muffin choices as the signature Morning Glory with raisins, coconut, almonds and carrots. Rolls filled with sausage or vegetables promise lip-smacking delight. Desserts take center stage when you bring home fruit-filled tarts, apple streusel squares, a Granny Smith apple pie or carrot cake. The hand-shaped breads vary daily and include multi-grain loaves, baguettes and croissants. Müsli is available, too. If you haven't stopped by Bear's Paw in a while, your dog may give you a nudge, because Stewart's lineup of dog treats enchants local canines. Bear's Paw creates special cakes for such occasions as weddings, birthdays or showers. Join the happy throngs who have made Bear's Paw Bakery a routine part of their day.

4 Cedar Avenue, Jasper AB
(Bear's Paw)
(780) 852-3233
610 Connaught Drive, Jasper AB
(the Other Paw)
www.bearspawbakery.com

Cargo & James Tea

Tea may be an ancient beverage, but it's speaking a trendy, modern language at Cargo & James, an Edmonton-based tea company that's a pioneer in North America's café tea industry. "We have created an environment where great tea is available to everyone without being considered too stuffy or having connotations with this stereotype of *old*," says founder and president Tim Grover, who opened the first Cargo and James café in 2000. The enterprise now boasts four Edmonton locations and has franchises popping up throughout Canada. You can drink your tea on the premises or take it with you. You can also take home bulk tea and tea paraphernalia such as presses, mate gourds, tea balls and strainers. The company sells more than 100 hand-blended teas from countries all over the world. You can find rich black teas from India and healthful green tea from China and Japan. Still other choices are chai tea, a rich and energizing fusion of spices, tea and milk; Rooibos or South African red tea, known for its antioxidants, minerals and vitamins; and the semi-fermented, fragrant leaves of the traditional Chinese oolong tea. Cargo & James is a leader among companies that are scrambling to meet the Canadian demand for tea. Consumption increased by more than 40 percent between 1996 and 2005. We want to "provide our customers with a stimulating drink that helps support their healthy lifestyle," says Tim, who invites you to enjoy your tea any way you like it at Edmonton locations in Whyte Avenue, City Centre, St. Albert and Sherwood Park Mall.

10634-82 Avenue, Edmonton AB
(780) 432-8152
www.cargoandjames.com

ELOISE'S

Eloise's specializes in health-conscious made-from-scratch baked goods. The bakery, owned by Head Baker Eloise Jacobson, offers more than 40 varieties of fruit and cream pies, tarts, muffins, Chapman's ice cream and even pet pastries. Over the past two years, Eloise's has evolved from a pie shop into a specialty bakery. Eloise has a strong family background in cooking, baking and creating, and when customers began requesting specialty items, she felt up to the challenge. When her wheat-free pies were a success, she moved on to gluten-free cookies and tarts. Eloise's seven varieties of gluten-free bread use nutritious sorghum and fresh-ground millet, are sweetened with agave nectar and are trans-fat free. The bakery has a selection of baked goods that use agave nectar as a sweetener, from cookies to pumpkin and banana breads. Eloise has also created items that are free of dairy, soy, nuts or corn. She wants everyone, regardless of dietary restrictions and allergies, to enjoy her baking. Try the rhubarb strawberry pie, flapper pie or a slice of lemon pie made with fresh-squeezed lemon juice. An oatmeal carrot muffin might hit the spot. Chapman's ice cream, made in Canada, is available in traditional style or in dairy, gluten, nut and lactose free versions. For an extra treat, try Chapman's on a homemade waffle cone or one of six varieties of Eloise's own ice cream sandwiches, all gluten-free. Your canine friends can sample one of the seven varieties of natural gluten-free dog treats. For a delicious and guilt-free experience, come to Eloise's and get your piece of the pie.

140B Main Street, Turner Valley AB (403) 933-4492 *www.eloises.ca*

Bean Brokers

You can find a meeting room, a comfy chair, ample parking or a drive-thru window and easy access back on Highway 27 at Bean Brokers, where owner Connie Harder wants you to have choices. Connie opened the coffee shop in 2002 after discovering Olds lacked a gathering place for enjoying specialty coffees and teas, fresh muffins and giant cookies. The Alberta native knew what she was doing because she previously owned a mobile coffee business. She uses Fair Trade espresso beans locally roasted by Mountain View Roasteries, as well as Swiss water decaf coffee and many healthful loose teas. The coffee and tea drinks were developed in-house and include such top selling selections as caramel macchiato and green tea lattes and chillers. On a hot day, the demand for frozen hot chocolate or Crunch Coffee, the coffee version of a chiller, goes sky high. Connie has noticed the rise in tea drinking and offers many healthful choices, including matcha, a potent green Japanese ceremonial tea that will give you an eight-hour pick-me-up with far less caffeine. The popular Rooibos chai latte features a South African plant known for its mineral and vitamin content. You can indulge in tulsi, a holy herb of India prized for its healing qualities. For coffee and tea that deserves your attention, visit Bean Brokers.

5020 46ᵗʰ Street, Olds AB
(403) 556-1069
www.beanbrokersinc.com

Tea...and Other Things

Opening her own business has brought Kelly Joyner of Tea...and Other Things more than just a new way of earning a living. It has brought her a new identity as the Tea Lady of Cochrane, purveyor of 250 different teas. The shelves of this tidy shop are lined with jars of loose varieties, many of which are valued for more than just their flavor and aroma. "Certain teas can be great inhibitors for particular health problems," explains the Tea Lady. "For example, if you start drinking tea young, your chance of getting arthritis is very small." Before 2003, Kelly was a ladies' wear specialist who was walking through a mall one day when she looked up at the sky

light and suddenly knew that she had to move to Cochrane and open a tea shop. She has been having a marvelous time ever since. "You meet the most wonderful people in this store," she says. Customers congregate around the sniffing bar, where you can sample teas by savoring their aroma. Choose a favorite to enjoy later and browse the delightful collection of teapots, teacups and other paraphernalia at Tea...and Other Things.

119 1 Avenue, Cochrane AB
(403) 932-7988
www.teaandotherthings.com

Rocky Mountain Bagel Company

Bagels are mainstays at Rocky Mountain Bagel Company, but the food choices have been growing since Darren Fischer joined Shanyn Young as co-owner of the café. This environmentally friendly spot with its steamy selection of gourmet specialty coffees has been

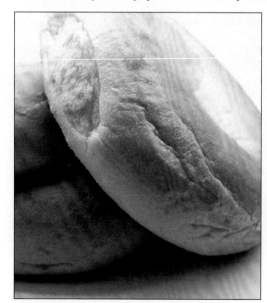

a community gathering place since it opened in 1998. A lively new menu includes 13 freshly prepared soups along with wraps, cookies and granola bars. You can order a box lunch for your hike or outing. Shanyn started as manager in 2000 and was instantly at home in the fast-paced environment. Darren joined the business in 2006, and helped attract still more customers with an expanded menu. A bilingual staff brings an outgoing, vibrant atmosphere to the café that adds to its appeal. The bagels, which come with a choice of six cream cheese flavours, naturally remain favourites. Discover Canmore's pulse at two Rocky Mountain Bagel Company locations.

830 8 Street, Canmore AB
(403) 678-9978
1306 Bow Valley Trail, #6A, Canmore AB
(403) 678-9968

Carol's Quality Sweets

If the smell of chocolate doesn't lure you in, all the jars of brightly coloured candy will. With more than 1000 varieties of chocolates and candy under one roof, you'll have loads of fun making your selection. Do you love chocolate? Whether it is a Carolmilk caramel, a champagne truffle or a piece of pure, dark, milk or white chocolate, you'll surely win. There is nothing artificial about Carol's chocolates. Chocolate from Belgium, real cream, natural flavours and real liquors blend together to form extraoridinary taste treats. Owners Grant and Carol Logan have been making sweets for 30 years, including special treats from the past, such as Grant's original marshmallow and crunchy peanut brittle. They want only the best for their customers. All chocolates and fudges are produced in their factory, using original recipes. Variety is their middle name. With British imported sweets, Dutch licorice, Haribo candy from Europe, sugar-free candy and chocolate, the hottest new kid candy, soap candy, Ganong chicken bones, licorice pipes and the list goes on, this sweet shop rivals Willy Wonka's factory. Seasonal items are sure to please. At Easter time, handmade chocolate bunnies and beautifully hand-decorated Easter eggs line the showcases, bringing back memories from your childhood. Christmas brings a wonderland of chocolate shapes, ribbon candy, old-fashioned mixed candy, barley toys and sweets from around the world. No matter the time of year, a gift basket of sweets from Carol's makes an awesome gift for any occasion: birthday, get well, anniversary or corporate. You won't want to forget Carol's when planning a wedding. The chocolatiers create sweet bridal favours that are both memorable and delicious. Stop by Carol's Quality Sweets, where they sell memories.

12519-102 Avenue, Edmonton AB
(780) 433-8650
www.carolsqualitysweets.com

Photos by Kris Nielson/www.krisdesign.ca

MacKay's Cochrane Ice Cream

The MacKay family has served gourmet ice cream to a delighted audience of customers since 1948. James MacKay started making ice cream to attract tourists and customers from nearby Calgary. Using only the finest ingredients and making each small batch by hand, he quickly expanded to offer new and original flavours. The word spread and soon customers came from all around Alberta for a taste of his knock-your-socks-off ice cream. Today, daughters Robyn and Rhona MacKay continue the family tradition of ice cream excellence with more than 50 magnificent flavours from which to choose, as well as a fine selection of frozen yogurts and sorbets. MacKay's Cochrane Ice Cream is an anchor business in Cochrane, attracting as many as 15,000 customers a week. On weekends, it's common to find a line of eager ice cream seekers curling right around the corner, happy to wait a few minutes for a little taste of heaven. The company now distributes its ice cream to dozens of stores and restaurants in Alberta, Saskatchewan and British Columbia. All of the famed ice cream shop's products are made right in Cochrane, in small batches, with ripples, candies and nuts still stirred in by hand. Don't miss a chance to visit MacKay's Cochrane Ice Cream to enjoy a scoop or two of this legendary treat.

220 1 Street W, Cochrane AB
(403) 932-2455
www.mackaysicecream.com

River Rock Fudge

River Rock Fudge makes living in or visiting Black Diamond a little bit sweeter. Husband and wife duo Tracy and Jason Pocherewny opened the fudge shop in 2003, but Tracy's experience in sweets goes back much further. She loves to bake, and making fudge seems to come naturally to her. River Rock Fudge handcrafts more than 25 delectable varieties of fudge, from classics like chocolate and maple walnut to more unusual varieties such as pumpkin, creamsicle and chocolate-orange-cranberry. You can order in a variety of sizes, from six-ounce boxes all the way up to the diet-busting two-pound tin. Christmas is one of the busiest seasons at River Rock Fudge, and Tracy and Jason offer an array of decorative holiday tins full of fudge for gifts. In keeping with the small-town feel of the business, Tracy and Jason enjoy placing their products in area country markets and fairs. They also offer a Fundraising With Fudge program for local organizations such as libraries and schools. Pick up some River Rock Fudge for a taste of the delicious morsels that are making life in Black Diamond sweeter, one bite at a time.

Black Diamond AB
(403) 933-2235

Le Chocolatier

John Spear acknowledges two categories of chocolate. There is premium dark chocolate, which, according to recent research, may be good for the heart in more than one way—and there is bad bargain chocolate, which is good for the backside. You will find none of the latter at Le Chocolatier, where John uses only the finest Belgian chocolate with the freshest ingredients and no preservatives in his truffles, bars and seasonal novelties. John's truffle selection is extensive, filled with everything from Canadian maple syrup and hazelnuts to Yukon Jack whiskey and fruity liqueurs. Le Chocolatier can also customize your chocolate order to your tastes and even print your design on a chocolate bar wrapper. Part of the fun of visiting Le Chocolatier is watching the chocolate making process through a glass window in the retail area. John and his crew make over 200 different chocolates there, so you never know exactly what will be happening in the kitchen when you drop by. John and his wife, Belinda, moved to Canada in 2000 from Windsor, England, where John was a chef. Taking over Le Chocolatier from the previous owner in 2004 allowed John to do something a little different while remaining in the food industry that he loves. In addition to its retail operation, Le Chocolatier supplies its products to five-star hotels, shops and restaurants in Canmore, Calgary, Banff and Lake Louise. Bite into, say, a Velvet Coffee truffle at Le Chocolatier, and let your smile tell John how well he is doing.

106 Bow Meadows Crescent, Unit 103, Canmore AB (403) 679-3351
www.lechocolatier.ca

Trains & Lattés

Photo by Jason Gale

TRAINS & LATTÉS
ESPRESSO BAR
RAILWAY GIFT STORE

People arriving in Jasper by rail know to schedule in a little extra time to stop in at Trains & Lattés. A life-long fascination with the railway by owners Michel Richer and Candice Verheyde grew into this unique bistro, gift shop and tribute to Canadian rail history. Even if you come to Jasper by auto, stop by and enjoy the specialty coffees, fresh homemade sandwiches, pastries and snacks. Spend some leisure moments with the shop's ice cream. Sit on the track-side patio and enjoy the soup of the day and one of the finest lattés in the land as you view the mountains and watch for railway cars. Inside you can browse through the train memorabilia that includes train miniatures and historic posters. You can find DVDs, books, train artifacts and souvenirs, all related to a bygone era. Other items include calendars, cards, maps, T-shirts, caps and whistles. The shop has antique china used on the Canadian National Railway and Canadian Pacific Railway. Stop by Trains & Lattés to indulge in some coffee and revisit history.

Rail Station, 607 Connaught Drive, Jasper AB
(780) 852-7444

Wonders Coffee House & Gift Shop

Linda Abrams, the owner of Wonders Coffee House & Gift Shop, wants visitors to feel the same way about Black Diamond that she does. Her shop functions as a visitors' center for the small town and its surrounding countryside in the foothills of the Rocky Mountains. The setting

provides endless inspiration to area artists. At Wonders, you will find art displayed on the walls as well as in your cup. Linda uses fair trade coffee, filtered water and the high pressure and temperatures of a Nuova Simonelli machine to produce quality espresso. She puts real chocolate in the mocha and finds many small ways to make Wonders an endearing stop. If you're following the Cowboy Trail, you'll enjoy the opportunity to view the local artwork, including wood carvings, pencil sketches and watercolours of the southern Alberta landscape. You'll also find jewellery as unusual as the shop itself, a 1929 former post office. Discover the rural splendours and gourmet refreshments of Black Diamond at Wonders Coffee House & Gift Shop.

130 Government Road S, Black Diamond AB
(403) 933-2347

Queen's Bakery & Café

Meeting over coffee and a pastry at Queen's Bakery & Café is a social ritual that many Hinton residents enjoy on a regular basis. Joining the regulars on any given day are numbers of initiates who have heard of the place from family, from friends or from somebody 200 kilometres out of town who said they just have to stop at Queen's Bakery if they are heading to Hinton. You would think that after 20 years, owners Peter and Annemiek Bundscherer wouldn't be amazed anymore to learn how people have found out about their business, but every day seems to bring a new surprise or two. Peter, a baker for a total of 50 years, and his wife, Annemiek, make pastries with flair and originality and they are famous for their spectacular cakes, including one that measured 24 feet long. Bring them a favorite photograph and they will reproduce it on a cake.

With soups and sandwiches on the menu, Queen's is a popular choice for lunch. Credit Peter for making Queen's the lively gathering place that it is, though the café represents only a fraction of his rich personality. He is also an avid book collector, chess player and mountain climber who has scaled many of the region's famous peaks. Grab a bite of something truly Hinton at Queen's Bakery & Café.

124 Market Street, Hinton AB
(780) 865-5050
www.queensbakery.com

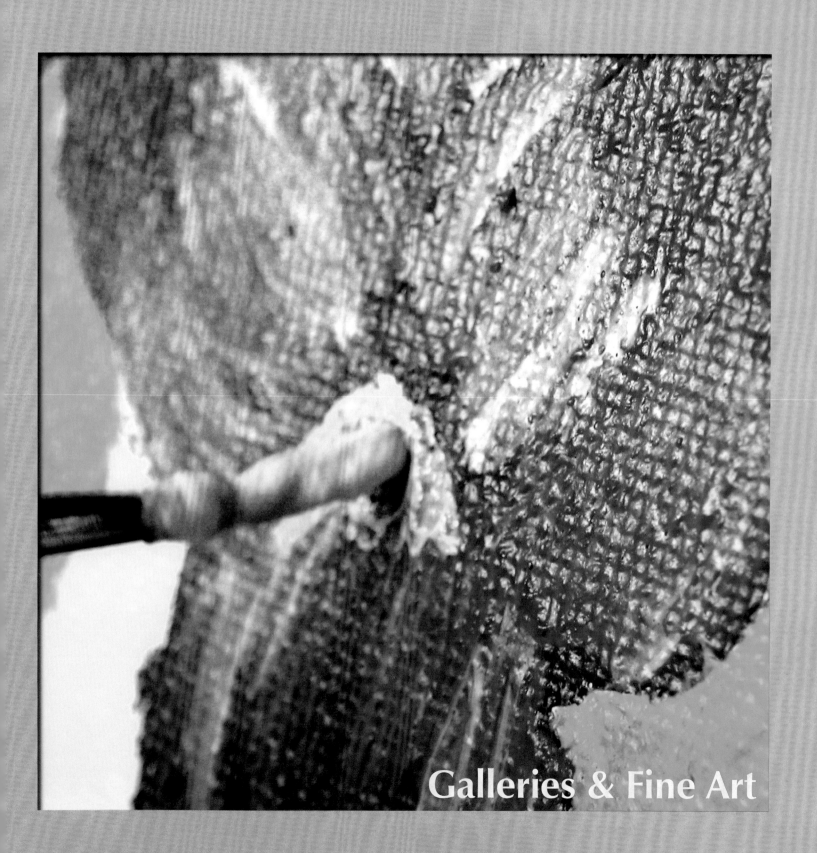

Galleries & Fine Art

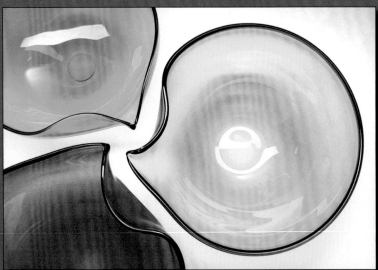

Alberta Craft Council

The Alberta Craft Council (ACC) is western Canada's largest member organization for fine craft. Founded in 1980 to stimulate and promote the craft arts in Alberta, the ACC is now best known for its extensive retail gallery with work by about 200 professional and emerging members, and its 15-plus Feature Gallery, Discovery Gallery and travelling exhibitions each year. The ACC sells work in the classic craft media such as clay, glass, fibre, wood, metals, as well as both traditional and experimental aspects of craft in Alberta. Look for ceramic and glass vessels, jewellery, stone and metal sculpture, furniture and furnishings, wearable art and more. The 2,000-square-foot Feature Gallery typically presents large survey exhibitions, which might include contemporary home furnishings, glass art or opera costumes. The Discovery Gallery offers exhibitions of emerging craft artists. Travelling exhibitions can be seen around the province and occasionally as far away as Ottawa, Washington DC or Korea. The ACC also organizes a quarterly magazine, weekly e-news and a comprehensive website, plus awards, publications, marketing ventures, education projects and information services for its members and the general public. Visitors will also be interested in the Alberta Craft Map, a printed or online guide to studios, shops and galleries that present fine craft. ACC member galleries in Calgary include Influx, the Croft, Arts on Atlantic, the Galleria and Leighton Art Center. You will also find Southern Alberta Art Gallery in Lethbridge, Terra Cotta in Black Diamond, Gallery on Main in Lacombe, Crooked Pot in Stony Plain, Forbes and Friends in Grande Prairie, and TU Gallery in Edmonton.

10186–106 Street, Edmonton AB
(780) 488-6611
www.albertacraft.ab.ca

Art Gallery of Alberta

As the province's leading institution for contemporary and historical art, the Art Gallery of Alberta (AGA) boasts an impressive permanent collection of more than 7,000 works. From classical to contemporary periods, the extensive curatorial program introduces local, national and international audiences to a diverse scope of artistic trends. From exhibitions featuring Baroque masters, Impressionists and Picasso, to cutting-edge contemporary art from China, the AGA draws great crowds with its first-rate programming. Its commitment to the arts in Alberta led to the exhibition *Capital Modern 1940-1969*, which appealed to local curiosity by exploring Edmonton's legacy as a leader in modern architecture. Similarly, Alberta's arts community celebrates its creative spirit with the 2007 Alberta Biennial of Contemporary Art: Living Utopia and Disaster, showcasing the best in painting drawing, sculpture and multimedia installation. In providing Albertans with the opportunity to experience art, the AGA's TREX program offers a series of travelling exhibitions that tour more remote areas of the province. Other community-focused programs at the AGA include symposiums, lecture series, artist talks, classes and studio workshops. In 2009, Randall Stout's winning design for the new gallery will open at Churchill Square as an 80,000-square-foot state-of-the-art facility for international, Canadian and Aboriginal art, education and scholarship. Explore the new building and keep in touch with the art of this region when you visit the Art Gallery of Alberta.

Enterprise Square, 100-10230 Jasper Avenue, Edmonton AB
(780) 422-6223
www.artgalleryalberta.com

Stone Productions Western and Wildlife Art Gallery

The subjects of John Stone's amazingly lifelike paintings often come in pairs, such as hummingbirds hovering among flowers or moose grazing in an alpine meadow. Like a latter-day Noah, he spends his days preoccupied with animals. From the smallest birds to the most majestic mammals, there hardly seems to be a creature native to the Canadian Rockies that hasn't captured John's imagination and inspired him to apply his brushes to canvas. When John isn't painting wildlife, he is using his incredible eye for detail to paint horsemen, ranches and other images that stir the heart. In *Iron Horse of the Rockies*, for example, a steam locomotive pulls a train through a gap in the foothills as a snow-covered mountain looms in the background. John has been selling his artwork for a living for nearly 20 years through Stone Productions Western and Wildlife Art Gallery, just off Highway 22 between Sundre and Caroline. His paintings are sought by collectors throughout the world who mention him in the same breath as Charlie Russell and Robert Bateman. He has illustrated three books, and his work has graced the cover of many magazines, including those of the Alberta Tourism office. Believe it or not, he never took an art lesson and didn't begin selling his paintings until he was about 50. Find a deep respect for all things great and small expressed through the art at Stone Productions Western and Wildlife Art Gallery.

James River Bridge, AB
(403) 638-2116

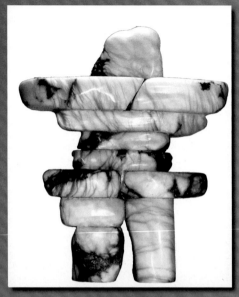

Our Native Land

Our Native Land celebrates the artwork of the native peoples of Canada as well as the continent's many natural wonders, which act as inspiration for much of the artwork. Eleonore and Joe Schuurman started the Jasper gallery 10 years ago, and today their children, Jackie Carmichael and Harry Schuurman, continue their passion for the art and culture of the continent's first nations. The 2,500-square-foot gallery brims with arts and crafts, including sculpture, jewellery and wall hangings of Inuit origin. In some cases these pieces are a primary source of income for northern communities as well as cultural expressions. The inspiration for many of the gallery's masks and decorative baskets comes from Indians living along the Northwest Pacific Coast. Still other artwork originates among artists of the Plains, who express their heritage with bark basketry, porcupine quills and soapstone carvings. From the Southwest regions of the United States comes jewellery fashioned of native stone and silver. In recent years, the gallery has added contemporary art with native or natural themes, especially from younger native and non-native artists. The gallery also carries jewellery made from ammolite, an opal-like gemstone from southern Alberta, and carvings from prehistoric ivory mammoth tusks, originating in Russia and northern Canada. Many tour groups stop at the gallery, where the staff can describe the history of individual pieces. For artwork that honours the land and its native peoples, visit Our Native Land.

601 Patricia Street, Jasper AB (780) 852-5592
www.ournativeland.com

Clayworks Studio-Link

"Working with clay or painting ceramics is an addiction that is safe, non-fattening and legal," according to the website for Clayworks Studio-Link. Once you discover the creative fun to be had here, you'll definitely be hooked. The only side effects are "numerous new friends and an increasing social circle." The full-scale clay studio offers classes for all ages in the various forms of clay art. Two sessions of children's pottery classes are offered every Saturday, with instruction, supplies, glazing and firing included. This is a great way for children to have some hands-on fun while also developing creative and technical skills. Adults aching to scratch their creative itch can take six-week courses or more intensive three-week sessions. Learn the art of sculpting, painting and glazing, and how to use the potter's wheel. For an afternoon's pastime, the studio hosts painting parties for adults and children with room for more than 30 guests. All of the pieces are pre-fired and ready, with paint and other necessities supplied by Clayworks. This is a great idea for gifts for friends and family. You'll also find a large variety of pre-made pieces for sale here, including vases, sculptures and attractive painted mosaics. Come on in and get your pottery fix at Clayworks Studio-Link.

10125 81 Avenue, Edmonton AB (780) 433-8866
www.clayworksstudio.com

AXIS Contemporary ART

Art Central

A visit to Calgary isn't complete until you visit Art Central, located in the heart of the downtown area. This three-story artist's complex features more than 50 studios, galleries, cafés and shops, all under one roof. You'll need comfortable walking shoes as you wander from level to level. Working studios bring you up close and personal with the finest artists Calgary has to offer. You can watch demonstrations of a variety of painting, sculpture, ceramic and jewelry-making techniques. Galleries showcasing traditional fine art and glassware, cutting-edge prints and wearable art invite you to stop by and explore. Shop 'til you drop at Art Central's creative and stylish gift shops. You'll love the one-of-a-kind floral creations, funky fashion accessories or handcrafted jewellery you won't find anywhere else. A wide selection of paper products and framing supplies are also on hand. When you're hungry, you'll enjoy a meal or a snack at the Siding Café or the Palette Coffeehouse. Either restaurant offers a menu rich in gourmet and comfort foods. Time-permitting, you can even attend a workshop. Connie Gibbens coaxes the creativity out of every participant with her jewellery-making classes at To A T Studio. Janine Vangool, in the Uppercase Gallery, specializes in the unusual art of button-making. Most workshops and demonstrations last from 45 minutes to one hour. You'll want to schedule plenty of time to enjoy the fun and creativity that Art Central offers those who come and stay awhile.

100 7 Avenue SW, Calgary AB (403) 543-9900 www.artcentral.ca

Shisomiso Boutique-
Locally designed and made

Photo by Lynn Ivall

Art Jewellery by Kari Woo of INFLUX Jewllery Gallery
Photo by Erin Wallace

The Melting Pot

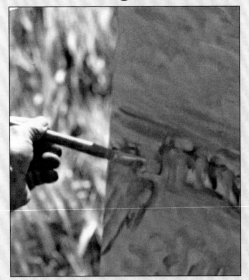

The Melting Pot Art & Gift Gallery offers an inviting and relaxed atmosphere in which you can view a wide variety of artwork and handcrafted treasures. The many styles of art include contemporary, modern and classic. This working art gallery and studio showcases more than 40 Western Canadian artists. In fact, 90 percent of the store's merchandise is by Alberta artisans. You'll enjoy the paintings, photography and metal art. Angela Hook's popular wire sculpture is on display. Pottery includes Japanese bowls and dishes with amazing glazes from Randall Clifford. You'll see stunning glasswork from Berting Glass. Gift ideas include handmade jewellery and other affordable handcrafted items. You can shop for art cards and books. Gift certificates and a gift registry are available. Owners Corinne Megarry and Vicki Myers opened The Melting Pot in 2001 in Calgary as one of the first stores in Artspace's Avenue of Shops. Over the course of five years, they developed a following of loyal clients. In 2006, they moved to a new location in Drumheller, into a cute 1920s house that they have renovated. For the best in arts and crafts from Western Canada, come to The Melting Pot. Also, be sure to visit Vicki's painting studio.

196 1 Street W, Drumheller AB
(403) 823-2483
www.meltingpotgallery.ca

Electrum Design Studio & Gallery

At Electrum Design Studio & Gallery, Wayne Mackenzie combines his love of fine art and of craft to create one-of-a-kind jewellery pieces. Wayne attended art school as a painter

before discovering sculpture and ultimately transitioning into jewellery. His studies under Swiss and German goldsmiths have imparted a distinct European flavour to his work. Lately, ancient Greek, Roman and Aztec influences in conjunction with the Alberta landscape have also begun to appear. Each piece is a reflection of the wishes and personality of the customer. Wayne enjoys the experience of meeting one-to-one with clients to determine what sort of piece will work best for them. While engagement rings are the most common request, Wayne also makes elegant brooches, pendants and other types of jewellery for special occasions. He works in gold and silver, platinum and precious stones. His gallery also features designs and crafts by leading Alberta artists. Find something one-of-a-kind at Electrum Design Studio & Gallery.

12419 Stony Plain Road, Edmonton AB
(780) 482-1402
www.waynemackenziegoldsmith.com

Scott Gallery

Contemporary art has found an enduring showcase at Scott Gallery. Marianne Scott was an art collector long before she opened the Edmonton gallery in 1986. She personally chooses the gallery pieces, integrating abstract and figurative paintings with sculpture, ceramic and original prints. Marianne handles more than 35 artists at all stages of their careers and puts on eight to 10 shows each year. You will find artwork by such established Canadian artists as Robert Sinclair, who captures the natural world in watercolour and acrylic stain. Doris McCarthy holds an international reputation for dramatic landscapes in oil, acrylic and watercolour. Douglas Haynes uses collage, gouache and acrylic to capture the essence of light in illuminated blocks set against dark backgrounds. Sean Caulfield was born in Rhode Island, but he was made for Alberta.

He studied printmaking at the University of Alberta and returned to the university in 2001 as the junior Canadian Research Chair in printmaking. His recent mixed media work renders industrial objects in rural settings. Marianne invites people from all walks of life who know and appreciate original fine art to become familiar with the work at Scott Gallery.

10411 124 Street, Edmonton AB
(780) 488-3619
www.scottgallery.com

Maryanne's Eden

Maryanne Jespersen expresses her love for the central Alberta scenery and rural lifestyle at Maryanne's Eden, The Art and Garden Gallery. The gallery displays such diverse works as ornamental garden art, sculptures and paintings by Maryanne. Born and raised in Alberta, Maryanne spent her youth exploring the foothills and mountains of the area. As an adult, she saw many more sights while working as a transport driver. Maryanne longed to interpret these sights and in 1990 began a serious study of art. With the opening of her studio and gallery in 2000, her dream of being a full-time artist had become a reality. The works on display at Maryanne's Eden are personal as well as objective. Her vibrant abstracts evoke the energy and life-force in nature. Her paintings of horses, cows and birds are full of color and light. Early morning and late afternoon are some of Maryanne's favorite times, and her landscapes perfectly capture those fleeting minutes of magic when the world seems to glow. In the garden, a friendly dragon or an unexpected cactus sculpture may greet you. You'll also find decorative bird baths and planters and even hand-crafted garden stepping stones for sale. Maryanne's works shine in many venues. Her artwork is in private collections around the world. Discover the soul of the Alberta landscape and find ways of elaborating your own backyard at Maryanne's Eden, The Art and Garden Gallery.

109 Centre Avenue E, Black Diamond AB
(403) 933-5524
www.maryanneseden.com

TU Gallery

TU Gallery has the selection of top-quality furnishings essential to satisfy your personal style. From handcrafted woodwork to exquisite photography and artwork, TU Gallery specializes in one-of-a-kind pieces. In fact, owners Alex and Lorna Paterson guarantee you will never find a mass-produced item in their gallery. TU Gallery carries a collection of only the most inventive, contemporary furniture. It was only a few years ago that the Patersons realized the desperate need for a high-end furniture gallery in Alberta. The couple opened TU to fulfill the demand for quality pieces that complement personal space and express personal style. Customers appreciate the fine work, most of which is created locally although still maintaining a universal appeal. In addition to furniture, more than 100 artists are represented throughout the gallery, and the store itself has eight in-house artists creating original oil paintings on a regular basis. All artists are carefully selected and are at the top of their craft, exemplifying the best in North American art. In sum, TU Gallery offers exquisite wood pieces, metal sculptures, innovative picture framing, and much more. With a recently expanded space, TU Gallery has an even larger collection of furnishings to match your spirit.

10718-124 Street, Edmonton AB (780) 452-9664 *www.tugallery.ca*

Highwood Art and Framing

For 11 years, Highwood Art and Framing has been providing quality art at half cost to the public. Owner Don Moore's philosophy is that it is important to surround yourself with beauty, and he wants to make that beauty available to all. This philosophy has made Highwood one of the highest volume dealers in Alberta. Don has framed pictures for 30 years and has taught framing at the college level. He is a tremendous resource of information, and loves to share his knowledge, experience and love of art through lectures at the store aimed at a range of listeners from beginner to expert. The gallery houses one-of–a-kind art from all over the world and locally based artists as well. You'll find prints, limited edition prints and originals under one roof. Artists are featured in well-attended studio events that are informative and enjoyable and come with music and food. Highwood does much framing for local artists exhibited at the Stampede and other special events. Whether you are purchasing for your own private collection or for your company, you will find something beautiful at Highwood Art and Framing.

413 First Street SW, High River AB
(403) 652-3538

Douglas Udell Gallery

Douglas Udell Gallery is home to some of the most admired contemporary art in Canada and the world. The three Douglas Udell Gallery locations each feature many established artists, including Jack Bush and Dorothy Knowles, as well as leading young artists gaining momentum in the Canadian and international markets, such as Dean Drever and Mara Korkola. Owner Douglas Udell is well-known for discovering artists and establishing their careers. He spent his childhood in art studios and has a special passion for sculpture. Udell is on a quest to "find those who have their own visual language." He opened his first gallery more than 40 years ago in the hopes of challenging and educating visitors and collectors. His galleries in Calgary, Vancouver and Edmonton produce several exhibitions a year. Discover something new and beautiful at Douglas Udell Gallery.

10332–124 Street, Edmonton AB (780) 488-4445 www.douglasudellgallery.com

Art Gallery of Calgary

For 30 years, the Art Gallery of Calgary has been dedicated to presenting the cutting edge of contemporary art. One of the largest non-collecting institutions in Canada, the gallery occupies 16,000 square feet with 6,000 reserved for exhibitions. Keeping no permanent collections allows the gallery to stay open and respond quickly to the latest developing trends. The gallery presents four exhibition cycles per year, showcasing group and solo exhibitions from Canadian and international artists as well as travelling exhibitions. The art experience is an interactive one, with artists' statements, curator's notes and a place for visitor feedback. You'll find many opportunities to meet the people behind the art. The gallery also offers a variety of educational programs, serving more than 1,500 school children a year. You'll find handcrafted jewellery, fashion accessories and ceramics in the gift shop, representing local, national and international artists. Visit the Art Gallery of Calgary for a glimpse of the latest trends in modern art.

117 8 Avenue SW, Calgary AB
(403) 770-1350
www.artgallerycalgary.org

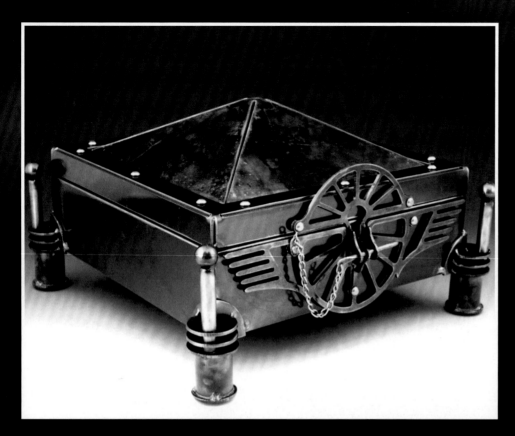

Pike Studios

The passion for creation is evident everywhere at Pikes Studios. Owners and artists Bob and Connie Pike ensure that visitors learn much about clay and metal work as they browse this working studio and gallery. Connie's work consists of functional porcelain dinnerware. Typically, the gallery contains more than 1,500 pieces of usable art including teapots, mugs, bowls, baking dishes and art plates. Connie loves to experiment with glazes. Colours range from the rich and vibrant Moss set to the cool and serene Celadon. Each is a one-of-a-kind creation. Connie's work is widely favoured—a quarter of a million pounds of her pottery are in personal and private collections around the world. Bob specializes in custom metal art work, including gates and garden accessories. His tables and boxes have a very architectural feel and reflect his 40 years as a craftsman. Bob also creates wall murals and metal sculpture as well as taking on client projects. At Pike Studios, there is always something new to delight the senses. Whether you want to add to your personal collection or enrich the life of someone else, Pike Studios has something to enjoy for many years to come.

70-9 Street SE, High River ALB
(403) 652-5255
www.pikestudios.com

Trianon Gallery

Located in the historic Hudson's Bay Building, Trianon Gallery is a bastion for artists, displaying largely contemporary exhibits and serving as the site for a lengthening parade of events. The building is remembered as the Trianon Ballroom, which opened in the 1930s and continued through the 1960s. Owner John Savill has an open-door philosophy that matches the airy spaciousness of the facility, encouraging the artistic community and transforming the structure into a vibrant artistic center. Trianon Gallery has hosted fundraisers and launched numerous exhibitions by nationally and internationally recognized artists, as well as student artists of all ages. Sculpture, paintings and architectural exhibits have all found their way into the gallery. It has also been a venue for workshops, plays, dances and musical events. Trianon often collaborates with other entities in the art world, such as the Southern Alberta Art Gallery and the University of Lethbridge Art Gallery, to enrich the artistic experience in Lethbridge. Savill appreciates the connection to the community that he has attained through the Trianon Gallery, but even more important to him is the community's strengthened connection to the art world. Check for upcoming events and shows at the Trianon Gallery, where change is the norm throughout the year.

104 5 Street S, Lethbridge AB
(403) 380-2787
www.savillarchitecture.com

The Croft Gallery

The Croft Gallery makes a major contribution to the growing community vibe along Calgary's 4th Street. Owners Eric and Robyn Giesbrecht provide a warm and inviting place for the community and visitors alike to appreciate the work of established and emerging Canadian artists. The Croft carries an amazing collection of great Canadian art for every budget. It features pieces from over 150 western Canadian artists and artisans. Ceramics are a focus, along with turned wood bowls and vessels. You'll especially want to check out the Croft's eclectic and often whimsical selection of pottery. The showroom displays a generous array of raku, glass and home décor items. You'll see paintings, sculpture and jewelry. Many of the gallery's repeat clients are collectors who consider the selection here to be the best in Calgary, both for its variety and quality. Organizers of the G8 summit chose plates from the Croft Gallery for use at that meeting of world leaders. While you are browsing, you will probably brush elbows with area residents who have dropped by looking for something that would fit a room perfectly. They know that with monthly exhibits from March to December, the Croft promises something new every time they come in. Let the energy along 4th Street carry you into the Croft Gallery for an encounter with Canadian arts and crafts.

2105 4 Street SW, Calgary AB (403) 245-1212 *www.thecroft.ca*

Gainsborough Galleries

Excitement, variety and a bright, airy showroom characterize Gainsborough Galleries, a tradition dating back to 1923, making Gainsborough the oldest gallery in Calgary. Owner Marie Wood has been involved in the family's art business since 1965. The colourful 3,000-square-foot gallery represents the work of some 45 artists, including several prominent Calgary artists, such as landscape artists Robert E. Wood and Ted Raftery. Vancouver artist Kal Gajoum, originally from Tripoli, paints in oils using a lively palette knife technique, while painter Tinyan Chan, born in China and designated a Master Painter by the Federation of Canadian artists, blends Western and Asian influences in his snow and floral scenes. Sculpture and bronzes are well represented here. You'll find soapstone carvings by Inuit and British Columbian sculptors along with lively jade animal sculptures by Lyle Sopel, called "one of the most accomplished contemporary jade sculptors in the world today," by *National Geographic*. The no-pressure sales staff at Gainsborough can help you decorate a corporate or private space with appropriate art and sculpture. They are glad to arrange for an in-home preview to ensure that the fine pieces you like most suit your surroundings. To surround yourself with fine art, visit Gainsborough Galleries.

441 5 Avenue SW, Calgary, AB (403) 262-3715 or (866) 425-5373
www.gainsboroughgalleries.com

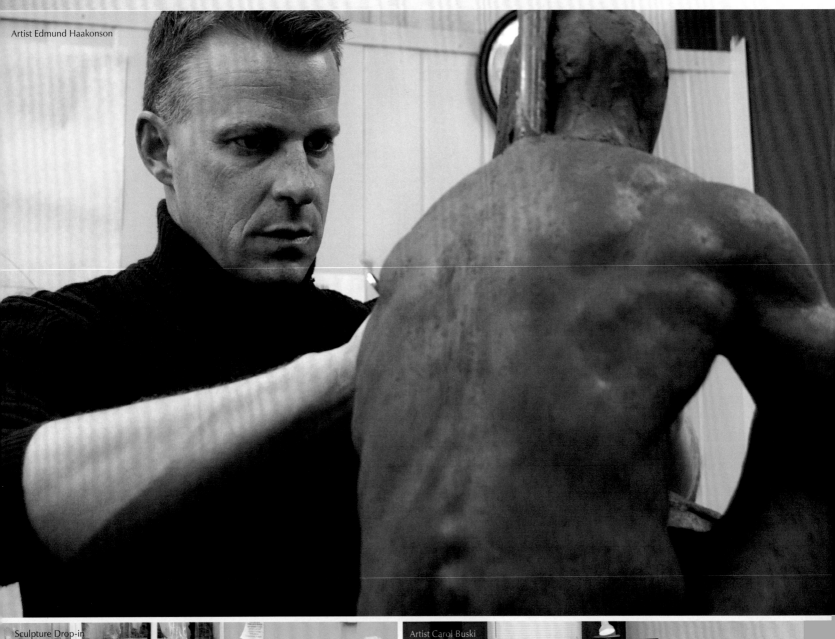

Artist Edmund Haakonson

Sculpture Drop-in

Artist Carol Buski

Sculpture by Ritchie Velthius, 2006

uru College drawing class outside Harcourt House

Harcourt House Arts Centre

Great things are often born of great tragedy. Such is the case with the Harcourt House Arts Centre. After a devastating tornado struck Edmonton in 1987, a group of artists organized Artists for Tornado Relief. A vision was born from that storm, and the artists incorporated as Where Edmonton Community Artists Network (WECAN). This organization sought to create a permanent arts centre, and in 1988 the Harcourt House Arts Centre burst into life. Harcourt House provides dynamic programs in 35,000 square feet of space that houses 42 studios, two art education spaces and three public galleries. The artist-run centre provides opportunities for practitioners of all the visual arts, including film, photography, painting, installation, sculpture, printmaking, drawing and performance art. All artists and art lovers are enthusiastically welcomed. Harcourt House offers an artist-in-residence program that is the only one of its kind in Western Canada. The centre's diverse programming includes exhibitions of the work of local and international artists, community art education, and art out-reach programs to educate and inspire. Come participate in one of the many classes that are open to the public and taught by professional artists. Each year, about 24,000 people see the exhibitions and take classes. Visit the Harcourt House Arts Centre and let your own creativity burst to life.

3rd Floor, 10215-112 Street, Edmonton AB
(780) 426- 4180
www.harcourthouse.ab.ca

Webster Galleries

The Inuit art of northern Canada is one of the focuses at Webster Galleries, opened in Calgary by John Herbert and Lorraine Webster in 1979. The Websters sell original artwork, particularly paintings and sculptures, in what has become one of Western Canada's largest galleries. Many well-known Canadian artists exhibit regularly at the 10,000-square-foot gallery. Réal Fournier is the artist in residence here. His paintings capture the happiness of childhood with houses and winter scenes in bold, swirling colors. Réal paints in the show gallery each day and helps customers with purchases, which allows the Websters to keep the gallery open seven days a week. The gallery is eclectic with respect to style, and the work of contributing artists is consistently high in quality. John has established close relationships of loyalty and respect with the artists. He understands the artists and their work and provides a level of service and quality that has gained the trust of many private collectors. Those looking for Inuit sculpture will find pieces of great integrity and value here. Paintings cover a range of styles and mediums, while sculpture can range from the whale bone and antlers used by the Inuits to ceramic and bronze pieces. You'll find work in pencil and pastel plus etchings, giclees and lithographs. This beautiful space can be rented by corporate or nonprofit groups hosting special events. Come and experience for yourself the powerful artwork that meets at Webster Galleries.

812 11 Avenue SW, Calgary AB
(403) 263-6500 or (888) 874-5519
www.webstergalleries.com

Bearclaw Gallery

Before there was a Canada, there were many nations across this land, each possessing its own language, traditions and art. The Bearclaw Gallery celebrates the traditional and continuing art of those nations. Established in 1975, the gallery was the first venture of renowned Canadian art figure Agnes Bugera. Bearclaw Gallery has greatly contributed to the growing respect and recognition of First Nations art. Agnes' daughter, Jackie Bugera, operates the gallery today. The gallery features surreal and realistic paintings from artists such as Daphne Ojdig, Norval Morrisseau and Linus Woods that depict both modern and ancient tribal culture and wisdom. Many of the artists, such as Alex Janvier, have become well-known in art circles around the world. You'll also find an impressive selection of Inuit soapstone sculptures by such master carvers as Mathewsie Iyaituk, Kananginak Pootoogook and Kiawak Ashoona.. A variety of Inuit dolls and other handicrafts rounds out the collection. The Bearclaw Gallery draws its client base from around the world through its easy-to-use website. Explore the art of Canada's First People at the landmark Bearclaw Gallery.

10403-124 Street, Edmonton AB
(780) 482-1204
www.bearclawgallery.com

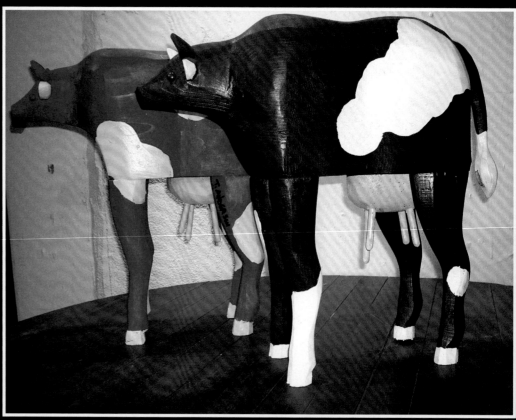

Gallery of Canadian Folk Art

Folk art lovers will rejoice when they discover this amazing gallery—the only gallery west of Ontario solely dedicated to folk art. Welcome to the Gallery of Canadian Folk Art. Owner Gail Carscallen's astonishing collection includes paintings, sculptures and carvings, furniture, textiles, antiques and artifacts. The gallery has pieces from every region of the country and therefore, presents the unique ethnic heritage of Canada in all its glory. Each folk art piece is unique and for sale. So, what is folk art anyway? Each piece of folk art is one-of-a-kind and handmade by an artist who usually has no formal art training. Folk art is the uncommon art of the common people. Folk art is also from the heart, to the heart and for the heart. Often folk art will evoke feelings of nostalgia, patriotism or religion, or, it may simply produce a laugh or a smile. The Gallery of Canadian Folk Art usually has three or four shows a year. A show may present the works of an individual folk artist or several artists who share a theme or work in the same media. A show may represent a particular region or help celebrate a holiday or ethnic tradition. A show can simply make you laugh. The sky's the limit. No matter what time or season of the year, there is always a lot to see and learn. The Gallery of Canadian Folk Art is very receptive to children and groups. For more information and the hours of operation, call, stop by or visit the website today.

2206A 4 Street SW, Calgary AB (403) 229-1300
www.galleryofcanadianfolkart.com

Image 54

A proud purveyor of quality artworks and custom framing, Image 54 is one of the top places to turn in Calgary for art prints and cutting edge exhibitions of original artwork by some first-rate Canadian artists. The Barrington sisters founded the studio in 1982 as a poster and picture framing shop. Since 2003, Daniel Lindley's ownership has nurtured Image 54's evolution into an art showcase featuring many solo exhibitions arranged through a thriving relationship with the Art Dealers Association of Canada. Visitors to Image 54 have been treated to the etchings of Meghan Armstrong, Kathy Barnson and Mychael Barratt. Other shows have featured photographs by Charles Britt, landscape oils by Nicole Bauberger and florals with an O'Keefe styling by Greg Pyra. Jack Roy's abstract acrylics and Marlessa Wesolowski's contemporary acrylic cityscapes represent just some of the variety you can expect at Image 54. The talented professionals here can also frame your treasured memorabilia and collections. The gallery's informative website takes you on a virtual tour of the artwork represented here with explanation of printmaking techniques. It took vision and dedication to move Image 54 from a simple framing shop to one of Canada's foremost independent art dealers. Come see what that vision offers you at Image 54.

709 - 11 Avenue SW, Calgary AB
(403) 265-5458
www.image54.com

Muttart Conservatory in Edmonton

Guy Roy—*La Tempete*
Oil on canvas, 30 x 36 in.

Claude A Simard—*La Villa en Toscane*
Acrylic on canvas–30 x 36 in.

Glen Semple—*Liquid Sunshine*
Acrylic on board, 48 x 36 in.

West End Gallery

For over three decades as gallery owners, Daniel and Lana Hudon have discovered and presented some of Canada's most compelling artwork at the West End Gallery. They have continually provided an exceptional selection of the best that Canadian painters, sculptors and glass artists have to offer. The West End Gallery in Victoria, B.C. was established in 1994 and is recognized as the city's most vibrant gallery. Both galleries carry an outstanding in-house collection of art glass displayed throughout the year. Each summer the Victoria gallery hosts the prestigious Annual Canadian Glass Show. Each gallery has a marvelous and diverse selection of emerging and well-established artists. Talented up-and-coming painters, such as Victoria's own Steven Armstrong and Quebec artists Claudette Castonguay and Guy Roy, have started their careers with West End Gallery and will undoubtedly continue to delight clients. Leading artist Rod Charlesworth captures the nation's special identity with his impressionistic landscapes. Alberta high realism painters Glen Semple and Len Gibbs have waiting lists to supply, and internationally acclaimed artist Claude A. Simard is featured by both galleries. With representation of over 40 painters, West End Gallery offers a wide selection of all styles and aesthetics. These days, Daniel and Lana's son, Matthew, joins them at the gallery. The Hudons are members of the Art Dealers Association of Canada and founding members of the Edmonton and Victoria Gallery Walk Associations. Art collectors will find work of lasting value and receive the very best in professional service. For the finest in Canadian contemporary and classical artwork, visit this Alberta treasure, the West End Gallery.

12308 Jasper Avenue, Edmonton AB (780) 488-4892 or (877) 388-0009
www.westendgalleryltd.com

Boot Hill Gallery & Gift Shop

When you think of images that define Alberta's prairie heritage and culture, your mind undoubtedly fixes upon horses, ranches and wildlife. These are the subjects of Bernie Brown's amazingly detailed pencil drawings. Boot Hill Gallery & Gift Shop in Okotoks has been the place to find his prints and originals since 1993. A self-taught artist, Bernie has established a worldwide audience for his depictions of everything from herds of running horses to prairie elevator scenes. His rodeo drawings capture bull riders and all the other arena action in vivid detail. Sometimes it's something away from the spotlight that inspires his imagination, like the sight of a steer poking its snout through the gate of its stall. Bernie is very adept at drawing children, whether they are playing baseball on the prairie or sitting on a fence in their cowboy hats. Bernie's artwork has earned him many awards and accolades. He is especially proud of being named Best of Show at the Calgary Stampede. In addition to displaying a wide range of Bernie's work, the Boot Hill Gallery offers an extensive selection of Western and wildlife sculpture, rustic furniture and gifts. A second location opened on the Cowboy Trail in the village of Longview in 2006. For art that captures the essence of the prairie, check out Boot Hill Gallery & Gift Shop.

41 Elizabeth Street, Okotoks AB (403) 938-8102
134 Morrison Road, Longview AB (403) 558-2386
www.berniebrown.com

A BOY AND HIS DOGS

Art by Bernie Brown

The Miller Gallery

The Miller Gallery has been established in the area for three years. It is the only gallery to showcase exclusively local artists and the only independent teaching studio in the area. To top it off, the Gallery offers a full selection of art supplies through its parent company, The Studio, which has been established for 18 years. The Miller Gallery features local artists, both established and newly arrived on the art scene. Exhibits encompass contemporary fine art prints, original fine art, lithography and wood blocks. Although the viewing experience is always richest in person, there is also a convenient online gallery where purchases can be made. Recent showings at the gallery include the organic, flowing and often monochromatic nature works of Julie Duschenes, the subtle landscapes of Judith Nickol and the bold, colourful Dreamscape series by Jill (E.J.) Moloy, who also teaches beginner through advanced classes in the studio. Moloy, a co-owner of the gallery along with Nadine Miller, teaches all of the two-dimensional art disciplines. She is a diverse and accomplished artist who excels at teaching and has a BFA from the Alberta College of Art & Design in Calgary. Moloy received the prestigious Instituto Allende scholarship, San Miguel de Allende, Mexico, and she has mentored many young artists. Moloy's work is a visual representation of the unseen dimensions of life, an expression of the emergence of the soul through the bonds of human consciousness. Find the spirit of Alberta shining through the works at The Miller Gallery.

407–A 5 Street S, Lethbridge AB
(403) 329-1050
www.themillergallery.ca

Summit Gallery of Fine Art

All of the art you'll see at the Summit Gallery of Fine Art is informed and inspired by nature. Like nature itself, it is also wonderful in its variety. Some express reverence for the natural world by capturing landscapes and wildlife in precise detail. Others use abstract colour, texture and light to explore what nature is, beyond mere appearance. Among the 60 local and international photographers, sculptors and painters represented at the Summit Gallery, some take an activist's stance, using their art to raise concern for the state of our natural world. It all makes for an engaging experience for the intellect as well as the emotions. Co-owners Bart Habermiller and Emily Barnett moved into this historical 1920s building following tenure by a fast-food restaurant. They ripped through layers of flooring until they found the original sprung maple that had once served as the town's dance floor. The restored interior pleases artists and visitors alike with its spacious design and aesthetic appeal. "Very few commercial galleries in Canada can boast 20-foot-high ceilings, skylights and hardwood floors," Habermiller points out. Head up the stairs and discover the Summit Gallery of Fine Art, where love of art and nature meet inside a Banff landmark.

120 Banff Avenue, Banff AB
(403) 762-4455 or (888) 358-4455
www.summitfineart.com

Southern Alberta Art Gallery

As with any great art facility, the value of the Southern Alberta Art Gallery (SAAG) cannot be measured solely by the art that hangs on its walls. Certainly its exhibitions are first-rate, and each provocative show that the curator mounts contributes to SAAG's status as one of Canada's top contemporary art galleries. Presenting exhibitions that stimulate thought and provide pleasure is, however, just one way in which SAAG strives to enrich the lives of everyone in the community. SAAG also serves a vital role in encouraging the public to participate in the arts through a variety of special programs. Several of these programs are geared towards young people, such as the No Boundaries Teen Art Club. By exploring teen issues and discussing how they relate to art making, participants in this club have the opportunity to express themselves and be creative. Adults take advantage of a full schedule of workshops, a film program, artist lectures, and the popular Art for Lunch series. Show your support for the arts by purchasing a SAAG T-shirt at the gift shop, which also carries works of local and regional artisans. Make the Southern Alberta Art Gallery, located in beautiful Galt Gardens, your destination for contemporary art exhibitions and so much more.

601 3 Avenue S, Lethbridge AB
(403) 327-8770
www.saag.ca

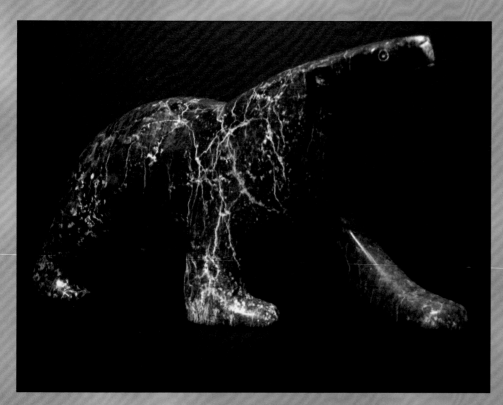

Cottage Craft Gifts & Fine Art

With half of a century focused on Inuit and Native art, Cottage Craft Gifts & Fine Art proudly retails an affordable selection of Canadian treasures. You will find a large collection of authentic Canadian Inuit sculptures as well as limited edition graphics and Native crafts. Cottage Craft also carries a collection of carvings and gift items symbolizing the Inukshuk, the stone figure traditionally built by the Inuit peoples of Northern Canada. The Inukshuk, the logo for the 2010 Vancouver Winter Olympics, is a symbol of world communication. This representation is also embodied in Cottage Craft's philosophy. During many successful seasons of buying and selling fine art, owners and sisters Lorraine and Avis Perry remain actively engaged in perpetuating and preserving traditional and contemporary Aboriginal expression. With their family heritage being Inuit, Lorraine and Avis' knowledge of Canadian First Nations culture, tradition and artistic styles is appreciated by art and history enthusiasts alike.

8330 Macleod Trail S, Heritage Plaza, Calgary AB
403-252-3797 www.cottage-craft.com

Agnes Bugera Gallery

For more than a decade, the Agnes Bugera Gallery has featured fine art by established and emerging artists from across Canada. The Agnes Bugera Gallery is well-regarded in Canadian art circles for offering a variety of fine contemporary art. Spring and fall exhibitions in the main gallery offer solo & group shows whilst works by other gallery artists are exhibited in the remaining sections of the gallery. You'll find paintings by Hong Kong-born Mandy Boursicot, whose still lifes represent a fusion of European and Asian cultures. Jamie Evrard paints florals in oil, in media ranging from copper to canvas and linen. Ernestine Tahedl's landscapes emphasize the essence of places in an impressionistic style. You'll also find bronze and steel sculptures from artists such as Patrick Meagher and Ben McLeod. Located in the heart of the Gallery Walk district, the gallery often features specialized exhibitions and offers meet-and-greet receptions with the artists. The atmosphere is elegant, but friendly. If you're looking for fine art from across Canada, see the Agnes Bugera Gallery.

**12310 Jasper Avenue,
Edmonton AB**
(780) 482-2854
www.agnesbugeragallery.com

Kinsella Art Galleries

Painting the natural wonders of the Canadian Rockies is a spiritual experience for Marilyn Kinsella, whose latest watercolors and prints are on display at her two galleries in Canmore. The artist's sense of awe and respect can be felt in every one of her wilderness scenes. Specific lakes and mountain peaks, such as Castle Mountain, Mt. Rundle and Maligne Lake, are the inspiration for her art. She enjoys portraying them from different perspectives and in different light. Marilyn has returned to her favorite subject, the Three Sisters, over and over while, she says, "truly never tiring of it." When not painting, Marilyn is busy shipping her work to customers all over the world. Her paintings are often used as prizes for corporate incentive programs. Her newly-published art book features a handmade paper cover, a beautiful print on

Marilyn Kinsalla—*Lake Louise with Poppies*

every page and blank space where you can record memories of your trip to the Canadian Rockies. Meet the artist at Kinsella Art Gallery or Kinsella Art Studio and Frame Shop, where she is always happy to pause from her work-in-progress to greet visitors and to encourage art discussions.

712 Main Street, Canmore AB (gallery) (403) 679-2014
#3, 1302 Bow Valley Trail, Canmore AB (studio and frame shop) (403) 678-4331
www.marilynkinsella.com

Hot Glass Studio

Since 2002, Hot Glass Studio has wowed Canmore with its stunning selection of blown glass art. Owner Susan Gottselig teams up with two other talented women, each with her own glass-blowing specialties, to produce uncommon works of beauty. Susan has a passion for sculptures from the animal kingdom, including whimsical bears, bison, chickens, penguins and fish that

Art Glass Bowl
Art by Nicole Tremblay

Cheeky Chickens
Art by Susan Gottselig

are simply irresistible. Her celebration figures, based upon the human form in glorious sweeps of color and with arms stretched high, are very popular. Nicole Tremblay creates famed friendship balls, as well as functional art pieces, such as bowls, vases, perfume bottles and ornaments. Beth Wooley Monod favours jewellery pieces with sterling silver and gold work. You'll also find handmade glass bead jewellery on display by both Nicole and Beth. If you'd like to know how blown glass is made, the women are happy to explain. Special projects and corporate orders are welcome. You are welcome to drop by to watch them at work, but the schedule varies so it is best to call ahead. The glass is hot, the music rocks and the process begins. It's magic at the Hot Glass Studio.

Unit 8, 111 Bow Meadows Crescent, Canmore AB
(403) 609-9333
www.albertacraft.ab.ca/susangottselig

Health & Beauty

The Worx Salon

Good hair gets noticed. Debi Seeley, owner of the Worx Salon, can tell you that. She has learned that the best way to advertise her business is to keep providing the best hair services possible. Customers who stride out of the Worx happy are like walking billboards. Friends and colleagues approach them to compliment them for their hair and ask where they got it done. You can feel the positive vibe in the air as you enter this salon inside a quaint house in Red Deer. Its eight chairs are often all going at once as Debi and her team provide cutting, coloring and conditioning for men and women. Children love getting their hair cut at the Worx, too. If you're looking for a new style, you might get an idea by checking out Debi's do. The hairdressers at the Worx are style ambassadors who display a variety of cuts and shapes. They even put on hair shows a few times a year. Debi always wanted to be a hairdresser. She started cutting people's hair when she was in high school and opened her first salon in 1988. The Worx, which has been buzzing since 2002, carries several different lines of hair products and offers eyelash extensions, tanning and waxing in addition to hair services. Get your hair done at the Worx Salon and start spreading the word when people tell you how great it looks.

3615 50 Avenue, Red Deer AB
(403) 352-7900

Rocky Mountain Soap Company

The Rocky Mountain Soap Company makes some of the most luxurious handmade soaps and bath products around. Tucked away in Canmore, the company's workshop employs more than 30 people dedicated to its core philosophy—be kind, be real, be natural. The company now has four store locations, but it remains committed to 100-percent-natural soap. Of course, this means the company uses absolutely no artificial ingredients in any of its products, which range from body butter to bath salts to baby care products. The firm's fearless leaders, Karina and Cam Baty (and daughter Ruby), are proud of a staff that helps each customer find the perfect product. Whether you're looking for pleasantly scented soap or a cure for dry, itchy skin, you're bound to find something that will work for you. Rocky Mountain's environmentally friendly product line includes earthy ingredients, including real grains and berries. Popular sellers include the Pumpkin Patch Soap, which is great for eczema, and a foot butter that is perfect for dry cracked heels. The company has received countless testimonials from customers who love the results. Drop into one of the Rocky Mountain Soap Company locations today and pick up one of Mother Nature's favorite soaps.

820 Main Street, Canmore AB (403) 678-9873
204 Banff Avenue, Banff AB (403) 762-5999
West Edmonton Mall, Edmonton AB (780) 732-0888
Calgary Eaton Center, Calgary AB (403) 269-SOAP (7627)
7-111 Bow Meadows Crescent, Canmore AB (866)-678-2678 (workshop/office)
www.rockymountainsoap.com

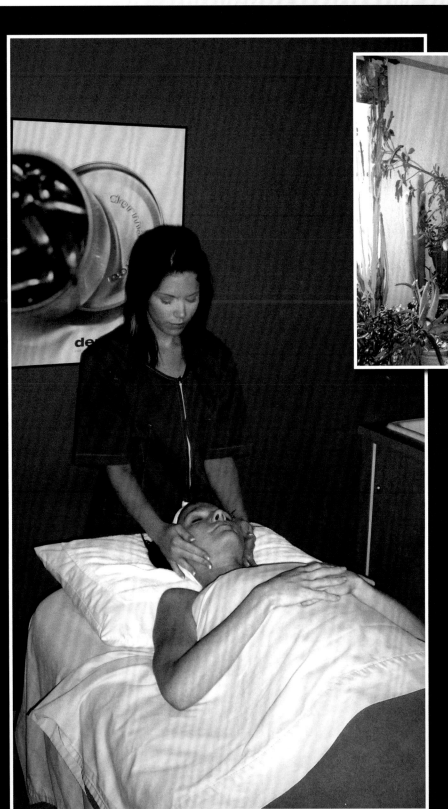

Cactus Club Salon & Spa

Compared to most other salons and spas, the Cactus Club is as spacious as the Sahara desert. Décor from the Mexico and Central America sets the tone at this 6,000-square-foot oasis. Roomy treatment areas host everything from hot stone massage to airbrush tanning. You can exfoliate your entire body with the Aromatherapy Salt Glow or seek a customized facial. Desert body wraps are the signature treatments, including the Desert Heat for stress reduction and the Desert Calm for muscular pain relief. Packages, such as the Orchid Cactus and Desert Rose, combine a number of services that leave guests with a renewed look, relaxed mind and revitalized body. Lunch is provided in the relaxation room for clients who come in for a full day. The salon offers hair cutting and styling for women, men and children as well as nail care, hand treatments and makeup updates. Owner Tamara Nadeau leads a team of 28 professionals who consider ongoing education to be part of their jobs. They attend local workshops and jet off to Los Angeles and Vancouver to stay up on the latest trends and innovations. With its result-oriented staff and therapeutically sound equipment, the Cactus Club seeks to become your choice for long-term treatments as well as occasional pampering. Next time you are looking for an oasis of healing, book an appointment at Cactus Club Salon & Spa.

11 Elizabeth Street, Okotoks AB
(403) 938-7310
www.cactusclubsalonspa.com

Totally Refreshed Steam & Spa

The healing quality of water is at the heart of Totally Refreshed Steam & Spa. The water used in its steam baths is carefully conditioned to ensure maximum health benefits. It's filtered, softened and dechlorinated, so you can bask in the warmth and moisture knowing that it's the pure stuff. Choose an intimate couples room or a family-size room for your steam bath. Young ones receive a special rate when you book a family room. You can even have rock or country music piped in to create a festive atmosphere. Do you prefer soothing environmental sounds? Try meditative ocean waves or bird songs. Each room has its own dressing and shower area. Owner Ken Tolsdorf, a construction expert, built Totally Refreshed Steam & Spa himself out of a genuine desire to give the gift of health to his community. He notes that while steam is wonderful for humans, it can be hard on some building materials. Therefore, designing the facility required painstaking attention to detail. For example, to protect the building and guests from mold, Ken used a special coating on the walls that creates a moisture barrier. The ceilings are sloped to prevent condensation from gathering and dripping down on guests as they try to relax. Totally Refreshed Steam & Spa offers a full range of massage therapies, spa services and aesthetic treatments in addition to its steam baths. Awaken your senses and experience relaxation at this community-minded business.

#2, 6200 67A Street, Red Deer AB (403) 314-1933
www.totallyrefreshedsteamandspa.com

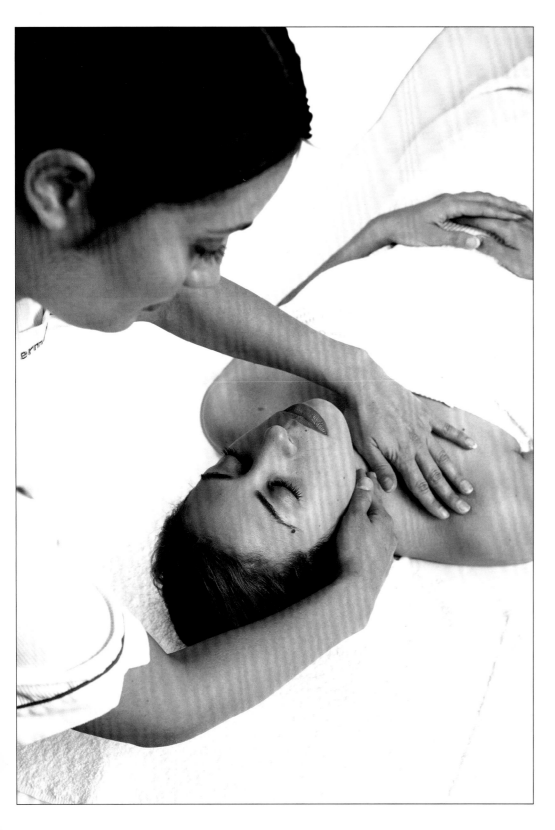

Milestones Spa

Marissa Willard understands that relaxation is an ideal state for body and soul and has made it her business to bring an oasis of calm to the citizens of Red Deer. She opened Milestones Spa in 2003 following seven years as a massage therapist. Relaxation starts at Milestones even before your therapist leads you to a private treatment room. You will take off your shoes and be offered herbal tea or water. Privacy, a lack of distraction and thoughtful scheduling are important parts of the spa experience, which is why Milestones has three massage therapists and three aestheticians ready to attend to your needs in two massage rooms and two aesthetics rooms. The spa is open Monday through Saturday with extended evening hours on Tuesday, Wednesday and Thursday. You can choose a spa package or individual services. For those spending the day, Marissa recommends the Sanctuary For Your Soul package with one exceptional experience after another, including a LaStone massage, which employs heated basalt stones and cool marble stones as an extension of the therapist's hands for a powerful effect. You also receive a customized body treatment and facial along with lunch, a pedicure and manicure. Couples can enjoy a night out with individual massages plus hand and foot treatments performed in the couples room. Marissa is particular about staff and has attracted long-term employees with professional certifications and a dedication to serving others. Step away from your busy life for a few hours of rejuvenation at Milestones Spa, recently voted #1 spa in the Red Deer Express 2007 Reader's Choice awards.

#165, 2004 50th Avenue, Red Deer AB
(403) 309-9474
www.milestonesspa.com

Spa Europa

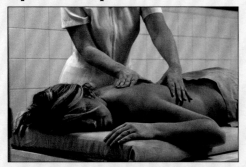

At Calgary's Spa Europa, the colours and textures of ancient Rome announce your escape from the modern pace. Laura Ezekiel and her daughter, Jennifer, opened the spa in 2004, offering European treatments that ward off aging and bring deep relaxation. Many treatments employ products from the Dead Sea, including a mud cherished for its healing properties. The spa treats up to 500 clients, one-third of them men, in a seven-day week. The signature Turkish *hammam* (steam bath) is particularly popular. This Turkish bath is over three hours long and includes head to toe exfoliation, aromatherapy steam sessions, hot and cold hydro treatments and a Swedish massage, enhanced by a fresh cucumber mint facial and a full body milk rinse. You can expect lunch, a scalp massage and hair shampooing, too. Originally from Russia, Laura is an aesthetician with 30 years experience in the skin-care field. Her customized facial is a luxurious event that varies in length and combines services and products to fit your skin. Other facials run as long as two hours and may include masks, microdermabrasion and nonsurgical facelifts. Massages take place on heated marble tables. For personalized spa services with many thoughtful extras, visit Spa Europa.

1029-17 Avenue SW, Suite 100-E, Calgary AB
(403) 229-1578
www.spa-europa.com

Diamond Oasis Salon & Day Spa

Diamond Oasis Salon & Day Spa believes in pampering you and the planet with organic products. Denise and Andrew Nichols want you to be able to count on innovation and a natural touch with whatever services you opt for. The salon uses organic shampoos, conditioners and styling products to obtain masterful results for men, women and children. The perms perform well without the heavy chemical load, and even the color in the salon's eyelash tints contains fewer chemicals. The nail polishes, scrubs and masks employ natural products, too. Diamond Oasis makes many of its own scrubs and lotions, so technicians can customize your treatment

and work around your individual sensitivities. Pedicures are a popular choice at Diamond Oasis. For extra soft feet, the spa mixes clay or honey with fresh fruit puree or yogurt. Still other pedicures heal, stimulate or moisturize the skin with peppermint, salt, chocolate paraffin and the spa's signature vanilla lotion. The spa offers holistic body treatments including aromatherapy and seaweed body wraps, and Reiki and crystal healings. Let the bounty of nature rejuvenate your body and soul at Diamond Oasis Salon & Day Spa.

114 Centre Avenue, Black Diamond AB
(403) 933-3535

ReNew You Studio & Day Spa

ReNew You Studio & Day Spa is dedicated to health and well-being through natural products and holistic spa services. Lee-ann Harder founded ReNew when she recognized the need to educate the public about new healing and rejuvenating spa treatments. At ReNew, clients find a comfortable and relaxing space to leave their daily troubles behind and surrender to one of the many stress-reducing treatments offered here. From Reiki and acupressure to body scrubs, herbal and seaweed gel body wraps, steam therapy and a wide range of massage therapy techniques, clients will find everything they want in a day spa. ReNew provides non-surgical facial treatments, facials and aesthetics. Set in charming Bragg Creek, ReNew is a place that combines all the best techniques in health and beauty to offer its clients a comprehensive

approach to wellness. Lee-ann also offers a full array of natural beauty supplies and cosmetics at her spa, and prides herself in stocking many products that are made with 100-percent, all-natural ingredients. The spa also offers a one-of-a-kind treatment called the Bowen technique, a series of gentle, rolling movements that improve the body's function without hard pressure. To unwind in plush surroundings while experiencing holistic and naturally wonderful spa treatments, visit ReNew You Studio & Day Spa.

Bragg Creek AB
(403) 949-8244
www.renewyoudayspa.com

Mountain Spa

The goal at the luxurious Mountain Spa is to nourish both your body and mind with beauty and health treatments, to pamper you with professional, private, individual attention. As you enter the shop, the elegant appointments and gentle music provide a relaxing atmosphere that only hints at the services available. A rooftop terrace with magnificent mountain views is a popular draw. You can also wait in the Mountain Spa Lounge. The spa offers a host of facial treatments for both ladies and gentlemen. Anti-aging and restorative eye treatments give instant and dramatic results. You'll find a full lineup of hair removal and electrolysis services, as well as eyelash and brow tinting and shaping. A variety of body wraps are available, from the moisturizing, replenishing Butter Me Up wrap to the detoxifying, regenerating Let's Play in the Mud wrap. The spa also offers several refreshing body scrubs. For the ultimate luxury, try the shop's Spa Days services, such as Body Bliss, which includes a Moroccan Spice body glow treatment, followed by a milk and honey wrap and Vichy shower. The relaxing hot stone massage is the blissful conclusion. You can also create a custom spa package to suit your needs. Spa Day services for couples are also available. All manicures and pedicures include a complimentary polish. At this spa, you are never rushed. When you visit the Mountain Spa, you'll leave feeling and looking your spectacular best.

111 Banff Avenue, 2nd Floor, Harmony Lane, Banff AB
(403) 762-0473

Angles Hair and Aesthetics

Owners Dominic and Lawrence Rizzuto can be proud of the accomplishments that fueled the Angles Hair and Aesthetics phenomenon. The company broke new ground in hair styling and colouring 26 years ago, gaining the attention of women throughout the Calgary area for its thoughtful consultations and attention to face structure and skin type. Today, Angles offers salon and spa services at 23 locations in Calgary and Edmonton as well as in Saskatoon, Saskatchewan. Second-generation family member Michael Rizzuto handles business development. Angles won Readers' Choice awards from the *Calgary Herald* in 2004, 2005 and 2006. Each salon has a different appearance and a somewhat distinct list of services, but all maintain consistent quality. Angles continues to be on the cutting edge of hair fashion and keeps its partners in the know on the latest techniques with quarterly seminars. One of the charms of Angles is its ability to appeal to a broad spectrum of women, including celebrities in need of camera-ready hair, brides, students and grandmothers. Often hair looks great when you leave a salon, but seems impossible to fix at home. The Angles staff helps you avoid this problem by teaching you how to reproduce your look at home. Angles offers spa packages that include facials, body wraps, aqua massage, brow waxing and hot oil manicures. You can arrange for a full body massage, professional makeup application, body polish or waxing. For glamour you can count on, come to Angles Hair and Aesthetics.

www.angleshair.ca

Curious Hair Skin & Body

Curious is what you'll be when you walk into this Calgary salon—well-coiffed and taken care of is what you'll be when you walk out. Owner Michael Rizzuto prides himself on providing an environment of relaxation and fun for customers. He and his wife, Shannon, who is in charge of the skin and body department, have gone to great lengths to distinguish this salon from others. The first thing you'll see when you come into this 4,400 square-foot store is a large variety of haircare products, including fine lines such as Kérastase and John Matter Organics. For Michael and Shannon, the goal of Curious is to provide all the services of a spa with twice the fun. That penchant for fun explains the old-school barbershop on the site, fully decked out with vintage gear and all the modern technology as well. As the team of expert stylists works its magic on your hair, you'll be able to enjoy watching the plasma screen television. Curious' stylists have an eye for detail, style and fashion. The atmosphere at Curious is vibrant and youthful, with an old-school appreciation for the history of style. Curious about how good you can look? Come to Curious and find out.

1740-1632 14 Avenue NW, Calgary AB (403) 210-1121

Optimum Health Vitamins

At Optimum Health Vitamins, optimum health is more than just a name; it's the goal for every customer. Shoppers will find a wide and varied array of supplements, a whole foods café where food is made fresh daily and an organic skin care spa to rejuvenate one's sense of well-being. Accented with an eclectic selection of jewelry, stones and crystals, the artistic atmosphere at the Optimum Health Centre achieves a one-of-a-kind mixture of body, mind and spirit. It is also a goldmine of information on holistic medicine. With 20 years of experience, owner John Biggs holds a Bachelor of Science degree in Foods & Nutrition, is a registered member of the International Organization of Nutritional Consultants, and is an active member of the Institute for Functional Medicine. This training allows John and his staff to provide accurate recommendations on the latest nutrition and health information, and to effectively match dietary supplements to individuals' needs. With more than 7000 vitamins and herbs to choose from, John, his wife Nicola, and their collection of excellent service-oriented staff will make your visit to the Optimum Health Centre worthwhile and interesting.

Centre: #2, 7115 109 Street, Edmonton AB (includes café and spa) (780) 432-5464
Downtown: 11646 104 Ave, Edmonton AB (780) 452-5705
Sherwood Park: #110, 101 Granada Blvd., Sherwood Park AB (780) 467-6650
www.optimumhealthvitamins.com

Mountain Bliss Spa

Stress is the enemy at Mountain Bliss Spa, and holistic techniques are the weapon of its defeat. The spa is at the forefront of a trend that regards spas as more than just places of pampering. These spas attract a new brand of client who desires health benefits in addition to beauty and relaxation. Raindrop therapy, reflexology and massage are among the therapeutic methods available at Mountain Bliss Spa. While sitting for facial and nail treatments, customers can enjoy the benefits of Himalayan salt lamps, a source of negatively charged ions that purify the air, elevate moods and increase alertness. Owner Hope Semeniuk has always been about holistic healing and was thrilled when the opportunity presented itself to fulfill her own vision. The response to Mountain Bliss Spa has been avid. As one recent customer told massage therapist Laurie Richardson, "I'm booking another appointment for one year from today because you are going to be the next hot spot in Canmore and I'll never get back in." Join the wellness revolution at Mountain Bliss Spa.

1, 1005 Cougar Creek Drive, Canmore AB
(403) 609-3505
www.mtnbliss-spa.ca

Edwards & Holloway Health and Wellness/ Alberta Institute of Massage

Now you can get a therapeutic massage or get a degree in it under the same roof. Brenda Grosenick and Carol Edwards are the owners and mentors of the combined Edwards &

Holloway Health & Wellness center and the Alberta Institute of Massage. At the institute, Brenda and Carol offer an intensive, hands-on massage therapist training program for part- and full-time students. They also teach such spa services as how to give pedicures and manicures, how to apply facials and body wraps and how to use essential oils for aromatherapy. Motivated by a sense of community service, they lead their students in reaching out to senior homes, sports events and community retreats. At Edwards & Holloway Health and Wellness, Brenda and Carol lead their students and graduates in offering massage, hot stone therapy and reflexology to clients. Unwind with a professional massage or help make the world a healthier place in which to live in by enrolling at the Alberta Institute of Massage.

#4,7710 Gaetz Avenue, Red Deer AB
(403) 340-1330
www.albertainstituteofmassage.com

Aromatic Massage & Skincare

You're in expert hands at Aromatic Massage & Skincare, hands that will massage the stress from your body using an arsenal of techniques from around the world. Husband-and-wife team of Pavel and Vlada Kropacek opened the spa together eight years ago. Pavel specializes in therapeutic, hot stone and Swedish massage, while Vlada, who has been in the industry for more than a decade, is constantly broadening her skills. She recently traveled to the Far East, where she learned the secrets of Thai and herbal massage as well as foot reflexology. Vlada also specializes in a variety of European skincare treatments that will leave you looking radiant. Aromatic Massage & Skincare uses some of the finest beauty products available,

including Sothy's of France, which is widely recognized for its high quality. Aromatic essential oils offer a myriad therapeutic benefits. Spend half a day at this oasis and feel your stress melt away. For hand-picked massage techniques, pampering treatments from head to toe and botanical products from around the world, visit Aromatic Massage & Skincare.

C-3440-50 Avenue, Red Deer AB
(403) 392-1863

Avanti Salon & Spa

Step into Avanti Salon & Spa and be ready to change your world. With 35 highly-trained professionals at your beck and call, a day at the Salon Spa offers a magical adventure you'll never forget. Head-to-toe beauty services are yours for the asking. You could begin the fantasy with a hot stone massage, pear and green apple sugar scrub or an elixir body wrap. Follow up with a mineral soak water treatment. Finish with an aromatic soothing facial and deluxe spa pedicure and manicure. First-class products from Schwarzkopf Professional are used throughout the salon. Avanti's loyal and growing clientele expect excellence and the staff is more than happy to meet the challenge. The award-winning aestheticians pride themselves on over-the-top pampering and over-delivery of service. For the past 20 years, this leading spa has provided cutting-edge European holistic practices for men and women alike. Avanti assists customers in exploring healthy alternatives to relieve stress and embrace well-being. Make a reservation to spend the day at Avanti Salon & Spa and experience a new you.

12520-102 Avenue, Edmonton AB
(780) 482-2396
www.youravanti.com

Canmore MediSpa & Laser Centre

Rick Balharry. M.B. Ch.B., thought he was going to spend one year working in Canada but ended up staying well over 30 years, a decision that has affected the health and beauty of many a Bow Valley resident. He introduced the first medical laser to the area in 1995 and developed the Canmore MediSpa & Laser Centre. "Our mission is to improve and maintain overall health by providing physician-supervised nutritional programs, skin care and cosmetic procedures," says Dr. Balharry. The staff is prepared to perform many cosmetic procedures, including laser hair removal, varicose vein removal and glycolic acid and other skin peels. You can receive Botox treatments for everything from wrinkles to back pain, remove fat with mesotherapy and pre-cancerous lesions or acne with photodynamic therapy. Many of the Centre's treatments are designed to counteract aging caused by exposure to the sun. "We do this by stimulating collagen and removing uneven pigmentation," said Dr. Balharry. The Centre offers non-surgical face lifts and microdermabrasion. You can also have an aesthetician analyze your skin and recommend products, including the right colour choices for their mineral makeup products. Clients can commit to specialized programmes in fitness and healthy eating. For beauty in skin, body and mind, visit Canmore MediSpa & Laser Centre.

901 B Main Street, Canmore AB
(403) 678-5511
www.canmoremedicallasercentre.com

The Beehive

The Beehive offers an array of soothing products made by hand from honey, beeswax, and fruit and vegetable oils, as well as specially selected pure essential oils taken from nature's fragrant pharmacy. The company uses no synthetic materials and all colors and fragrances are plant-derived. The only preservative used is grapefruit seed extract. Because many people are allergic to nuts, the Beehive uses no nut oils except in the Sweet Almond Soap, which is clearly marked. Sandra L. Wells and friend Stan Hay instead hand-select a cornucopia of remarkable plant oils and extracts that have been used around the world for centuries to beautify, heal and soothe skin. In 1992, Wells and Hay joined forces in a tiny basement, huddling together over a hot plate to create the first of a long line of all natural lip balms, personal products and candles. The duo took their first wares to a local market where they quickly sold out. Demand grew from there. Today, the Beehive boasts two busy stores housed in vintage buildings and a buzzing website. Treat yourself to a daily dose of nature's bounty with rejuvenating products from the Beehive.

311 10 Street NW, Calgary AB
(403) 270-2622
831 17 Avenue SW, Calgary AB
(403) 244-1616
www.thebeehiveonline.com

The Lavender House Esthetics & Day Spa

Lavender is the reigning color, fragrance and overall inspiration for The Lavender House. Cochrane's only day spa offers an abundance of aesthetic treatments and services. In the warmer months, it offers hot stone massage outdoors among the fresh lavender gardens. Lavender is traditionally known as a natural remedy believed to relieve anxiety, depression and notably enhance relaxation. Indulge in an array of treatments, while basking in the surroundings of an original 1910 Victorian home. Conclude your journey with a stroll through the lavender gardens and sense the warmth and tranquility of lavender. Candy Pente and Sue Garland are the gracious hosts who will assure your stay at The Lavender House is a first class experience. Candy and Sue invite you to walk through their doors and unwind in the serene surroundings exclusively known as The Lavender House.

308 3 Street W, Cochrane AB
(403) 932-6811

Aurora borealis lights up the sky over Odysseum in Edmonton, Alberta, Canada.

Little Off the Top Barber Shop

You'll have an easy time locating Little Off the Top Barber Shop, thanks to the two full-size cowboy silhouettes framing the entry of the shop in the ever-so-Western town of Cochrane. Like the rest of historic Main Street, the four-year-old shop, owned and operated by Darrell Sharpe, has a Western outlook and a certain old-fashioned charm. This is a shop exclusively for men and boys, which makes it easier for Darrell and his staff to provide the atmosphere and services that bring in customers from miles around. You'll find cowboys and country gentlemen visiting with Darrell, who will know you by your haircut even if you haven't been in for a year. Not only does Darrell take pride in his haircuts and his memory, he also entertains his customers with stories and often sings their favourite country tunes, earning the nickname, "the singing barber." No matter how long you have been on the range, Darrell and his barber posse can provide exactly the straightforward cut or trim you seek. They'll treat you to a manly atmosphere reminiscent of earlier times and take just a little off the top. Catch up on local talk, hear a story from the Old West or listen to Darrell put heart and soul behind a favourite country tune with a visit to Little Off the Top Barber Shop, the only barber shop in these parts that caters just to men.

504 1 Street W, Cochrane AB
(403) 932-5070

Rainy Daze Medi-Spa

Saving for a rainy day? Rainy Daze Medi-Spa is the perfect way to spend a leisurely indoor afternoon. Owners Lorraine Schiele, Tanya Crawford and Meghan Berg opened the spa together in 2006. Their motto is *Live, Laugh, Love,* and the spa's menu of nurturing and relaxing treatments helps guests to do just that. If the stress of life has left you in need of some tender, loving care, come in and let a registered massage therapist fix you up. Combine massages with secondary treatments such as salt glows, paraffin hand dips or an infrared sauna session. Unlike a traditional sauna, this one uses infrared rays to heat the body, resulting in a more cleansing detoxifying experience. If you're looking for a makeover, Rainy Daze can provide you with a Microdermabrasion or a glycolic peel. These advanced facial treatments gently remove surface layers of skin, along with fine lines, age spots and acne scars for a fully refreshed appearance. In addition, Rainy Daze specializes in laser treatments from hair removal to muscle pain. The Rainy Daze staff maintains a soothing atmosphere to replenish your spirit as well as your body. Let Rainy Daze Medi-Spa wash away your stress and leave you with a sunny glow.

5002A-50 Street, Sylvan Lake AB
(403) 887-0660

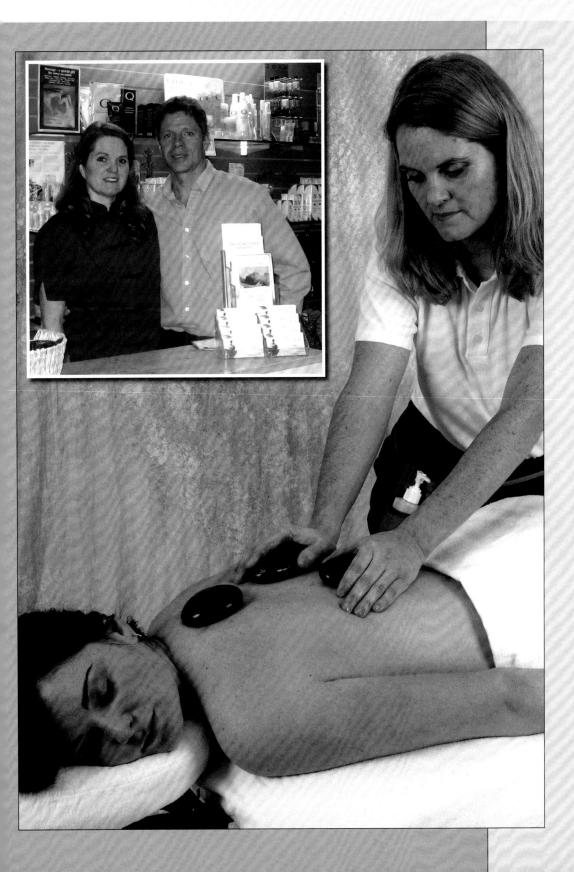

NeuroMuscular Therapy Center & Holistic Health Spa

The world's cultures have long honored natural healing therapies as a means of maintaining health. In 2004, Shirley and James Aberle launched NeuroMuscular Therapy Center & Holistic Health Spa, bringing state-of-the-art technologies based on the latest scientific research to re-awaken these age-old-healing-traditions. This small, unassuming health spa, nestled back off Main Street offers a variety of highly effective western medical body therapies as well as therapeutic relaxation massages. All-natural rejuvenating skin care for healthier, younger looking skin and therapeutic nail care using only non-toxic products won't sacrifice health for beauty. Looking good and feeling young is an important part of feeling great. The health properties of heat and detoxification are now made available to everyone through the gentle infrared sauna therapy and ionic foot bath. You'll be introduced to a plethora of health information, seminars and products to keep you on top of the world, happy, healthy and feeling good. James and Shirley have spent their lives amassing knowledge on health, fitness, nutrition, relaxation, meditation, esthetics, and massage while travelling, working and studying abroad and in Canada. In addition, while serving the world's most affluent patrons' onboard private luxury yachts and the World of ResidenSea Ship, they have learned the fine art of five star service, which comes through in their attention to detail and in creating a health spa in harmony with nature. To learn more, visit the website, where you can also reserve your services on-line.

#104, 820 Main St., Canmore AB
(403) 678-0717
www.NMTCanmore.com

Marista Spa

Customers at Marista Spa know Marek Mroczkowski has found his calling when they experience what many have called the best massage of their lives. Marek came to Canada from Greece in 1988, working at all sorts of jobs before focusing on the pleasure his massages gave family and friends. In 2000, he trained in Alberta to be a masseur, opening his spa in 2003 with help from his daughters, Joanna and Magdalena. Massage choices include therapeutic, sports, deep tissue and hot stone massage, plus Reiki and reflexology. Upon entering the spa you'll find a friendly multilingual staff along with two massage rooms, two aesthetics rooms, a manicure and pedicure room, a steam room and a relaxation room designed as a transition space between services. Your comfort extends to a choice of beverages, including coffee, tea, hot chocolate, juice or cider. The spa uses many products by the Hungarian firm Éminence Organic Skin Care. Topical phytohormones are designed to restore hormonal balance to skin and slow the signs of aging. People with sensitive skin or rosacea benefit from the Couperose-C serum. Whether you have concerns with wrinkling, acne or loss of skin radiance, the aestheticians at Marista can customize a facial for you. Spend a couple of hours or all day indulging in your well-being at Marista Spa.

#6 – 5108 52nd Street, Red Deer AB
(403) 341-3720

Hickory Stix Salon & Spa

Aveda spas are world-renowned for their all-natural products, sustainable business practices and professional training. Hickory Stix Salon & Spa is Okotoks's own Aveda spa. Owners Angela and Wade McLeod have created an inviting atmosphere with soft lighting and muted colors that leave clients fully relaxed during their salon and spa treatments. Offering the full range of body, facial and hair services, Hickory Stix's excellent staff are graduates of Aveda institutes for advanced training. Clients know that they can expect creative stylists, nurturing therapists and a collective commitment to wellness. Aveda makeup, skin and hair products are made of organic, plant-based ingredients and non-petroleum mineral ingredients that protect your body and the earth. In addition, Aveda sources many of its ingredients from traditional communities

around the world to promote a more sustainable global economy. In accordance with the South Asian tradition of Ayurveda, Aveda products and treatments incorporate aromatherapy to balance the elements in your body. Aveda massage training incorporates several traditions of pressure point technology. Expect a facial or scalp massage with your facial or hair treatment at Hickory Stix. Enjoy yourself from head to foot at Hickory Stix Salon & Spa, where you'll find world-class services with a community spirit.

103-29 N Railway Street, Okotoks AB
(403) 938-3378

Bodyworks Salon & Day Spa

Bodyworks Salon & Day Spa is located in the middle of Canmore on the Bow Valley Trail. Nearby shops and hotels offer a convenient location to slip away for an hour or two. Locally owned and operated, Bodyworks Salon & Day Spa has been the choice of locals for over a decade and specializes in catering to weddings and large spa groups, coined by the highly trained staff as *spaties*. The shop's wide range of services includes massages, wraps and scrubs,

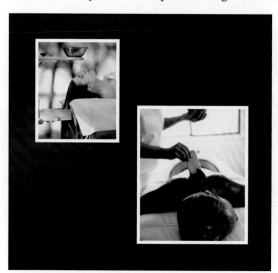

facials and advanced skincare treatments. Naturally, you can enjoy manicures and pedicures, nails or hairdressing, makeup or waxing. Mix and match services to create you own special day. Are you on a romantic holiday? A couples massage is a popular way to relax together. The Mountain Mud Wrap releases toxins. Try a Shirodhara massage, in which warm oil flows over the third eye to calm the nervous system. Bodyworks Salon & Day Spa uses the Decleor Paris product line exclusively. Leave relaxed and restored after your day of shopping, golf or skiing.

1702 Bow Valley Trail, Canmore AB
(403) 678-5746
www.bodyworks-salon-spa.com

Sylvan Steam & Spa

After a week of hard work, many Finnish immigrants in Sylvan Lake once looked forward to spending their Saturday night at Anderson's steam bathhouse. Located in the same building that opened as Anderson's in 1947, Sylvan Steam & Spa is as popular today with out-of-towners as with locals. The spa offers private steam baths in fragrant cedar wood rooms. More than a comforting way to relax, steam therapy is full of health benefits, according to owner Cynthia Leigh. It stimulates the immune system, enhances circulation and detoxifies the organs, skin and fatty sebaceous glands. In addition to steam baths, Sylvan Steam & Spa offers massage and a wide range of other spa services, including facials, body wraps and nail care. On rainy days, many vacationers abandon their tents to seek warmth and relaxation at Sylvan Steam & Spa. Cynthia has decorated the historic building with period photographs and memorabilia to keep its heritage alive. Experience the refuge that has been a Sylvan Lake tradition for more than 60 years at Sylvan Steam & Spa.

4916 48 Avenue, Sylvan Lake AB
(403) 887-2413

Amatsu Eastern Healing Arts Clinic

Amatsu Eastern Healing Arts Clinic embraces an Eastern approach to healing that safeguards health and longevity with early intervention. The clinic uses many forms of Japanese healing disciplines and specializes in helping those with chronic conditions. If you've never heard of Amatsu before, you aren't alone. This form of massage therapy is a regulated profession in Japan, where Dr. Christian Perez received his formal training. In North America, he is the only practitioner of his kind. His doctorates are in natural medicine and missionary medicine, and he is certified by the World Health Organization. Two years ago, Dr. Perez left Toronto to work in Canmore, a place he believes is better situated for healing. At the core of his practice is Amatsu, a form of bodywork that incorporates Japanese clinical massage, acupuncture, Chinese herbs, diet, exercise and lifestyle counseling. Amatsu improves circulation, removes toxins, positions vital organs, increases body tone and coordination and strengthens the immune system. Patients usually make Dr. Perez's treatments an ongoing part of their lives, and some have moved to Canmore to be near him. For a life filled with meaning and health, visit Amatsu Eastern Healing Arts Clinic.

#202–729 10 Street, Canmore AB
(403) 609-3059
www.amatsu.ca

Pleiades Massage and Spa

Pleiades Massage and Spa is renowned for quality treatments at reasonable prices. The staff members, all certified massage therapists, have built a reputation that prompts clients to return again and again. Upper Hot Springs is at the doorstep of the Banff spa, and you can

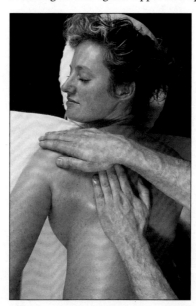

take a refreshing dip there when you visit. Owner Blake Johnson makes all of the products used in the various treatments. The spa uses Swedish massage and oils to reduce stress, aches and pains, while enhancing vitality and well-being. Deeper therapeutic massage speeds healing and recovery from illness or injury, as well as conditions ranging from headaches to back pain. Reflexology, Reiki, Shiatsu and hot stone massage are available. Enjoy an all-natural facial—Blake's own formulas provide a perfect match for your skin. A body treatment or wrap will leave your skin wonderfully soft and supple. Combination packages and couples massages are also offered. For a perfectly relaxing experience, make an appointment at Pleiades Massage and Spa.

Top of Mountain Avenue, Banff AB
(403) 760-2500 or (866) 760-2502
5420 Highway 93, Radium Hot Springs BC
(250) 347-9485
www.pleiadesmassage.com

Wildflower Massage & Esthetics

Wildflower Massage & Esthetics is a locally owned day spa in the heart of Canmore. Owner Kamila Borutova, a registered massage therapist and licensed esthetician, has been with the spa since its opening in 2000. In 2006, she and her husband Richard purchased the spa and spent hours renovating it to meet their high standards. Kamila promotes the personal approach, and clients soon feel at home here. A hard-working team of massage therapists and estheticians keep Wildflower open seven days a week, so you can improve your well-being at a time that best fits your schedule. Kamila has been a massage therapist for the Biathlon National Team, helping athletes on the World Cup circuit and the 2006 Olympics in Torino. She can help you to achieve your ideal performance, too. Wildflower's regular clients include many recreational and Olympic level athletes. The most popular treatments are the deep tissue, therapeutic, hot

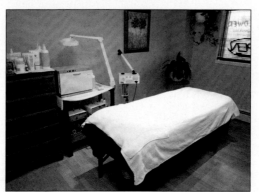

stone and Swedish massages for those who are looking to reward their body. The rosehip wrap, which includes a body polish, mini-facial and foot massage, remains a favorite treatment. Wildflower Massage & Esthetics is also well known for its great facials, manicures and signature Wildflower pedicures. Call or visit the website to find out more about the treatments, meet the friendly staff and schedule your appointment.

#5-713 Main Street, Canmore AB
(403) 678-4644
www.wildflowercanmore.com

Red Earth Spa

The forecast at the Red Earth Spa calls for showers, though not the kind that you would mind getting caught in. These are Vichy Rain Showers, calming cascades that flow from a bar of seven showerheads to imitate a warm tropical rain. Your skin will tingle and the tension in your muscles will release as the warm waters pour over you. With the Wet Earth Signature Treatment, you can even experience a hydro massage under the Vichy shower, following a full body exfoliation and mud wrap. The Red Earth Spa embraces a holistic philosophy of re-connecting individuals with Earth's elements for treatments that heal the soul as well as the body. Featuring a full menu of body treatments, aesthetics and facials, it uses Phytomer products to feed the senses and enhance natural beauty with 100 percent natural active marine ingredients. Among the most popular treatments are the Pure Earth Signature Facial with particle-free microdermabrasion and the couples side-by-side massage. The nurturing Deep Earth Signature Treatment involves a private soak in aromatic oils, seaweed or detoxifying mud. Located at the beautiful Banff Caribou Lodge, the spa employs warm, earth-toned colors, muted studio lighting and a clean modern design to put your mind at rest. Relax in the rain, sea and mud at Red Earth Spa.

521 Banff Avenue, Banff AB
(403) 762-9292
www.redearthspa.com

Divine Serenity Spa & Massage Therapy

A day at the spa is a treat for all ages at Divine Serenity Spa & Massage Therapy. Indeed, you might meet four generations of customers, from toddlers to grandmothers, in the lounge of this Red Deer retreat. Many mothers and daughters have been coming together for years for a special girl's day out. Divine Serenity Spa & Massage Therapy is located downtown in the historic Red Deer courthouse, a wonderful building with elegant stairwells leading to the spa's private rooms.

Owner Pamela Carrier has transformed the interiors into peaceful, inviting coves for individuals, couples and groups such as bridal parties. Pamela leads an experienced and energetic team of professionals in offering a full range of therapeutic and esthetic services at the spa, including massage, facials and nail care. Treat yourself to a date with bliss at Divine Serenity Spa & Massage Therapy.

#103-4836 50 Street, Red Deer AB
(403) 346-4922

Latherup Canada Salon 'N' Spa

All natural soaps are not created equal. Latherup Canada offers a superior product with a base of pure olive oil and canola oil instead of the beef tallow or pork lard used by some manufacturers. The difference is readily apparent. Latherup soaps will not clog pores or irritate skin, and they provide moisturizing qualities. The soap bars are made with natural preservatives, herbs, essential oils and plant colors, with no artificial additives. They are blended with scents and textures that address the different facets of skin care. The lavender soaps act as an oily skin tonic, promote restful sleep and alleviate tension. A Citrus Sand Bar pampers feet by exfoliating dead skin with a zesty, uplifting scent. Besides the soaps, every inch of the body is carefully considered in a product line that ranges from scrubs and bath eggs to eye tea, hair, aesthetics

and nail treatments. Latherup also provides a luxurious muscle therapy treatment, infrared sauna and spray tan. The namesake salon and spa is located in an historic post office originally built in 1895. Owner Robyn Shackleton is a certified cosmetologist with the professional background and dedicated staff to back it up. Grateful for the support of her family and community, she makes it her mission to offer excellent, individualized care. Come by and revitalize at the Latherup Canada Salon 'N' Spa.

4908 50th Avenue, Lacombe AB
(403) 782-3038

Restaurants & Cafés

SoHo Bar & Grill

When you take the name of your business from one of Manhattan's most fashionable neighborhoods, you know the pressure is on to provide a chic and electrifying experience for your patrons. Roque De Obieta welcomes the challenge of bringing New York flash to Calgary and even adds splashes of South Beach style to his SoHo Bar & Grill. At the heart of any sophisticated urban experience is a cosmopolitan menu. The third floor dining room at SoHo is the setting for just such a meal that transcends the ordinary and takes you to Manhattan for New York strip and to Madrid for paella. There are soups, salads and appetizers for lighter appetites, including spicy East Indian samosas served with SoHo's signature dipping sauce. The dance floor gets quite crowded on weekends when local DJs mix up some party tunes. We advise that you plan your approach to the action while sipping a martini or mojito. Yes, Roque and his team of bartenders are committed to the art of bartending as it is practiced at the hippest of New York nightclubs. Dress the part of an aspiring artist, fashion designer or trendsetter and step out for eating, drinking and dancing at SoHo Bar & Grill.

801 6 Street SW, Calgary AB
(403) 237-6453
www.sohobargrill.com

Namskar Fine East Indian Cuisine

Calgary Living magazine calls Namskar Fine East Indian Cuisine the spice of life. *Where Magazine* named it the Best Ethnic Restaurant in Calgary in 2005 and 2006. Owners Trilochan and Jaswinder Sekhon have created an oasis of peace and quality. The name of the restaurant reflects its hospitality—it means *I bow to you* or *there is no one like you.* Unpretentious, yet with warm saffron yellow tablecloths and crisp white folded napkins, the décor is a perfect balance of elegance and appeal. The roomy stand-alone building is divided into two sides, providing an intimate feel and the ability to accommodate private functions. It takes more than great ambience to make an outstanding dining experience, though. It takes excellent food and superior service, and that is where Namskar Fine East Indian Cuisine shines. The cuisine ranges from subtle to spicy and includes both vegetarian and non-vegetarian fare. Diners return frequently to try tangy dishes such as the tandoori prawns, tandoori chicken or two kinds of kebab. Namskar offers goat curry or vindaloo, dishes most people have not tried but which have excellent flavour. *Biryani* and *naan* bread complete the feast. Whatever you choose, save room for the wonderful deserts. Some customers come just for the *ras malai,* chilled homemade cheese patties in a sweet creamy sauce. Come back to Namskar again and again to enjoy the wonderful food and warm Indian hospitality.

202 16 Avenue NE, Calgary AB
(403) 230-4447
www.namskar.ca

Bona Roma

For more than a decade, pizza at Bona Roma has been a Calgary institution. The restaurant, which bills itself as a Little Italian Eatery, has two locations in Calgary. Owners Jason and Justin Richter have maintained the family tradition of excellence established by their parents, Brian and Eunice. Their presence is still keenly felt at Bona Roma, with everything from appetizers to salad dressings and main courses taken from their original recipes. Get an authentic Neapolitan pizza with all the toppings or the signature Chicken Marsala. Bona Roma uses only the freshest ingredients, with many purchased from small suppliers locally. The company's motto, Pizza and Pasta You Deserve, reflects its deep dedication to the community. Beyond knowing the names and favorites of its regular customers, the company sponsors an annual scholarship. If you're not local, though, you can still enjoy Bona Roma pizza by delivery. The restaurant's special delivery trucks include ovens that allow your pizza to be made en route, a popular feature with movie sets and corporate events. If you're looking for pizza, pasta and a family tradition of dining excellence, come to Bona Roma.

6915 MacLeod Trail SW, Calgary AB
(403) 252-6686
www.bonaromapizza.com
89 Bowridge Drive NW, Calgary AB
(403) 247-3327

Rockyview Hotel

Established in 1904, the Rockyview Hotel is a classic image of an old western hotel and saloon. Today, the hotel celebrates the fusion of old and new, pairing décor from the early 1900s, such as hardwood floors, cherry wood finishes, tin ceilings and antique fixtures, with a menu featuring regional cuisine at its best. The Canyon Rose Steakhouse is a rare gem serving timeless steakhouse classics inspired by contemporary and fresh culinary ideas in a setting immersed in a fascinating and charming past. Weekend brunches are fresh and delicious and dinner will bring you AAA Alberta beef and bison as well as game, seafood and organic local produce. Guests can stay in one of the 15 rooms located above the Steakhouse and get down to live Country Western Music in the Stageline Saloon Friday and Saturday nights. Sunday is all about champagne breakfast and the live acoustic jam session, so get up early. Come to Rockyview Hotel and enjoy the timeless flavour that will surround you.

304 - 1 Street W, Cochrane AB
(403) 932-2442
www.rockyviewhotel.com

Orchid Room

Featuring a superbly crafted blend of Thai, Vietnamese and French cuisines, the Orchid Room isn't your average restaurant. Each plate comes adorned with fresh flowers from Owner Ken Nguyen's flower shop, where he specializes in growing, caring for and selling spectacular, delicate orchids. With fare that sizzles with superb flavors, it's no wonder lunchtime can get crowded. The restaurant is located 15 feet above street level, features a novel indoor patio and can seat up to 100 people. Despite its quirky locale, the Orchid Room boasts of a cozy atmosphere bedecked with stylish French-inspired décor. For a real treat with which to start your meal, try the mango-shrimp salad rolls, an enticingly sweet appetizer made with only the freshest ingredients by experienced chefs. Next, you can move on to caramelized salmon, tamarind prawns, lemongrass chicken or a host of other entrée choices. Each embodies fusion cuisine at its finest. The dessert menu entices with exciting combinations, like the restaurant's specialty, mango crème brûlée, plus with a host of traditional French crème brûlées and classic Asian desserts. The service is swift, friendly and accommodating, but that doesn't mean you won't want to linger over your delectable meal. For a stylish gourmet adventure, visit the Orchid Room for lunch or dinner.

244-315 8 Avenue SW, Calgary AB
(403) 263-4457

Leto Steak & Seafood Lounge

For more than 25 years, Leto Steak & Seafood Lounge has been drawing food lovers from near and far. Leto serves the best in AAA Black Angus beef and generous portions of fresh seafood with top-quality service. The Super Leto's Special Seafood Platter for Two has been called the richest plate in Central Alberta. The platter holds two lobster tails, King crab legs, a filet shish kabob and a dozen giant prawns and scallops, served together with rice, potatoes and vegetables. Owner Evagelo Saganis is a gracious host who always has time to say hello. Customers have claimed to travel miles for the shish kabob stacked with filet mignon. The prime rib is also legendary. Leto's complements these traditional favorites with a selection of classic Greek dishes such as souvlaki—bite-sized pieces of pork marinated in fine herbs and broiled, served on a bed of rice with greek salad and vegetables. The restaurant often features live entertainment, so you get not only a great meal, but a show, as well. One tip: reservations are a good idea for this community favorite, especially on weekends. The restaurant accommodates 145 diners and an additional 120 in the separate sports lounge. Whether for a party for 100 or an intimate dinner for two, you'll have a great evening at Leto Steak & Seafood Lounge.

4944 Hwy 2A, Lacombe ALB
(403) 782-4647

Fusion Café

You'll taste a fusion of flavours from Vietnam, Asia and North America at the Fusion Café. The café has deliberately avoided specializing in one cuisine or another in order to offer the widest variety of flavours for guests to choose from. With more than 200 items on the menu, there's something here for every taste. The menu is categorized by meats with a separate column for noodles, making it simple to navigate in spite of its size. You'll find several varieties of Asian noodle soup, along with Vietnamese spring rolls and szechuan beef. You'll also find seafood options, including prawns, scallops and squid. The Fusion Café is also the only restaurant in Red Deer to sell bubble tea, a fun Asian drink that combines fresh fruit with bubbles of tapioca in many different flavors. For an international menu with something for everyone, make your way to the Fusion Café.

6, 6842-50 Avenue, Red Deer AB
(403) 348-5268 or (403) 348-8238

Guido's Ristorante

Since 1973, Guido's Ristorante has been a destination of choice for those seeking fresh, authentic Italian food, with a beautiful second-story view of the mountains. Mike and Vivian Derondeau have owned and operated Guido's using only the freshest ingredients, never compromising the quality of the food. To ensure this, the pasta is homemade and the trout appetizer and salmon entrée are smoked in their kitchen. The ever-popular French onion soup is hearty and rich, baked with a topping of crostini and double Gruyère cheese. Entrées include traditional pasta dishes, lasagna, cannelloni and chicken or veal Parmagiana and veal Valdostana, a local favourite served with a creamy wild mushroom sauce. The wine list complements every meal selection and palate. A dinner at Guido's would not be complete without sampling a dessert of homemade ice cream, fruit sorbet or Belgian chocolate mousse. The many guests who make return visits from all over Alberta, eastern Canada, United States and the four corners of the globe are welcomed in a friendly, casual atmosphere year after year. Stop by—the welcome is always warm, the conversation full of life and of course, the food is oh so good.

116 B Banff Avenue (above McDonalds), Banff AB
(403) 762-4002
www.dininginbanff.com/restaurants/guidos.shtml

French Quarter Café

There's a Mardi Gras for your taste buds every day at the French Quarter Café, a New Orleans-inspired restaurant that has been adding spice to Canmore's restaurant scene since 1995. Beneath photos of smiling jazz musicians, diners feast on jambalaya, seafood gumbo and all those other flavourful Cajun and Creole dishes that have made New Orleans synonymous with good eating. Chef Michael Raso has too much fun to call what he does working. "I feel like I retired the day I first opened the doors at the French Quarter," he says. His love affair with Cajun and Creole cuisine began with his first trip to Louisiana in the 1990s. Each time he goes back, he adds some new dish to his repertoire and some new way to blend the exotic spices that are key to his cooking. Kick off your day with a breakfast of Eggs Bourbon Street—eggs served on crab cakes with shrimp Creole sauce and Cajun potatoes. Po' boys, New Orleans' favorite sandwich, are popular for lunch. From the alligator skewers and pecan-crusted catfish to the blackened red snapper and crawfish ètouffèe, the menu at the French Quarter will make you as happy as a street party. Chef Michael loves adding his own touches to traditional recipes with his daily specials, so be sure to ask what the special is on the day you drop by. An extensive wine list, live jazz every second Friday and cooking classes complete the picture at the French Quarter Café. Strut right in for a meal, and let the good times roll.

4, 102 Boulder Circle, Canmore AB (403) 678-3612 *www.frenchquartercafe.net*

Melrose Café & Bar

Melrose Café & Bar is ideally located, as the trademarked motto states, in the Heart of the Red Mile, a section of Calgary made famous by thousands of Flames fans who, decked out in their team's colour, celebrated victories here in 2004. Thousands of patrons watched the games from the Melrose Lounge. This popular bar and restaurant, owned by Wayne Leong, has been celebrating sports victories and engaging in spirited hospitality for over 15 years. On weekends the three-level bar, complete with a lounge and restaurant, takes on a nightclub feel, with more than 60 flat-screen televisions on each level to bring sideline thrills of major sporting events while you enjoy international cuisine in a casual setting. You'll find plenty of satisfying food to add to the fun here. Starters are popular and include bruschetta, quesadillas, goat cheese bake, calamari and the popular ginger beef. Thin crust pizzas, salads and pasta join such Melrose specialties as coconut curry mussels and fajitas to create an enticing variety. The kitchen at Melrose uses the latest technology to deliver quality and efficiency. Technical innovations serve patrons in ways you are unlikely to find elsewhere. The four-level Melrose patio, with its trendy 17th Avenue location and lush greenery, is widely considered the best place to see and be seen. Revel in the scene, in the game and in the food with a visit to Melrose Café & Bar.

730 17 Avenue SW, Calgary AB
(403) 650-0063
www.melrosecalgary.com

Whistle Stop Café

The Whistle Stop Café is housed in a restored 1940s Canadian National Railway dining car. The menu emphasizes healthy choices while serving comfort food, a mix you just may be able to get behind. One of the most popular dishes is mulligatawny, an interpretation of a spicy meat and curry soup from India. Another favourite is Flapper Pie, an old family recipe. Healthy sandwiches and other light lunch fare are also on the menu. The owners of the café, Dwayne and Patti Johnson, take a hands-on approach to the daily operations of the restaurant. All of the food is made from scratch, including the bread, which is baked by Donna, Patti's mom. Donna also bakes up some terrific cinnamon buns. You may also come to the Whistle Stop Cafe for afternoon tea. During the cold months, most of the customers are local professionals. In spring and summer, the Whistle Stop Café is a destination spot, with visitors from around the world, particularly from Britain. Just next door you'll find the Museum of the Highwood with its many exhibits and kid-friendly activities. When in High River, be sure to visit at the Whistle Stop Café for some healthy comfort food in a friendly atmosphere.

406 1 Street SW, High River AB
(403) 652-7026

Colossi's Coffee House

Until just three years ago, the quaint town of High River had no real coffee house where people could meet with friends to enjoy a variety of coffee fancies and each other's company. This prompted coffee-loving owners Dwayne and Patti Johnson to open the sophisticated and now flourishing Colossi's Coffee House. Inspired by Dwayne's Italian grandfather, Jack Colossi, they gave Colossi's Coffee House a warm Italian décor that breathes camaraderie and hospitality. As you enter, you see an impressive brick wall that displays local arts and craft items. Comfy couches surround the fireplace, an altogether inviting scene. Stone and wood floors complete the rustic but refined ambience. Colossi's menu lists cappuccinos, lattes and iced coffees, along with regular coffee made of a variety of coffee beans and blends. Smoothies are popular in summer. Colossi's does not neglect the sweets—it offers tempting desserts to go along with your cup of Joe. Freshly baked muffins, wraps and other light fare are some of your choices. You can also take home a bag of coffee selected from the many varieties on hand. Dwayne and Patti also provide coffee beans by special order. Do yourself a favor and take a respite in this relaxing Italian-style shop, Colossi's Coffee House.

114 4 Avenue SW, High River AB
(403) 652-2181

Pizza Bob's Classic Pie

What Bob Collins knows about pizza says a lot about his knowledge of people. A Neapolitan pizza from Pizza Bob's Classic Pie just might make your date swoon with its similarity to the pizzas of Italy. Mom will approve of its MSG-free crusts and sauces, and kids won't know why they like it better than others, but these pizzas could cause them to develop a taste for fresh vegetables, vine ripened tomatoes and gourmet meats. Pizza Bob's pies feature thin crusts, made crisp and flavourful in a European style brick oven. Those who love meat and nothing by meat will doubtless zero in on the Croc-O'-Bull, which features ham, pepperoni, lean ground beef, salami and Italian sausage. If everything but meat is your preference, the Veggiemaniac is the pie for you. You can find pizzas featuring chicken, garlic, pineapple or classic Greek ingredients here. The Heart Smart pizza replaces tomato sauce with olive oil, seasonings and a topping of spinach, mushrooms and green onions. Just in case you don't see a combination to your liking, you can always build your own pizza here. Pizza Bob's offers a few more foods worth mentioning, such as chicken or meat lasagna, Greek or Caesar salad, and such starters as chicken wings or garlic bread. You can have your pizza delivered to most areas of the city or bring your own wine to the small dining area and take advantage of the free corkage. For a pizza from a master, come to Pizza Bob's Classic Pie, and be sure to say hi to Bob while you are there.

2610 Kensington Road NW, Calgary AB (403) 521-BOBS (2627)
www.pizzabobs.ca

Rouge

Rouge has discovered a restaurant style that suits Calgary and defines that style as cosmopolitan with global, particularly French, influences. *Avenue* magazine named it a top pick, and *Wine Spectator* gave it the 2006 Award of Excellence. "Texture, temperature, colour, nutrition and most importantly flavour. These are the components I consider," says co-owner and Chef Paul Rogalski. "Food is the medium for my art." Paul assures his food will be fresh with herbs and produce from Rouge's own on-site garden. For dinner, you might enjoy a superb rack of lamb or the duck, which many say is the best in Calgary. Beef tenderloin or a beef ribeye roast are excellent choices, but Rouge also can also treat you to such exotic meats as wapiti or ostrich. Rouge is located in the Cross House, built in 1891 on the banks of the Bow River and listed as an Alberta Heritage Site. Dining takes place in an atrium and parlour as well as in the dining room. A second floor gallery displays artwork and can seat a group of up to 40 people. All rooms offer a warm and vibrant atmosphere. An enormous garden filled with trees, flowers and shrubs covers six city blocks. It is available for dining and private functions in warm weather along with an outdoor patio. Paul and co-owner Olivier Reynaud love to meet their guests. Join them at Rouge and see why the critics are talking.

1240 8 Avenue SE, Calgary AB
(403) 531-2767
www.rougecalgary.com

Chef's Studio Japan

Yoshiteru Morikawa and Akiko Toshimitsu are renowned in Canmore for sushi that pleases all five senses. When they opened Chef's Studio Japan, they were certain that they could create a restaurant that would truly stand apart. They do so by relying on their extensive experience in food service and in making sushi, plus their knowledge of what they call healing food. Featuring fresh, organic and wholesome ingredients, the restaurant's menu is a perfect melding of traditional Japanese cuisine and modern healthful options. Workers at Chef's Studio, which is named for its artful presentation of food, pay attention to each little detail, from beautifully symmetrical arrangements of superbly crafted pieces of sushi to delightful, one-of-a-kind salads

built for two. It's not just the food that will delight the senses. The work of local artists is always on display and available for purchase, providing a rotating décor that never lacks for excitement. Natural Japanese themes back up the ever-changing art, creating a welcoming and relaxing atmosphere in which to enjoy your meal. Visit Chef's Studio Japan for a taste of Japan with a healthy twist on your next visit to Canmore.

108, 709 Main Street, Canmore AB
(403) 609-8383
www.chefsstudiojapan.com

Saltlik, A Rare Steakhouse

Written up in the *New York Times* and *Martha Stewart Living*, Saltlik, A Rare Steakhouse serves premier quality beef. The two-storey chalet-style restaurant resembles an upscale ski lodge, with its fireplace, brass-and-wood warmth and original art work. The bar, on the main level, has a long and impressive wine list. The restaurant is on the second storey. Casual and comfortable in an elegant way, Saltlik serves you fine food, with great service and reasonable prices. You'll

find a steak to write home about, seasoned and cooked to perfection, along with the chef's array of delectable sauces. The butcher's cut prime rib is offered on Friday and Saturday nights. Other signature dishes include the chili-rubbed baby back ribs and veal strip loin with wild mushrooms and cream reduction sauce. Seafood lovers can indulge in the Pacific wild salmon with chili butter. Side dishes are generous, enough to satisfy two or three. Most menu items are made from scratch. Owner James Sachkin travels often, shopping international markets for ideas and premium ingredients, and he reinvents the menu at least quarterly. (The favorites always remain.) In Banff, stop in at the Saltlik, A Rare Steakhouse, for a fine lunch or dinner.

221 Bear Street, Banff AB
(403) 762-2467
www.saltlik.com

Café de Ville

A touch of sophistication accents the casual dining at Café de Ville. Sounds of soft jazz play overhead, inviting you to leave your cares and worries behind. An aura of warmth and elegance welcomes you to your table. As the fireplace flames cast a golden glow on the cozy brick and wood interior, feast your eyes on the menu. It spans the world—Thai prawns, trois tapas, rack of lamb, smoked salmon and of course Alberta beef. Appetizers such as escargot, bouillabaisse or polenta soufflé can jumpstart your culinary journey. House specialties include duck confit, a savory blend of spices, honey, ginger, soy and garlic chili glaze, and Kashmir, chicken escallops smothered in banana chips, coconut, chutney and curry cream. Chef Paul Campbell prepares pasta dishes with unusual flair. Cran-pesto pasta features sun-dried cranberries. Wild boar bacon adds panache to the pasta carbonara. Pastry Chef Mark Marynowski completes the affair with a sampling of sinful delights that change daily. Servers bring trays of delectable desserts right to your table. Local suppliers deliver fresh ingredients daily to ensure the high quality diners have come to expect. Restaurateur Anita Lewis brings 20 years of culinary expertise to your dining experience. She purchased Café de Ville in 2000 after years as a patron. Reserve a table at Café de Ville for a night of sumptuous food and graceful service.

10137-124 Street, Edmonton AB
(780) 488-9188 or (866) 988-9188
www.cafedeville.com

Evelyn's Memory Lane Café

Evelyn's Memory Lane Café has a time-capsule quality that makes this 1950s-style diner a nostalgic return to the past. Don and Evelyn Zabloski took over the restaurant four years ago, having previously made a hit with their award-winning coffee shops in Banff. At Evelyn's Memory Lane Café you'll find a lunch counter lined with red leather stools and a jukebox at every booth. Memorabilia from the '50s and '60s adorn the walls and a model train circles the restaurant. Chef Dorte Gensky prepares classic comfort foods from Evelyn's recipes, which have appeared in international publications. The homemade ice cream, the fresh baking and the roast chicken sandwiches are especially popular. Customers who can't find a seat often order the specials to-go. These hot specials change daily, and when the Zabloskis call something *special* you can be certain it lives up to its word. Bring your appetite for nostalgia to Evelyn's Memory Lane Café for an old-fashioned diner experience.

118 4 Avenue SW, High River AB
(403) 652-1887

Kane's Harley® Diner

Kane's Motor Cycle Shop combines two of life's great pleasures in one location. It's a restaurant with antique Harleys® on display and a Harley-Davidson® dealership across the lane. Inside Kane's Harley® Diner, the legendary Mick Cawthorn has translated the biker's passion into a fun, upbeat decor. He personally hand-laid the tile design in the diner. Cawthorn's magic is evident everywhere, including the food. A breakfast favorite is the Biker Bowl—hash browns topped with scrambled eggs and ham, tomato and green onions, cheddar and hollandaise sauce and served with your choice of toast. For lunch or dinner, choose from dishes such as the Inglewood Classic, grilled cheese stuffed with sautéed onions and tomatoes, or Hogs In Flight, a half rack of ribs and a full chicken breast smothered in barbecue sauce and served with vegetables and your choice of potatoes or salad. That's just a small sample of the customized favorites you'll find on the Kane's Harley® Diner menu. Stop in at Kane's Harley® Diner for the kind of meal that will give you the energy you need for a long ride.

1209 9th Avenue SE, Calgary AB
(403) 269-7311
www.kanesharleydavidson.com

Cuisine Concepts

You will be embarking on a culinary adventure when you try the distinct flavors at each Calgary restaurant in the Cuisine Concepts restaurant group: Big Fish, Diner Deluxe, Vue Café and Open Range. Dwayne and Alberta Ennest met when they worked together at the same café. In 2001, they married and opened the first of their own Cuisine Concepts venues. For this food journey, you'll want to grab your Palate Passport, a fun little booklet you can have stamped and redeem for goodies from Cuisine Concepts. At Diner Deluxe, you will join the regulars who know this retro diner is the best place to find a hearty breakfast all day long. The comfort food here gets a gourmet twist. Right next door is Urban Baker, where bakers start early each morning handcrafting slow-rise breads, such as a chocolate cranberry loaf. In 2005, *Avenue Magazine* called the bakery's apple-flax-rosemary sourdough one of the 25 Best Things to Eat in Calgary. Located inside the Virginia Christopher Fine Art Gallery, the Vue Café is an upscale wine, cheese and lunch spot decorated with work by some of Canada's most talented artists. Big Fish seafood and oyster lounge offers an easygoing atmosphere and exciting flavours. Open Range brings Southwest style to Alberta elk, buffalo, beef and lamb. Though the restaurants vary in flavours and style, Dwayne and Alberta remain dedicated to using organic and locally sourced ingredients whenever possible at their restaurants. For a world of inventive menu options, savour the variety at the Cuisine Concepts restaurants.

www.cuisineconcepts.ca

Big Fish

Big Fish brings excitement to the table, along with inventive seafood dishes. Opened in 2004 by Dwayne and Alberta Ennest, the Calgary restaurant welcomes diners with a classy fishing theme, blues music and antique wood tables. Lunch choices include a delectable soft shell crab sandwich with wild boar bacon and a fried oyster po' boy. The raw bar offers six varieties of fresh oysters, with such sauce accompaniments as caper chive mignonette and a chili and tomato cocktail. As an appetizer, you may opt for the spicy winter squash bisque with lobster and root vegetables or pan-fried frog legs with lemon preserves and roasted garlic. White wine, leeks and creamy green curry allow the freshly steamed mussels to really shine. Popular main courses include seared organic salmon, East Coast lobster tail and seafood *pot-au-feu* with saffron and grilled Tuscan bread. Come in on the weekends for a delicious brunch, and enjoy one of the inventive martinis any day. Dwayne and Alberta are concerned about sustainable practices within the fishing industry and take steps to purchase seafood that is responsibly harvested and farmed. For seafood that defies the norm, try Big Fish.

1112 Edmonton Trail NE, Calgary AB
(403) 277-3403 *www.big-fish.ca*

Diner Deluxe

Diner Deluxe reminds you of the 1950s with hearty meals and all-day breakfasts, but the mom and pop team who put together this pretty Calgary diner wanted to surprise their customers with accents from the new millenium—in the food and the surroundings. Owners Dwayne and Alberta Ennest opened the retro themed diner in 2001 and put a clearly modern twist on home cooking classics from the Fifties. Start off with a cup of Kicking Horse organic Fair Trade coffee while you look over the breakfast menu. Your taste buds will awaken with thoughts of the sun-dried tomato and chicken apple sausage frittata or the Southwest scramble with cheddar, salsa and cilantro sour cream. A basic dish of French toast evolves into something divine in the sourdough French toast stuffed with Canadian bacon and Gouda cheese. Lunch options include grilled AAA Alberta sirloin steak with homemade pork and beans, baked macaroni with sun-dried tomatoes and a double smoked pork chop with roasted applesauce and yam wedges. Ingredients for the meals come from local suppliers whenever possible, including Farmer Cliff, who supplies the restaurant with homegrown veggies and free run eggs, and a Quebec family who delivers maple syrup harvested on their land. Pastel vinyl, chrome kitchen tables and space-age lamps add cheerful notes here. Experience the next generation in home-style meals at Diner Deluxe.

804 Edmonton Trail NE, Calgary AB (403) 276-5499 *www.dinerdeluxe.com*

Vue Café

While customers enjoy fine foods and wine at the Vue Café, they appreciate a view provided by some of the most talented artists in Canada. In March 2005, Dwayne and Alberta Ennest teamed up with Alberta's mother, a respected Calgary art dealer, to combine their joint love of food and art in a chic setting inside Virginia Christopher Fine Art Gallery. Here, the cheese bar treats customers to artisanal Canadian and imported cheese served with a choice of preserves. You can sample tapas, such as red lentil hummus or a platter of cured and smoked fish. For lunch, you will find a sophisticated choice of panini sandwiches, including a cashew and chickpea burger with mango chutney on a baguette or smoked buffalo sausage with Manchego cheese on herbed focaccia bread. Select from a list of thoughtfully chosen wines to accompany your meal. Whatever you order, feel confident that the chef prepared everything from scratch, including the sauces, dressings and even the mustard. If you are looking for an impressive venue for your next cocktail party, wedding reception or other special event, the Vue staff can provide catering to meet your needs. Come to the Virginia Christopher Fine Art Gallery and enjoy the Vue Café.

816-11 Avenue SW, Calgary AB (403) 263-4346 *www.vuecafe.com*

Open Range - steaks and chops

Open Range opened in July 2006 with the goal of creating a whole new steakhouse experience. Beef continues to be the main food ingredient people speak of when referring to Calgary, and it seems people never tire of eating it. However, Dwayne and Alberta Ennest felt that their clientele would want a steakhouse menu that was new and interesting. In keeping with Dwayne's food philosophy—simple ingredients, prepared with expertise—and his commitment to regional farmers, Open Range offers locally raised beef, elk, bison and game, seasoned with southwestern flare. The steaks are familiar, but they are prepared so creatively that even the most jaded palates will sit up and take notice. The restaurant's wine list emphasizes producers who make outstanding wines to perfectly compliment a fantastic meal. Open Range has a long wine list, but not too long. The dining room is comfortable, making people feel right at home. It is composed of a mixture of reclaimed wooden tables and black table cloths by a large fireplace that casts its glow throughout the dining areas. The ambience is western elegance with subtle cowboy accents. As with the other restaurants in the Cuisine Concepts family, the contemporary artwork on display is available from Virginia Christopher Fine Art gallery. Open Range - steaks and chops, an easygoing neighbourhood eatery.

1114 Edmonton Trail NE, Calgary ALB 403.277.3408 *www.cuisineconcepts.ca*

Cat 'n Fiddle

If the extensive menu and 17 varieties of beer on tap are not enough to entice you into the Cat 'n Fiddle, there's always the chance that you'll encounter something supernatural. When transplanted Scots named Stuart and Jean McAllister bought the pub several years ago, their dream of owning a cheerful neighborhood watering hole came true. Little did they know that a few of their regulars had already passed from this world. The spooks at the Cat 'n Fiddle specialize in harmless pranks, such as switching the television off and on or flipping the pages of the jukebox when the machine is unplugged. According to Stuart and Jean, they fit right in with the regular crowd of earthly merrymakers. Because the living must eat, the kitchen at the Cat 'n Fiddle stays busy throughout the day, preparing breakfast, lunch and dinner. The menu features a long list of appetizers, salads and sandwiches. Fish and chips are a favorite, with cod all week and halibut on Friday. On any occasion, drop in and you might find a full Scottish pipe band playing. Grab a bite, have a pint and catch the happenings at the Cat n' Fiddle.

540 16 Avenue NW, Calgary AB (403) 289-0414

Riverstone Pub

The western décor of the Riverstone Pub suits the menu perfectly. Rocky Mountain Ribs, Cow Poke Potato Skins and Wild West Wings are highlights among the appetizers. Munch away to your heart's content as you gaze at the photographs of Calgary's pioneering days that adorn the walls. Portions are as ample as the Western prairie celebrated in the photos and in entrée names such as the Prairie Sunset and Prairie Fire pizzas. Riverstone's wait staff is adept at serving large groups and keeping track of many names and tabs. At 6,000 square feet, the pub easily accommodates parties and banquets. Relax in the expansive game room, which features pool tables, darts and the latest electronic games. Riverstone features live bands on weekends and accepts reservations for that special table. Find excellent pub fare and western charm at the Riverstone Pub.

773 Northmount Drive NW, Calgary AB
(403) 509-1560

Villa Firenze

It takes the entire Nicastro family to ensure that your dining experience at Villa Firenze will delight you in every way. After all, when you spend several hours enjoying a meal, those hours should be filled with wonderful flavours, service and surroundings. Villa Firenze has been providing this special mix of comforts in Calgary for 16 years, and word is out that an evening spent here is as romantic as the food is delicious. As one diner put it, "It's not just a simple dinner, but a great dining experience." That experience is built on the décor, the soft music and the meticulous consistency of Chef Joe Nicastro, who owns and runs the restaurant along with his wife, Pina. The fine wines and authentic Italian cuisine prepared with Chef Joe's culinary expertise will gain your attention, while Pina's charming service will win your heart. You can't help but feel like honoured guests of a big Italian family when you meet Mama Teresa, who frequents all areas of the restaurant. Peter and Mary Ann assist with dinners, including those held in the restaurant's semi-formal banquet room. Chef Joe's specialties include homemade pasta, sauces and sausages. Diners consistently rave about the portobello mushroom appetizer. The limoncello liqueur makes a nice finish to your meal. Prepare to awaken all of your senses with a visit to Villa Firenze, Calgary's destination for dining perfection.

610 1 Avenue NE, Calgary AB (403) 264-4297

Pulcinella

Pulcinella brings the flavors of authentic Neapolitan pizza to Calgary—and chef Domenic Tudda has the paperwork to prove it. Pulcinella has met the stringent standards of the Associazione Pizzaioli Napoletani, the group that essentially has the final say in what constitutes a genuine Italian pizza. To get that certification, Domenic had to train with the organization when he was in Italy learning to be a master chef. The organization had to approve of the restaurant's blueprints and equipment lists and inspectors were even flown in to view the final result. The end result is that Pulcinella is one of only 20 restaurants outside Italy to gain the association's seal of approval. Adding to the authentic Italian feel is Pulcinella's huge wood stove oven, made with stones from Mount Vesuvius, as required by the association. It's the biggest pizza oven in Western Canada. The crust here is the traditional very thin variety, slightly browned on the bottom for just a hint of crunch, and each pie is topped with the restaurant's own extra-virgin olive oil and fresh basil. Toppings include prosciutto and other delectable Italian meats, in addition to a variety of vegetables. For dessert, try some of the delicious tiramisu or sweet, chocolate-filled cannoli. The atmosphere here is vibrant, with splashes of green and red against the bright white walls and dark floors. If you're looking for authentic Italian flavor in your pizza, come in to Pulcinella for a slice of pure *amoré*.

1147 Kensington Crescent NW, Calgary AB
(403) 283-1166

Chez François

Innovative cuisine and panoramic views come together to create a sophisticated dining experience at Chez François. Chef Jean François Gouin, along with wife and partner Sylvie, opened Chez François in 1990 and were delighted when it quickly became one of the Canmore area's most favored eateries. Chef Jean combines the fine traditions of French cuisine with locally grown organic produce, AAA Alberta beef and other quality ingredients to produce original, flavorful dishes with international flair. Patrons can dine on award-winning creations, such as cream of wild mushroom soup and coquille St. Jacques, as part of a sumptuous multi-course meal or take a more casual approach and stop in for one of the café's famous breakfasts. Start your day with gourmet pancakes, eggs Benedict with the chef's special Hollandaise sauce or an airy omelette filled with savory ingredients and cooked to tender perfection. Chez François can also cater your next private event and offers a private dining area for more intimate occasions. Jean and Sylvie came to the Canadian Rockies from Montreal, where Jean refined his culinary skills. Feast on incredible views and truly delicious foods at Chez François, centrally located near the Bow Valley Trail.

1604 2 Avenue, Canmore AB
(403) 678-6111

North Shore Bar & Grill

North Shore Bar & Grill brings the surfing luau atmosphere of the Hawaiian beach to Sylvan Lake, offering diners a casual, fun place to hang five with friends. Owner Kevin Bargholz brings years of experience in the travel and hospitality industries to work every day. Before opening the restaurant in 2006, Kevin had fallen in love with the North Shore of Hawaii, with its laid-back attitude, music and great food. That love is reflected in the restaurant, which features a décor of surfboards and Tiki masks that Kevin collected during his travels. Guests can enjoy their food

and drink inside or in the large comfy chairs on the restaurant's outdoor patio. True to its Hawaiian flavor, special events are commemorated here with a pig roast and luau. The most popular item on the menu is the Big Kahuna burger, glazed with Jack Daniels barbecue sauce and topped with cheese, mushrooms and pineapple, plus onions, lettuce and tomato. North Shore also features an extensive tropical cocktail menu. The house specialty, the High Tide, is best prepared by Kevin himself. If you're looking to catch a wave of fun, food and drink, come to North Shore Bar & Grill.

A1-5043-50A Avenue, Sylvan Lake AB
(403) 887-1939

Rocky Mountain Flatbread Company

During the day, the folks at Rocky Mountain Flatbread Company handcraft and partially bake their handcrafted flatbread pizzas for distribution as a frozen food product to health stores and grocers throughout Alberta and BC. In the evening, diners enjoy food that uses quality ingredients, local producers and organics. Everything you eat here is made here including the

hearty soups, salads, flatbread pizzas, pastas and desserts to live for! The idea of sharing is a key feature, portions are large and food is brought to the table as soon as it is ready for optimum taste. Strong emphasis is placed within the restaurant on recycling, sustainability and community values. You can look at pictures of local heroes nominated by local schools, discover where produce originates and read about the latest school projects and recycling initiatives happening in and around the Bow Valley. An ideal spot for families, friends and couples, the restaurant offers something for everyone. The warm, wood-fired oven is one of the largest in Canada. In the play area for kids, children can pretend to prepare and bake their own flatbread pizzas. In the summer months, floor-to-ceiling windows let in the fresh mountain air. For a whole new take on pizza, visit Rocky Mountain Flatbread Company.

101-838 10 Street, Canmore AB
(403) 609-5508
www.rockymountainflatbread.ca

Glory of India

Indian cuisine is a combination of subtle tastes, with flavors that are as varied as the climate and as exotic as the people of India. Fragrant, pungent and warm spices, from the four corners of the country are delicately blended in meticulous proportions to create the dishes Glory of India presents to you. Each dish has its own distinct flavor and aroma which can only come from spices that are separately prepared each day afresh for each individual dish. The blending and preparation of spices is a centuries-old craft and indispensable to Indian cuisine. At Glory of India, the presentations, as they like to call their dishes, are rooted in the soil of northern India and are prepared in the restaurant exactly as India natives prepare them in their own homes. Glory of India has achieved many recognitions and awards, such as Best New Restaurant 2002 by *Calgary Herald*, Best Ethnic Restaurant 2003 by *Where Magazine*, and as the Best Indian Restaurant 2006, they received the Most Memorable Meal award from *Where Magazine*. Most acclaimed food critic John Gilchrist, from *CBC Radio*, says he had "the best Indian meal of his life at Glory of India." Kathy Richardier, of *Calgary Herald*, claims that they have the, "most tastiest Indian food in the city." Glory of India's most popular lunch buffet was recognized by Miles Pittman, of *Fast Forward*, as "a flavourful surprise." What else can be said about Glory of India? Your taste buds need to be taken for a trip to the Far East to quench the craving at Glory of India. It is the most elegant, exquisite, romantic and comfortable setting right in the heart of downtown Calgary. Celebrate the best moments of your life at Glory of India.

515 4 Avenue SW, Calgary AB (403) 263-8804 *www.gloryofindia.com*

Muse Restaurant

Muse Restaurant features eclectic French and Canadian cuisine served in casual yet elegant surroundings. This contemporary atrium-style space consists of several dining levels, including a special 8-to-10 person chef's table and a comfortable full-service lounge. The Muse staff combines the finer points of service with a friendly demeanour free of pretentiousness. Owner Christien Hurlburt and General Manager Bal Ramos lead the service team. The creativity of the kitchen is unsurpassed. It uses the freshest local ingredients and whenever possible, organic meats and produce. You'll often find chef Cam Dobranski scouring the local farmers markets. Begin your evening with a soup or salad course. Then move on to appetizers such as sautéed tiger prawns and Roma tomato *concassé* with herbs and white wine, or French escargot and forest mushrooms in a tarragon *beure blanc*. The entrée might be wild boar bacon-wrapped venison tenderloin, green tea marinated duck breast or Yukon potato lobster lasagna with weathervane scallops, sauce American and flying fish caviar. Finish up with apple pie, a banana split or a cheese selection. As an alternative, consider the nine-course chef's tasting menu. Planning a special event? Muse can help you celebrate with style and class. Muse is in the heart of Calgary's fashionable Kensington area, near the Jubilee Auditorium, and is a favourite destination for the theatre and concert crowd. For the best of what fine dining has to offer, come to Muse Restaurant on your next night out.

107 10A Street NW, Calgary AB (403) 670-6873 *www.muserestaurant.ca*

Sushi Club

During lunchtime at the Sushi Club, the sun streams through the front window and the staff are equally bright. It's the sushi, however, that really brightens your day. Owners Koki Miyashita and Katsu Inoue keep close ties to their native Japan, assuring that their sushi is as authentic as possible. Special orders of fish arrive frequently from Japan, and the sake is imported as well. The Sushi Club's intimate setting provides seating for about 30 diners who enjoy Koki and Katsu's original creations. The presentation is lovely. The sashimi melts in your mouth, especially the toro and the red tuna. Try one of the Crunchy Calamari Jalapeno Rolls or a Sunkissed Roll. Hanabi, which translates colorfully as the firecracker sushi tower, is perfect for sharing. Some of the sushi, such as the smoked black cod roll with prosciutto, is very modern. The sushi/sashimi special comes with a generous array of sashimi and sushi, plus miso soup, salad and rice. As the name suggests, the menu at the Sushi Club is mostly sushi, but you can also get tempura or teriyaki dishes. The deep fried baby octopus is a must. The Sushi Club offers great cocktails with all kinds of wacky liqueurs. Since opening in 2003 in the heart of Kensington, the Sushi Club has earned the respect of sushi aficionados. If you love sushi, tell your friends to find you at the Sushi Club.

103 - 1240 Kensington Road NW, Calgary AB
(403) 283-4100

Photos by Ken Chow; Lighting/Production by Josh Wong

Peters' Drive-In

Peters' Drive-In has always turned out a consistently great burger, and since its 1964 founding it has transformed into a Calgary landmark. The food is extraordinarily tasty, which is why the lines to the drive-through are constantly packed, sometimes right up until closing time at midnight. The experienced staff can sell 6,000 burgers and nearly as many milkshakes on a summer day. Shakes come in 30 basic flavors, and you can order them in any three combinations. The result is that Peter's actually offers more than 4,000 different milkshakes. Mango and marshmallow sound intriguing. Of course, you could keep it simple by ordering vanilla, chocolate or strawberry. Peters' uses only the best ingredients; the fruit in many of the milkshakes is fresh, and the drive-in serves real whipping cream on its sundaes and banana splits. Peters' Drive-In was founded by Gus Pieters, who emigrated from the Netherlands to Canada with a baker's background and exactly two dimes in his pocket. He lived in the Arctic for five years, working for an oil company and saving money to start his own business. More than 40 years later, his restaurant lives up to its slogan, the Drive-In You Can't Drive By.

219-16 Avenue NE, Calgary AB
(403) 277-2747
www.petersdrivein.com

Ironwood Stage and Grill

The Ironwood Stage and Grill is a steak lover's paradise, and Calgary knows it for the AAA Flatiron Steak Sandwich, topped with blue cheese butter, housemade onion rings and Portobello mushrooms. The options don't end there. Savor eclectic Alberta cuisine with mouth-watering appetizers such as Grilled Spolumbo's Sausage with tequila butter and green chili cornbread. For a lunchtime treat, try a flatbread topped with honey peppered bacon, roasted corn, green onions, tomatoes and blackbean mayo or a sandwich stacked with roasted rare lamb with grainy mustard slaw and red onion marmalade. Entrées such as cumin crusted chicken breast strips with orange ginger glaze and fresh battered halibut with artichoke tartar are perfect for an evening meal. The Ironwood, a local favorite, was The Tradesman Club for more than 20 years before it became one of the cities best music venues. New owner Patrick MacIntyre stepped up in 2006 to revamp its menu and style. Patrick and his gracious, outgoing staff take pride in serving quality food that tastes good and is budget friendly. The Ironwood is a stop on the route of many great musicians, local and international. You can check for up-coming special events, entertainment schedules and menus online. Enjoy splendid food and great music with a visit to Ironwood Stage and Grill.

1429 9 Avenue SE, Calgary AB (403) 269-5581
www.ironwoodstage.ca

Original Joe's Restaurant & Bar

If you're an average Joe looking for feel good food in a neighborhood atmosphere, Original Joe's Restaurant & Bar is the place for you. Original Joe's offers a dining experience that provides a respite from our increasingly fast-paced and image conscious world. The menu goes way beyond typical pub grub. You'll find fish and chips, along with our signature Red Tractor Nachos and burgers, as well as a variety of soups including chili corn chowder, salads and sandwiches, plus pizza and pasta dishes. Be sure and save some room for a delicious dessert, such as the aptly named Chocolate Therapy Cake. Original Joe's has more than a dozen different beers on tap, including Original Joes micro-brewed originals. The bar also offers a variety of wines and spirits. Looking for a satisfying meal at a reasonable price in a casual atmosphere? Come enjoy the company, friendly staff, food and drinks at Original Joe's Restaurant & Bar. With locations to serve you in Calgary, Edmonton, St. Albert, Red Deer, Lloydminster and Lethbridge.

www.originaljoes.ca

The Living Room

The dim lighting and comfortable surroundings in the 1940s urban bungalow may remind you of a particularly pleasant living room, but once you try the five-course meals and magnificent wine pairings, there'll be no doubt you are in The Living Room. Executive Chef Kevin Hill puts a Canadian twist on classic French and Italian cuisine in this cozy restaurant, a popular place for a romantic dinner for two or a special occasion event. Once you have tried this fresh, flavorful fare, your definition of living room will be altered for all time. The emphasis here is on local foods and organic, natural ingredients with a sheet appearing daily to announce what is fresh. Kevin doesn't stop with diverse offering and creative wine pairings, either. He offers cooking demonstrations as well. The owners of this jewel—Jay Blackford, Patrick Hill, Cliff Harvey and Michael Miller—take pride in all aspects of this delightful space, including a patio that manages to be truly special. With two outdoor fireplaces and cedar fencing, this cozy outdoor dining location makes a great spot for a tete-a-tete or some amusing people watching. The lucky traveler will find a diverse local crowd at The Living Room, a place that attracts both urban executives and their families. For all the comforts of home in a restaurant rated as one of the top five restaurants in Calgary, come to The Living Room.

514 17 Avenue SW, Calgary AB
(403) 228-9830
www.thelivingroomrestaurant.com

Tipperary's Pub

Does this experience sound familiar? You are watching a championship game when the coverage shifts from the action at the stadium to the boisterous scene at a neighborhood pub, where a crowd of die-hard fans is following the game on the big screen and cheering for their team. Tipperary's is a pub just like the ones you have seen in those shots. With seating for 250, it's big enough that you'll definitely feel it when everyone lets out a roar after the favourite team has scored. What's more, thanks to the 15 big-screen televisions, every seat in the room brings you close to the action. Combine the lively atmosphere with fabulous food and drink specials, and you might not ever want to leave Tipperary's. No matter what night of the week you drop by, you'll find a great deal on something to eat or drink, whether it's half-price pizza on Tuesday or wings for 25 cents on Wednesday. The regular menu features an array of 60 items. Wash down your meal with a pint of a featured beer, such as Alexander Keith's or Sleeman's. Gabe Nicks and Dan Ruzsvanszki lead a staff that is ready to accommodate your next party with several event options, ranging from full dinners and buffets to appetizer packages. The action tonight is at Tipperary's Pub. Be there when it starts.

2002-16 Avenue NW, Calgary AB (403) 289-5566 *www.tipperaryspub.com*

Shillelagh's Pub

The nightly special at Shillelagh's Pub sometimes strays a bit from what you would expect at an Irish pub, but no one seems to mind. Customers are too busy enjoying the taste and the price of the pizza on Pizza Tuesdays to get worked up over the break from tradition. Order your burger on Monday with a brogue, if it makes you happy, or wait it out until Friday when the fish and chips will satisfy your appetite for something Irish and the beer special will quench your thirst. The sounds of Calgary's best Celtic musicians fill the room on Steak Thursdays, when this low price gets you steak and fries all day. Pints of Alexander Keith's beer are popular here. Saturdays feature a deal on prime rib. If you prefer to order from the menu, you'll find homemade soups in addition to everything from grilled shrimp skewers and perogies to crab cakes, nachos and quesadillas. A *shillelagh* is a wooden club associated with Irish folklore. When in Calgary, know it as the name of the neighborhood pub on the city's west side that serves something for everyone. Come to Shillelagh's Pub to enjoy two stories, two outdoor patios with views of the city and a good-natured crowd aged 18 to 80.

#323-1851 Sirocco Drive SW, Calgary AB
(403) 255-4747
www.shillelaghspub.com

Q Haute cuisine

Q Haute cuisine is the result of an inspired collaboration between four energetic and accomplished restaurateurs. When Carmello Sangregorio and Michele Aurigemma joined forces with Gaston Langlois and Marcello Belvedere in 2005, they created a restaurant offering contemporary European cuisine in a warm, sophisticated atmosphere overlooking the Bow River. The business strives to deliver the highest quality meals and uncompromising attention to detail, and the name of the restaurant is derived from those goals. The *Q* stands for quality, and *haute cuisine* refers to elegant and skillfully prepared food. Q offers a full à la carte menu, with delectable offerings, such as bison strip loin with pea barley risotto and stuffed pheasant breast. In addition, the restaurant offers a chef's tasting menu, which includes several courses and is based on seasonal ingredients. Choices such as the wild boar sausage with chickpea cream, roasted duck breast and jumbo prawns with pea shoots satisfy the most discerning palate. Allow the sommelier to recommend wine to complement each course. With five dining areas, the restaurant can tailor its spaces to perfectly fit your next special event. The food, presentation, service and ambience all come together exquisitely to make your next corporate or personal occasion a success. Visit Q Haute cuisine to experience the merging of four dynamic culinary experts.

100 La Caille Place SW, Calgary AB (Upper Level, 7 Street & 1 Avenue SW) (403) 262-5554
www.qhautecuisine.com

Buchanan's Chop House & Whiskey Bar

Buchanan's Chop House & Whiskey Bar feels like an old-fashioned neighbourhood hangout, where you can count on friends to welcome you in with good conversation, sizzling hot steaks and, oh yes, more than 200 varieties of whisky. Owners Michael and Carol Buchanan opened the restaurant in 1988, and have earned a well-deserved reputation for delicious food. Buchanan's features thick cuts of Alberta beef steaks and chops, and many hungry diners enjoy taking on the monumental 28-ounce, grade AAA Porterhouse steak, or the 26-ounce prime rib chop. Customers say the cheeseburgers are legendary, and the pasta and sauces are made fresh in the restaurant each day. Wine lovers are sure to be pleased with the extensive selection of vino, but the whisky list is simply astounding. The bar offers more than 200 fine malt whisky choices, and even offers seminars to educate customers on the finer points of scotch. Feel free to ask the waitstaff about the choices, as they are all knowledgeable about the drinks and can discuss the various single malts or blends on hand. Buchanan's convenient location and inviting atmosphere makes it a great place to head for a downtown lunch or to unwind after a day at work. You'll feel like you are connecting with an old friend when you stop by Buchanan's Chop House & Whiskey Bar.

738 3 Avenue SW, Calgary AB (403) 261-4646
www.buchanans.ca

Metropolitan Grill

With its fashionable atmosphere, global cuisine and live music and dancing, the Metropolitan Grill beckons people from all over Calgary to spend a fun evening out. The staff members, carefully selected by owner Jeff Hannah, are at once friendly and professional, a true reflection of the spirit of the room. The Met dishes up a variety of flavors, with a Mediterranean theme running throughout. Start out with one of the flavorful appetizers, such as lemon pepper calamari, a jumbo shrimp cocktail or vine ripened bruschetta. The Delmonico salad, with chicken, avocado, blue cheese and bacon on a bed of crisp greens, is a popular choice. Customers say the AAA Alberta beef steaks are some of the best in town, and there are several to choose from, from the Metropolitan Sirloin topped with jumbo prawns, to the Wild Mushroom Filet, the chef's favorite. Any of the dessert choices will bring you sweet satisfaction. The chocolate pecan flan is one of the Met's most famous dishes, and the white chocolate crème brûlée is infused with wild berries. Come by for a delectable brunch on the weekends and live music and dancing in the lounge on Friday and Saturday nights with no cover charge. Your friends are calling. They want to Meet You at the Met.

318 8 Avenue SW, Calgary AB (403) 263-5432
880 16 Avenue, #16, SW, Calgary AB (403) 802-2393
www.metropolitangrill.ca

Vic's Steakhouse & Bar

You are in for a Canadian steak experience at Vic's Steakhouse, where all the beef is local Alberta Angus Pride. A high-heat searing process locks in the juices, resulting in the highest degree of tenderness and flavor. Try Vic's signature steak, a 10-ounce rib steak grilled and basted with the restaurant's own special butter. All steaks are served with rich veal demi, wasabi mashed potatoes and fresh baby vegetables. While Vic's plays the role of traditional steakhouse with excellence, other entrées reveal that it is also a restaurant for the adventurous palette. Lavender Honeycomb Roasted Quail and Miso Bronzed North Pacific Cod are a couple of the intriguing offerings. For a twist on the standard surf and turf, consider the Seared Digby Scallops with Braised Wild Boar Belly. The atmosphere and décor set the tone for an upscale though relaxed dining experience. The interior fuses dark woods and local stone. The many windows looking out at the mountains give the room a well lit and open feel. Located inside the Radisson Hotel, Vic's Steakhouse & Bar provides cozy mountain charm for hungry travelers and locals alike. Join the folks gathered there tonight for a Canadian feast.

511 Bow Valley Trail, Canmore AB
(403) 678-3625
www.radisson.com/canmoreca

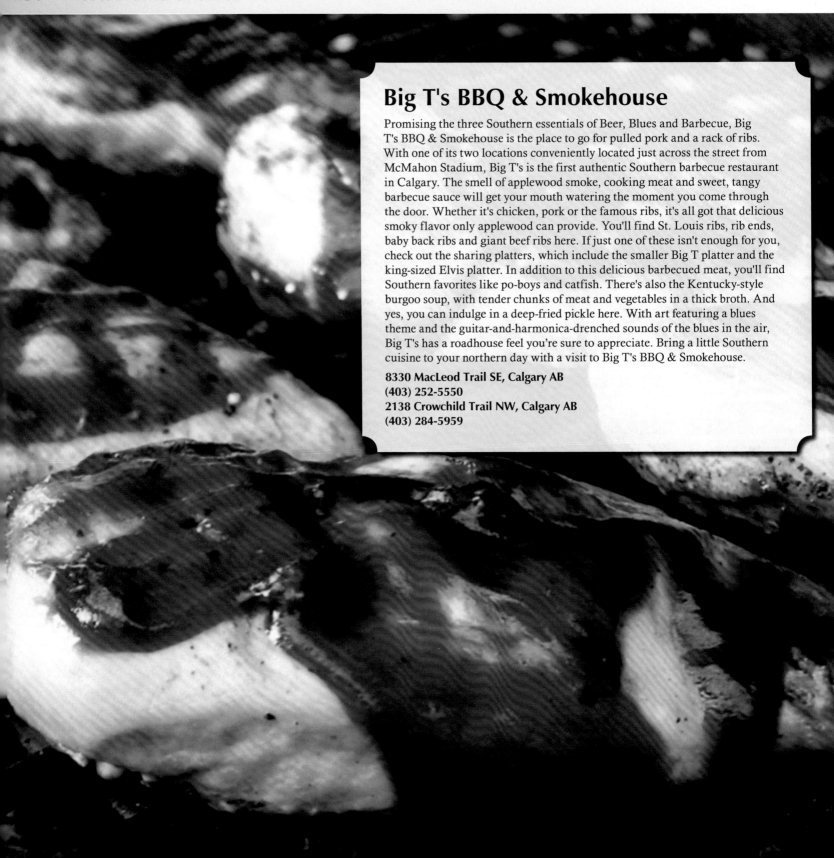

Big T's BBQ & Smokehouse

Promising the three Southern essentials of Beer, Blues and Barbecue, Big T's BBQ & Smokehouse is the place to go for pulled pork and a rack of ribs. With one of its two locations conveniently located just across the street from McMahon Stadium, Big T's is the first authentic Southern barbecue restaurant in Calgary. The smell of applewood smoke, cooking meat and sweet, tangy barbecue sauce will get your mouth watering the moment you come through the door. Whether it's chicken, pork or the famous ribs, it's all got that delicious smoky flavor only applewood can provide. You'll find St. Louis ribs, rib ends, baby back ribs and giant beef ribs here. If just one of these isn't enough for you, check out the sharing platters, which include the smaller Big T platter and the king-sized Elvis platter. In addition to this delicious barbecued meat, you'll find Southern favorites like po-boys and catfish. There's also the Kentucky-style burgoo soup, with tender chunks of meat and vegetables in a thick broth. And yes, you can indulge in a deep-fried pickle here. With art featuring a blues theme and the guitar-and-harmonica-drenched sounds of the blues in the air, Big T's has a roadhouse feel you're sure to appreciate. Bring a little Southern cuisine to your northern day with a visit to Big T's BBQ & Smokehouse.

8330 MacLeod Trail SE, Calgary AB
(403) 252-5550
2138 Crowchild Trail NW, Calgary AB
(403) 284-5959

Mercato Italian Gourmet Cultura

The sounds of opera and the aromas of spices and olive oil have been filling the air at Mercato Italian Gourmet Cultura since 1974. This Italian restaurant and market, located in Calgary, specializes in making people's mouths water. It's one big family operation in the kitchen, and you're invited to watch as the open design dares you to catch all of the ingredients that go into making the sauces and other family recipes served at the restaurant. Dominic Caracciolo works alongside his children, siblings, aunts and uncles in turning out authentic Italian dishes that will make you shout "amore." The gourmet market next door features handmade bruschetta and sausages. Racks of oils and beautifully displayed produce convey the feel of a real Italian market, right there in the middle of funky 4th Street. Fix an easy lunch or dinner at home with prepared pastas and sauces from the market, and don't forget to pick out some pastries, too. Dominic is carrying on the family tradition begun by his parents, Victor and Cathy, who were born in Italy and immigrated to Canada in 1957. Hard work, dedication and an obvious love for what they do are the reasons for this family's success. Satisfy your appetite for Italian cuisine in a big way at Mercato Italian Gourmet Cultura.

2224 4 Street SW, Calgary AB (403) 263-5535 *www.mercatogourmet.com*

Continental Treat Restaurant

The Continental Treat Restaurant is a family affair. Two generations of the Borowka family work together to bring their romantic turn-of-the-century dining vision to life. Owner Richard Borowka oversees the entire operation. His wife, Helena, is the main chef, son Sylvester is host and maître d' and son Christopher serves as head waiter. The ambience is one of pure charm, combined with an air of luxury and elegance. Classical music selections waft overhead, reminding you to take your time and enjoy the journey. Staff members tend to your every need. The entrées reflect a central European influence with the tastes of Poland, Switzerland and Austria well-represented. Regional delicacies include steak a la tartare, Dutch herrings, Hungarian goulash and wild mushroom sauerkraut perogy. Roast duck, lamb chops and Belgian pork tenderloin make a good choice, or try the rainbow trout. Other delicious choices include the Hunter Plate, wiener schnitzel and filet mignon. The crepes Florentine, stroganoff and wild mushroom paste are more favorites. Both lunch and dinner menus offer extensive choices. The wine list is varied and reasonably priced. For a special evening of candlelight, linen tablecloths and Mozart, reserve a table at the Continental Treat Restaurant, where family and staff take pride in making you feel special.

10560-82 Avenue, Edmonton AB (780) 433-7432
www.continentaltreat.com

Oceana Seafood Steakhouse & Bar

Oceana Seafood, Steakhouse & Bar presents customers with a large classy restaurant. The 200-seat Calgary restaurant manages a fine dining experience while retaining a welcoming, family-oriented atmosphere. Nick Papaioannou, along with partners Chris Papaioannou and Harry Safaris, opened the restaurant in 2000 and recently moved it to a stunning location overlooking the Bow River. The restaurant offers patio dining in warm weather and a contemporary lounge. Nick credits his wife, Voula, with helping him to be a successful businessman and restaurateur, beginning when they were both only 17 years old. The extensive menu choices are impressive, with nearly 40 fresh seafood options. The Sterling Silver AAA beef is tender and juicy, cooked to your liking. Lemon oil, oregano and olive oil are key ingredients in Oceana's focus on healthful, Mediterranean style foods. Stir-fries, pasta dishes and oysters are popular here. The flavours are sophisticated and the portions, generous, which leaves diners satisfied on all fronts. Oceana appeals to a wide cross section of tastes, and you will likely find a large sampling of the city's population here, from young professionals stopping by after work to retired people and families with kids in tow. Enjoy gourmet cuisine in a relaxed setting with a visit to Oceana Seafood, Steakhouse & Bar.

101 7 Street SW, Calgary AB
(403) 245-8787

New Asian Village

Hundreds of years before health food became a craze, the people of East India were cooking with spices whose benefits were proclaimed in ancient Sanskrit texts. Harmeet Kapur, owner of New Asian Village, knows these spices well. He sprinkles ginger, saffron and many other spices into the dishes that have been tantalizing customers since 1983. Curries and kabob platters are popular, while lunch and dinner buffets offered seven days a week give guests the opportunity to sample a variety of genuine Indian dishes. There is no extra charge to dine in the sumptuous luxury of one of the private, silk-curtained Maharaja rooms, although reservations are recommended. What clse makes the Indian food at New Asian Village beneficial? After being trimmed of fat, the meat is marinated in yogurt and spices. Any remaining fat is seared off when the meat is cooked in a high-temperature Tandoor oven. It all results in a cuisine that is as aromatic and flavourful as it is healthful. Harmeet recently added special selections to the menu of diet-specific choices for those with diabetes, high cholesterol and hypertension. Follow an ancient tradition by eating well at one of the three New Asian Village locations.

Central: 10143 Saskatchewan Drive, Edmonton AB (780) 433-3804
West: 17507-100 Avenue, Edmonton AB (780) 488-6666
South: 9308-34 Avenue, Edmonton AB (780) 463-9997
www.newasianvillage.com

Chianti Café and Restaurant

Since 1987, Chianti Café and Restaurant has been the perfect place to dine before catching a show in old Strathcona, Edmonton's entertainment and theatre district. After all, it's the rare eatery that serves meals that are quick, reasonably priced and prepared from scratch. These are just a few of Chianti Café's attributes. Add consistent quality and Chianti's support for the arts, and the logic behind your choice becomes crystal clear. Owner Ken Rubuliak is proud to sponsor many local arts and theatre festivals, and in 1996, the café received an award from the mayor for Sustained Support of the Arts. Ken is equally proud of the service and Italian cookery that has earned Chianti the title Best Italian Restaurant from *Edmonton Journal*. Air Canada's *enRoute* magazine lists Chianti as one of Canada's top 100 restaurants. You will find pasta, chicken, veal and seafood prepared the way you like them. Because Chianti creates each meal when you order it, the restaurant is happy to meet dietary requests. Half portions are available on most menu items, and those on gluten-free diets can choose the brown rice pasta. Chianti is open 11 am to 11 pm seven days a week and has 160 seats indoors and another 50 on the patio. Chianti is not only a reasonable place to dine, it's a beautiful one. It is lodged in the picturesque old Post Office building at the corner of 105 Street. Give in to your common sense with a visit to Chianti Café and Restaurant.

10501 82 Avenue, Edmonton AB
(780) 439-9829
www.chianticafe.ca

Photos by Zinger Photographics

Swans of Inglewood

If not knowing where your next pint of Guinness can be had causes you to fret when you travel, then stop worrying. It's always on tap at Swans of Inglewood, a friendly gathering place in Calgary's oldest neighbourhood. A local favorite since 1994, Swans features a varied menu to go along with the quaffable beverages. The marinated baby back ribs or chicken fingers are great as starters or a snack. The main menu includes everything from shepherd's pie for a traditional taste of the Old Country to a jambalaya that will have you thinking of Mardi Gras. If pizza is your preference, don't be afraid of eating some Smog. The name refers to the ton of yummy toppings, namely sausage, mushrooms, onions and green peppers. Entrées, such as the Dijon Chicken and Red Wine Steak, come with veggies, garlic toast and your choice of baked potato or pasta. Owners Nadina Stainsby and Barry Fairbrother pride themselves on providing a comfortable atmosphere suitable for conversation. If you're tired of places where shouting is the only way to be heard above the overpowering music, then you will appreciate the mellow experience that Swans offers. Raise a pint of Guinness and settle in with friends or the regulars at Swans of Inglewood.

1336 9 Avenue SE, Calgary AB
(403) 233-7574

Infusion Contemporary Cuisine

A drive to Bragg Creek is an opportunity to change gears and drink in some bucolic charm. It's also a chance to change flavour gears at Infusion Contemporary Cuisine. Owner and Chef Air Bouphasiry named his restaurant to describe the cosmopolitan quality of his food, which combines French heritage with Asian accents. When the weather is fine, guests often choose to dine on a deep veranda decorated with flower baskets. Expect rich cream sauces with finely balanced flavours. The beef tournedo fillets come in a brandy sauce, while a Thai-influenced basil and curry sauce transforms deep-fried salmon. An intense Beaujolais sauce sets off escargots wrapped in pastry. Air's high standards show up in every dish, from appetizers, such as fried calamari with an appealing spicy-sweet-hot dipping sauce, to the many chocolate

desserts. Sunday brunch loses the Asian overtones but retains the rich sauces with a celebrated eggs benny and a generous seafood crepe. Air's wife, Soledad, deftly handles the front of the restaurant operation. Infusion may be hidden in the trees, but it's well known, and reservations are recommended. For a refreshing change of pace, plan lunch, dinner or Sunday brunch at Infusion Contemporary Cuisine.

23 Balsam Avenue, Bragg Creek AB
(403) 949-3898
www.infusionbraggcreek.com

Mirabelle

Charlson "Charlie" Cheung brings 30 years of dining expertise to Mirabelle. As owner, executive chef and manager extraordinaire, Cheung oversees every step of your stay at this well-known Edmonton restaurant. The cheerful staff works as a team to provide you with a cozy home-away-from-home atmosphere. Many of the smiling faces you'll see there have been serving at the restaurant for more than 15 years. You'll find classic chicken, lamb, seafood and pasta entrées, with Beef Wellington as the house specialty. Locals consider Mirabelle a weekend destination spot. Gathering in the spacious lounge, sports fans eye the television screen and root for the home team. Located near downtown, Mirabelle is a prime location for large group events. The well-appointed dining room seats up to 100 people comfortably. For a reasonably priced meal and an exceptional value, make a point to stop by Mirabelle restaurant. Charlie Cheung will be there to greet you.

9929 109 Street, Edmonton AB
(780) 429-3055

Seventy-Nine Restaurant & Lounge

Seventy-Nine Restaurant & Lounge has built its outstanding reputation on a perfect combination of upscale cuisine, a refined adult atmosphere and friendly service. Julie Lockhart and Tiffany McKenna wisely chose not to tamper with success when they became the owners not long ago. They maintained the ambience that makes Seventy-Nine an ideal choice for romantic dining. Under their leadership, the restaurant began serving lunch and introduced a lounge concept at night. As a result, the restaurant is versatile enough to suit your needs, whether you are looking for a place to enjoy a casual lunch, an intimate dinner or an after-hours cocktail with dessert. Executive Chef Jaryd Baceda provide the top-notch menu. As for the lounge, the owners say, "We want people in the area to see that they don't have to drive to Calgary for a nice martini or glass of wine." Located in downtown Okotoks, the restaurant always shows up on the Best of the Foothills list of favourite places. In recent years, it has even won in multiple categories, including Best Restaurant Atmosphere, Best Wine List and Best Dessert. Experience excellence day and night at Seventy-Nine Restaurant & Lounge.

79 Elizabeth Street, Okotoks AB
(403) 938-7918
www.seventyninedining.com

Cook County Saloon

The Cook County Saloon offers a rootin' tootin' good time for fans of country music and cowboy culture. Located in Edmonton since 1981, this club has been voted Canada's #1 Country Nightclub 10 times. Top-of-the-line acts including George Strait, Toby Keith and Rascal Flatts have graced its stage. Catering to the rodeo crowd in Edmonton, it doesn't get any more honky tonk than this. The space includes a full seven bars and three different beer tubs to help quench your thirst. Things get especially rowdy on Risqué Thursdays, when women compete for a $1,000 shopping spree by riding a mechanical bull—judged by the men, of course. Those looking to dance to the latest country tunes or live bands can scoot their boots onto the dance floor. The saloon offers party packages for those looking to celebrate special occasions, including such benefits as limo service and a decorated, reserved table for no cover charge. V.I.P. membership packages offer discounts and privileges, allowing members to bypass the traditional outside lineup and get in right away. So round up a posse of your friends and head on in to Cook County Saloon.

8010 Gateway Boulevard, Edmonton AB (780) 432-2665
www.cookcountysaloon.com

La Table de Renoir

Amid the hustle and bustle of the city, La Table de Renoir offers a respite for diners who crave comfort and camaraderie. For the past three years, owners Pierre and Sujo Renoir have combined artistry and ancestry to create a French oasis in the heart of the city. Paintings by Pierre grace the walls, all reminiscent of the masterpieces by his great-grandfather. His wife, Sujo, is the executive chef, and she prepares all menu items a lá minuté from her original recipes. Start with soupe du jour, salade maison or hors-d'oeuvres such as escargot tossed in garlic butter and flambéed in brandy. Lunch features sandwiches such as the croquet-monsieur, a combination of grilled Gruyère cheese, smoked ham and Béchamel sauce. At dinner, Les Plats de Résistance feature médaillons de porc and *magret de canard* (duck breast) with mission figs and balsamic sauce. All entrées are prepared in the rustic Provençial tradition. Heighten your pleasure with a bottle of wine selected from the extensive wine list. Dessert classics such as *tarte tatin* (apple tarts), crème brûlée and mousse au chocolat compliment meal's end. Sit back and enjoy an espresso or cappuccino. Finish off the consummate dining experience with a cognac, brandy or glass of port. Pierre and Sujo Renoir invite you and your friends to come together at La Table de Renoir in celebration of joie de vivre, the good life.

10046–101A Avenue (Rice Howard Way), Edmonton AB
(780) 429-3386
www.latablederenoir.ca

Villa Caruso Steak House & Bar

A meal at Villa Caruso Steak House & Bar is a feast for the senses that includes international cuisine, scenic views from every seat in the house and the ambience of a stone and log building. Litsa Perperidis, who moved to Canada from Greece 44 years ago and opened the Jasper restaurant 30 years back, marries Western foods with Greek recipes and traditions. You can start your meal with British Columbia smoked salmon, Nova Scotia mussels, or calamari and tzatziki dip. Wild game selections include buffalo and elk. Popular entrées include prime rib and an entire slate of Alberta AAA beef cuts. You will find seafood, pasta and baby back ribs along with a children's menu and such Greek dishes as souvlaki, moussaka and rack of lamb. The house-made ice cream is an all-time favourite. Litsa runs Villa Caruso with her husband, Tim, and a loyal staff that has operated as a team for the better part of a decade. Just as visitors find themselves returning to Jasper for the inspirational mountain setting, so they return to Villa Caruso with its comfortable lounge and three outdoor patios. The warmth you experience comes from the people who serve you and the people who visit the restaurant as well as from gleaming woods, high ceilings, chandeliers and two fireplaces. You can watch your chef prepare charcoal-broiled steaks and other delicacies while you visit the martini bar. For a Grecian slant on steaks and seafood, come to Villa Caruso Steak House & Bar.

640 Connaught Drive, Jasper AB (780) 852-3920 *www.villacaruso.com*

Yianni's Taverna and the Kasbar Lounge

The clash of finger cymbals and jingle of gyrating belly dancers are your first clues that Yianni's Taverna is a big, fat, fun Greek restaurant. A favorite with college crowds and others looking for some fun with their food, the restaurant has been in business for 23 years. Owners Jim and Tammy Anast have gone out of their way to make dining at Yianni's an authentic Greek experience, with large tables huddled together to increase the social atmosphere. You'll find happy regulars sharing from each other's plates, laughing and enjoying the music and conversation. The food is traditional Greek fare such as lemon and oregano marinated lamb, souvlakis and spanakopita. There's also plenty of seafood on the menu, with swordfish frequently offered. During the weekends, you'll find belly dancers gyrating to both traditional Greek sounds and more modern ones, including disco favorites. If you want to get in on the action, that's more than OK—it's expected. Unleash your inner Zorba, as the dance line extends right out the door and onto Whyte Avenue. If you're looking for something a little quieter, check out the Kasbar Lounge downstairs. The room features a romantic Moroccan décor and refined atmosphere to encourage more intimate conversation. Bask in the exotica of Mediterranean Europe at Yianni's Taverna and the Kasbar Lounge.

10444-82 Avenue, Edmonton AB
(780) 433-6768
www.eatmorelamb.com

Ouzo Greek Taverna

Ouzo Greek Taverna is the place to go to satisfy a big, fat appetite for Greek food. Owners Tom and Laurel Luzzi pride themselves on the freshness and quality of the traditional Greek cuisine you'll find at their Calgary restaurant. Tom, who is the chef at Ouzo, honed his craft under Connecticut Chef Nick Pappadakis for more than two years. His skills are reflected in the rave reviews Ouzo has received from both the *Calgary Herald* and the *Calgary Sun*, whose food critic praised the restaurant for its "classy, colourful and fun approach to dining." The lamb dishes at Ouzo have been especially singled out for praise. *Action* magazine lauded the Roasted Taverna Lamb basted with Grecian herbs and the *kleftiko*, which is lamb shoulder, slow roasted for 12 hours and served with a demi-glaze. You'll also find excellent *souvlaki* at Ouzo, with skewers of chicken, beef or lamb basted in lemon-oregano marinade and charbroiled. The My Big Fat Greek Dinner platter will feed two people with a salad, lamb chops and ribs offered along with pita bread. Two people stopping by for a late night nibble will enjoy the appetizer platter. Ouzo offers an extensive wine list as well as the Greek anise-flavored liqueur that gives the restaurant its name. The décor is a soothing traditional Greek blue with Greek landscapes and seascapes decorating the walls. For an experience that will have you eating and thinking like a Greek, come to Ouzo Greek Taverna.

2005 B 4 Street SW, Calgary AB (403) 229-1400 *www.ouzo.ca*

The Main Dish

When most of us hear the term fast food, we think of anything but haute cuisine. Thanks to entrepreneurs and partners Jason Zaran and Mike Kadri, fast food has a whole new meaning. Zaran and Kadri are the founders of the Main Dish, a new concept company that beautifully merges convenience and quality food. The Main Dish relies on the talents of two executive chefs, Kevin Pelissier and Kevin Outhet. Together, the team has created a fast, fun and fabulous place where hip and healthy denizens of Calgary can pick up tasty meals to go. Upon entering you'll see a glass enclosed Chef's Fare Showcase with an array of fresh meats, vegetables, salads, sides and desserts that are ready for your home oven or microwave. To the left is a grocery section where you can pick up fresh fruits, local cereals, Vita eggs and gourmet sodas. In the Hot Cuisine area you can grab ready-to-eat meals, which you can enjoy on the go or in Main Dish's 30-seat dining room. When weather permits, you can dine outside. The Getaway Gourmet corner has fine selection of made-to-order sandwiches, along with hearty soups and salads. Zaran and Kadri take great pride in their knowledgeable staff and their popular one-stop eatery and market. The next time one of your friends puts down fast food, open their eyes by taking them to the Main Dish.

903 General Avenue NE, Calgary AB (just off 1 Avenue NW, between 8 and 9 Streets) (403) 265-3474
www.tmdish.com

Von's Steak and Fish House

Since 1988, Von's Steakhouse has been serving Edmontonians the highest quality of beef and fish available. Von's serves Sterling Silver beef, which is the top 12 percent of AAA Alberta beef. Von's also takes pride in using local suppliers and serving wild fish. The chefs at Von's handcut the beef, which has been aged a minimum of 21 days to ensure maximum flavour and tenderness. This dedication to quality has earned Von's several honours, including Best Steaks, Best Steakhouse and Best Fish in Edmonton. Von's is especially renowned for its prime rib which is slow-cooked a minimum of 16 hours at low heat and crusted with savoury spices. The rustic building, located in the trendy Old Strathcona entertainment district, was built in the 1930s and features original exposed brickwork. This building once housed a bottling plant. The restaurant now has four distinct areas and a lounge featuring only the finest in wines and spirits. Serving more than 30 wines by the glass and more than 100 bottle selections, Von's has quickly become one of the leaders in the finer dining segment. The service at Von's is attentive yet casual in its approach, assuring each guest a comfortable yet professional experience. Von's has several private dining rooms catering to group functions from 10 to 60. If you're looking for award-winning steak and seafood, come to Von's Steak and Fish House.

10309-81 Avenue, Edmonton AB
(780) 439-0041
www.vonssteakhouse.com

Royal Thai Restaurant

Nadine Huyah and Kevin Tran acted upon their dream of bringing Thai cuisine to south Calgary in 2006. Serving soups, curries and noodle dishes just as you would find in Bangkok is the goal at Royal Thai Restaurant. With a nod to tradition, the curries come in clay pots. Choices abound, and the only problem is selecting just one from the long list of vegetable, meat and seafood options. One of the Chef's Favorites that has already become a huge customer hit is the Cashew Nut Chicken and Shrimp. The Hot Wok, another dish that became instantly popular, offers a choice of chicken, shrimp or squid stir-fried with vegetables, sprinkled with peanuts and served with three different delicious sauces. Aficionados of lemongrass soup are invited to try Kevin's spicy version and judge how it ranks with others they have tasted. The Tom Kha Gai is a renowned soup from southern Thailand that features chicken in coconut milk flavored with lime juice and Siamese ginger. As for salads, recent visitors pronounced both the mango and papaya salads "exceptional." Kevin is always willing to cook something that you don't see on the menu, though chances are the menu will suffice. If your taste buds have become complacent, let Royal Thai Restaurant give them the jolt they need.

12101 Lake Fraser Drive SE, #500, Calgary AB
(403) 278-8018

Maligne Canyon Restaurant

Everything about Maligne Canyon Restaurant provides unexpected pleasures. Originating as a tea house in 1962, the restaurant sits atop one of Jasper National Park's most popular scenic attractions. Owner Galal Helmy fell in love with the spot 1970 and built the restaurant into the landmark it is today. The restaurant serves breakfast, lunch and dinner buffet-style. It's worth visiting just to look out over the canyon through the glass walls of the warm, inviting room, with its high ceilings and stone fireplace. An unexpected delight is an adjoining art gallery that features one of the world's best collections of native Indian and Inuit art. From Norval Morisseau, one of the most renowned native artists in the world, to the large collection of stone and ivory carvings, you'll see works of enormous historic and cultural value. Wedding parties love this setting. Whether you go for the food or the art, don't miss the Maligne Canyon Restaurant.

Maligne Lake Road, Jasper AB
(780) 852-3583
www.malignecanyon.com

La Tapa

Ten years ago, sisters Monica and Sheila Gordulic renovated a 70-year-old house to create a warm and inviting dining spot on a quiet street in downtown Edmonton. Their tapas have become well-known throughout the city and their Patatas Alioli have become a festival favourite at the annual Taste of Edmonton. The restaurant is a wonderful place to meet with friends – the downstairs and patio are always packed during the summer and the inviting window tables are especially popular year-round. In addition to a delicious variety of soups, salads and entrées, La Tapa offers more than 30 tapas to choose from and you can enjoy a great meal just selecting a few from the bountiful offerings on the menu. Pasta, meat and seafood entrées arrive at your table bursting with Spanish spices and sauces. Paella, a dish of chicken or seafood, gently simmered with saffron rice and vegetables, serves as the house specialty. Order a pitcher of Sangria to round out your meal and allow at least two hours to enjoy the ambience, good conversation and, of course, the tapas. The restaurant is ideal for group functions and special events. In July, La Tapa hosts the Running of the Bulls party, a celebration that mirrors the famous festival in Pamplona, Spain. Flamenco dancers swirl, revelers take to the streets and tables filled with tapas to please the crowds. Space is limited, so call early to reserve your table.

10523 - 99 Avenue, Edmonton AB **(780) 424-8272** *www.latapa.ca*

Banzai Sushi & Teriyaki House

Fast, fresh and affordable Japanese food awaits diners at Banzai Sushi & Teriyaki House. The Calgary restaurant has introduced many diners to the joys of Japanese cuisine. One of the common misconceptions about Japanese food is that it is expensive. Not so at Banzai, which offers generous portions at reasonable prices. The restaurant is renowned for its popular *donburi*, which means rice bowl. Banzai presents these dishes as teriyaki chicken, tempura or a combination of beef and chicken served over rice. Japanese noodle soups offered here include beef and curry varieties. Sushi rolls, a combination of sticky rice and toppings, which may be raw, cooked or marinated, are popular at Banzai. The Alaskan Roll features smoked salmon, while the Banzai Roll combines tuna, salmon and the brightly coloured flying fish roe known as *tobiko*. The California roll with crab, cucumber and avocado is always a favourite. You can also indulge in fresh raw seafood known as sashimi. The tuna or salmon sashimi can be purchased separately or as a combination plate that gives the diner a bigger portion of each. Banzai also serves tantalizing shrimp and veggie tempura. There's virtually no waiting for your food here; most entrées come to your table within five minutes. If you haven't been introduced to Japanese cuisine yet, let Banzai Sushi & Teriyaki House at two locations bring the Far East to your table.

526 A 4 Avenue SW, Calgary AB
(403) 253-8120
470-9737 MacLeod Trail SW, Calgary AB
(403) 262-9060

Ducks on the Roof Restaurant & Sports Bar

Whether you're looking for private evening out with a loved one or a night of food, drink and fun with friends, Ducks on the Roof Restaurant & Sports Bar has it covered. The restaurant, which opened 16 years ago, features two separate dining areas. The sports bar maintains a pub

atmosphere, where you'll enjoy chatting and watching sports with friends both old and new. There's also an elegant dining room, suitable for more formal occasions. Owners John and Kelly Scondrianis struggled for months to find the perfect name for their restaurant. When one day their 4-year-old son pointed to a family of ducks on the roof of the building, they took the name from out of the mouth of their babe. The menu is semi-casual and international, ranging from Greek souvlaki and Asian stir-fries to pizzas, pastas and sandwiches. The service is fast and friendly. Ducks on the Roof offers delivery in the Cochrane area. For both fine dining and casual fun, visit Ducks on the Roof Restaurant & Sports Bar.

Westwinds Shopping Mall, Cochrane AB
(403) 932-5959

La Casa Pergola

The pace is brisk and the atmosphere bright during lunch at La Casa Pergola. Later, the lights are turned down low and the tables are set for romance. Cheerful by day, the restaurant provides an elegant and intimate setting for dinner. Candlelight flickers and Placido Domingo plays softly in the background as diners feast on veal, seafood and pasta. Chef Guy Kinniard uses only the freshest ingredients in his authentic Italian recipes, down to the sauces, dressings and

soups. Savor the salmon with mustard cream sauce or enjoy lamb marinated in raspberry and rosemary. The filet mignons are two inches thick and the truffles are imported from Italy. By the time you finish your dessert of Frangelico Cheese Cake or chocolate walnut budino with caramel sauce, your seduction will be complete. Consider bringing your colleagues to La Casa Pergola for lunch at noon and returning later, when the candles are glowing, for dinner with that special someone.

4909- 48 Street, Red Deer AB
(403) 342-2404

Village Cantina Tropical Grill

In the Caribbean vacation of your dreams, a festive place serving tropical drinks and the fresh catch of the day sits just up from the beach. When it's time to get out of the sun, you can wander in for a tasty margarita or mojito and some appetizers. The Village Cantina Tropical Grill is Calgary's version of such an establishment. Even when the Canadian winter is raging, this bar and grill feels bright and warm. The décor evokes lazy, sun-soaked climes. None of the food is deep-fried, so it all tastes fresh and flavorful. You and a few friends can make a light meal out of ordering several tapas for the table. The Cancun-style ceviche, a house favorite, features delicate sole marinated in lime juice with tomatoes, onions, peppers and cilantro. Complement the ceviche with baked brie, smoked salmon quesadilla or warm artichoke dip. Tequila is treated with respect at Village Cantina Tropical Grill—it serves only 100 percent blue agave tequila. You'll even find it in some of the dishes. Calgary's hottest new venue, Club Paradiso, is above the Cantina and on Saturday nights, Carly's Angels, a troupe of female impersonators, performs funny, edgy, Vegas-style entertainment for sell-out crowds. Leave your cares behind at the paradisiacal Village Cantina Tropical Grill.

1413 9 Avenue SE, Calgary AB
(403) 265-5739
www.villagecantina.ca

Tonquin Prime Rib Village

Tonquin Prime Rib Village has a reputation for excellence, and in one visit you will see why. Owned and operated for 35 years by Nick Bartziokas, the restaurant is a labour of love. Known as Jasper's authority on prime rib, Nick prides himself on only buying and serving the highest quality products, including the AAA beef for which Alberta is famous. His prime rib is legendary in these parts, prepared from a secret recipe and method that lasts seven hours. His menu has a decidedly international flair, to the delight of his many international visitors. Appetizers include, when available, a wonderful fresh mussels marinara. From mild to wild, the soups du jour include selections from Italy to Thailand. While many come for the sumptuous steaks, just as many come for the seafood. Be sure to try the scallops en brochettes, plump juicy scallops sautéed together with bacon in a seasoned burre blanche. If you are up for something different, try the Greek-style lamb chops with baked potato or the veal Marsala, veal scallopini sautéed with mushrooms in a Marsala wine sauce. There is even a children's menu. The dining room seats 140 with wonderful views from the large windows. About 50 can be seated on the beautiful patio, and 60 at the bar. For great food in a casual atmosphere, don't miss Tonquin Prime Rib Village.

100 Juniper Street, Jasper AB (780) 852-4966

Zona's Late Night Bistro

Zona's has been a festive late night destination for 10 years. Owner Chris Dmytriw strives to keep the atmosphere fun, fresh and exciting, and keep the food cutting-edge. The room has a Mediterranean feel with a touch of Greece. Chris studied art before opening the bistro, and Zona's reflects his creativity. The décor is always evolving—Chris changes the art on the walls regularly to keeping it interesting. Zona's has brought world food and fusion food to Canmore. The menu includes many ethnic dishes with Canadian ingredients, as well as fully vegetarian options. All of the meals are handmade and health conscious, and are flavourfully made with a variety of spices. You can start with the avacado Caesar salad or the in-house maple-smoked salmon, artichoke heart and cream cheese dip. For an entrée, try the popular Moroccan molasses leg of lamb curry, a specialty since day one, or the pomegranate glazed stuffed chicken. Zona's is jumping after dark, especially on theme nights. Come in on Wednesdays for a jam session or on Thursdays for the popular Zen lounge night. Whichever night you can make it in, you'll be sure of an enjoyable time.

709 10 Street, Canmore AB
(403) 609-2000
www.zonaslatenightbistro.com

The Blue Olive

The Blue Olive offers a quick, nutritious lunch to get you through a busy workday or for a refreshing dinner at day's end. The bustling street outside the Calgary restaurant is a people-watcher's delight, open to only foot traffic during the day. Owners Tom and Laurel Luzzi completely renovated the inside space of the Blue Olive, turning it from a counter-style deli to a sit-down restaurant with some of the deli elements remaining intact. Sandwiches here are packed with turkey, ham, chicken, smoked meats or vegetables and come on several breads, including ciabatta and rye, as well as in wraps and paninis. Salads, soups, pasta and hot entrées are also popular. Expect a creamy coleslaw and a Kosher dill pickle with your sandwich as well as rustic bread served with the restaurant's signature blue olive spread. Caesar, Greek or Cobb salads offer light and lively choices. If you're looking for seafood, try the marinated seafood antipasto with squid, shrimp, mussel, octopus and clams combined with olive oil, artichoke hearts, peppers, lemon and garlic. The portions here are generous, and business people appreciate the fast and friendly service that lets them eat well and still return to their offices on time. "What a delightful place this is," wrote an enthusiastic *Calgary Herald* food critic. For big salads and big sandwiches in a bustling central location, come to the Blue Olive.

225 8 Avenue SW, Unit X, Calgary AB
(403) 233-0564

Koi

If a bit of gallery hopping followed by a meal at a hip restaurant sounds like a pleasant way to pass the time in Calgary, you will be happy to know that you can satisfy both your hunger for art and your appetite for innovative nutritious cuisine at Koi. Philip Wong is a chef by trade, though you sense, as you marvel at the many original works on display at Koi, that he would be just as happy with a career in art. Co-owner Natasha Peace followed a career in the corporate world with training as a yoga instructor. Together, they have created a community feel at their restaurant by inviting local artists to bring the room alive with their works. The community vibe is enhanced by a tapas-style menu that encourages sharing. A typical meal might begin with a house favorite, the yam wedges, which are served with a spicy coconut curry dip. From there, you can opt for more appetizers for everyone or decide to have the soba salad, smoked

salmon or tiger prawn curry bowl all to yourself. Most drinks and many items on the menu are organic, and the food is prepared without sugar, flour or deep frying. Days start early at Koi, which opens at 8:30 am for breakfast and stays open well into the night to cater to the cocktail crowd. For local art, healthful dining and a community atmosphere, check out Koi.

#100, 1011-1 Street SW, Calgary AB
(403) 206-1564

Red Door Bistro

The Red Door Bistro blends the flavors of fine dining with a casual atmosphere—it's just the spot to gather with friends for an evening out. Owner Darren Gurr opened the lighthearted restaurant in the heart of Calgary's design district in 2006. He puts a modern spin on traditional French cuisine, and is equally caught up in the art of creating the perfect cocktail. Start your meal off with a cup of the daily soup, a Moroccan lettuce wrap with roasted lamb or the house specialty, fresh oysters. One bite of the La Grande grilled cheese sandwich, made with cinnamon-raisin brioche, smoked bacon and Gruyére cheese, will change the way you think of

the classic combination forever. Entrée choices include the beer-braised lamb shank, seared rare ahi tuna and lobster ravioli. Cocktails range from century-old recipes to originals such as the Drunken Carrot. If you prefer something non-alcoholic, try the freshly made lemonade or minted apple-berry drink. Meet up with friends at the Red Door Bistro to break bread in a relaxed, casual atmosphere.

607 11 Avenue SW, Calgary AB
(403) 233-2433
www.reddoorbistro.com

The Cross-Eyed Giraffe Café

Before owners Loretta (Lori) and Charles Johnson earned their culinary degrees, Lori entered a cross-country cooking contest in Toronto. Her Tangy Topped Salmon Casserole won first place in the main-course category. The prize was an all-expenses-paid trip-for-two to Nassau in the Bahamas. This accomplishment must have given her long-term inspiration, because many years later, Lori and Chuck opened their own café in Bentley called the Cross-Eyed Giraffe Café. Genuine friendliness and superb customer service pervade the Cross-Eyed Giraffe Café. The prices are fair, the food is fantastic and the atmosphere is comfortable. Fresh soups and two specials a day are standard offerings. Sandwiches are bistro-style and the baked goods are just like home. A cappuccino bar and extensive selection of teas make it easy to stop in for a beverage and a visit. Breakfast is served all day. When Chuck and Lori met at a summer camp outside of Bentley in 1960 it was a twist of fate that benefited the whole community. The Cross-Eyed Giraffe Café warmly welcomes locals and visitors, giving everyone a friendly place to gather as they share their life experiences over a fine bit of food and drink.

4926 50 Avenue, Bentley AB (403) 748-3700

Tapas Restaurant and Bodega

Embrace a blend of Spanish and Portuguese culture and cuisine at Tapas Restaurant and Bodega, where owners Gail and Greg Elford specialize in creating food for sharing. Tapas Restaurant and Bodega made its debut in 2003 and has since become a favorite haunt for locals and visitors alike. Just one short year later the establishment was named as one of Canada's Best New Restaurants by *enRoute* magazine. Diners can kick back and relax while sampling a diverse array of captivating entrées served in small quantities. The small plates allow patrons to try several dishes that can cover a full range of taste sensations. Popular favorites include the tapas tomato tostada, made with garlic and basil and topped with smooth Brie, and the grilled *pollo brocheta*, or chicken skewers seasoned with fresh rosemary and citrus zest and served with a sweet potato and vanilla bean puree. The entrepreneurial Elfords originally worked in the hospitality and hotel industry before purchasing a vintage home, which they decided to turn into a tapas-style restaurant after vacationing in Spain (where they were wed). Discover one of the worlds must diverse culinary traditions at Tapas Restaurant and Bodega.

633 10 Street, Canmore AB
(403) 609-0583

Balkan The Greek Restaurant

Balkan the Greek Restaurant is a Banff institution that has served the authentic flavors of Greek and Mediterranean cuisine in a warm and festive atmosphere for 25 years. Reviews, in media that range from the Canadian Broadcasting System to newspapers, applaud this restaurant for ambience, excellence of cuisine and exceptional value. As locals know, you'll get hearty Greek home cooking and warm hospitality. Each Tuesday and Thursday, the restaurant features Greek Night, with belly dancing, plate smashing and of course, plenty of ouzo. All of the dishes are made from scratch, using the freshest and finest quality ingredients available. The signature dish is the fabulous roasted lamb, *arni psito*. Other favorites are the souvlakis and an assortment of Greek grills. All of the dishes capture the authentic flavors of Greece. Owner Jason Karlo personally trained chef Jason Bloomfield, who has been creating his masterpieces for more than 20 years. All of the staff are energetic, friendly and knowledgeable about both

food and wine. The wine list is extensive, carefully chosen to complement the flavors of the food. You'll find a variety of imported Greek wines, as well as Canadian, Chilean and Australian classics. Your visit to Banff is not complete without a stop to enjoy a fine meal with family and friends in the lively Balkan the Greek Restaurant.

120 Banff Avenue, Banff AB
(403) 762-3454
www.banffbalkan.ca

Monkey Top Saloon

The Monkey Top Saloon is a community favourite that was created in the early 1990s in a historic mercantile building built in 1914. A Western theme permeates the saloon with Old West pictures and branding iron markings from local ranches on the interior timber. The saloon is famous for its steak sandwich and a drink known as the Monkey Top Cæsar. There is an outdoor patio for diners or drinkers who want to party under the stars. Dick Damron, of country music fame, hosts a Mexican fiesta and hangs his hat at the Monkey Top when he is in town. The Monkey Top offers a special function each month hosting activities that range from lobster

parties, fishing derbies and a winter sled event to rodeo days and golf tournaments. The Monkey Top Idle is a popular annual event. Owners Karen Oberg and Annie Thyr have a strong community support ethic and the saloon participates regularly in fundraising activities. Referred to as the Biggest Little Bar in Alberta, the Monkey Top is wheelchair accessible and always friendly. Enjoy the hospitality and charm of the Old West at the Monkey Top Saloon.

5002–50 Avenue, Bentley AB
(403) 748-3141

The Trough Dining Co.

The smell of roasting coriander. A candle dancing on your glass of Grand Cru. That Marvin Gaye remix you love so much. Dinner becomes magic. Partners Rosie Gair and Michael Western have used their extensive food and beverage experience to create a restaurant that is capable of delivering this ethereal feeling. As with any great restaurant, the foundation for the Troughs success is the food. Rosie has turned a passion for ingredients and flavours into a labour of love. With the input of her creative team of chefs and an emphasis on fresh locally grown ingredients, she is continually coming up with new dishes that keep her ever growing legion of fans coming back. Michael has created a setting worthy of Rosie's food. The cozy dining room of 10 tables was built for a personalized dining experience focusing on the details. This is highlighted by a sound system that boasts a separate volume control for each table, cotton plush hand towels in the washrooms and red wines always served at a perfect 61 degrees. To facilitate the seamless experience they have assembled a group of top servers from the area necessary to deliver the Troughs' attention to detail style of service, world class wine list and eclectic back bar. This quality dining experience is executed while maintaining a sense of humour. Even the name gives you a glimpse into the Troughs cheeky style. Located one block off busy Main St., Canmore's newest restaurant has become a jewel in this beautiful mountain town.

725 Walk of Champions (9 Street), Canmore AB
(403) 678-2820
www.thetrough.ca

Hardware Grill

Plenty of restaurants get good reviews, but few receive accolades at the level of Hardware Grill. The local press has described it as the best restaurant in town. Air Canada's *enRoute* magazine names it as the best restaurant in the prairies. Toronto's *Globe and Mail* has simply called it the best restaurant in Canada. The brainchild of Larry and Melinda Stewart, the Hardware Grill is where French culinary traditions meet the best West Canadian produce. Located in the heart of Edmonton's arts district, the spacious and elegant restaurant is decorated in warm earthy tones, with plum hardwood floors and with lovely river valley views. With a well-worn copy of *Larousse Gastronomique*, Larry delivers his Canadian Prairie cuisine *à la minute*. There are no warming ovens or shortcuts. Bread is baked on the premises twice daily. Sausage is made in-house and salmon is smoked on the premises. A sample first course is the pepper-crusted Ahi tuna (rare) with a warm Provençale tomato tart. Entree examples include the 42-day aged sterling New York steak with pea-shoot-grape tomato sauté, prosciutto-wrapped asparagus and black coffee barbecue sauce. Another is the porcini-crusted sea bass with lobster-truffled potato crêpes. Vegetarians enjoy the English pea ravioli with Mediterranean bread pudding and portobello mushroom stuffed with onion jam and goat cheese. The Hardware Grill offers a list of 700 fine wines and has received ten consecutive awards of excellence from *Wine Spectator*. No one does it like Hardware Grill.

9698 Jasper Avenue, Edmonton AB (780) 423-0969
www.hardwaregrill.com

The Blue Pear

A meal at the Blue Pear is an opportunity to take time out from your fast-paced life for a quiet, elegant meal. Chef Darcy Radies carefully balances pure and simple flavours to create the five courses that change monthly at the Blue Pear. Conversation begins to flow as diners relax into surroundings that, like the food, are deceptively simple and completely elegant. The carefully orchestrated procession of appetizers, soup, salad, entrée and dessert offers a visual and flavourful feast for the senses. Beef tenderloin, grilled fish and rack of lamb were among the choices when we visited. Darcy and Jessie Radies were married in 1999, and opened the Blue Pear as business partners in 2000. Jessie offers management skills that complement Darcy's culinary know-how. After graduating from the culinary arts program at Caribou College in Kamloops in 1985, Darcy worked at first-class establishments throughout Canada, Europe and Australia before opening the Blue Pear. He established himself at Toronto's Centro, then headed to the Youville Court Hotel in Somerset, England and Aquaries restaurant in Morges, Switzerland. Following stints at hotels in Sidney and Queensland, Australia, Darcy returned to Canada to work at Lake O'Hare Lodge near Lake Louise and Jack's Grill in Edmonton. The Blue Pear opens four nights a week with room for about 40 people; reservations are necessary. Discover the power and elegance of simplicity when you dine at the Blue Pear.

10643 123 Street, Edmonton AB
(780) 482-7178
www.thebluepear.com

River Roadhouse Bar

Kick up your heels at the River Roadhouse Bar, a full-blown country joint for juicin' and jumpin' cowboy-style. The River Roadhouse boasts a big dance floor and live country music every weekend, a rarity for a small town like High River. The rustic wood décor is complete with cattle brands on the walls. Owned and operated by the fun-loving Rogers family, natives of High River, the bar offers locals a chance to commune and celebrate. Brothers Rob and Jim and their wives, Lisa and Becky, decided to open the bar together after Rob's success in the restaurant industry. A certified chef, Rob serves up juicy steak, ribs and down-home cooking at the River Roadhouse while Jim manages the bar. The girls are in charge of the behind-the-scenes stuff, but everyone is hands-on when necessary to keep the party rolling. "We all know how to cook, serve and bartend," says Rob. Guests can enjoy pool tables, big-screen televisions and a video lottery terminal for entertainment. The large outdoor patio is a great place to kick back and enjoy good brew and company. The Rogers keep things interesting throughout the week with specials such as Tuesday Wing Night and karaoke on Wednesdays. On special occasions, they host community parties in the parking lot with a chili cookout and beer garden. Join the Rogers family for a fun time at the River Roadhouse Bar.

420 Centre Street N, High River AB
(403) 652-1555

Wild Tangerine Cucina Domestica

Modern Asian cooking is the focus at Wild Tangerine Cucina Domestica, which *Where Canada* magazine named the Best New Restaurant in Canada in 2004. *EnRoute* magazine felt that the imaginative cuisine, exemplified by such originals as the Shrimp Lollipop appetizer, deserved Top Table of Canada recognition in 2004 and 2005. Wild Tangerine was the only new Edmonton restaurant included in the *Top 70 Best Buy in Canada* 2005/06 and *Where to Eat in Canada* 2006/07. Owners Wilson and Judy Wu were stars of the Edmonton restaurant scene long opening Wild Tangerine. From 1993 to 2003, this dynamic brother and sister team was the driving force behind Polo's Café, which consistently earned the highest ratings from the *Edmonton Sun* and *Edmonton Journal*. Wilson and Judy keep things light, healthy and nutritious at Wild Tangerine, while adding large helpings of style. Their pot sticker-style perogies are stir-fried in a yummy lotus sauce and served with bison sausage. Loyal customers say that you just have to try them. Small and intimate enough to be called a café, this modern, urban establishment features a wine bar with Edmonton's first complete wine menu offered by the glass. Bite into something that's wild at heart and deep in soul at Wild Tangerine Cucina Domestica, or grab a meal at Wild Tangerine Mobile Cuisine, Wilson and Judy's hip take-out place on the main floor of Manulife Place downtown.

10383 112 Street, Edmonton AB
(780) 429-3130
www.wildtangerine.com

Packrat Louie

For more than 13 years, Packrat Louie has been a destination in Edmonton for those looking for an upscale but casual dining experience. Located in the middle of the city's bustling arts district, the restaurant enjoys a great deal of walk-in traffic from the neighbourhood as well as many guests who make a special trip from other areas. With a friendly, talented staff to take care of your needs and a large, varied menu that includes many European and North American favourites, it's easy to see why Packrat Louie has such a dedicated clientele. Lunch options range from elegant French escargot to good old meatloaf—with a twist, as it's made of bison and lamb. The restaurant is renowned for its authentic wood-fired pizzas, which appear on both the lunch and dinner menus. Also for dinner is a large variety of succulent seafood, including caramelized prawns and Chilean sea bass. The restaurant's extensive wine list has something to complement every meal. Whether you're seated in the comfortable dining room, in the lounge or on the cozy outdoor patio, you'll enjoy first-class comforts, an elegant menu and a casual vibe when you dine at Packrat Louie.

10335-83 Avenue, Edmonton AB
(780) 433-0123
www.packratlouie.com

Jasper Brewing Company

When Brewmaster Brett Ireland and Managing Partner Alex Derksen opened Jasper Brewing Company in 2005, they did more than provide Jasper with local microbrews. They also added an important gathering spot to Jasper's main street. The partners played with the idea of opening a brewery back in high school and eventually did just that. A tour of the brewery provides the inside story on the making of such beers as Rocket Ridge Raspberry Ale, Rockhopper India Pale Ale and Liftline Cream Ale. Whether you choose an ale or lager, you can expect eight innovative beers that combine premium hops and malts from around the world with the brewing company's

own yeast strains and natural Canadian Rocky Mountain water. The pub seats 85 people and the restaurant seats 60. Sports fans can follow their favorite teams on high-definition plasma televisions. The restaurant offers a deluxe assortment of sandwiches, salads and entrées that pair up nicely with the beers. Sirloin steak, beer-battered fish-and-chips and chicken marinated in bourbon and dark ale are popular choices on a menu that combines several cuisines and throws in a generous splattering of Cajun cooking. For beer crafted with attention to the details, visit Jasper Brewing Company.

624 Connaught Drive, Jasper AB
(780) 852-4111
www.jasperbrewingcompany.ca

Strathcona Tea House & Restaurant

In 1992, Marlhine Lothian saved the 1905 Bank of Commerce building in Vegreville from demolition by moving it to Androssan to house Strathcona Tea House & Restaurant. Marlhine uses the fine old building as her home and as a place for you to connect with family and friends. The restaurant serves breakfast, lunch and tea every day but Monday and offers extended dinner hours on weekends. Diners enjoy the ambience created by original chandeliers and a solid oak mantle and front door. Dining is a leisurely experience at Strathcona, which offers live entertainment in the evenings and country meals created from scratch. Dinner choices include bison or ostrich patties, pan-fried liver and onions and roast chicken. The restaurant

is a four-time winner of the Golden Fork Award from the Gourmet Diners Society of America, most recently taking the prize in 2006. Marlhine's mother, Jeannette, and daughters Shelley and Teddi attend to the tea house and adjacent shop, Desiderata–A Woman's Haven, which offers spa services, ladies fashions and carefully chosen home décor, including antiques and silk flower arrangements. Make your reservations for a country outing at Strathcona Tea House & Restaurant.

52404 Range Road 221, Ardrossan AB
Tea house: (780) 922-6963
Desiderata: (780) 922-2279
www.strathconateahouse.com

Treo Restaurant

James Patchell gives new meaning to the concept of global cuisine at Treo Restaurant. Along with his wife and partner Pamela, James has created a masterpiece of a restaurant that combines fine foods and welcoming vibes. James has more than 30 years of experience as an executive chef and now uses his extensive training and expertise to follow his own culinary path. Treo Restaurant offers new concept dining, which James and Pamela call small plate. Under this plan, diners order several petite entrées that they are encouraged to share around the table, turning a simple, flavor-packed meal into a truly communal activity. *Bon Appetite* has contacted James for recipes. Both *London Vogue* and the *Montana Travel Guide* have featured Treo, a testament to this charming restaurant's broad appeal. In addition to its expansive menu, Treo also has a large international wine selection filled with vintages selected for quality and their ability to compliment James' creations. Forget about deciding which entrée looks the best and sample all your favourites at Treo Restaurant.

**1005 Cougar Drive, Canmore AB
(403) 678-8802**

The Créperie

For more than 30 years, the Créperie has been serving up fine French cuisine in a cozy, romantic atmosphere. Owner Hans Kuhnel opened this Edmonton restaurant in 1976. He left his native Germany in 1967 and worked his way toward Alberta with restaurant jobs in France and Switzerland. Hans borrowed from the Swiss and especially the French in creating his menu for the Créperie. True to its name, the Créperie serves crépes as everything appetizers to main courses stuffed with chicken or beef. You can even enjoy a chocolate crépe for dessert. You'll also find a wide variety of other favorites, including ribeye steak, lamb and baked salmon. The Créperie serves delicious soups and salads. The quaint cellar that serves as its setting seats up to 175 amid flickering candlelight. The cuisine, service and atmosphere at the restaurant have garnered many awards, including *Vue Weekly*'s Golden Fork Awards for Best French restaurant and Most Romantic restaurant. *Where* magazine gave the Créperie its Most Memorable Meal Award. Despite having opened several restaurants since, the Créperie has remained Hans's favorite, and it is easy to see why. Find fine French cuisine in a romantic atmosphere at the Créperie.

111, 10220 103 Street NW, Edmonton AB
(780) 420-6656
www.thecreperie.com

Mikado

Alberta's first Japanese restaurant, Mikado has been serving Edmonton since 1972. Owner David Okumiya has cultivated a menu and atmosphere that rigorously uphold the traditions of his native culture. Fresh fish is flown in from the world's largest fish market in Tsukiji, Japan as well as from California, Nova Scotia and the B.C. coast. Okumiya has imported Japanese Robata grills to allow for the high temperatures that keep his meats and vegetables juicy and tender. Certified Japanese sushi chefs prepare the sushi and sashimi, which *See* magazine recently named the Best in Edmonton. *Where* magazine named Mikado as offering the Best Japanese cuisine in general. You'll find traditional favorites such as beef or chicken teriyaki and tempura on the menu, as well as many other flavourful delicacies. Bento boxes are a favorite way to sample a variety of tastes. For something a little modern, try the sushi pizza—a pancake of grilled rice topped with chopped onions, seaweed, masago and fish in a spicy sauce. The décor is simple yet elegant, with large sushi bars and private tatami rooms available. Mikado's also caters with a portable sushi bar and sushi chef. For Japanese dining fit for an emperor, visit Mikado.

1903–98 Street, Edmonton AB (780) 432-4500
10350–109 Street, Edmonton AB (780) 425-8096
www.mikadorestaurant.com

O'Sullivan's Restaurant & Bar

Whether you are a restless native of Calgary or just passing through, O'Sullivan's Restaurant & Bar is a popular place to find good food and a fun atmosphere. Owners Kevin Langen and his wife, Kerry, were among the first to bring an upscale pub to Calgary. The place they've created fosters friendship, warmth and conversation. O'Sullivan's exceptional service has earned it the local Service with Style award. There is also plenty of entertainment, including karaoke three nights a week. Real chefs make exceptional food in-house, including the must-try steak sandwiches. Daily specials include Monday madness, when chicken wings are only 10 cents apiece, and happy hour Sundays, when happy hour prices apply all day. The restaurant is conveniently located and with ample free parking for all your friends. If you are ready for a vacation from your everyday life, check your cares at the door of O'Sullivan's Restaurant & Bar.

5809 Macleod Trail S #104, Calgary AB (403) 253-5886

Athens Greek Restaurant

At Athens Greek Restaurant, guests are served and treated like family. The owner, Andy Triadopoulos, was born and raised in Greece. His wife, Natasha, and daughters Kristina and Irene also help at the restaurant, where the authentically prepared food is superlative. Andy loves what he does and believes in attention to detail. Even the yogurt is prepared the old-fashioned way, by hand, using all-natural ingredients. Natasha oversees the preparation of the homemade ice cream and baked-from-scratch breads. The menu boasts a number of traditional dishes such as humus, *tzatziki* (a yoghurt-based dip) and *spanakopita* (spinach pie). You can also try any of a host of Greek salads, *souvlaki* (shish kebabs) and *moussaka* (eggplant casserole). Traditional lamb dishes are a menu staple. Vegetarian, seafood and steak entrees are also available in abundance. Athens Greek Restaurant has played host to famous world travelers and regular folks alike. It can prepare off-the-menu dishes for diners who call ahead with their wishes. For a dining experience that's like coming home to a Greek villa, Athens Greek Restaurant is the place.

71 N. Bridge Street, Drumheller AB
(403) 823-3225

Bob the Fish Tavern

Fans keep coming back for more at Bob the Fish Tavern. Sports fans relish the beer and big screen television. Food fans savor the Big Fish burgers and lemon-pepper chicken wings. Specialties of the house include Clam-jammed Chowder, battered fillet of hake, salads and fries to die for. The dinnertime menu features more substantial fare such as pork dumplings with ginger and chili sauce or a plate of spicy jambalaya. Golden Tee golf machines and the Buck Hunter video game offer a welcome distraction when you're not hungry. Catch a hockey playoff game, sit and chat with friends or grab a table outside and watch the locals strut their stuff. Live bands rock the joint occasionally. Manitoba-born owner Bob Goodwin sets the stage for first-class eats and customer service to match. He modeled his business on taverns he visited while touring the U.S.A. "The people in American taverns take their job seriously, and they do their job very well," he says. Old, young, cowboys and families form a melting pot of fun and frolic at this popular hang out. Where did the name originate? Goodwin is a purveyor of service, hospitality and tummy-pleasing food, but he's also an avid fisherman. Once you're there, you won't want to leave Bob the Fish Tavern.

501 17 Avenue SW, Calgary AB
(403) 244-4471

Michael's Restaurant Pizza Bar

There's more in store for you than pizza and beer when you step inside Michael's Restaurant Pizza Bar. Don't be surprised if a National Hockey League player pulls up a chair next to you. Since 1981, this popular sports bar has been a hot-spot for star sightings. The thick-crusted pizza, pasta plates, salads and sizzling steaks lure them in. The main dining room is a virtual hall of fame. Authentic NHL jerseys, sweaters and hockey sticks line the walls. You'll find an autographed photo of U2's lead singer Bono among the treasures as well. You can sit upstairs, downstairs or grab a table on the rooftop patio where it's sunny and sheltered. If you sit near the kitchen, you'll see a steady parade of pizzas heading out the door. Throughout the workweek, downtown businesses order 50 to one 100 pizzas for lunch. At night, the restaurant sends pizzas over to the NHL dressing room after hometown hockey games. Owners Michael and Helen Batas are casual, friendly and full of community pride. Their son John now oversees day-to-day operations. If you're looking for pizza oozing with cheese and baked to perfection, Michael's Restaurant Pizza Bar scores every time.

139 10 Avenue SW, Calgary AB (403) 264-6731

Ranchman's

Ever since its doors opened in 1972, people who know have been calling Ranchman's Canada's greatest honky tonk. Owners Harris Dvorkin and Kevin Baker describe their restaurant as the place to be for dining, dancing and glancing. Ranchman's is the official hospitality location of the Canadian Professional Rodeo Association, and one look around will show you why. This dance hall and restaurant is a virtual museum of rodeo memorabilia with photos displaying more than 90 saddles of Canadian and world champion pro-rodeo cowboys. There's even a mechanical bull to test your mettle. The restaurant here served as a location in the Academy Award winning film *Brokeback Mountain*. You can dance the night away to great country music that's guaranteed to make your boots scoot. Canada's own Shania Twain and Terri Clark have played here, as have country greats like Toby Keith, Loretta Lynn and Ronnie Milsap. Those with two left feet can take dance lessons here. The food and drink is classic Western fare, including delicious chicken, beef and ribs dripping with barbecue sauce. The restaurant holds more than 1,000 people on the inside and more than 900 on the patio. Ranchman's offers catering and can even arrange for entertainment at your event through its talent agency. With all this, it's small wonder the Canadian Country Music Association has named Ranchman's Club of the Year six times. Come to Ranchman's to enjoy rodeo gear, delicious food and a rootin' tootin', boot-scootin' good time.

9615 MacLeod Trail S, Calgary AB (403) 253-1100 *www.ranchmans.com*

Caesar's Steak House

"More oil deals have been cut here than anywhere in the West," say Gus Giannoulis and Nick Kaketsis, owners of Caesar's Steak House in Calgary. For more than three decades, this restaurant has been captivating diners with the best aged and charbroiled prime beef Alberta has to offer. The rich surroundings of the lounge, a combination of burgundy leather and dark wood finishes, live up to the rich flavours found here. Expect a choice of 70 fine wines and such steak specialties as rib eye, filet mignon or T-bone. The highlight of the sumptuous dining room with its Romanesque interior is the Olympic Torch grill, designed to look like the real torch and to cook your steaks just as you like them. Returning patrons often ask for their father's table with a view of this grill, flanked by elegant columns. You can start your repast with such specialties as scampi, escargot or barbecue ribs. Choose a steak for the Olympic Torch grill or a tenderloin for two prepared at your table. Other specialties include steak and lobster tail, Chicken Neptune and rack of lamb. The staff is as loyal as the patrons, and more than half of the employees have worked here for 20 years or longer. Whether you are cutting a deal or simply dealing with your favourite cut of beef, come to Caesar's Steak House ready to answer one overwhelming question: How would you like that done?

512 4 Avenue SW, Calgary AB
(403) 264-1222
www.caesarssteakhouse.com

The Embarcadero Wine and Oyster Bar

The Embarcadero Wine and Oyster Bar, named for the waterfront district in San Francisco, is inspired by eclectic international cuisine. The signature oysters are a variety of northern Atlantic and Pacific fresh oysters on the half shell, as well as Oysters Florentine, Rockefeller and the house specialty, Embarcadero Oysters sautéed with Italian sausage, marinated fresh tomato and Asiago cheese. Imaginative gourmet offerings are featured daily in addition to favourite specialties such as the Seafood Symphony (a dazzling mix of salmon, prawns, orange roughy, mussels and lobster tail), and mixed seafood in pasta or jambalaya. Entrées include AAA Alberta beef (flame broiled steaks and slow cooked prime rib), rack of lamb and Brome Lake breast of duck. A large assortment of casual fare is also available: tapas and appetizers, Buffalo style chicken wings, burgers and pizzas. An extensive wine cellar and a continually changing selection of wines by the glass will provide the perfect wine to complement your meal. The historic red brick house features a main floor lounge with a European style wine bar, big screen televisions and an adjoining casual dining area. Upstairs, the Gallery dining room with its original artwork has a fine dining ambience, ideal for special dinners and private functions. In the summertime, the street-side patio with its goldfish pond and apple tree is a shady retreat from the city bustle.

208–17 Avenue SE, Calgary AB
(403) 263-0848
www.oysterbar.ca

Ed's Restaurant

Ed's Restaurant is a Calgary institution that has been in its landmark, circa 1911 house for over 20 years. Best known for pioneering Buffalo style chicken wings, Ed's is all about choices, both in food and ambience. The extensive menu for lunch or dinner features AAA Alberta beef, steaks and prime rib, and also ranges from filet, lobster, pastas and seafood, to casual fare such as creative pizzas, sirloin burgers freshly ground in-house, and a huge assortment of finger food appetizers. Ed's famous Buffalo style wings, dry and crispy, come in five degrees of hot, as well as sweet or spicy Asian flavours. The six dining rooms emulate spaces in the original residence, from the cozy wood-paneled Boardroom and the sunny Garden Terrace, perfect for quiet intimate dining, to the spacious main-floor Solarium for larger groups, offering big-screen TV's for viewing sporting events. In the summertime, a sheltered ground-level patio and a breezy balcony offer sun and shade for al fresco dining. Centrally located just one block west of the Calgary Exhibition and Stampede Grounds, Ed's is a favourite of corporate Calgary for business lunch or dinner meetings, with its private dining rooms for 10 to 50 people, complimentary audio/video equipment and customized menus to suit any occasion. Ed's Restaurant can be described in two words: sensible indulgence.

202 17 Avenue SE, Calgary AB
(403) 262-3500
www.edsrestaurant.com

Blues on Whyte

The soulful moan of a harmonica blending with a sweet guitar lick is the first sound you're likely to hear at Blues on Whyte. The club, located in the historic Commercial Hotel, is one of Canada's premier live music venues. True to its name, Blues on Whyte is dedicated to that foremost of North American music, the blues. Whether you're a fan of the early country Delta Blues of Robert Johnson or the electrified Chicago variety practiced by the likes of Muddy Waters and B.B. King, you'll feel right at home at Blues on Whyte. Some of the biggest names in the blues have played here over the past 27 years, and you'll never know when they just might show up again. The club features live music every night, with acts ranging from local and regional favorites to international stars. On Saturday nights, the house band hosts an open stage jam that attracts talent from all over. It's best to show up early for that. The atmosphere, like the music itself, is free and casual, with suit-and-tie grooving next to blue-collar. Come to Blues on Whyte and let the soulful music wash your blues away.

10329-82 Avenue, Edmonton AB
(780) 439-5058

Surahi

Sam and Babbi Boyal, husband and wife team, say that the recent opening of their restaurant, Surahi, is a dream come true, and they are happy to be able to share the flavors of the northwest Indian state of Punjab with customers. The family originally hails from India, where they had experience in the restaurant business, and believes that Calgary was ready and waiting for them.

The name Surahi refers to a traditional piece of pottery used for storing water. The upscale eatery reflects the family's values, with a warm, casual atmosphere, perfect for sharing a meal with friends and family. Indian décor, much of which was brought from India by Sam and Babbi, adorns the walls and lets customers know they will be experiencing a truly authentic meal. Regulars love the beef and lamb curry, as well as the tandoori style chicken. The restaurant offers several specialties, including some that are dairy free. *Gulab jamun*, a traditional dessert in a sweet syrup, is a delicious ending to a meal here. Discover the exotic spices and flavors of India with a visit to Surahi.

8906 Macleod Trail SE, Calgary AB
(403) 212-1324

Dakota Bar & Grill

A warm respite from the cold winds outside, Dakota Bar & Grill offers cuisine that's inspired by the American Southwest and served in a laid-back atmosphere. In the day, urban professionals flock to this downtown Calgary restaurant, located across from Bankers Hall. They come back after hours, too, making Thursdays and Fridays particularly busy. The extensive menu

offers dishes ranging from quesadillas to chipotle steak. Try the spicy enchiladas or the corn chowder soup, or simply sit with a drink and enjoy one of the big-screen televisions. The Dakota is an excellent place to meet with your pals for a game of pool or darts. It features a large selection of draft beers. The comfortable Alberta décor is red brick and dark mahogany. In the warm season, you'll enjoy sitting on the Stephen Avenue patio and watching the vibrant street life. Plant life and urns add a private ambience to the patio. The Dakota is completely non-smoking. David Venini is the proprietor of this family-owned establishment. He invites you to come make yourself at home at the Dakota Bar & Grill.

310 8 Avenue SW, Calgary AB
(403) 262-4967

Houlihan's Restaurant

Houlihan's Restaurant offers award-winning food and service in a relaxing, contemporary atmosphere. This Red Deer restaurant has been a neighbourhood fixture for the past 30 years. It recently earned the Best of Red Deer People's Choice award for best all-around restaurant. The atmosphere at Houlihan's is relaxing and comfortable, with a flower-draped cabana and gently trickling water feature in the centre of the restaurant. There's plenty of space for you and your guests to enjoy yourselves as you eat. The lunch menu features such delicacies as prime rib sandwich topped with gravy and served with aromatic garlic toast and vegetables. Other options include chicken, pasta and seafood salads, as well as stir-fry and barbecued chicken. The dinner menu has renowned filet of beef Wellington, stuffed with paté, covered with mushrooms and wrapped in a puff pastry. You'll also find a variety of pasta dishes, including seafood fettuccini. Houlihan's maintains an extensive wine list with something to complement every meal. Make sure to save room for a delicious dessert. The menu is regularly updated, so you'll find new delicacies when you return. Come to Houlihan's Restaurant for award-winning food, service and atmosphere.

#11-6791 Gaztz Avenue, Red Deer AB
(403) 342-0330

Aussie Rules Foodhouse & Bar

Aussie Rules Foodhouse & Bar is a dueling piano bar in a class of its own. Its three star piano players—Bob Cunningham, Scott Fooks and Mike Szekely—rotate between two pianos for a non-stop four hour performance that will have even the most timid guests standing on their chairs singing their hearts out. Aussie Rules talented piano players take requests from the audience and incorporate them into the show, whether it is oldies, 80s rock, country or hip hop. The show involves hilarious comedic stunts and provides an atmosphere where anything can happen, which makes Aussie Rules an ideal place to hold a birthday or stag party. The stage does not belong to the piano players alone. If you feel the need to get up there and join in the show Aussie Rules encourages you to do so. At Aussie Rules, you'll find casual comfort food, a busy bar and a night to remember. Doors open at 5 pm Thursday thru Saturday and shows take place from 8 pm to midnight on Thursday, and from 9 pm to 1 am on Friday and Saturday. Aussie Rules also books private parties, such as corporate functions, Sunday through Wednesday. It books up fast here at Aussie Rules so be sure to make reservations four to six weeks in advance. For a rockin' good time and a night you won't soon forget, make plans to visit Aussie Rules Foodhouse & Bar.

1002 37 Street SW, Calgary AB
(403) 249-7933
www.aussierules.ca

Ming Eat Drink

As you walk through the proletarian portal of Ming Eat Drink in Calgary, the enthralling aroma of masterfully prepared Chinese cuisine invites you to have a seat, and the sophisticated martini bar invites you to share a drink with your fellow revolutionaries. Owner Wayne Leong yanks you straight out of the mainstream with the controversial ambience of his hip Chairman Mao/Che Guevara décor. Ho Chi Minh would approve of this people's paradise, serving Food, Drink and Fine Propaganda since 1997. The Chairman would proclaim that the Red Room must be seen. El Che would give his approval to the Martini Mingle. Every party approves of the fun and individuality that are key to Ming's dining experience. Beyond classic Chinese fare and outstanding drinks, you'll find proof of Ming's artistic sentiments at the annual Ming Short Film Festival, which you, comrade, can enter. With entries chosen by the end of July, Ming screens the selections for this popular festival in late August. Ming features music and a trendy cocktail bar where customers of all political persuasions come to see and be seen. A 2003 readers' poll at the *Calgary News & Entertainment Weekly* lavished Best of Calgary awards on Ming—for best bar to have a conversation in, best vibe and friendliest staff, to mention just some of the honors. For an enlightened meal or cocktail in an exotic environment, come to Ming Eat Drink.

520 17 Avenue SW, Calgary AB
(403) 229-1986
www.mingeatdrink.com

La Chaumière Restaurant

La Chaumière Restaurant celebrates the distinct flavours of each season's fresh market ingredients. The Calgary restaurant's French market cuisine has been attracting a devoted local clientele since 1978. Executive Chef Bob Matthews brings over 20 years experience to the ambitious job of reinventing an artful menu every season. Savor such concoctions as Pâté Maison with milkweed cornichons and fig Cumberland sauce or seared scallops wrapped with eggplant on caramelized zucchini. Sample the seasonal flavor of the dessert menu's classic French parfait in hazelnut, mango or cranberry-orange. La Chaumière also offers a list of more than 800 international wines. Boasting a setting for every occasion, the restaurant even makes the attractive wine cellar available for private gatherings, such as wine tasting and cocktail parties. You'll find dining tables set upon a clay tile floor in a golden room lined with wooden wine cases and tapestries. La Chaumière also offers a private dining room and two banquet rooms for parties and business meetings. The banquet rooms include their own patio and are separated by a soundproof folding wall that can be opened to accommodate up to 100 guests. The banquet menu offers 10 to 15 delectable appetizers, both hot and cold. La Chaumière attracts a talented and dedicated local staff that serves with genuine pride and hospitality. For a distinctive dining experience, plan your next special event at La Chaumière Restaurant.

139 17 Avenue SW, Calgary AB (403) 228-5690
www.lachaumiere.ca

La Dolce Vita Ristorante

Chef Franco Cosentino captures his philosophy of cooking in a single word, which he repeats with more emphasis each time he says it. *Fresh. Fresh. Fresh.* You can find him practicing his craft at La Dolce Vita, a community cornerstone since 1981. Franco was trained in Italy, and he is very picky. The salmon that he serves is wild, and the pasta is made by hand on-site, as is the bread, sausage and ice cream. Franco makes a point of never using frozen meat in his kitchen, where much of the action takes place around the wood-burning oven. In season, he serves wild boar, venison and pheasant. This family business is located in Calgary's Italian district, just minutes from downtown but in its own corner of the city. Lunch upstairs is popular with businesspeople, while families fill the main room on weekends. Many regulars recommend starting with the savory bruschetta followed by the grilled shrimp or veal picatta. You'll find salmon and a variety of pasta offerings here. An outstanding selection of wines complements the menu. Chef Franco was developing his own personal style way before beginning formal training. "When I was growing up in the kitchen, no one taught me recipes," he recalls. "I had to steal with my eye." Enjoy this master's fresh approach to cooking at La Dolce Vita.

916 1 Avenue NE, Calgary AB
(403) 263-3445

1886 Buffalo Café

Thanks to the 1886 Buffalo Café, breakfast is the favorite meal of the day for many folks in the downtown Calgary area. Regulars flock to this small wood building, rubbing elbows on some mornings with professional hockey players and television personalities. Proving that not all celebrities go for glitz, the café is as unpretentious as famous restaurants get. A sign across the front for both a lumber company and a power company commemorates the building's historical use as an office for these operations. Calgary's pioneers used to pay their lumber and electric bills here. The décor inside the 1886 Buffalo Café is true to the theme of the 1880s. As for the menu, hearty choices abound, including breakfast burritos and fluffy omelettes that are something of an art. The most popular dish is the egg scramble known as Kenny's Special. Be sure to check out the photo museum while you are here for glimpses of Calgary as it once looked. The café serves breakfast until 3 pm and is not open for dinner. Turn breakfast into something special by eating at the 1886 Buffalo Café.

187 Barclay Parade SW, Calgary AB (403) 269-9255 *www.1886.ca*

La Trattoria D'Italia

The Old World flavors of Italy are on delicious display at La Trattoria D'Italia. The Calgary restaurant is owned by Giovanni Cipriani and Mario Rossi. Giovanni was born in Terracino, Italy, near Rome. He learned the art of cooking from his mother, a chef. Five years ago, Giovanni and Mario used their training to bring their heritage to life at La Trattoria D'Italia. The restaurant offers 22 different varieties of pasta alone, all made from scratch. The restaurant's thin-crust pizza has gained great renown, with *Ffwd Weekly* writer Miles Pittman declaring that "the cooks at La Trattoria make the best, most traditional thin crust pizza I've had in town." Seafood lovers will delight in the options—the calamari has gained a large following. Those looking for a bit of culinary variety will delight in the constantly changing daily lunch and dinner specials. The restaurant maintains an excellent wine list, with many varieties of both red and white wine. The elegant but casual dining atmosphere features white linen tablecloths and friendly hosts who visit and attend to your every need. That spirit of service is also reflected in La Trattoria's support for community activities, including youth sports and charitable organizations. If you're looking for an authentic Italian meal in a friendly, family atmosphere, come to La Trattoria D'Italia.

3927 Edmonton Trail NE, Calgary AB
(403) 276-6026

Sobaten Japanese Noodle House

Sobaten Japanese Noodle House proves your meal can be nutritious and delicious at the same time. Owner Yosh Shima opened the restaurant four years ago with the vision of bringing healthy, authentic Japanese food to the Calgary area. Sobaten specializes in Japanese noodle dishes and sushi. The restaurant takes its name from the *soba* noodle, which is made of buckwheat. Soba is a staple of Japanese cuisine and is often served in hot broth as a noodle soup. Soba yu, water used to boil the noodles, is even drunk as a delicacy following a meal. At Sobaten, delicious soba soup contains seaweed, shrimp and chicken. Sobaten also serves another Japanese noodle mainstay, *udon*. A thick noodle made from special wheat flour imported from Japan, it figures in sweet and sour dishes and can accompany curried chicken and many other flavor combinations. You'll also find a full range of sushi options, as well as many vegetarian dishes. The atmosphere at Sobaten is casual and friendly. Feel free to slurp the noodles. As Shima-san says, "If you don't slurp, it just doesn't taste good." This is not a joke. The inrushing air from the slurping cools the noodles and makes them taste better. When you're looking for a healthy, delicious and authentic taste of Japan, come to Sobaten Japanese Noodle House.

#105 550 11 Avenue SW, Calgary AB
(403) 265-2664

Toad n Turtle Pubhouse & Grill

With a menu that extends beyond traditional pub fare and an impressive variety of beers and spirits, the Toad n Turtle Pubhouse & Grill is a great place to hang out with old friends or meet some new ones. Try one of the 24 beers on tap from all over the world or sample the amazing collection of over 60 single malt scotches. The Toad n Turtle takes food very seriously and provides an ample variety for different palates and ever-changing weekly features that the locals flock here for. On weekends you must try the Hang Over breakfast with a Caesar or two, while watching a game or reading the paper. The building is an impressive design featuring vaulted ceilings, separate rooms with comfy seating and a fireplace. The Toad n Turtle has a great atmosphere and is filled with friendly staff and customers. When it's nice out, the huge rooftop patio is simply magical. With its own kitchen and bar and a view of the spectacular Rocky Mountains and the city's skyline, it's hard to leave, so come early. The Toad n Turtle is located near the airport and numerous hotels, so you'll find a mix of locals, travelers and regular patrons sharing the food, drinks and fun. Meet old and new friends for excellent food, drink and service at the Toad n Turtle Pubhouse & Grill, or drive up the highway and enjoy the Toad n Turtle in Red Deer.

2475 27 Avenue NE, Calgary AB (403) 717-0670
S Common Point, Red Deer AB (403) 352-4420

Tom's House of Pizza

How is the crust at Tom's House of Pizza? If you truly love pizza, that's undoubtedly the question that is foremost on your mind. The crust is, in a word, delicious. It comes out of the brick hearth oven thin and delicate and is topped with generous amounts of fresh ingredients. The dough and sauces are created right on the premises. The pepperoni, salami and sausage are prepared especially for Tom's. Founded in June 1963, Tom's is the oldest existing pizza parlour in Calgary. With two dozen choices on the menu and an emphasis on local, healthful ingredients, it's easy to see why there are now four locations and another two on the way. Tom's House of Pizza uses only 100 percent Canadian mozzarella and cheddar cheeses. The crusts, sauces and toppings contain no MSG, oils or eggs. The menu options cover all bases to satisfy meat lovers, vegetarians and even anchovy addicts. There is no typical order at Tom's, because the team in the kitchen is just as happy to fix you a pizza with no toppings but cheese, a pizza with six or more toppings and anything else in between. The common bond is that each pizza is made to perfection. To taste how Calgary likes its pizza, try the Tom's House of Pizza nearest you.

17103 James McKevitt Road SW, Calgary AB (403) 254-4410
7730 Macleod Trail S, Calgary AB (403) 252-0111
4812 Centre Street N, Calgary AB (403) 230-2122
3908A–17 Avenue SE, Calgary AB (403) 272-4232
www.tomshouseofpizza.com

Rajdoot Restaurant

At Rajdoot Restaurant, meats marinated with 35 spices and herbs are pushed through five-foot long skewers and laid in clay ovens. It all happens right before your eyes, as the ovens are situated in a windowed viewing area visible throughout the dining room. Rajdoot's Butter Chicken and other Punjabi and Pakistani-based delicacies that arrive at your table are, according to many food critics, the best of their kind in the area. Readers' choice polls in Calgary have bestowed such honors on Rajdoot as Best Indian Restaurant and Best International Dining. The clay ovens not only make for quite a spectacle, but the extremely high heat that they contain is the key to this restaurant's healthful cuisine. The fat on the meat is burned away, leaving chicken, lamb and beef that are as lean as they are flavorful and aromatic. Owner Raj Mall is proud to point out that as a member of the local vegetarian society Rajdoot provides many vegetarian options, too, including curries, stir fries and a delicious roasted eggplant dish called Eggplant Bharatha. "Every diner is like a guest in our home," says Raj, whose guests over the last 18 years have included movie stars and dignitaries visiting from all over the world. Let Rajdoot Restaurant be your destination for fine cuisine from the Indian subcontinent.

2424 4 Street SW, Calgary AB
(403) 245-0181

Catch Restaurant & Oyster Bar

Whether you're planning a casual night out with friends or an elegant event, Catch Restaurant & Oyster Bar can meet your needs. *EnRoute* magazine named this Calgary eatery its Best New Restaurant in 2002. Located in the historic Imperial Bank of Canada building, Catch Restaurant & Oyster Bar is actually two restaurants in one. On the first floor, you'll find the casual San Francisco-style oyster bar with its seafood specialties. The fresh fish is flown in by jet every day from both coasts. With its live lobster and crab tank and a view into the kitchen, you'll swear you were at Fisherman's Wharf as you enjoy your shucked oysters and favourite beers and ales at the bar. Upstairs, Catch becomes elegant, with white linen tablecloths, hardwood floors and crystal stemware. The upstairs menu features a blend of fine Canadian and international cuisine prepared in the French tradition. You'll enjoy fine seafood and fresh, Celtic beef here. The top floor of Catch features a glass roof with a spectacular view of the Calgary skyline and is reserved for catered and special events, such as wedding receptions or business luncheons. You'll find state-of-the-art presentation equipment here and a staff willing to tailor the décor, cuisine and entertainment to suit your taste. Whether you are dressing up or down, bringing one person or a party, come find out what Catch has flown in from the sea.

100 Stephen Avenue, Calgary AB
(403) 206-0000
www.catchrestaurant.ca

Hidden Bistro

Betty-Anne Schafer had worked in the hospitality industry, but a café was a new horizon for her. She drew on her independent spirit and sense of adventure to open the Hidden Bistro. The cozy and intimate bistro was soon the talk of the town. Located just off of the main street of Lacombe, Hidden Bistro is open for breakfast and lunch as well as for that afternoon mocha or specialty tea complimented by a fresh pastry. You can enjoy home-style breakfasts all day long at the bistro. Lunch offerings include hearty soups and sandwiches with fresh coffee always available. Everything is freshly made, and Betty-Anne keeps deep fryers off of the premises. The creative menu offers something new and interesting every day. For traditional favorites made with heart, visit the Hidden Bistro.

3B, 5010-50 Street, Lacombe AB
(403) 782-9490

Il Portico Restaurant

In true Italian spirit, every guest is the guest of honor at Il Portico Restaurant. For 15 years, Il Portico has been a downtown favorite for those in Edmonton looking to raise their spirits. With its earth-toned décor, fine wood tables and large windows, the restaurant feels both settled and spacious. The street-side patio seats up to 70. Those looking for a more private affair can dine in the cellar, which seats 32. Chef Kevin Lendrum serves up the finest in Italian flavors and aromas, including a renowned grilled Alberta beef tenderloin with Chianti butter sauce. In the

Italian tradition, he uses nothing but the freshest ingredients. Diners can watch their food prepared in the restaurant's open kitchen for an enticing preview of sights and smells. Il Portico's extensive wine list has won the Award of Excellence from *Wine Spectator* magazine 10 times. You'll find fast and friendly service at Il Portico, where the customer always comes first. If you're looking for Italian cuisine in a vibrant atmosphere, try Il Portico Restaurant.

10012-107 Street, Edmonton AB
(780) 424-0707
www.ilportico.ca

Edgemont Bar & Grill

When it comes to supporting good health, the Italians know there's no better combination than exercise, good food and time spent with friends and family. Chris and John Pietrovito set out to be a part of that equation three years ago by opening Edgemont Bar and Grill, a restaurant capable of being many things to many people. The Edgemont is located in the World Health Club, one of the largest fitness and spa facilities in Western Canada. You can have breakfast here with your family, try a specially made protein or energy shake after a workout or relax in good-looking surroundings for a dinner that ought to suit kids, couch potatoes and fitness buffs. Thanks to Chef Norm Klettke, the cuisine is about as international as you can get. Appetizers range from sushi to chicken wings. You can indulge in a gourmet pizza, choose from such pub fare as club sandwiches and burgers, or settle down to savour *osso bucco* or a meal-sized salad. Sunday means brunch, and Tuesday brings a gourmet pasta bar with a chance to watch Tony the Pasta Man in action. Edgemont is also a place to play a game of pool or watch your favourite team on a 100-inch projection screen while enjoying one of the draft beers, quality wines or liquors. "People make the business," says Chris, and his staff knows most customers by name. Raise a glass to the good things in life with a visit to Edgemont Bar and Grill.

7222 Edgemont Boulevard NW, Calgary AB
(403) 374-1006
www.edgemontbarandgrill.com

Moti Mahal Restaurant

No city can truly call itself cosmopolitan unless it can boast excellent cuisine from all over the world. Among Calgary's exciting mix of ethnic restaurants, Moti Mahal stands out. Here, the discerning palate may detect Turkish and Iranian influences to go along with the strong East Indian flavours. Owner Harjit Mann calls his hybrid-style Kashmir, noting that it is very appealing to Western tastes. Indeed, Moti Mahal's huge following includes folks who got hooked when this family business started in the 1980s and have remained faithful through its move to its present location in south Calgary. The curries are perfectly spiced and the naan is amazingly tender. According to some, the vegetable samosas are not just the best to be found in Calgary but in all of Alberta. One reviewer said it all when he raved that Moti Mahal exceeds expectations every time he eats there. If you have never tried Indian food before, Moti Mahal offers a great way to experiment with its lunch buffet. Everything is labeled and staff members are more than willing to explain each dish and make recommendations based on how spicy you like your food. Get into the cosmopolitan swing of Calgary by eating at Moti Mahal today.

38–240 Midpark Way SE, Calgary AB
(403) 201-7336

Marv's Classic Soda Shop & Diner

Have you ever had a real old-fashioned ice cream soda? Marv's Classic Soda Shop & Diner in Black Diamond is Canada's only working traditional soda fountain, offering the best in classic beverages from the 1940s and now introducing Marvello Carbonated Ice Cream. Specially made booths and tables, a nickelodeon piano and other antiques take you back to a bygone era, or a scene from *American Graffiti*. The diner-style menu features homemade hamburgers such as the James Dean. Classic hotdogs are made from 100 percent Alberta beef. A candy store offers classics such as Blackjack gum and licorice. An even better reason to come to the shop is to hear Marv Garriott himself, a singer and guitarist. The Canadian Country Music Association nominated him for Duet of the Year 1982. Marv entertains you with Elvis tunes and other 1950s-era favorites while you enjoy your meal. Marv spent 35 years in the entertainment business before starting an antique store and candy shop in the old Mt. View Theatre seven years ago. After reminiscing about the soda fountains of his youth, he put the cherry on top by purchasing vintage ice cream freezers, a soda fountain and other equipment from as far away as New Jersey. Marv uses ancient soda recipe books to create concoctions such as Canary Island and Black Cow ice cream sodas, malts and The Cowboy Trail sundae featuring saskatoon, a Canadian berry that gave its name to a city. To rekindle old memories and create delicious new ones, experience Marv's Classic Soda Shop & Diner, where the past is present.

121 Centre Avenue W, Black Diamond AB
(403) 933-7001 *www.marvsclassics.ca*

Regal Beagle Pub

Most beagles only wish they had wings, but the Regal Beagle Pub in Calgary actually has them—the plump, meaty variety that won *Fast Forward*'s Best Wings poll six years in a row. It's standing room only on wing nights, when customers crowd in for owner Sid Gotmy's flavourful wings and ribs. You are bound to develop your own list of favourites from such variations as salt and pepper, teriyaki, barbecue, honey garlic, suicide and the house specialty, Beagle sauce, which would be hard to reproduce since Sid's recipe is a well-kept secret. Thirteen draft beer choices and a menu that includes salmon and hand-cut steaks promise you will be happy even when the wings and ribs aren't at special prices. Sid's 13-year-old pub is a labour of love for its owner and for such long-time staff members as 13-year veteran Chef Rod Burt and Managers Mike Shupenia and Zee Sayadi. The décor is old school with antique signs and collectibles hung from walls, ceilings and rafters. Sports lovers can find a front row seat for the game at one of 10 television screens. On a sunny day or balmy evening, customers often choose to eat on the patio. Sid took the name of the restaurant from the neighbourhood pub in the television sit-com *Three's Company* that aired from 1977 to 1984. The menu features trivia questions about the show, which you might recall starred John Ritter as a clumsy culinary student. Bring your sense of humour and your appetite to Regal Beagle Pub.

410–14 Street NW, Calgary AB (403) 283-6678
180–94 Avenue SE, Calgary AB (corner of 94 Avenue and MacLeod Trail) (403) 640-7775

Il Sogno

Taking its name from the Italian word for *dream*, Il Sogno has been living up to expectations since opening in August 2000. "If you're dreaming of some outstanding Italian cuisine served with as much joy as it's prepared, then pinch yourself awake and head on down to Il Sogno," writes a food critic for the *Calgary Sun*. Executive Chef Emil Shellborn uses only superior, fresh, organic ingredients for his sophisticated and cosmopolitan clientele. His attention to such details as AAA beef has made the Beef Carpaccio a signature dish. It is served with organic baby arugula and finished in Barolo mustard and Parmigiano Reggiano. Chef Emil makes all of his pastas, including the sumptuous lobster tortelloni. For a full taste of Il Sogno, Emil and his team will serve a four-course meal for the entire table, infusing the traditional flavours of Italy with a New World presentation. An outstanding wine list offers 150 selections. The setting for your Il Sogno experience is a 1910 Heritage Building with hardwood floors and high ceilings. When Il Sogno won *Where Magazine's* Rising Star award in 2001, it was clear that this restaurant had made a strong, favorable impression in a short time. In 2006, the magazine named Il Sogno in the top four fine dining restaurants in Calgary. *Calgary Magazine* has ranked it as number six among the top ten restaurants in Calgary. For lunch or dinner, consider Il Sogno, the restaurant that Calgary has collectively proclaimed *magnifico*.

#24- 4 Street NE, Calgary AB
(403) 232-8901
www.ilsogno.org

Java Jamboree

Les and Ottilia Jaworski opened Java Jamboree in 2002, and have since drawn quite a crowd of followers who pass through to get their daily dose of artfully presented coffee. Your sensory experience doesn't begin with the first sip. It starts, instead, the moment you receive your cup and find that the barista, an artist in an apron, has created a foamy work of slurp-able art right atop your beverage. Latte Art, which has become very popular throughout Canada and the United States, consists of imaginative designs drawn in the milk foam produced when the drink is made. Artists deftly form hearts, *fleurs de lis,* apples and other images while serving up a steady line of cappuccinos, espressos and lattes. The Jaworski's dream was to bring the sensuous coffee drinks of Italy to Alberta. To do so they began by searching for the perfect coffee blends, which they found at a trade show in Seattle. Blended from specially selected beans, Java Jamboree's signature coffee exudes a rich, perfectly brewed flavor that is highly prized by professional cuppers everywhere. Become a patron of the arts, while indulging in your coffee passions with a stop at Java Jamboree.

9-312 5 Avenue, West Cochrane AL (403) 932-6240

Aida's Mediterranean Bistro

The day we dropped by Aida's Mediterranean Bistro, a lady walked in the door and exclaimed, "I love this place." No doubt she was one of the many loyal customers that owner Aida Abboud had just been telling us about, one of the faithful who comes here three or four times a week to feast upon Aida's Lebanese cuisine. *Feast* is no exaggeration, as Aida's is known for its generous appetizer platters for two, featuring many of the delicacies that Aida most enjoys preparing. These include grape leaves stuffed with rice, tomatoes and onions as well as hummus that many say is the best in town. Aida's spinach and lentil soup is just the thing to take the edge off the Calgary chill. For entrées, the Middle Eastern lamb chops baked in a tangy oregano and sumac sauce earn raves, as does Fish Tajen, a halibut steak baked in tahini sauce, onions and cumin. Dawood Basha, meatballs sautéed in a medley of vegetables and pomegranate juice, is one of the many house specialties. It's served with couscous, the Middle Eastern alternative to rice. Famous as well for the Mouhammara dip, a red pepper, walnut and pomegranate juice blend that was liked so much it was once shipped to a wedding in Winnipeg. Healthful ingredients and preparations are Aida's trademarks, so much that health-conscious folks from all over the city are part of the crowd who come here for lunch and dinner. Numerous awards won through the seven years of business include Best New Restaurant in 2000 by John Gilchrist, Best International Restaurant in *Fast Forward* magazine a few years running, and Most Memorable Meal Award (Mediterranean) in 2006. Visit Aida's Mediterranean Bistro and you too will be declaring your love for this restaurant.

2208 4 Street SW, Calgary AB
(403) 541-1189

Black Cat Bar & Grill

Black Cat Bar & Grill welcomes one and all with a friendly neighbourhood vibe, urban casual food and an extensive wine list. This downtown Calgary restaurant serves sandwiches, salads and pasta as well as grilled chicken, steaks and salmon. When owner Val Gaudon opened the Black Cat two years ago, she brought many loyal customers with her. Customers like the intimate atmosphere, where the staff knows them by name and they know the staff. Janice Fell coordinates and manages the bar and grill's upbeat activities, which have a way of bringing people together. Mellow wood floors and warm earth colors help you get comfortable, whether you are discussing world affairs over cocktails or bellying up to the bar with friends to watch sports on televisions scattered around the room. The Black Cat is a flexible establishment, open for breakfast, lunch and dinner. Customers also enjoy stopping for cocktails and conversation after work. The restaurant offers numerous menu choices and features a daily soup, sandwich and entrée special. The Canadian sandwich, made with bacon and sharp cheddar, is a crowd-pleaser; the fish and chips are a great favourite, too. Happy hour packs the house with customers sampling their favourite wine or the vast selection of beers on tap. This bar has so much to offer to everyday life that you owe it to yourself to sample the food, the drink and the company at Black Cat Bar & Grill.

150-635 6 Avenue SW, Calgary AL
(403) 233-7654

The Belvedere Restaurant & Lounge

At The Belvedere Restaurant & Lounge you enter a world of understated elegance and Old World charm. First, unwind in the lounge with a martini and soak in the atmosphere. Relax in the custom-made furniture as you enjoy the view of the Calgary Tower through the Belvedere's two skylights. Then, ready yourself to be amazed at the magic you'll experience amongst the plush draperies, walnut woodwork and discreet lighting as you order from a menu that can only be described as true haute cuisine. Everything at The Belvedere is prepared in-house with regional produce and meats to ensure freshness and variety as well as a keen attention to detail. With a menu that changes at least three times a year, you can rest assured the ingredients are always fresh and always of the highest quality. With your palate satiated by the perfect pairing of food and your selection from one of 750 wines served in Riedel crystal, you'll experience why awards and reviews have placed The Belvedere as the Best Restaurant Overall in Calgary. It is routinely in the top ten in Canada and was voted for the past five years by *Wine Spectator* magazine as having one of the top 500 wine lists worldwide. The Belvedere is as renowned for its exceptional service and deft handling of its accomplished clientele as it is for the wonderfully wrought food. Satisfy all your senses with a visit to The Belvedere.

107 8 Avenue SW, Calgary AB (403) 265-9595 *www.thebelvedere.ca*

Tubby Dog

This is not your ordinary hot dog dive. Though catering to a casual, universal crowd, Tubby Dog offers fast food of real quality in a fun and funky atmosphere. Owner Jon Truch hails from the restaurant and bar business, and his concept is as comprehensive as any professional undertaking. In contrast to the city hot dog stands one walks away from, customers at Tubby Dog will want to stick around for the show. You may watch projections of obscure vintage cartoons and movies, and on the weekend Tubby Dog engages live DJs. The joint is open late for students and other late night fun seekers but upholds a family atmosphere, and Jon's whole family works here. The family makes chili, corn dog batter and pickled eggs from scratch using family recipes; they steam the dogs the old-fashioned way. And lest you think it's all about the trappings, Tubby Dogs are a full meal, in portions up to a half a pound. With the perfect hybrid of food, beer, music and visuals, Tubby Dog has found a hidden niche in the Calgary community and is fast becoming a vibrant destination on the Red Mile. Stop in and rediscover the hot dog for the 21st century.

103–1022 17 Avenue SW, Calgary AB (403) 244-0694 *www.tubbydog.com*

Black Swan Ale House

One of South Calgary's most popular pubs, the Black Swan Ale House serves a vast range of clientele while still maintaining the feel of an English neighbourhood pub. With its vaulted ceilings and airy 7,000 square feet, it can accommodate up to 400 but is run in spirit by a core of loyal regulars. Owners Wayne and Archie Sim have tailored their menu to their regulars' tastes and requests, accruing an impressive selection of domestic and imported beers and some of the best pub fare around. While their breaded calamari and oven-baked chili fries are still favourites, they have recently moved away from the predominantly deep-fried pub foods of old and are featuring a healthier selection of appetizers and salads. The décor at the Black Swan is in the best English tradition—rich with woodwork, stained glass and stand-up tables. On Sunday nights, the pub features live music from the up-and-coming bands of Western Canada. A row of indoor televisions makes the Black Swan a favourite place to watch sporting events. You can enjoy the patio even during the cold seasons, thanks to special outdoor heaters. The Sims take pride in their immunity to trends, offering a reliable and comfortable ambience that hinges on friendly service. For English flavour in the heart of Calgary, visit Black Swan Ale House.

**10455 Southport Road SW,
Calgary AB**
(403) 271-8776

Oh! Canada Restaurant & Bar

Murray Drope is clearly a patriotic person. His restaurant, Oh! Canada Restaurant & Bar, is all about this great country, with a focus on Canadian-inspired dishes using ingredients from within Canada's borders. The three-story restaurant, located inside the Nexen Tower in the heart of downtown Calgary, offers a great view overlooking Century Park through numerous large windows. Chef Justin Kukak prepares patriotic dishes, such as the Gretzky, a smoked turkey sandwich on ciabatta bread. Newfie fish and chips plus Atlantic salmon baked on a cedar plank are other all-Canadian classics. An extensive selection of wines represents vineyards from across the country. In addition to enjoying the delicious food, you just might learn a bit more about Canada from the quirky bits of trivia on the menu. The casual, contemporary space offers patio seating in fair weather. With its great views, relaxed attitude and carefully prepared food, Oh! Canada is an ideal place to share a meal with friends or family, and the Alberta Restaurant Association agrees, honoring it for the Best Casual Dining Menu. The restaurant also offers a large conference centre, flexible catering services and many breathtaking backgrounds for parties and weddings. Oh! Canada Restaurant & Bar invites you to come Eat, Drink and Be Canadian at a restaurant that celebrates the flavours of a nation.

815 7 Avenue SW, Calgary AB (Nexen building) (403) 266-1551
www.ohcanadarestaurant.com

Da Lat

In just three years, Da Lat has become a runaway favourite in Calgary for authentic Thai and Vietnamese cuisine made from scratch. The intimate restaurant serves no more than 30 tables but presents the menu of a much larger restaurant, including such favourites as house-made beef satay and a list of fresh curries served from a traditional clay pot. In addition, you can sample a full selection of Vietnamese coffees, exotic teas, fresh fruit shakes and bubble teas. Chef Kevin Tran, who brings more than 18 years experience to the menu, prepares all dishes personally. Da Lat owner Nadine Huynh met and married Kevin in Regina after emigrating from Vietnam in 1978. There they opened their first Da Lat restaurant and named it for a famous Vietnamese city on a mountaintop, representing lofty standards and a coveted retreat destination. Their success in Regina allowed them to create an even better restaurant in Calgary. "We have put our hearts and souls into Da Lat," says Nadine. "People leave happy. They love the variety." The restaurant offers catering and patio seating in warm weather. For age-old Thai and Vietnamese recipes made right, visit Da Lat.

**1314 17 Avenue SW, Calgary AB
(402) 228-5425**

Divine

Since 1996, those looking for market fresh food with a world influence have been enjoying Divine dining experiences. Divine is more than a name for this restaurant—just ask the readers of the Okotoks *Western Wheel* newspaper. They've voted Divine the Best Place for Lunch and the Favourite Place for a First Date, and said that the restaurant had the Best Homemade Soup and Best Dessert. Owners Darren Nixon and Lareina Wayne won these awards by their dedication to quality and freshness. Nearly everything at Divine is made from scratch, and the restaurant uses a great deal of locally grown and raised food, guaranteeing fresh, vibrant flavours. The food at Divine incorporates flavours from all over the world. Whether it's an Asian noodle bowl with sweet ginger chicken and vegetables for lunch, or a thin-crust pizza for dinner, there is something on the menu for every taste. Want to learn to cook some of these delectable items at home? Darren and his sous chef Adrienne Penny offer cooking classes monthly, giving students hands-on instruction as well as a recipe book and—of course—a meal. The atmosphere at Divine is fun and upbeat, with helpful staff ready to answer your questions and ensure your enjoyment. If you're looking for great, fresh food, treat yourself to a Divine intervention.

42 McRae Street, Okotoks AB
(403) 938-0000
www.divinefood.ca

Jasmine Palace

Drinking tea while eating snack-sized portions called dim sum is an ancient Chinese custom that has taken hold in Red Deer since husband and wife team Jime and Rena Jim opened Jasmine Palace in 1998. The restaurant serves Hong Kong-style dim sum, and diners choose from an array of complementary dishes that may be salty or sweet, including vegetable-filled dumplings, meat and shrimp. The morsels are cooked under high-pressure steam and served in bamboo vaporization bowls. Other offerings at Jasmine Palace are equally authentic, including

a giant Chinese buffet worthy of a hearty appetite and close to 100 á la carte menu items. Jasmine Palace is rightly proud of its fresh seafood, which includes many shrimp and scallops dishes, plus mussels and squid. You will also find vegetarian offerings and a full slate of pork, beef, chicken and noodle dishes. The atmosphere is pleasant with a helpful staff who can customize meals for those with food allergies or particular preferences. Jime studied hotel and restaurant management in Red Deer in 1989 and worked for several restaurants before setting out on his own to recreate the foods of his homeland. Eat in, take out or take advantage of free delivery at Jasmine Palace, open for lunch and dinner seven days a week.

3731 50th Avenue, Red Deer AB
(403) 309-5566

Classic Lunch & Cakery

A classic is something that has stood the test of time and never went out of style. This definition certainly fits Sundre's popular gathering place, known as Classic Lunch & Cakery. It has been

around since 1990, serving the kinds of food that everyone from Grandma to Junior loves. Customers say "excellent" to the potato soup and "even better than last time" to the hamburger soup. Combine one of them with a sandwich for a tasty and wholesome lunch. Everything here is made right here, including the sensational muffins and pies. When you are finished eating and sipping a specialty tea, you will want to visit the gift shop. It is a browser's paradise full of local arts and crafts as well as antiques and collectibles. Travelers from all over the world feel right at home at Classic Lunch & Cakery, rubbing elbows with the regulars who can't get enough of the homemade goodness. Owners Sharon and Reanna Cummins invite you to spend a lazy afternoon with them at the cheerful Classic Lunch & Cakery.

106 Centre Street, Sundre AB
(403) 638-2015

Joe's Blarney Stone Pub & Restaurant

They say that kissing the Blarney Stone in Cork, Ireland will give you the gift of gab. If that's true, there must be a lot of puckering people at Joe's Blarney Stone Pub & Restaurant, one of the friendliest places you'll find. Many of the regulars are on a first-name-basis with the staff and with each other. Owners Joseph and Katherine Ng have been serving up pints and smiles at the Red Deer pub for the past four years. The Blarney Stone is renowned for its excellent selection of draft beers on tap. If you're looking for pub grub, you'll find plenty of it here, with options ranging from nachos and potato skins to chicken wings and a seafood platter. Those looking for something a little lighter can pick from an array of soups and salads. There's always plenty to do at Joe's, with pool, darts and even karaoke for those looking to show off their pipes. With room for more than 200 people, Joe's makes a great place for events and gatherings. If you're looking for spirited conversation, food and drink, pucker up and head to Joe's Blarney Stone Pub & Restaurant.

**38, 6320-50 Avenue, Red Deer AB
(403) 343-7880**

Photo by Simon Law

Taj Mahal Restaurant

The Taj Mahal Restaurant was Calgary's first East Indian restaurant when it was established 34 years ago and remains in a class of its own. A family business, the Taj Mahal serves home cooked northern Indian recipes directly from the table of Amrit and Bassant Chandna. Their children, Sunny and Narula, share in presenting their mother's cooking to the Calgary community and are in training to become the next generation owners of the restaurant. Several generations of customers have become friends of the family over the years. The restaurant is marked at the entrance with a real marble replica of the original Taj Mahal, engraved with the same designs by descendants of the original builders, further symbolizing the legacy that the Chandnas brought from India to Calgary. Inside, the Taj Mahal Restaurant presents a casual dining atmosphere in ambient reds and golds. The Chandnas offer a typical buffet-style lunch and a full dinner menu. The northern Indian or Mogul food is a relatively refined style, concerned with complex spicing rather than heat factor. It revolves around the traditional tandoor, an urn-shaped clay oven in which foods are quickly seared to seal in maximum flavor. The Taj Mahal's menu has won the Best Food award from the Spirit of the West Food Festival for eight years in a row. The restaurant has also been named the Best Restaurant and Best Vegetarian Restaurant in Calgary and continues to win readers' choice awards year after year. The Chandnas invite you to their table at the Taj Mahal Restaurant.

4816 Macleod Trail SW, Calgary AB (403) 243-6362

Quarry Bistro & Wine Bar

As you visit the Quarry Bistro & Wine Bar throughout the year, you will find that the menu changes to feature ingredients at the height of their flavour and freshness. The Braised Rabbit with Pea Risotto or the Prawns Provencal that you enjoyed in the spring may have been replaced by other fabulous dishes from Chef David Wyse's kitchen, but the light and airy atmosphere will not have changed. Your server may be the same person who took your order last time and recommended just the right wine to complement your meal. Don't be surprised if he or she remembers you. David and his sister, Naomi Wyse, have put their hearts and souls into the Quarry, winning strong customer and staff loyalty. Having spent more than 30 years nourishing their love of food and good company in the restaurant business, this sibling team opened the Quarry in 2003. They see their bistro as an expression of their long-held dream to have a little place of their own in the heart of the mountain community of Canmore. Call the menu classic French and Italian provincial. Everything on it stems from local and organic ingredients. Chef David adds his own touches to create meat, seafood and pasta dishes that are equal parts traditional and modern. Discover a favorite dish every season at the Quarry Bistro & Wine Bar.

718 Main Street, Canmore AB
(403) 678-6088
www.quarrybistro.com

Vegetarian spring rolls

Shrimps and scallops in a nest

Coconut mango ice cream cake

Blue Willow, 2007

Blue Willow Restaurant

When you dine at the Blue Willow Restaurant, you'll enjoy wonderful food, excellent service and a rich history that reaches back 50 years. Owner Victor Mah, his son Stan and grandson Patrick have set the standard in Cantonese cuisine for the region and are looking forward to introducing new tastes from the west and east. The current menu is large and includes an array of vegetarian dishes: vegetarian spring rolls or the vegan-friendly green onion cake. This restaurant's entrées will tempt the taste buds with dishes such as shrimp and scallops in a nest with wok-fried mushrooms and pea pods in rice wine, served in a crisp potato nest. Whether you prefer the hot and spicy or the sweet and sour, you will find something to delight your tastes —delectable coconut mango ice cream cake for dessert, perhaps? Cap off the evening with the traditional fortune cookies, and the untraditional: a spinning hot towel to refresh yourself. Each dish is a reflection of Victor's love for the restaurant. "He's married to his business," says his wife, Esther. Born in Saskatoon and raised in China, Mah returned to Canada and eventually started his first café in Fort Saint-John. After marrying and gaining a bit more experience, he opened the first Blue Willow (named after an old Chinese fable) in 1958. The current Blue Willow opened in 1983 and has been the proud recipient of the Best Business award, *Vue Weekly's* Golden Fork award, and *Where Edmonton Magazine* readers' choice for Best Chinese Food and an Unforgettable Dining Experience. With such a history, it's no wonder that members and former members of the Edmonton Oilers and visiting teams stop by. Visit the Blue Willow and dine like an emperor.

11107-103 Street, Edmonton AB
(780) 428-0584
www.bluewillowrestaurant.com

Uncle Louie spinning a hot towel

Bistro Provence

As the seasons change, so does the menu at Bistro Provence, because Chef Nicolas Desinai is committed to using fresh, homegrown ingredients. Remarkably, the local produce goes into recreating the natural flavours of Nicholas' native France. He trained for 20 years in Europe with many recognized chef's before moving to Canada in 1999. His French cuisine is fifty percent bistro style and fifty percent fine dining. He participates in the annual Dine Alberta event, which pairs chefs with local producers to create a special menu for the occasion. Chef Nicolas admits that the only challenge in creating his menu is checking for what is available locally, but he likes working with local food. Bistro Provence is known for its delicious fresh food and an excellent French atmosphere. Nicolas teaches French cooking classes on Mondays, connecting people together with fun and joy. Catering is also available year-round for all occasions. The house, originally built in 1882 as a trading post, boasts character and charm, complete with a little patio for summertime dining. For French cuisine originating from Alberta's soil, try Bistro Provence.

52 N Railway Street, Okotoks AB
(403) 938-2224
www.bistro-provence.ca

The New Dynasty Restaurant

If you aren't in the neighbourhood, it's worth twice the price of gas to drive across town to eat at the New Dynasty Restaurant. That was the way one of Calgary's food critics described this wonderful Chinese restaurant. Of course, tourists and Calgarians from the other side of the city are not the only ones that the New Dynasty Restaurant serves. It has been serving local residents since the team of Dick and John Chan first opened the doors in 1994. Some regular customers even claim that since it opened, they had no need to eat Chinese food anywhere else. The success at the original northwest location sprung the need to satisfy customer demand and Dick and John opened another location in the northeast a few years later. Whether you choose the bountiful buffet of many tasty Chinese cuisine favourites or traditional and authentic dishes from an à la carte menu, you will always leave satisfied. Mix that in with the elegant décor and wonderful service and you'll soon discover that the Chan family has created a classy atmosphere that makes for a festive night out. Visit either location of the New Dynasty Restaurant to find out what everyone is raving about.

#201 - 150 Crowfoot Crescent NW, Calgary AB
(403) 239-3300
#400 - 388 Country Hills Boulevard NE, Calgary AB
(403) 226-5828
www.internetcentre.com/newdynastyrestaurant

The Atlantic Trap & Gill

The eastern coast of Canada reaches far into the West, thanks to the Atlantic Trap & Gill. You'll find knee-slappin' music on the weekends and a laid-back, lively East Coast party atmosphere every day. Owners Tracy Johnson and Jill Johnson opened the Trap eight years ago to give Calgary's homesick maritimers a place to call home and others a chance to let down their hair East Coast style. A ceiling slung with fishing net and an assortment of lobster traps, banners and flags set the mood in this pub. You will find an extensive assortment of beer on tap and seafood at moderate prices. The beer-battered fish and chips is a celebrated favourite here. You will also find steamed mussels, bacon-wrapped scallops and Atlantic lobster. For a Nova Scotia beef dish, try the Halifax donair. Finger food is popular here, too. For a sampler of the Trap's favourite starters, try the Scoff, a platter of wings, ribs, garlic fingers, popcorn shrimp and veggies with dip. Live Celtic music and a big dance floor invite your foot stompin' participation. The vibe is lively and youthful; the clientele, a mixed bag of friendly folks of many ages and backgrounds. You say you've never experienced the East Coast? Well, you can skip the airfare and head straight to the Atlantic Trap & Gill for a pint, a chance to swap stories or to dance the night away.

3828 Macleod Trail S, Calgary AB
(403) 287-8811
www.atlantictrapandgill.com

Sahara Restaurant & Lounge

Sahara Restaurant & Lounge serves the cuisine of Lebanon. This is one of the healthiest cuisines in the world, but your taste buds wouldn't know it. Voted among the top 10 restaurants in Canada by *Where* magazine, Sahara consistently provides high-quality food and ambience to its loyal patrons. From an extensive selection of luscious hot and cold appetizers, soups, salads and dazzlingly diverse main dishes, the Sahara's menu offers everything a discerning gourmet could want in authentic Lebanese cuisine. Patrons can choose from appetizers meant to be shared and savored, the freshest seafood dishes, classic Lebanese dishes such as *shish taouk* (grilled marinated chicken breast with garlic sauce) and Western dishes such as filet mignon cooked

to tender perfection. Dinner guests can choose from two levels of spacious and intimate seating, softly lit and tastefully decorated with murals of the desert, an oasis, the Mediterranean Sea and beautiful green pastures. At night, diners can indulge in lively conversation. Entertainment comes from a belly dancer who winds her way through the tables to the traditional rhythms of Lebanon. The Sahara is open for lunch and attracts a wide selection of people who come for the healthy, exotic cuisine. For a taste of excellence, dine at Sahara Restaurant & Lounge.

739 2 Avenue SW, Calgary AB
(403) 262-7222
www.saharacalgary.com

Photo by Jarusha Photo

Tiffin Curry and Roti House

Named for the *tiffin*, a traditional East Indian lunch box, the Tiffin Curry and Roti House serves up a menu of quick, delicious and authentic Indian food. The restaurant, which opened its doors more than three years ago, is owned by the Ramji family and operated by brothers Aly and Cassim. The father, Bill, provided the idea for the restaurant, while their mother, Naznin, provided all of the recipes. The tiffin is a traditional Indian lunch box that keeps the food fresh and hot. Authentic tiffin boxes are on sale at the restaurant, and patrons who buy one can get a discount on combination meals. The menu is Northern Indian cuisine with a dash of African influence to spice things up. The food is specially prepared every day, using the freshest ingredients picked up by Aly on his daily run to the market. The butter

chicken is an especially popular item, as is the authentic *roti* bread. Roti (*chapati*), a staple of the Indian diet, is a flatbread made with light whole-wheat flour. Roti is used both for dipping and for rolling up with curries. You'll also find traditional *samosas* (stuffed pastries) and many other delicious offerings. The atmosphere is light and friendly, with modern décor. Televisions show Bollywood musical films for an authentic Indian touch. If you're looking for a nutritious, delicious taste of India served in less than 15 minutes, come to Tiffin Curry and Roti House.

188-28 Street SE, Calgary AB
(403) 273-2420

Redwater Rustic Grille

When Lance Hurtubise of the Vintage Group and Ned Bell, the Food Network's Canadian celebrity chef, collaborate, the results are bound to be fresh, vibrant and thoroughly contemporary. That's what diners can expect at Calgary's Redwater Rustic Grille, where West Coast cuisine gets a remake, thanks to Bell's menu and the stylings of Executive Chef Mauro Martina, a seasoned traveler who incorporates influences from around the world. The décor is a combination of casual and sophisticated with soft lighting, burnished cherry wood and travertine tile. A glass-enclosed wine cellar, housing 1,400 bottles of wine, serves as the centrepiece of the dining room. Many of the wines are seasonal specialties from smaller boutique wineries and cannot be found elsewhere in the city. Meals here begin with the Redwater's signature Redwater Redichi, a rustic spread of tomatoes and peppers served on an oven-dried baguette. Popular entrées include rotisserie chicken tacos, double-cut pork chops and seasonal fresh fish. Signature sauces offer a choice of flavourings for meat, fish and poultry dishes. Two in-house pastry chefs make desserts a serious consideration. Look for such specialties as coconut cheesecake with pineapple salsa or a warm brownie with hot fudge sauce and banana gelato. For sophisticated food and surroundings at reasonable prices, try lunch or dinner at Redwater Rustic Grille.

9223 Macleod Trail S, Calgary AB
(403) 253-4266
www.redwatergrille.com

The King & I

At the King & I, brother and sister Bingo and Helen Chung, along with business partner Mel Sanders, offer vibrant Thai food in an elegant atmosphere. The trio opened the restaurant nearly 20 years ago, and over the past two decades has refined the style of the restaurant to reflect their passion for food and customer service, as well as Bingo and Helen's cultural heritage. With Bingo specializing in curries, and Helen, in a variety of sauces, the two head chefs please their customers with a complementary blend of specialty flavors and seasonings. The three owners travel to Thailand periodically to keep up with the latest in Thai cuisine. The menu offers numerous choices, all made without MSG, including meats, seafood and several vegetarian options. It could prove challenging to choose from such mouthwatering selections as tiger prawn curry, Thai barbecue beef and lemon grass chicken. If you are having trouble making up your mind, simply order the King's Feast and receive a variety of appetizers, entrées and coconut rice, all selected by the chef. The restaurant's richly colored dining area and soothing atmosphere invite a leisurely dinner, while the flexible dining areas can accommodate both small and large groups. Come to the King & I for fine Thai cuisine prepared to perfection.

822 11 Avenue SW, Calgary AB
(403) 264-7241
www.kingandi.ca

Japanese Village

Japanese Village delivers fresh and fun meal options by cooking and grilling individually for each and every honored guest partaking of Japanese fare here. With unparalleled flair, owner John Arasaki proudly continues his dramatic 30-year tradition of sensational teppanyaki dining. This form of preparation involves every customer in the creation of his or her own meal grilled over a hibachi. John proudly delights his guests with a myriad of tempting sauces, including ginger, sesame, and John's own Bon Appetites brand of sauces. Since leaving Japan, John has worked extensively in breweries and restaurants under the tutelage of such masters as the renowned Hiro Matsuba and Ted Asai. He is quick to point out that, in the tradition of a Japanese-style steakhouse, Japanese Village consistently focuses on steak and seafood. Sushi is not part of the menu here. For an exceptional blend of Old World technique in the new world setting of Calgary, visit Japanese Village.

317 10 Avenue SW, Calgary AB
(403) 262-2738

Eat! Eat! in Inglewood

Eat! Eat! in Inglewood has a modern sounding name but an old-fashioned feeling. The restaurant, which opened in 2004 in Calgary's oldest neighbourhood, is tucked away among the antique stores, trendy shops and galleries of this charming area. Owners Joanne Bachynski and Dennis Kazakoff will make you feel like an honoured guest when you come for brunch, where you can dine on fabulous food, just like Mom used to make. You can also view the Western themed creations of local artisans here. The restaurant is meticulously clean, and the owners

describe their fare as "good honest food." Dennis insists on fresh garlic and wouldn't even consider the powdered version. Joanne must put some magic in her eggs Benedict, because they cast a spell over all who try them. Inglewood is home to several nature preserves, the Calgary Zoo and the Deane House. When planning a day filled with Inglewood's attractions, be sure to include a visit to Eat! Eat! in Inglewood.

1325 9 Avenue SE, Calgary AB
(403) 532-1933

Shopping & Gifts

greengate
Garden Centres

Greengate Garden Centres keeps an
eye out for innovative products and new
plant cultivars that help southern Alberta
gardeners succeed with their gardens.
Greengate is located on a five-acre lot next
to Fish Creek Park in Calgary, and features
a knowledgeable staff with many members
who go back 30 years with the garden
centres, giving them a superior background
in gardening in Alberta's challenging climate.
Employees at Greengate collaborate with
customers to bring together the right plants
and supplies and to keep you educated on
new innovations, such as mycorrhizae, a
beneficial fungi that delivers consistent
plant nutrition. Pick up your complimentary
copy of *Gardensense* and find out what's
going on in Calgary gardens. You can shop
online or use the website as a veritable
encyclopedia of information on how to
succeed with everything from annuals to
wildflowers. Greengate's Cravo greenhouses,
some of the largest retail greenhouses in
North America, feature retractable roofs
and offer a comfortable environment for
both people and plants with constant
temperatures and floor heating. Greengate
Garden Centres is the official garden centre
of the Calgary Horticultural Society and
contributes support to area gardeners at
many local garden events. You will want to
return often to Greengate Garden Centres,
where special events and sales events take
place throughout the growing season. Plan
a garden that will thrive in Alberta with
a visit to Greengate Garden Centres.

14111 Macleod Trail S, Calgary AB
(403) 256-1212
www.greengate.ca

The Goldworks Ltd

Lethbridge is one of the warmest, sunniest cities in Canada, and a friendly city for families. It is also home to the Goldworks, the Mereski family business. The Goldworks specializes in custom jewellery design and repair. Using new technologies such as laser welding and Matrix CAD/CAM services has increased the design and repair capabilities of the shop, including the redesigning of worn jewellery into fresh new pieces using the original materials. There are five skilled, full-time goldsmiths on the staff. The repair services are so exceptional that the local word is if the Goldworks can't fix it, nobody can. The shop is also known for a large selection of colourful Ammolite that is polished, beveled and ready to be set into jewellery. Owner Dave Mereski comes from a family of jewellers. He branched out to open his own shop because of his keen interest in goldsmithing and jewellery servicing. His staff now includes his wife, Teresa, their two sons, Elliot and Graham, and the talented Earl Hammond, who have all caught his enthusiasm and developed their own specialties in the business. You can expect extraordinary craftsmanship and attention to detail at the Goldworks.

412–13 Street N, Lethbridge AB
(403) 320-0846
www.thegoldworks.net

Lost Ark Antiques

Kevin Praud loves the treasure hunt of the antique business, tracing the historical value of artifacts and revealing them as the treasures they are. He named his Nanton shop, Lost Ark Antiques, in honor of his favourite movie, *Raiders of the Lost Ark*. At the end of the movie, the ark is left unsuspectingly on a shelf in an abandoned warehouse, lost again. It's an inspiring image for an antique hunter: you never know what you'll find. Kevin strives to make the treasure hunt just as rewarding for visitors to his shop, a downtown landmark located in the oldest commercial building in town, a former dry goods store dating to 1902. His stock is diverse, ranging from furniture to jewellery to toys, but he specializes in regional historical artifacts. Nanton, like

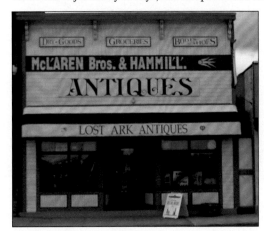

many towns, traces its origins to the arrival of the Canadian Pacific Railroad, and Kevin collects historical Alberta memorabilia. Another chapter in local history involves a brigade of Northwest Mounted Police that were sent to quell a liquor rebellion during the 1870s, items from this episode in history would epitomize both what Kevin hopes to collect and sell. You'll find cowboy heirlooms such as spurs and chaps and Indian art, pottery and beadwork. You may even find something truly unexpected when you go treasure hunting at Lost Ark Antiques.

1915–20 Avenue, Nanton AB
(403) 646-3003

MyFilosophy

Tannis Davidson loves the pursuit of fashion and understands the desire for traffic-stopping style. She knows that the clean lines and exceptional comfort of the clothing and accessories she carries at MyFilosophy translate into expressions of well-being for the wearer. She puts her philosophy of fashion to work at MyFilosophy, with two Edmonton locations. The 142 Street shop carries clothing and shoes for men and women, while the Whyte Avenue store caters strictly to women, taking a modern, urban approach to fashion in keeping with its location. You will find exclusive offerings and many designer trunk shows. By creating a store where she would shop, Tannis appeals to many fashion-conscious women aged 25 to 55. You can arrange for a personal shopping night and locate styles for casual, business and evening occasions as

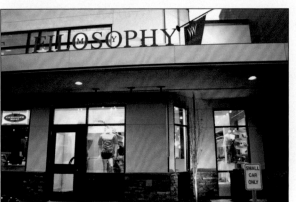

well as lingerie, shoes, handbags and jewellery. Canadian designers include Jacqueline Conoir, Gloria Gaudette and Joeffer Caoc. Experience the feeling of opening a closet filled with possibilities for self expression at MyFilosophy.

10744–82 Avenue (Whyte Avenue), Edmonton AB
(780) 432-8001
9674–142 Street, Edmonton AB
(780) 488-2334
www.myfilosophy.com

Elysion Florals, Antiques & Gifts

Deb Bottomley, the proud shop owner, travels throughout Canada seeking unusual items for Elysion Florals, Antiques & Gifts. Deb, together with Diane Beirnes and a team of friendly, competent staff, lovingly, create inspired custom floral creations. You can order flowers for any occasion, request a gift basket or just browse the eclectic shop for items that surprise and delight the senses. The shop is a feast for the eyes—merchandise is artistically arranged in still-life vignettes. You may find silk and beaded purses for that special occasion, vases in all shapes, sizes and colours, beautiful silver jewellery, handcrafted kaleidoscopes, tiaras, a shawl or other special accessories and, of course, an abundance of flowers and potted plants. Elysion is a member of the Teleflora network of florists, so flowers can be sent around the world, but its mainstay is work for local residents, hotels and businesses, weddings and conventions. Elysion understands the language of flowers, and creates floral artistry that lingers in memory long after the blooms fade. If you are planning a wedding in Jasper, Elysion can help with all phases of planning, including flowers as beautiful as the inspirational setting. Come and enjoy all that Jasper has to offer and check out this little treasure in the Rocky Mountains.

614C Connaught Drive, Jasper AB
(780) 852-3230
www.flowersjasper.com

Old Strathcona Farmers' Market

There has been an Old Strathcona Farmers' Market every Saturday since 1983. One of Edmonton's most cherished traditions, the market started small with about 30 vendors selling fresh vegetables and fruit in a parking lot on the east side of 103rd Street and 83rd Avenue. If 1,000 customers showed up in those early years, the sellers considered it a busy day. Multiply the turn out by about ten, and you'll have some idea of the size of the crowd that will be packing the aisles this Saturday. The mission of the market has always been to bring a touch of the farm to the heart of the city. Therefore, you can expect to find fresh flowers and plants along with seasonal produce, cheese and eggs. The concept has also evolved beyond farm products to include anything that the vendor has personally brought to fruition. As the informal slogan says, You Make It, You Bake It, You Grow It, You Sell It. You might find fresh seafood next to a local potter displaying her latest creations from the kiln. In all, the Farmers' Market attracts about 130 regular vendors offering everything from carrots and cookies to handcrafted furniture and woven clothing. The market moved across the street to an indoor site in 1986, ensuring visitors a comfortable day of shopping no matter what the weather has in store. The market is located in the historic Old Strathcona neighborhood and is open Saturdays from 8 am to 3 pm, year round. Ask a bunch of Edmonton residents what they are doing this Saturday, and someone is bound to tell you that he or she is going to the Old Strathcona Farmers' Market. Don't leave Edmonton without experiencing it.

10130 83 Avenue, Edmonton AB
(780) 439-1844
www.osfm.ca

Spirits West Wine & Liquor Merchants

Bragg Creek boasts many fine shops of an artistic flavour, and Spirits West Wine & Liquor Merchants is one. Owned by Walter and Dale-Shea Cross, this wine and liquor shop boasts an eclectic selection of Old-West style paintings and Native American art. A panoply of collectibles is on display around the shop. Look up to spot the full-sized cougar, poised to leap, an ever-present mascot surveying the patrons. With more than 40 imported beers, an extensive choice of single-malts and a collection of fine wines, you're sure to find something you can relax with that suits your fancy. Among the novelty wines, check out the Marilyn Merlot and Elvis Jailhouse Red. The store holds tastings each Friday and Saturday, along with formal seasonal tastings with an impressive door prize: a case of fine wine and/or Scotch valued at $1,000. The Crosses are active and generous benefactors and participants in Bragg Creek community life. For example, they host an annual Bragg Creek Parade Day complimentary breakfast. The Crosses and Tammy Moon, the shop's manager, warmly invite you to come in and enjoy yourself.

15 Balsam Avenue, Bragg Creek AB
(403) 949-2497

The Heavenly Outhouse

Against the striking backdrop of snow-capped Canadian Rockies, rolling foothills surround the town of Cochrane, just a few miles out of Calgary. Cochrane is an artist's community, bristling with shops that reflect both history and whimsy. The Heavenly Outhouse is one such shop. Dedicated to the legacy of the true Western town with all its quirks, the Heavenly Outhouse bespeaks elegance and humor side by side. The outhouses of the past century have faded away, and the modern-day bathroom demands decoration. Here is where the Heavenly

Outhouse excels. Owners Brenda Poffenroth and Valerie Vassie don't neglect elegance, should that be your desire. Brenda and Valerie stock their shop with every nicety to make your bathroom inviting. Scented candles, lotions and sweet-smelling soaps fill the shop. Fine towels and bathrobes make a fine addition to your bathroom comfort. Whimsical gift items are available to strike a charming country note. It makes perfect sense to have a shop such as this in Cochrane, where the Great Western Outhouse Race closes the streets of the town on the first Saturday of September. Brenda and Valerie invite you to stop in and appreciate the Heavenly Outhouse in all its glory.

312 1 Street W, Cochrane AL
(403) 932-9288

Serendipity Café and Home Décor

For the past five years, Serendipity Café and Home Décor has been a happy refuge in Calgary, offering warm food and fun browsing. Owner Karin Sorensen stocks a colorful array of unusual products, gifts and home décor items that you'll be sure to admire. Look for contemporary furniture, including special pieces for smaller homes and condos. Serendipity specializes in custom gift baskets that draw from its ample inventory. You'll surprise your loved one with the variety and taste of the items in these baskets. Whether you're shopping for a friend or for

yourself, you can expect the unexpected at Serendipity. Smells and tunes from the café will eventually draw you in from your shopping. The café serves gourmet coffee, breakfast and light lunch in a warm and inviting ambience. Cozy yet classy, it has earned a loyal base of regulars over the years. You can mingle and enjoy the conversation while browsing through a diversified mix of home accessories when you visit Serendipity Café and Home Décor.

1319 9 Avenue SE, Calgary AB
(403) 261-2661

Headcase Hats

Do you know a pork-pie from a fedora? If your hat IQ is low, you need to get to Headcase Hats and start studying the subject. The store is stocked wall to wall with hats for men and women. Hats from Canadian suppliers are well represented, though influences from around the world and from every era are evident. Of course, if you're one of those people who remembers movies by the hats the actors wore, then you are an advanced student who will enjoy continuing your education at this fun place. The merchandise is neatly arranged to make browsing easy. You will find sections of classic, formal hats and trendy, casual hats for men and women. The staff members at Headcase have witnessed women transform into seductive divas and men into self-assured gentlemen just by slipping the right hat on their heads. Inspiring people to discover a new side to themselves is what the owner, Sandra Mattar, says her store is all about. Headcase Hats has been supplying the public with everything from top hats to panamas since 2004. Drop by and tip your hat to Sandra and her staff for creating such an entertaining store.

#301, 10368–82 Avenue, Edmonton AB
(780) 435-6601
www.headcasehats.com

Photos by crystal.puim.photography

Freya's Jewellery & Currency Exchange

Freya's Jewellery & Currency Exchange offers exquisite handcrafted jewelry and Canadian gemstones. The shop stocks a large selection of Canadian diamonds in a variety of styles, and each diamond is laser-engraved with pride. Specialties of the shop include hand-wrought and hand-carved rings, pendants and earrings. You'll find contemporary, casual, and elegant traditional designs. The shop's line of hand-carved rings features bands with animal carvings such as bears, wolves and eagles. You can supply the shop with a picture of your favorite pet or animal, and its skilled artists will carve a band design from the image. In addition to a full line of jewellery items, the shop also offers museum-quality Indian handcrafts, as well as a line of Royal Canadian Mint coins, jewellery and watches. The shop also stocks gold and silver charms and Rundle rock. Other services include currency exchange and jewellery and eyeglass repairs. The studio workshop is open to view so that you can watch the three staff goldsmiths at work. All of the staff are knowledgeable and friendly, eager to find that just-right piece for you, or to design a one-of-a-kind treasure. For the finest jewellery and custom, handcrafted designs, come to Freya's Jewellery & Currency Exchange, a proud member of the Canadian Jewellery Association.

108 Banff Avenue, Banff AB (403) 762-4698 *www.freyas.ca*

Ammolite in the Rockies

Ammolite in the Rockies is a shop with a unique focus: the ammolite gemstone, rarer than diamonds, is featured in all of its jewellery. Ammolite is formed from a fossilized marine creature which lived more than 70 million years ago. The fossil is called *ammonite*. While ammonite is found the world over, only Canadian ammonite yields the gemstone *ammolite*, with its brilliant iridescence that rivals the famed black opal. Ammolite stones may display one color or the full visible spectrum. Multi-coloured ammolites reveal different hues from every angle. As early as the 15th century, the Blackfoot people considered ammolite to have magical powers. Today, feng shui masters declare ammolite to be the most influential gemstone of the millennium, with exceptional positive properties. When you see this fabulous stone, you're quite likely to agree. Ammolite in the Rockies offers a variety of jewellery pieces, such as necklaces, pendants, rings and earrings. Other selections include cufflinks and bolo ties. Each piece in the shop's collection is custom-mounted to showcase the stone's full brilliance. You may order custom-made pieces, choosing your own stone. The shop offers silver, gold and platinum settings in any design you wish. A section of the shop serves as a presentation area, where you can learn the history and the processes involved in ammolite production, from mining to the finished gemstone. When in Banff, visit Ammolite in the Rockies to see glorious, luminous jewellery.

110 Banff Avenue, Banff AB (403) 762-4652 *www.ammolite.ca*

Springbank Cheese Company

The Springbank Cheese Company has been operated by three generations of the Hemsworth family, who have been in the cheese business since 1960. A new addition to the Springbank Cheese Co. family includes husband and wife team, Carie Lee and Adrian Watters who opened the Willow Park Village location in Calgary in October 2006. Springbank Cheese Co. features a world of cheese including 360 types of cheese available in their retail stores. Their elaborate website catalogs more than 700 cheeses by alphabet and by type, including goat's milk, sheep's milk, reduced fat, organic, lactose free and rennet free. Another page features gourmet recipes using specific cheeses. You can receive still more personalized guidance at the company stores. Have fun discussing your preferences and tasting with the Springbank Cheese staff. You can even attend classes at the Willow Park Village Shopping Centre location on Macleod Trail. You can learn about blue cheese at the Night of Blues or gain perspective about the different processing of cheese at the Raw Milk vs. Pasteurized Cheeses: The Great Debate. Additional services include custom cheese trays, baskets and seminars. The staff are always interested in different cheeses form around the world so if there is a cheese you wish to acquire, let them know and they will do their very best to source your request. For a friendly and educational cheese shopping experience, visit the knowledgeable team at Springbank Cheese Company.

10816 Macleod Trail S, Calgary AB
(403) 225-6040 or (800) 265-1973
2015 14 Street NW, Calgary AB
(403) 282-8331 or (800) 661-2349
www.springbankcheese.ca

Keltie's Fine Gifts & Collectibles

Personal collections, whether of figurines, plates or music boxes, offer hours of pleasure. Collectors immerse themselves in the intricacies of their subject and remember the hunt for each piece. Dixie and Brian Le Vesconte make such moments possible at Keltie's Fine Gifts & Collectibles. The Calgary shop carries some of the most recognizable names in collectible art objects. It also offers an array of fine gifts made in Alberta. Among the M.I. Hummel figurines you will find at Keltie's are the special Canadian editions. You will find Canadian Mounties from Cherished Teddies and exclusive cottage miniatures by Lilliput Lane. Porcelain figurines are plentiful and stylistically diverse, from classic figures by Armani and NAO by Lladro to baby-faced Pendelfin bunnies and exclusive Disney classics. The shop carries Waterford crystal,

Belleek vases and handblown glass paperweights by Glass Eye Studio. Look for amazing sculptures from Thomas Blackshear and the All That Jazz collection. Red Hat fans will find a growing collection of official Red Hat items. Revel in the details with a visit to Keltie's Fine Gifts & Collectibles.

Willow Park Village
#570-10816 MacLeod Trail SE,
Calgary AB
(403) 271-6661 or (888) 600-3220
www.keltiesfinegifts.com

Community Natural Foods

Community Natural Foods' two locally owned stores have been the hub of Calgary's holistic health community since 1977. Those who shop and work at Community fervently believe in

supporting local organic farms, fair trade suppliers and family farms. Community offers a wide variety of quality products, including organic produce, bulk foods, organic and free range meats, and organic and GMO-free grocery items. You will find nutritional supplements, bath and body care items, ecological and natural household products, holistic books and culinary supplies. Also, look for vegan, wheat-free and celiac appropriate selections and more. The 10th Avenue market is home to the Sunflower Café with hearty lunch and snack options. The knowledgeable staff at Community Natural Foods are eager to help you achieve your lifestyle goals and make your shopping experience a true education in health and well-being.

1304 10 Avenue SW, Calgary AB
(403) 229-2383
202 61 Avenue SW, Calgary AB
(403) 541-0606
www.communitynaturalfoods.com

Blooms & Butterflies

When you purchase any floral arrangement or a fine gift from Blooms & Butterflies, chances are you will be impressed by the Oriental influence that the owner, Jorene Mei Law, brings with her from her home city, Hong Kong. Jorene and her team have a passionate attachment to flowers, just as butterflies have an intense relationship with blooms. The team approaches every order with creativity and a dedication to their customers, traits that have won them a loyal following and many referrals. Blooms & Butterflies arranges worldwide deliveries of floral gifts and fruit baskets, promising to go that extra mile to ensure you and those you care about are well looked after at reasonable prices. Furthermore, Jorene and her husband, Alan, use uniqueness and affordability as guides in their gift selection process. They bring back porcelain treasures such as collectible tea sets and figurines as well as Northern Ice candle holder art pieces from around the world. Since floral creations and special gifts say more than words ever could, the Blooms & Butterflies team sincerely invite you to experience the Blooms & Butterflies flower power.

#228 Willow Park Village, 10816 Macleod Trail SE, Calgary AB
(403) 271-5352 or (888) 877-5199
www.bloomsandbutterflies.ca

Cobblestone Corner

Sometimes Shelley Keane has to pinch herself to prove she isn't dreaming. She loves owning her own shop and stocking it with those special finds that make her and her customers smile. Home décor, jewellery and a complete line of gifts and apparel for baby are among the reasons women have found to browse the Cobblestone Corner since 1999. Local arts and crafts, garden décor and accessories are among the unexpected finds they will bring home. Shelley travels and searches to find the items that fill her shop and keep the merchandise turning over regularly. She loves interacting with her customers, who share with her an eye and a taste for the unusual. Men shopping for their sweethearts know to come to Cobblestone Corner for its huge selection. The wonderful staff are always on hand for friendly advice. For an upbeat and eclectic shopping experience, check out what just came in at Cobblestone Corner.

#319 1851-Sirocco Drive SW, Calgary AB
(403) 686-8880

The Scottish Shoppe

If you've got a reason to dress up in Highland wear, then you understand the importance of proper fit, from your Prince Charlie or Argyll jacket and wool tartan kilt to your ghillie brogues. That's why people who need Scottish garb come to the Scottish Shoppe. The shoppe has a 34-year history in Calgary and prides itself on genuine clothing and other imported Scottish goods. Irishmen find products from their homeland, too. Owners Jim and Freda Osborne understand the importance of Scottish heritage to Calgary, where a quarter of the population is of Scottish descent. They rent kilts in several well-known tartans and use a local kilt maker for made-to-order kilts. They also sell tartan scarves and ties. The Osbornes are members of the Scottish Tartans Authority, an organization of tartan weavers and retailers dedicated to tartan documentation. For weddings, couples find the items they need for an authentic Celtic wedding, including rings, bridal tiaras and tartan ribbons for bouquets and bridal garters. You can even arrange for a Scottish piper. Giftware includes pewter and hand-cut crystal. The quaich, Scotland's traditional cup of friendship is particularly suited to bridal toasts. You will find jewellery featuring clan crests, fine art prints, shoes for Highland and Scottish country dancing and traditional musical instruments such as penny whistles and Celtic hand drums. When heritage matters, visit the Scottish Shoppe.

1410 4 Street SW, Calgary AB
(403) 264-6383

Durand's Limited Editions

Whether you are a serious collector in search of a high-end collectible, a casual shopper looking for a gift or a Corporate buyer, you'll find something delightful at Durand's Limited Editions. Owners Monty and Susan Durand, with son Jon, take a personal interest in their clientele and keep a lookout for items they know will please individual customers. The spacious Calgary store is loaded with such treasures as Swarovski crystal, Walt Disney Classics Collection, Lladro and Bradford Exchange products. Durand's features a varying range of products from plush Bearington Bears to Lord of the Rings pewter, Windstone Dragons and Myth & Magic. You will find Swedish art crystal by Mats Jonasson, animal sculptures by Sandicast, Mill Creek Studios and Country Artist as well as porcelain by Franz. Durand's provides gifts and collectibles for any price range or taste. The shopping experience at Durand's is a relaxing one, letting you explore its wide selection of products from around the world. Anyone who collects Lilliput Lane's tiny English cottages or the Comic Art of Guillermo Forchino, will know they've come to the right place. Monty and Susan have been in business more than 12 years. Before them, Monty's parents, Dan and Hazel Durand, owned Durand's Diamonds and Jewels, a store equally respected for its discernment. Discover for yourself why Durand's Limited Editions inspires customer loyalty.

2404 Centre Street N, Calgary AB
(403) 277-0008 or (866) DURANDS (387-2637)
www.durandslimitededitions.ca

Cozy Corner Creations

Shopping for kids is a breeze at Cozy Corner Creations. Handcrafted wooden furniture makes the perfect gift for the special little ones in your life. Picnic tables, benches, chairs and toy boxes fit the lifestyles of the young and fun-loving. Custom-made rocking horses promise to deliver years of entertainment. You'll admire the fine craftsmanship and high quality wood used at this shop. The smell of pine and sturdy spruce fills the air. Each piece is coated with oil for a long-lasting finish. Notice the attention to detail and smooth surfaces. All pieces are constructed with functionality and safety in mind. Furniture comes fully assembled and ready to paint. It's up to you to grab a brush and apply the colors of choice. Co-owners Elvin Janzen and Colleen Buchanan, a father-daughter team, combine their talents to bring you the best that wood has to offer. Adult-size picnic tables, folding RV tables, desk top video shelves and coat racks are also available. Cozy Corner Creations invites you to take a peek at the wonderful world of wood.

4522 Shannon Drive, Olds AB
(403) 507-8910

Stan Groff Saddlery

Stan Groff keeps alive the Western Alberta traditions of artful saddle making and leatherwork at his studio, Stan Groff Saddlery. Growing up in Saskatchewan, Stan received a belt-making

kit. This small gift led to a love of leather-crafting and all things relating to the cowboy lifestyle. As a young adult, Stan made his way to the Northwest Territories to become a gold miner. The life of the cowboy called to him, though. He found work with a large saddle making company and, for 10 years, learned the skills involved in turning leather into saddles, chaps and harnesses. In 1980, Stan ventured out on his own, starting out of his basement and then quickly expanding as word of his talents grew. Stan specializes in a style of leather carving called *Sheridan*, which features intricate floral detailing. Using the techniques and skills learned over many years, Stan produces high-end custom saddles, clocks inlayed with tooled leather, harnesses and other cowboy accessories. Stan's list of satisfied customers includes many celebrities, Jackie Chan and Tom Selleck amongst them. Bring home your own piece of Western Alberta tradition with an exquisite leather saddle from Stan Groff Saddlery.

608 Centre Street S, High River AB
(403) 652-7190

Rose Cottage Gifts & Accessories

A stroll past the brightly painted murals and historic stone facades of downtown High River takes you to a shop with a 20-year history of welcome. Rose Cottage Gifts & Accessories is a holdout from a simpler time and a refreshing change from big city shopping centres. Even the prices let you know you have left the big city behind. The store takes its name and much of its inspiration from the previously owned Briar Rose Tea Room. Today, casual shoppers and serious collectors seek out Rose Cottage for its popular collectibles, gifts and home décor. The colorful displays and stained glass accents set a relaxing tone. Owners Tom and Naomi Coates can provide insight into the product lines and place special orders for the collector with

something specific in mind. Look for such sought-after products as Bearington Bears, Franz porcelain and Bohemia crystal. You'll also find scented candles and Carol's Rose Garden stationery. The large selection of costume jewellery is an attention-getter. For a shopping experience that combines country friendliness with first-rate merchandise, visit Rose Cottage Gifts & Accessories.

110 3 Avenue W, High River AB
(403) 451-7657

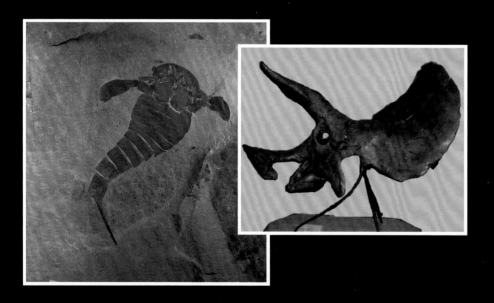

The Fossil Shop Inc.

The Fossil Shop invites customers to peer millions of years into the past with fascinating displays of fossils and minerals. Since 1986, the dedicated team have stocked an amazing series of finds from around the world. Whether you have a beginning interest in fossils or are a serious collector, the Fossil Shop has something to pique your interest. See the complete skeleton of a cave bear or a beautiful spiral shell of an ammonite. The shop carries dinosaur, mammal, insect, sea life and plant fossils as well as minerals. Each fossil has a unique story of how it is a clue to the past. As you examine a fossilized bone complete with bite marks, it is easy to let your imagination wander to all the possibilities of how the creature died. The Fossil Shop also carries a variety of gift items, including educational books, t-shirts and miniature model dinosaurs. For the fossil lover who has everything, consider a dinosaur bone belt buckle or pair of trilobite earrings. The store serves collectors from around the globe and ships items worldwide. Visit the Fossil Shop—come touch the past.

61 Bridge Street, Drumheller AB
(403) 823-6774
www.thefossilshop.com

Heirlooms Antiques Calgary

Bill and Bente Picken bring more than three decades of experience in antique dealing to Heirlooms Antiques Calgary. Before opening their Calgary store they spent 35 years as traveling antique dealers, doing antique shows. In 2006, Bill and Bente moved their collection of more than 12,000 pieces to a central location. The fine furniture selection includes many Victorian pieces in heavy oak, walnut, mahogany and maple. Heirlooms carries many rare figurines from Hummel, Doulton, Worcester and other makers. The store also displays beautiful jewellery pieces in gold, silver and costume, including cameos and Sherman rhinestones. It has artworks ranging from oil paintings and watercolors to needlepoint pieces, Inuit carvings and pottery. You'll also find fine china from Moorcroft, RS Prussia, Royal Nippon and others. If you're a photography buff, be sure to check out the Heirlooms collection of cameras, some of which date to the 1850s. Die-cast models and dolls are just a few of the antique toys at the store. Everything is beautifully displayed. Bill, Bente and their staff are available to answer any questions. If you're looking for one-of-a-kind antique pieces that will become your family's heirlooms, visit Heirlooms Antiques Calgary.

#101 7004 MacLeod Trail SE, Calgary AB
(403) 301-4822
www.antiquescalgary.com

Dragonfly Creations

Owners Clair Wilson and Jane Keelan have spent the last 12 years specializing in distinctive gift baskets at Dragonfly Creations. If you walk into this Calgary shop, you can ask to participate in the basket design, but most customers rely on the expertise of the owners and their staff. The themed baskets found here are beautifully designed and customized to suit every recipient personally. For those who love fine foods, Dragonfly concocts such delights as the Pasta Please basket, a colander loaded with Italian specialties, or a basket filled with the makings for the

ultimate Canadian breakfast. You'll find baskets just for chocolate lovers, for gardeners or for the person in your life who mans the barbecue grill. Clair and Jane put together the kind of bath and body products that offer spa style luxury at home. They also know just how to greet that newborn baby with soft toys, blankets and such specialty clothing as no-scratch mittens and Robeez slippers. You will find a basket for a pizza party or a movie party. Any cook would be delighted to receive a stylish container filled with stainless steel kitchen gadgets or a set of mixing bowls complete with specialized measuring tools. You could spend countless hours collecting thoughtful products to create a personalized gift, or you can come to Dragonfly Creations, where the products and the presentation are flawless.

1611 14 Street SW, Calgary AB
(403) 209-8609
www.dragonflycreations.ca

A Baskethound Gift Baskets

A Baskethound Gift Baskets hand delivers gift baskets in Calgary and surrounding areas and can ship lovely ready-made gift baskets anywhere in Canada. Through its website, you can ship a basket filled with gourmet treats and unusual gift items 24 hours a day, seven days a week. Owner Gayle Impey loves custom work. If you have an idea or theme in mind, she can work with you to craft a basket that will capture your vision. *Gift Basket Authorities Digest*, a leading trade publication, has featured Gayle's designs. Gifted Associates, Inc., a leading industry organization, has honoured her work. A Baskethound carries a large assortment of chocolates, sweet and salty goodies, and luxurious bath and body products. For children of all ages, Gayle

offers plush pets by Webkinz. Each comes with a secret code that lets you enter Webkinz World on the Internet. The Magnetic Classic Games Collector Tin is an interesting choice for someone with time on their hands, such as a hospital patient. A Baskethound offers adorable items for babies and new parents that are both useful and humorous. You can slip some Oil of Old Age into a birthday basket or make a car wash fanatic happy with a combination of sponges, cleaning supplies and treats. For sympathy, celebration or romance, consult A Baskethound Gift Baskets. You'll make someone's day.

Calgary AB
(403) 201-1166 or (877) 570-0757
www.abaskethound.com

Lina's Italian Market

Lina's Italian Market brings the flavors of Italy to Calgary. Lina Castle, proud Italian, opened the store and restaurant 15 years ago to share the joys of her heritage. Lina, along with her son Marino and husband, Tom, make sure shoppers get an authentic taste of Italy. The bakery specializes in all manner of Italian and Sicilian pastries and delicacies. The cheese shop has more than 80 fresh, delicious varieties from which to choose. You'll love the delicious deli meats. A variety of fresh pastas, coffee and similar goods are in stock, as well as ceramic ware and other items from Italy and around the Mediterranean. The market has many books on Italian cooking that will teach you how to prepare a delicious, authentic Italian feast. The friendly, knowledgeable staff is there to answer any questions. Those looking for a delicious meal will delight in the restaurant's offerings, which include that greatest of all Italian imports, the freshly made pizza. Or try one of Lina's cold cut sandwiches, stuffed peppers, sausages or veal scallopini. For dessert, there's luscious gelato in many flavors. Enjoy a steaming cup of cappuccino with your meal. Come to Lina's Italian Market for a taste of great Italian food, plus Italian goods and culture.

2202 Centre Street NE, Calgary AB
(403) 277-9166

Ashwood's Home Décor

Ashwood's Home Décor is a lovely Cochrane shop of country furnishings with a little touch of shabby chic for good measure. Barb and Heather Gould, the mother-and-daughter owners, have a flair for home design and furnishings that's reflected in the casual elegance of the shop's vintage and new furniture. The eclectic mix of antiques, modern furnishings and home accessories makes for an exciting shopping experience. Antique art is definitely a focus, with the vintage chandeliers, stained glass pieces and metal Amish barn stars. As an Alberta exclusive, the shop carries the Bridgewater Pottery line of earthenware from England. You'll find home décor items from Quebec and Nova Scotia and from Europe. The shop stocks bath and kitchen accessories, linens and carries a huge bedding line called Pine Cone Hill. To keep your home sparkling clean, try the Caldrea line of natural cleaning products. Barb and Heather are always pleased to share their knowledge of home decorating with you. With the store's kaleidoscope of ever-changing treasures, you'll want to visit more than once. Don't miss a chance to browse Ashwood's Home Décor for that just-right piece for your home.

110–2 Avenue W, Cochrane AB (403) 932-5252 *www.ashwoodshomedecor.com*

Son of the Pharaoh

The mystique of ancient Egypt has been drawing people to a curious shop on Calgary's 17th Avenue since 1990. At Son of the Pharaoh, owners Emad Adly and Carol Card have assembled a collection of beautiful jewelry, home décor and gifts that will make you dream of the land of pyramids. Necklaces like the ones that queens once wore, jewelry boxes inscribed with hieroglyphics and bowls made of alabaster and marble are just some of the treasures to delight the most exotic and discerning of tastes. Statues of gods and goddesses stand guard throughout the store. Drums and other exotic instruments invite you to resurrect an ancient rhythm. Whether you are inspired by Egyptian spirituality, a student of its history or just someone who enjoys distinctive handcrafted imports, Son of the Pharaoh is the store for you. Emad is always happy to share his vast knowledge of what each piece represents. He is proud to carry belly dancing and other folk costumes along with the art, jewelry and décor. Looking for a chair shaped like a royal throne that will make you feel like Ramses at home? Find this and so much more at Son of the Pharaoh.

1512 17 Avenue SW, Calgary AB
(403) 265-5152
www.sonofthepharaoh.com

Jungling Works

A store overflowing with gifts for the home, Jungling Works stocks everything from duvet covers to hand-spun glass. Form, Function, Fun is the mantra that Debra Jungling and her husband, David Carter, keep in mind when deciding on new products for their store. The selection changes with each season and keeps up with the latest trends in design, fashion and innovation. Many home décor items are one-of-a-kind pieces crafted by Canadian artisans. The savvy home chef will find a wide array of kitchen accessories of the highest quality. Debra and David pride themselves on their personal relationships with the store's loyal customers. If you can't find something here, they are happy to find it for you. Jungling Works is the perfect place to purchase a wedding or other special occasion gift, and Debra offers artistic gift wrapping, which is often admired as much as the gift itself. Debra is a third-generation Drumheller resident. Her store is housed in an historic building that was once Drumheller's first bakery, built in 1920. Surrounded by history and family traditions, Debra and her husband work to keep their storefront looking beautiful, and have planted the boulevard in front of Jungling Works with wooly thyme and a breathtaking garden display. As a result, they have received a revitalization award for contributions to the Drumheller Valley. For a shopping experience that'll please everyone, visit Jungling Works.

299 1 Street W, Drumheller AB
(403) 823-2208

That's Crafty!

The perfect punctuation to an afternoon's drive into the countryside, That's Crafty! is housed in a 1,800 square foot barn in the midst of a prairie panorama. When June Evans opened her combination antique and gift shop, tearoom and lunch spot nearly 18 years ago, it was with the help of neighbors and friends and the belief that a personal greeting can brighten everyone's day. That attitude is still reflected in the personal service June and her staff give to each customer. Inside the quaint barn, patrons will find a mind-boggling array of gifts, from hand-painted refrigerator magnets to hand-stitched quilts and antique Hoosier cabinets. The shop displays the work of more than 300 Western Canadian artisans, and more than 50 professional consigners supply antiques. Items from as many as 300 individual consigners are also on hand, ensuring that everyone will find something they love. The tearoom, open for lunch or tea, features a patio with a breathtaking view of rolling hills. The tearoom's bakers pride themselves on their much-lauded cinnamon buns. There's nothing like a sweet, gooey fresh-from-the-oven bun when you're out shopping. Sip from a steaming cup of tea and enjoy the shop's yearly changing theme wall. Past themes have included chocolate and the Alberta centennial. Get away to the country for a day at That's Crafty! and you'll surely find just what you're looking for.

26 km. W on Highway 9, Drumheller AB (403) 677-2207 *www.bigblueteapot.com*

The Gift Designers

If you find yourself wandering the aisles of department stores looking for the perfect gift for that special someone, spending hours but still coming up empty handed, a call to the Gift Designers is in order. Noreen Giesbrecht, a gift specialist, opened the shop in 2002 to offer customers a wide range of gifts for every occasion. Gourmet coffee, chocolates and fruit, candles, picture frames and body products are among the goodies in Noreen's bag of tricks. Choose one of many pre-designed theme baskets or tailor your gift or basket specifically to your friend. Golfers will love the package designed just for them, with golf balls, tees, a book on improving their game and even a gift certificate to a local course. Other themes include Summer Fun and Movie Night. Noreen's gifts come in baskets, bowls and platters worth preserving, so your friend will enjoy the container long after the goodies are consumed. In addition to baskets, you can order fresh flower arrangements and stuffed animals from the Gift Designers. Noreen is proud to make her living by helping make people happy and shares her fortune by contributing to an international organization that helps women start micro-enterprises. So take back your free time and let the Gift Designers create the perfect gift for your business associates, friends and family. Visit the shop or online store today.

Calgary AB
(403) 201-5021
www.thegiftdesigners.com

Gorgeous Glass

Perhaps the word Glennie McKirdy hears most frequently when people look at her dichroic glass jewellery and gifts is "gorgeous." With that accolade in mind, Glennie and co-owner Doug Pickles named their five-year-old business Gorgeous Glass, and proceeded to live up to their business name with every new creation. They display and sell their eye-catching jewellery and gifts every week at the Calgary Farmers' Market. Their dichroic glass, with an iridescent quality similar to fire opals or the feathers of a hummingbird, makes art of all sorts of items, from pendants and rings to tiles, nail files and plates. Dichroic glass is a spin-off from the space industry. The multiple colour effects come from thin layers of metallic oxide, such as titanium, silicon or magnesium, fused to the surface of the glass in a high temperature kiln. Gorgeous Glass also produces high-end beaded jewellery from some of the world's finest glass beads, including Swarovski crystals and Venetian glass beads. For gleaming jewellery and gifts, contact Glennie and Doug or visit their booth at the year-round Calgary Farmers' Market, open Fridays, Saturdays and Sundays.

4421 Quesnay Wood Drive SW, Calgary AB
(Calgary Farmers' Market)
(403) 933-2912

The Cactus Trading Co. and Neon Cactus Wines

The Cactus Trading Co. and Neon Cactus Wines are two stores in one spot. You can browse through fine gifts for your friends or discover wine or spirits for any get-together. The Cactus Trading Co. has several rooms full of jewellery and gift items. The fabulous jewellery selection includes sterling silver, amber and wood designs, along with interesting shell, leather and beaded pieces. The one-of-a-kind stone rings, earrings, pendants, bracelets and watches will astound you. Distinctive gift items run the gamut from Himalayan salt lamps and T-Lite holders to handmade paper products and Rocky Mountain soap gift sets. Special candles and holders are on display alongside crystals, home décor items and much more. The Cactus Trading Co. also stocks clothing items and accessories, such as designer sweaters, denims, Montana suede jackets and handbags. On the other side of the business, Neon Cactus Wines offers a full selection of wines and champagnes, as well as dozens of single malts and specialty beers. The shop also carries glassware and wine accessories. The knowledgeable staff members, all of them well-versed in the inventory, are happy to help you choose the perfect accompaniment to your gathering. For a truly distinct shopping experience, come to the Cactus Trading Co. and Neon Cactus Wines.

204 5 Avenue W
(Points West Shopping Centre),
Cochrane AB
(403) 932-4475

Pots 'n Peppers

Your mama knows, being home at the range was never like this. Except for the warm country welcome, the only thing old-fashioned about this upscale, fresh, funky and completely functional kitchen store is its charming plank floors. You'll want to spend an afternoon just browsing, never mind catching up, on the latest gadgetry, cookware and table linen designs offered in the Pots 'n Peppers culinary repertoire. Discover new materials, such as heat resistance silicone, that have revolutionized the kitchen tool market. See the latest fashion trends for your table designed by April Cornel. The store also stocks knives, bakeware and stemware from high-end brands such as Henckel, Emile Henry and Riedel as well as everyday basics like a quality peppermill. Delight in the fine balance and weight of an exceptional knife. Marvel at the bright colour selection and superior performance of the baking products. Come and see the stemless wine glass line from Riedel, perfect for picnics or informal entertaining. Learn how the latest cappuccino machines can deliver a latte on demand and sample a brew on-site. The shop stocks gourmet foods perfect as a hostess gift or for those special dinners, along with candles and music to set the mood. Owners Claire Breeze and Alex Souvairan see cooking as a fun, memory-packed way to bring family and friends together. Drop in today and you can look forward to improved food preparation, exciting entertaining ideas and items to make cleaning a breeze from the friendly and knowledgeable staff at Pots 'n Peppers.

**212 1 Street W, Cochrane AB
(403) 932-1175**

Chinook Honey

Art and Cherie Andrews began their life among bees with a few hobby hives. At the time it was an enjoyable way to relieve stress and now, over a decade later, Chinook Honey Company has grown to 300 hives with a retail store on the honey farm. Art and Cherie have developed a passion that they love to share with others. With the use of their indoor observation hive they demonstrate to young and old alike the many fascinating aspects of honey bees. Some bee activities, such as the queen bee laying eggs and perhaps even a new young bee emerging from its cell, can be witnessed. Worker bees bringing in pollen and performing the wag tail dance are also frequent sights. Sampling all the bee bounty is educational as well. Whether it's health products such as bee pollen, propolis or healing creams, or tasty treats such as the many specialty honeys and candies, you are invited to try it before you buy. That includes their new product, mead (honey wine). Mead, also known as the Nectar of the Gods, is the oldest fermented beverage in the world. Art has been perfecting his recipes for years and now produces it onsite as well as offering it for sale in their store. In addition, Art and Cherie host a Harvest Festival every year in late August. Whether you want to learn more about the amazing honey bee or just shop for great honey, mead and other unusual products, Chinook Honey Company is the destination for you.

16 Street W at Highway 7, Okotoks AB
(403) 995-0830
www.chinookhoney.com

When Pigs Fly

When pigs take wing, anything can happen, and When Pigs Fly is a store name that lets you know right away you are in for something special. Owner Jenny Sherwin searches high and low to find fun gifts that you won't find elsewhere. Unusual jewellery, home décor items and garden pieces are waiting to be discovered. The extensive collection of jewellery ranges from the fashionable upper end to everyday wear. You'll enjoy browsing through the kitchen and household section, which stocks a large selection of pottery from Hillborn Potteries, as well as Zen-inspired pieces. Would you like a toucan can opener or a parakeet garlic press? The shop has it. After all, the store is about fun. When Pigs Fly carries a wide range of stained glass artwork that will turn any ordinary window into something that will brighten your day. It also specializes in high-quality, high-fragrance candles for any occasion. Whimsical garden accessories such as wind chimes are ready to adorn your indoor or outdoor garden. You'll find a zoo-full of animals—stuffed, ceramic and porcelain. When Pigs Fly has portraits of animals and animal statues for the garden. Naturally, you'll find piggy banks, including the granddaddy of all piggy banks, the 25-pound, 24-foot porcelain bank that will save enough loonies and toonies to pay off your mortgage. For gifts that will make you smile, or roar, come in to When Pigs Fly.

10470-82 Avenue, Edmonton AB (780) 439-9127 *www.whenpigsfly.ca*

Bat Sheba

Taking its name from the wife of King David in biblical times and from an imported fragrance by the same name, Bat Sheba offers a wide variety of gift items that make everyone feel like royalty. Owner Meg Paulsen strives to provide beautifully crafted gifts that are diverse and elegant. There is something for every occasion, and the staff is knowledgeable about all of the products. Meg takes pride in offering many products made locally or elsewhere in Canada, for example, Derek Alexander leather handbags and Warm Buddies. Indulge yourself in bath products by Crabtree & Evelyn as well as the ever popular Canadian-made Zen products and more. Perhaps you know a very small person who could use a pair of Robeez, the perfectly posh baby shoes. Bat Sheba also carries Bella glass made in Syria, stunning glassware that includes plates, bowls and vases and brings magic to any room. Equally beautiful is the Arabeska glassware from Poland. Each piece is a mouth-blown creation that is alive with colour and shape. Glassware made in Thailand is also a beauty to behold with silk embedded in each piece. You will also find Bradford exchange collectables to add to or complete your collection. For a truly special gift, stop by Bat Sheba.

103 3 Avenue W, High River AB
(403) 652-3944
www.batsheba.com

Gracie and Gruff Fine Toys

When you look through the window at Gracie and Gruff Fine Toys, you know you are in for a magical time. Kids of every generation deserve a toy store such as this. Owner Duane Schreiner envisioned a store where children and parents could have a fun and memorable experience while enjoying wonderful service and selection. One visit and you will see that he has succeeded. *Toys and Games Magazine* named this shop Canadian Toy Retailer of the Year, the *Calgary Herald* gave it the Readers Choice award and *Alberta Venture* called it the best little toy store in Canada. As an independent toy store, Gracie and Gruff is free to offer toys and books from all over the world. The ever-changing inventory ensures that you'll always see something new. Educational toys, plush, books, puzzles and games are only a few of the items you'll find at Gracie and Gruff. Combined with classic tin toys and collector's items, the selection appeals to the young and young at heart. While the Macleod Trail and Bankers Hall locations are stocked with treasures, they are uncluttered and have wide, accessible isles, inviting all to come and explore. A 12-foot gazebo at the Macleod Trail site gives children a place to read or try out toys while parents and grandparents locate the perfect gift. From books and revived classics to the new favourites, come to Gracie and Gruff Fine Toys.

9309 Macleod Trail S, Calgary AB (403) 692-6644 Bankers Hall, 315 8 Avenue SW, Calgary AB (403) 264-6678 *www.gracie-and-gruff.com*

Itinerant Flowers

When Ken Nguyen started Itinerant Flowers, his mission was to provide floral masterpieces to suit everyone's budget. Nguyen had a love of orchids and a knack for creating resplendent floral arrangements, but he opened Itinerant Flowers in 2004 with little more than a dream and a love of beauty. Today, the original downtown location is a hub serving a number of satellite locations throughout Calgary, providing loyal patrons with beautiful flowers for every occasion. Nguyen and his staff love to create gorgeous arrangements of dried flowers that will last for years to come, and can easily craft exotic fresh or dried arrangements to suit any style. From corporate gatherings and elaborate weddings to everyday arrangements for loved ones, Itinerant Flowers has done it all. Nguyen's customized approach guarantees each customer will leave his shops satisfied and with an armload of something sublime. Careful delivery is a major part of the service provided at Itinerant. Every arrangement, no matter how great or small, receives the personal attention it deserves, and is guaranteed to arrive in the same splendorous condition it was in at the shop. With its superb service, attentiveness and high-quality selection, Itinerant Flowers is a place you'll want to visit.

315 8 Avenue SW, Calgary AB
(403) 292-0566

Touchstone Gallery

Touchstone Gallery nestles on the main floor of the historic Davey Block, a 1926 building. Combining art and history, the gallery breathes charm. Gifts of all kinds fill every nook and cranny. The gallery features an impressive list of Western Canadian artists and is known for its unusual collection of pottery. Expansive picture windows display glass and metal artwork sure to lure you in. Once inside, the handcrafted jewelry, eye-catching wall décor and framed paintings dazzle the eye. Green thumbs may take note of the charming garden figurines. Owner Lorraine Shippobotham relocated from Calgary a short time ago and is enjoying the rural feel of Olds. Much to her delight, customers arrive at her door from all over Southern Alberta. Lorraine takes great care when selecting her inventory. Her choices reflect her philosophy of life: The simpler it is, the better the statement. Take some time to explore Touchstone Gallery and see how that idea has been translated into reality.

5002 50 Avenue, Olds AB
(403) 556-8188

Honey B's

It's a long way from California to Calgary, but Honey B's has shortened the distance considerably, at least for those seeking great design. Honey B's, which opened in Kensington in 2004, is devoted to the Shabby Chic style that started in California and has gained popularity as it moves north and east. Barb and Murray Brown, owners of Honey B's, understand the style. Shabby Chic's cottage feel integrates old and new. Furniture is often painted white or ivory. A worn or distressed look accentuates texture rather than colour. You'll find refurbished antiques here, many refinished by Barb. You'll also see accessory pieces, such as crystal, silver and pottery, with the pale colors and vintage overtones of the style. Honey B's popular chandeliers are exclusive to the shop. They are made of wrought iron that has been painted ivory with clear or pink crystal drops hanging from every arm. Honey B's casual, livable look invites you to find new uses for items you already own. A repainted dresser could end up in an entryway. An antique window frame might become wall art. The Browns' shop is a study in how to achieve Shabby Chic elegance. Use a wrought iron gate as a headboard or stack up antique suitcases for a nightstand. Put some California casual in your home with a visit to Honey B's.

28 12 Street NW, Calgary AB
(403) 283-0272
www.honeybs.com

The Colourful Cook

Do you like discovering that perfect stocking stuffer or personalized gift? At the Colourful Cook you will. A charming, specialty kitchen shop, the Colourful Cook offers a wide selection of kitchen knickknacks and cooking tools. Packed from top to bottom, this little shop is so full that it is easy to spend hours browsing through all of the amazing products. Zwilling JA Henckels knives, Le Creuset cast iron cookware, Riedel wine glasses, Cuisinart small appliances, OXO Good Grips and Zyliss gadgets and Emile Henry dinnerware are a few of the well known products carried in the store. Come in and find out how a mango splitter or a pineapple slicer make eating fruit a delight. Test the edge of a fine knife blade and learn how to maintain it properly. Discover how a Lampe Berger can eliminate most of the bacteria in the air when you are cooking and then sit prominently on your mantelpiece as a work of art. Watch how our glass cleaning E-Cloths wash a window with just water and leave no streaks. Never clean the bottom of your oven again with one of our Chef's Planet oven liners. Find that specialty item you've always wanted, or simply discover something new with the help of the experienced staff. From great bridal or hostess gift ideas to practical kitchen tool innovations, the Colourful Cook has it all. Come in and check them out for yourself!

**721 8 Street, Unit 103/104, Canmore AB
(403) 678-3922**

Photos by Char Woodman

The Replenishing Shoppe

Dee Berryhill, founder of the Replenishing Shoppe, welcomes you to her world of relaxation with a complete line of stress-relieving products. Soothing music filters through the aisles—the pleasing sounds of nature, piano, flute and harp carry your worries away. Enticing smells of incense sticks, cones and smudge bundles fill the air. You'll find a complete line of fragrant bath salt fizzes, body soaps, scrubs and lotions. Blended aromatherapy oils promise relief from the pressures of the day. Scented and unscented candles beckon in a wide range of colors, shapes and sizes. A wide variety of books on inspirational topics, meditation, self-help and spirituality guide you down the path to a calmer life. Blank journals invite you to record your journey. The shop has power bracelets, wish bracelets, dream catchers and wishing wands that invoke magic. Pre-packaged gift sets for the man or woman in your life and Bliss Boxes for weddings make gift-giving a delight. You can add an inspirational greeting card to complete your package. Most of the products are made in Canada, and quite a few of Dee's suppliers are located in Calgary. Orders arrive quickly, making your wait time shorter and your items more affordable. The Replenishing Shoppe expects to add an aroma therapist and a Reiki master to the long list of services available to patrons. Leave your hectic day behind and enter the world of the Replenishing Shoppe.

907 Heritage Drive SW, Calgary AB (403) 301-0961 *www.replenishingshoppe.ca*

Willow Haven Flower Shop

The Willow Haven Flower Shop is more than just your average flower shop. It's an enchanted wonderland filled with vibrant colours, fragrant scents and a glittering array of baubles that attract the eye and delight the mind. Willow Haven is owned and operated by Netherlands native Leo, his wife, Jules Nugteren, and staff, who use creativity and community awareness to find the ideal gifts and décor pieces to complement their customer's tastes. The shop is filled with everything from jewellery and peacock feathers to live finches that chirp merrily in antique birdhouses. You'll also find exotic yet simple furniture, rustic plant holders, candles and many other home décor items. Leo's passion for flowers, however, is evident at every turn. Fresh flowers, ordered directly from the Netherlands each week, pack the large refrigerated room, which is filled with nature's sweet floral scents. From these, Leo and his staff create flower arrangements and bouquets that are elegant and lavish, yet simple. Their work decorates wedding parties, corporate events, gala celebrations and everyday occasions. In addition to roses, chrysanthemums and lilies, Willow Haven uses calla lilies, gloriosa, traditional hyacinths, plus a myriad of more exotic flowers. Take a mini-vacation to a blossom-filled paradise with a trip to the Willow Haven Flower Shop.

105-826 Main Street, Canmore AB (403) 678-6775 *www.willowhaven.ca*

Rose's Stuff

Rose's Stuff is more than just a craft supply store. It's a place where friends and neighbors gather to share ideas and learn new skills. Owners Rose Goerzen and Ila Bonnell enjoy crafting every bit as much as their customers. Keeping current on emerging trends in the cottage craft industry is what they do best. You'll find the latest designs in stickers, decorative papers, ribbons and scrap booking supplies. Rubber stamps used to create handmade greeting cards come in every size, shape and theme imaginable. A whirlwind of colour whips through the shelves, and inkpads and paints display a rainbow of choices. You can personalize your masterpiece with supplies from Inkadinkado, Art Impressions, Stampendous, Karen Foster Designs and many more. Rose's Stuff also offers classes. Join a group or bring your friends and create one of your own. Planning a special event such as a wedding, birthday, graduation or baby shower? A wide selection of invitations, balloons, streamers and thank you notes await you. For all of your creative needs, experience the joy of one-stop shopping at Rose's Stuff.

2025 19 Avenue, Didsbury AB
(403) 335-9210
www.rosesstuff.com

Ribbons & Bow Gifts

If variety is the spice of life, shopping at Ribbons & Bow Gifts is a gourmet's delight. *Eclectic* sums up this nifty little showplace that has surprises around every corner. Co-owners Myra Dykstra and Amy Kohut enhance your experience with their knowledge and top-notch customer service. A selection of food items, fashion accessories and jewelry pieces fulfill your hankering for the unusual. You'll find no generic products here. Looking for products to warm your spirit

and soothe your soul? Try the one-of-a-kind bath salts, body lotions and aromatherapy candles that are hand-picked by Myra and Amy. Select items for your home while you're walking the aisles. Choices range from dazzling wall décor to luxurious bed linens. There are so many goodies, so little time. The inventory constantly evolves and changes. New products are added daily to pique your interest each time you pay a visit. A little retail therapy is yours at Ribbons & Bow Gifts.

2023 19 Avenue, Didsbury AB
(403) 335-8840

J & D Gifts

Amidst the majestic Rocky Mountains of western Alberta, Jasper's J & D Gifts is a local institution. Entering the shop, you're likely to find locals playing a game of cards, chess or backgammon in the shop's warm and inviting atmosphere. Native Indian and Canadian artist's work are abundantly represented at this shop, along with many unusual locally made clothing items. Intriguing porcelain figurines depict the history and rich lore of the area. You'll also find a terrific selection of kid's gifts and games. For kids and grownup kids, J & D Gifts stocks

a beautiful selection of stuffed animals. Take one home in lieu of the real thing. Owner John Dobrota carries on his mother's business, begun in 1974, which brings the legend and lore of native and Canadian arts to you. John, a native of Jasper, is a well-respected source on the history and geography of this breathtaking part of Alberta. He's pleased to share his knowledge of the area with you. Jasper creates memories and this shop preserves them. Stop in and see the magic of Jasper at J & D Gifts.

600 Patricia Street, Jasper AB
(780) 852-4262

Victoria's Flowers & Gifts

Step into Victoria's Flowers & Gifts and feel the glow of a gentler era. The store, built in 1925, sets the stage for your encounter with expertise and first-class service. A fireplace seating area, flanked by hardwood floors, glass panels and high ceilings provides a charming centerpiece. Both the lovely building and the arrangements created by Victoria's floral and gift-giving experts demonstrate impeccable attention to detail. If you're planning a special event, let the staff walk you through the process. According to their motto, they don't just sell flowers, they sell emotions. Simply put, staff members match your arrangement to the emotion you wish to convey. Gift items include elegant baskets of luscious fresh fruit, dish gardens and green or blooming plants. Don't fight the urge to buy a little something for yourself. Brighten up your home or office with a floral fantasy from Victoria's Flowers & Gifts.

1816 20 Street, Didsbury AB
(403) 335-3444
www.victoriasflowersandgifts.com

Photos by Leah Dawonik Photography

Perfume Emporium and Gift Shop

If it is new and hip in New York, it is new and hip at Perfume Emporium and Gift Shop. This is the place to go for high-quality apparel, accessories and rare fragrances. Browse the fragrances from Paris, Italy and New York City and check out the wide selection of bling, including Jacob watches. The store specializes in the most current urban street wear for men and women, including hard-to-find oversizes and brands such as Snoop Dog, Sean John, Baby Phat and LRG. Owner Paula Bramble imports limited-edition fashions from the States and offers many exclusive designs. She is glad to accommodate special orders for fashions not readily available in the city. The shop is a favourite with professional athletes and musicians and those who appreciate hip hop fashion. Even shorties are accommodated here, with kid's sizes at reasonable prices. The kids will love the brand-name gear from Baby Phat, J-Lo, Rocawear and many more. Stop by Perfume Emporium and Gift Shop to get street smart.

10038 164 Street NW, Edmonton AB
(780) 489-4731

Jasper Camera & Gift

When you walk into Jasper Camera & Gift, you sense a tradition of knowledge, service and community. These are the values of owner Ross Pugh. Housed in an historic building that dates from 1924, Jasper Camera & Gift is three stores in one. In addition to selling quality cameras and binoculars and traditional developing services, the shop also specializes in large-format printing. Staff can take your photo and resize it or put it on canvas. Your photo can be transformed into a wonderful piece of art by digitally recreating it. A gift section features local Canadian gifts such as stationary and home décor items. The store also has a selection of beautiful books on

Jasper, the Canadian Rockies and Canada in general. The history of the store reaches back 64 years and three generations. It began with two of Ross's grandparents, Orren and May Olson, who saw a need to help visitors preserve memories of their visit and to record the history of the area they loved so much. By the time Ross's parents, Jack and Barb Pugh, assumed responsibility for the store, it had already gained a reputation for friendly and professional service, which continues to this day. Come to Jasper Camera & Gift, where you can find what you need to sustain important memories.

412 Connaught Drive, Jasper AB
(780) 852-3165
www.jaspercameragift.com

Around the Town

Everyday is a holiday at Around the Town. You'll smile when you walk in the door. Displays for every season and any special occasion will delight even the most reluctant shopper. Owners Gayle Martin and Janice Johnston showcase the largest selection of Department 56 in Edmonton. Finely-crafted, lit buildings from Dickens, North Pole, New England, Snow Village and Christmas in the City are available year-round. If you can't find that special piece, let Around the Town track it down for you. Customers can also register their villages and get notification of

yearly limited edition, numbered pieces so they don't miss that special treasure. If Halloween is your thing, you'll be delighted by more of Department 56 handpainted buildings as well as spooky life-sized display pieces that will make your house a favourite stop for all the little ghosts and goblins. Around the Town is also home to Winston and Millie, two great dogs that product-test all the great doggier treats. Don't forget the great pet clothes by Coco Napoleon and locally made pet soaps and pet toys, so perfect for that new pet. Whether you need a great wedding gift, baby gift or some over-the-top holiday decorating, Around the Town is the place to go. If you need help, Around the Town offers seasonal home and corporate decorating to make your life a little easier. Get into the holiday spirit every day of the year with a visit to Around the Town.

10428-82 Avenue, Edmonton AB
(780) 433-8696

World Antiques & Interiors

You'll find Lorraine Dalen's World Antiques & Interiors in Calgary's trendy Inglewood district. It's of the longest established antique shops in Inglewood and has one of the finest collections of antiques and collectibles in Calgary. Housed in an historic 100-year-old building, the shop contains treasures ranging from a 1700s Georgian clerk's desk to a 2007 pewter vase. Depending on the day you visit, you may find an Edwardian armoire, a Georgian tilt-top table or a hand-carved, museum quality Victorian dining room hutch. Stained glass, Tiffany and Art Nouveau lamps are well represented in the collection, as are fine paintings and Canadian antique pieces. Looking for jewellery? Whether your taste runs to vintage or the hottest new looks, the shop's large selection has something just right for you. If you're looking for home accessory items, the shop has fine china sets, vases and clocks. Whether you just want to browse for an afternoon or you are hunting for a specific piece, you'll be entranced by this lovely shop. You'll also be pleased with the reasonable prices. Lorraine's newest addition is the Retro line of furnishings and accessory items. Make a point to come see the delights at World Antiques & Interiors. Open the door and enter this fabulous mix of the past and present.

1312 9 Avenue SE, Calgary AB
(403) 237-8686 or (888) 855-8686
www.worldantiquesandinteriors.com

Frog Kisser's Den

Unexpected pleasures await you at Frog Kisser's Den. Like the frog that was kissed by the princess, everything in the store has been magically transformed by Lucia van der Meer's paints, brushes and needles. Lucia recreates common objects to give them a new life that transcends their intended life span. Her store is a funky, colourful collection of handmade and imported jewellery, clothing, furniture and more. Her workshop is inside, so you can see all kinds of creative projects in the works when you visit. Nothing is dull or ordinary when Lucia gets her hands on it. Old jeans become skirts and army fatigues sport multi-coloured frills. Lucia also selects handmade and vintage pieces from around the world that express the individualistic spirit of the store. You never know what you will find at Frog Kisser's Den, but it's bound to be a new, exciting treasure every time. Come and see what Lucia is up to today.

10836 124 Street, Edmonton AB
(780) 488-0329

Rustic Residence

Whether you are furnishing a country cottage or seeking a striking piece for a contemporary condo, Rustic Residence has ideas. There is no limit to the places where you can add rustic charm, say owners Dwayne and Ally Morberg. Their inventory of furniture, accessories and décor includes many one-of-a-kind pieces that may be here today and gone tomorrow. "If there is something you really like, make an inquiry, because it may be the last," says Dwayne. Melanie Schmitke, an interior decorator by trade, oversees the design of the showroom, her creations flowing from one space to the next and into the basement of this store in historic Inglewood. She assists customers in all phases of home design, from initial concept to color selection, and even makes home visits. If a piece intrigues you, Dwayne and Melanie suggest that you take it home to try on for a few days. Then you can make payment arrangements if you decide to keep it. Each item in the store has personality, as does the 90-year-old building itself. Customers are charmed by the tin ceilings and squeaky floors. After they have browsed the merchandise, they often comment that they want to take all of it home with them. Find furnishings for an entire home or just that right piece at Rustic Residence.

1215- 9 Avenue SE, Calgary AB
(403) 205-4200

Earth's General Store

Michael Kalmanovitch, owner of Earth's General Store, is a man with a mission: save the world one customer at a time. Since opening the doors in 1991, he's championed environmental causes. Consume less, consume wisely, consume locally and love lots more—that's the message the store conveys. This eco-friendly attraction offers an array of environmentally friendlier products. Fair Trade certified and organic products take the lead. The wide variety of coffee, tea, spices and chocolate will entice anyone. Bamboozles, pre-folded diapers made from bamboo, are just one of the variety of diapers offered as an earth-friendly alternative for the littlest ones. Best selling titles like *Heat* by George Monbiot and *The Last Generation* by Fred Pearce present the readers with the latest in environmental thinking. You'll discover a plethora of chemical-free cleaning products for every room in your house. Organic fruit blend deodorants, Burt's Bees lip balm, shampoo and conditioners are among the many animal-free body care products. Unique to this store is the wide assortment of healthier menstrual products. Come to chat, share ideas and shop. You'll leave Earth's General Store with new ways to live lighter on Mother Earth.

10832 Whyte (82) Avenue, Edmonton AB
(780) 439-8725
www.egs.ca

Janice Beaton's Fine Cheese

Janice Beaton believes in good food and taking time to enjoy it properly. She's the owner of Janice Beaton's Fine Cheese, which has two successful stores in Calgary's Mt. Royal and Kensington districts. She's also president of the Calgary chapter of Slow Food International (www.slowfood.com), an organization devoted to fostering local food traditions. Artisanal cheeses from such sources as Neal's Yard Dairy in London, England and David Wood's Salt Spring Island Cheese Company in British Columbia will spark a desire to share your finds with friends. At the shop, you will find up to 250 cheeses from small producers and many exclusive products. You can order a cheese tray for your next party and buy tapenades and pestos, too. The store stocks everything for making fondue, including the cast iron pot, special mix and crusty baguettes. You can buy raclette cheese rounds and the machine for warming them. Both stores give classes in cooking and presenting cheese as well as pairing it with wine. Take time to savour

cheese made in small quantities at Janice Beaton's Fine Cheese.

1708 8 Avenue SW, Calgary AB
(403) 229-0900
1249 Kensington Road NW, Calgary AB
(403) 283-0999
www.jbfinecheese.com

Le Papier

As the name implies, the products at Le Papier are mostly paper-based. This Edmonton stationery and gift store is a favourite place to find a humorous card or rubber stamps. The shop carries nicely bound journals and scrapbooks. You will find indigenous art on some of the note cards as well as handmade paper. You can frame your treasured photos or line them up in good-looking albums, thanks to the gift collection at Le Papier. Long-time customers make regular stops at Le Papier, which opened in 1989. Says one such customer, "I've been going to Le Papier for ages now, and they really do always have what I want . . . even when I'm not quite

sure what that will turn out to be." Owners Audrey Chipeniuk and Anne Boisjoli enjoy updating their product lines and seeking new items not commonly found in gift shops. Some of the gifts that don't involve paper include candles and stuffed animals. Humor extends beyond cards into many gift items. Le Papier started small, but now boasts 2,100 square feet packed with charming variety. Next time you are on Whyte Avenue, have some fun shopping for cards and gifts at Le Papier.

10352 82 Avenue, Edmonton AB
(780) 431-0322

Elegant Expressions

For the past three years, Elizabeth and Elyse Moland have been adding a touch of elegance to homes and offices across Edmonton through their exceptional gift and décor shop, Elegant Expressions. This charming and creatively designed shop features a variety of delightful vignettes that showcase hand-crafted items from around the globe, including award-winning jewelry pieces, richly textured textiles and an assortment of fossil art that would make a statement in any setting. Elizabeth and Elyse, an outgoing mother and daughter team, have become experts in choosing just the right accents for their discriminating clientele. They have built up the company's reputation for excellence in a short time by offering exceptional service at every turn. In addition to providing a fine array of quality products from Asia, notably Tibet and India, Elegant Expressions also offers in-home consultations and custom-ordering options that will let you design the home interior you've dreamed about. Elegant Expressions takes pride in displaying items that are unusual, elegant and practical, as well as visually stunning, which makes it the ideal place to browse for everyone on your gift-giving list. The luxuriously understated atmosphere of Elegant Expressions is welcoming to men and women alike. The Moland's gracious; expert service will make any do-it-yourselfer feel like a design pro in no time. Give your home a new spark of life with Elegant Expressions.

**628 Riverbend Square,
Edmonton AB
(780) 988-7944**

Mulberry Lane

Mulberry Lane's owner, Dianne Clay, believes that the character and soul of your home is directly related to the character and soul of the things you put into it. Her store offers gorgeous pieces of furniture, clocks, lamps, gifts, home accessories, and bath and body items. You will discover a large selection of unique jewellery from around the world, including silver and gemstone jewellery from Israel and Mexico. The store space is open and uncluttered, yet filled with things that delight. Pieces in the showroom reflect not only impeccable quality, but also a true individuality that cannot be replicated. Mulberry Lane combines the old and new, the simple and complex, the bright and subdued, quality and utility, with great results. You will love browsing through the collection of must haves and are sure to find that perfect piece for your home. Mulberry Lane is an excellent place to find beautiful gift items that will be appreciated for years to come. The staff members are friendly and helpful, and they clearly enjoy what they do. They are always available to make design suggestions or provide gift ideas. Mulberry Lane provides a bridal registry, plus wish lists that are very helpful in fulfilling those holiday dreams. Be sure to sign up for the mailing list to stay up to date on new items and offers. For a delightful fusion of the fresh and funky, classic and contemporary, visit Mulberry Lane.

110-5227 Lakeshore Drive, Sylvan Lake AB (403) 887-6211
www.mulberrylane.ca

Mildred's Collectibles & Antique Furniture

Mildred's Collectibles & Antique Furniture is more than just a store, it's a community meeting place. If you like antiques and good conversation, you'll love spending time in this antique emporium. Owners Mildred Towsey, Robert and Linda Mohr and long-time employee Klaus welcome collectors from near and far. All of the pieces displayed are acquired from the Alberta area but originally hail from around the world. Treasures in the 7,000 square foot showroom range from classic china tea cups and saucers to turn-of-the-century clocks and furniture. Most of the pieces are from the 19th or 20th century. Brand-new collectibles include keepsakes from Cherished Teddies, Royal Doulton, Disney and Hummel. More than 50 coffee cups hang on the wall, but they're not for sale. They belong to the members of four collectible clubs and customers that meet regularly at the gathering spot. Local chapters of collectors, enthusiasts and connoisseurs come together to share both information and their passion for the art of collecting. For a little bit of nostalgia or expert craftsmanship, you'll find that one-of-a-kind antique or special collectible at Mildred's Collectibles & Antique Furniture.

6814 104 Street, Edmonton AB
(708) 438-0368

Maligne Canyon Gift Shop

The Maligne Canyon Gift Shop is a gift shop like no other. Most stores boast that you can find a gift to fit every budget, but here you really can. You can find quality gifts that range from a 25-cent post card to a piece of authentic art valued at over $800,000. Owner Galal Helmy is proud to provide high-quality jewellery, garments and leather goods, as well as an extensive collection of history books to inform you about the area and its people. The shop's location allows for a spectacular collection of original Native Indian and Inuit art. Well-known artists include Norval Morrisseau, Eddy Cobiness, Jackson Beardy and the Hunt family of the Kwakiutl Nation. The First Nations Group of Seven, a famous group of landscape artists from the 1920s, is well represented. You'll also find one of the largest collections of Legends sculptures anywhere. Don't forget to pick up film. For gifts that capture the spirit of Alberta, visit Maligne Canyon Gift Shop.

Maligne Lake Road, Jasper AB (780) 852-3583 *www.malignecanyon.com*

Your Divine Indulgence

Everywhere you look at Your Divine Indulgence, the best of Canadian arts and crafts are on display. Owner Danna Melnyk selects only well-made, high-design gift items for her shop. From handcrafted jewellery, stained glass and wall art to fragrant candles, soft bathrobes and delicious gourmet foods, Your Divine Indulgence is a treat for the senses. The 2,000-square-foot showroom devotes whole departments to kitchen wares, baby items and bath products and separate rooms for western and nautical themes. You'll find inspiring displays and delightful surprises from floor to ceiling. "If a piece of furniture catches your eye and it isn't bolted down, just ask for a price," says Danna, who has watched her business grow incredibly since opening in 1980. It originally occupied a humble, 500-square-foot space above her father's pharmacy. The Sylvan Lake shop is her second location, which opened in 2000. The seasons bring in new tones and styles to reflect the time of year, so come often to Your Divine Indulgence for distinctive gifts with local origins.

5004 50 Street, Sylvan Lake AB
(403) 887-4498

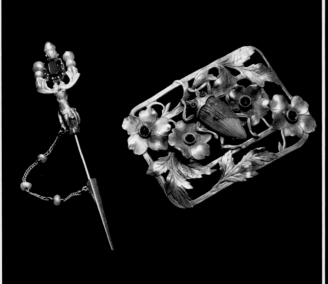

The Black Swan

The Black Swan showcases the finest jewellery available. It carries thousands of exquisite and rare pieces of antique and modern jewellery, and each piece comes with its own story. Hand-picked heirloom pieces date from 1800 to 1950. For the past 18 years, owner Michèle Gallant has built a solid reputation as a purveyor of fine antique jewellery and other objects. Michèle's passion for rare beauty shines through—her impeccable taste is apparent throughout the store. Exquisite Japanese jade necklaces and rings draw your attention. Try on a Victorian glass bracelet and admire the fine craftsmanship. Italian mosaic and micro mosaic broaches are handmade from dozens of tiny tiles, often arranged in a colourful floral motif and set in brass. Vintage objects made from unusual materials stand out in the extensive collection. You'll find jet, a lightweight black material from the coal family. Bakelite is one of the first plastics ever developed. Bringing jewellery and *objets d'art* to you from around the world, Michèle catalogues the story and heritage of every piece she acquires. If questions come to mind while you tour the well-appointed store, just ask. Michèle loves to share her knowledge and passion with new customers as well as her regulars. Visit the Black Swan and discover treasures from the past that you'll cherish far into the future.

10822 Whyte (82) Avenue NW, Edmonton AB
(780) 414-6768

Castle Mountain Home Furnishings

If you prefer your fittings to be comfy, cozy and warm, Castle Mountain Home Furnishings is the store for you. It's Canmore's largest and longest-established furniture store. Voted best home décor shop in 2005 by a local readership poll, this popular Bow Valley store stocks items specially designed for a Rocky Mountain ambience. With 8400 square feet of space, the showroom features a broad collection of wares from quality manufacturers. Dining room sets by Broyhill, Lane and Live Edge Design catch your eye. For that perfect night's sleep, select from the gallery of Serta mattresses. Show off your style and panache with a lamp from Pacific Coast Lighting or a carpet designed by Dash & Albert. Interior decorators on staff can assist you in coordinating styles, textures and fabrics. A wide selection of custom-designed upholstery lets you pick just the right piece for your home. You can also be your own designer and order from a catalogue of fabric and color choices. Local deliveries are free. Owners Don and Beryl James have been at this location since 1997, and they are committed to finding the perfect mix of furnishings and accessories to complete the mountain home look that you love. Home-sweet-home dreams come true at Castle Mountain Home Furnishings.

1310 Railway Avenue, Canmore AB
(403) 678-6037
www.furnishcanmore.com

Calgary Farmers' Market

Looking for some of the finest food, produce, arts and crafts in Alberta? The Calgary Farmers' Market offers these products directly from local producers. Inaugurated three years ago, the market brings vendors from across the province together in the centrally located hangar at Currie Barracks. One of the expressed missions of the market is to bring country food to city tables. To that end, you'll find a huge variety of locally grown produce, much of it organic. Vendors proffer fruit trees, mushrooms and herbs. You'll also find artisan cheeses, fresh seafood and meat ranging from grass-fed beef to bison. Those looking for prepared foods will find dozens of options at the market, from pies and ice cream to Chinese and Mexican foods. Local artisans show handmade clothing, soaps and crafts. The atmosphere is lively and friendly, harkening back to the old-fashioned town-center markets of yesteryear. For good times and homegrown products that nourish your community as much as your family, shop the Calgary Farmers' Market.

H6, 4421 Quesnay Wood Drive SW, Calgary AB (403) 244-4548 *www.calgaryfarmersmarket.ca*

Coyote Trading Company
—Offering an Alternative Shopping Experience

Coyote Trading Company is proud to be in their 16th year of business and prouder yet to offer unique, quality handcrafted gifts and home and garden décor to Central Alberta. The goal of the shop has been to offer items that are alive with the warmth, spirit, sun and soul of Mexico. They have been gradually introducing beautiful handcrafted items from other areas across North America. Today, when you visit what appears to be a quaint little store in Lacombe, you will be pleasantly surprised. Be sure to look up and see the stunning life size figures of a Moose and Rearing Stallion displayed on the building's overhang. When you step inside the shop, your senses will be overwhelmed with the soulful energy of the many Artisans' crafts. You will immediately be stimulated with the pleasant scents of handcrafted, natural spa products, and Beautifully Handcrafted Natural Perfume Pendants. Great things come in small packages is certainly true of Coyote Trading Company. What appears to be a little shop is really a 3000 sq foot Treasure Chest of many unique Artist created products. The Coyote's goal is to offer a shopping alternative to the huge box stores by providing handmade quality products at reasonable prices with great customer service. Come for the experience and stay for the shopping. Handmade, handcrafted products are the order of the day at Coyote – Coyote Trading Company, your unique shopping alternative.

5019 B–51 Street, Lacombe AB
(403) 782-5004

Stychen Tyme Quilt & Yarn Shop

No matter which of the fibre arts attracts your fancy, Stychen Tyme Quilt & Yarn Shop can support your interest with a comprehensive array of supplies. Romy and Ken Quackenbush opened the Jasper shop seven years ago as an inspirational setting for knitters, quilters and other crafters. The shop acts as a resource centre for the fibre arts and arranges many classes and retreats. You will find Canadian cross-stitch and quilt patterns with mountain motifs, Lopi and Peer Gynt yarns for Nordic sweaters and 3,000 bolts of fabric, including many featuring lodge and wildlife prints. Whether you create multidimensional contemporary pieces or use traditional patterns, Romy and Ken understand that crafters reach into the past to make present creations that endure into the future. This artistic focus, shared by the owners and their customers, leads to many long-term friendships, making the store a gathering place in the community. The work of local quilters hangs on the walls. You will find books, special threads and a wealth of knowledge, which Romy is quick to share with her customers. Whether you seek a lesson in technique or the inspiration for your next creation, come to Stychen Tyme Quilt & Yarn Shop.

402 Patricia Street, Jasper AB
(780) 852-7490 or (866) 852-7490

Brooklyn Clothing Co

Calgary may be a long way from Brooklyn, but, guys, you can dress with New York style and attitude up here in Alberta. All you have to do is shop at Brooklyn Clothing Co., a clothing store exclusively for guys. Notice it's *guys* and rather than *men*. If you're looking for suits and ties for the executive lifestyle, you'll have to try elsewhere. Brooklyn Clothing Co. is a denim-friendly den carrying cool stuff for the male who isn't ready for pinstripes, and may never be. Brooklyn Clothing offers more than 50 styles of jeans from 575, Energie and True Religion, to name just a few of the lines. The store stocks shoes from Puma, Dayton and Bronx (New York again), leather jackets from Brogden Track and clothing from Andrea Palombini, Encore and Nudie. Brooklyn Clothing is a must whether your goal is to look good on campus, on a date or at your job at the music store. You'll receive service without pressure from the staff. Brad Tien and Heng Sim run the show. They keep an outstanding selection of apparel and accessories available at all times and search constantly for new lines. Belts, watches and caps are part of the mix here. You won't see brownstones from the window, but you can feel the vibe of the streets at Brooklyn Clothing Co. Check it out today.

201–1211 Kensington Road NW, Calgary AB
(403) 283-4006
www.brooklynclothing.com

Wicker Tea & Spice

Along the boardwalk of the Bragg Creek Shopping Centre, you may brush shoulders with travelers from all corners of the globe browsing through the wares at Wicker Tea & Spice. Owned and operated by Wendy Argent for the past 12 years, Wicker Tea & Spice houses an extensive assortment of gifts, treats and collectibles that appeal to the tastes of locals and travelers alike. Along with a variety of teas and gourmet food products, Wendy's collection includes art, cards, porcelain dolls, ceramic bears and stuffed animals. You may even run into a well known artist signing one of their creations on site. Wendy, a former first-grade teacher,

has a warm and welcoming manner and clearly enjoys meeting her many customers. She will happily show you around, answer questions and arrange custom shipping for you so that you don't have to carry your gifts when you travel. Equally eager to make friends is Tyaa, Wendy's Cavalier King Charles Spaniel, who will greet you with a waggy tail. Come down to this gem at the heart of Bragg Creek and let Wendy and Tyaa show you the charms and flavors of Wicker Tea & Spice.

Balsam Avenue, Bragg Creek AB
(403) 949-4262

Kensington Wine Market

Your next good bottle of wine is just steps away as you stroll through trendy Kensington. The knowledgeable staff at the Kensington Wine Market is at your service. They can help you find a tried-and-true or make great recommendations for new favourites. Whether you are looking for an everyday easy sipper or something perfect for that special person or occasion, you won't be disappointed. If you are a wine novice, you can reserve a spot in the Introduction to Red

Wine class, one of the many regularly scheduled in-store tastings. Try the Kensington Wine Market for specialty beers from around the world and one of Calgary's largest selections of single malt scotch. Gifting is another specialty of this fine store. Whether you're turning 50 or sending thanks to your corporate clients, the Kensington Wine Market does it all. It's that easy.

1257 Kensington Road NW, Calgary AB
(403) 283-8000 or
(888) 283-9004
www.kenningtonwinemarket.com

Canuck Gifts

Owner Mahnaz Bourouiba is as concerned about upholding values as she is in selling her collection of specialty products at her cute little store, Canuck Gifts. The shop opened in 2003 with a sophisticated urban blend of merchandise that celebrates Canada's unique cultural mix as well as its many contributions to the world. You will find many unique crafts, home decorations and kitchen products. The shop has sculptures, vases, jewellery, paintings and fine foods, including Canada's many maple delights. Canuck Gifts even features gourmet food tastings. Books on Canadian heritage gives the interested gift shopper an insight into the many cultures of Canada. Unlike most gift stores aimed at tourists, this shop attracts the entire community—it's a gathering spot for browsing and sharing experiences with the neighbours. Every product is authentic and individual in nature, so the inventory is attractive to a broad range of customers. Mahnaz refreshes the store regularly, keeping the contents and the overall look exciting and new. She is very particular about her staff, which must exemplify the store's values as well as know the products. You will be seen and heard at Canuck Gifts, where Mahnaz makes a point of forming a relationship with every customer. Take part in the Canadian experience with a visit to Canuck Gifts.

858 B Carmichael Lane, Hinton AB
(780) 865-5538
www.canuckgifts.com

Livingstone & Cavell Extraordinary Toys

Remember when you could escape into a universe of your own making, with the help of a dauntless imagination and some great toys? Now you can revisit that land of childhood wonder and innocence at Livingstone & Cavell Extraordinary Toys. Opened in 1992, this retail treasure was born of a couple's shared passion for distinctive, well-made toys of the past and present. A stylish shop designed to appeal to adult sensibilities as well as to the child at heart, Livingstone & Cavell features nostalgic collector toys from childhoods past, quirky novelty items, and lovingly crafted dolls, tricycles and puppets of the present era. Hand-painted toy soldiers, old-fashioned model railroads and real steam-powered engines recall the romance of history. Made of durable wood, metal and plastic, these timeless toys carry sought-after brand names such as Märklin, Wilesco, and William Britain. From tin wind-up toys to potato guns, the selection bridges generations in its appeal. Whether you are a serious collector, in search of a one-of-a-kind gift or just want to experience the world of fine artisanship dedicated to play, stroll through the aisles of Livingstone & Cavell Extraordinary Toys and find something curious and delightful at every turn.

1124 Kensington Road NW, Calgary AB
(403) 270-4165

Scentchips N' Stuff

The sweet smell of success fills the air at Scentchips N' Stuff. The shop offers a robust array of Scentchips and related products which will complement your home, office or that special room of your own. Scentchips are the original wax potpourri, shaped like flowers and leaves, with hundreds of combinations available such as Sea Breeze or Apple Pie. Light the tea light under your favourite blend and enjoy the aroma. The shop also carries the very popular Lampe Berger, a decorative home accessory with a patented catalytic burner that destroys all airborne

odours and helps purify the air before the fragrance is diffused. Aromatherapy products come in a wide variety, such as candles, soaps, pendants and more. You're sure to find that one-of-a-kind gift. Owner Sandy Lee started the business in 1999 and has worked to perfect the trade and offer the widest range of home fragrance products. Scentchips N' Stuff is worth a visit if you're looking to transform any room into an aromatic haven.

1335-9 Avenue SE, Calgary AB
(403) 710-2800

Rob Rae Clothiers

Men who want to look good at the office, on the golf course and at the nightclub know to shop at Rob Rae Clothiers. Located in the downtown core of Red Deer for nearly 40 years, the shop features made-to-measure suits, sports wear and lifestyle wear from many top lines, including Hugo Boss, Tommy Bahama and Lacoste. The Tino Cosma line of gentleman's wear offers ties and other accessories. Because the inventory of shirts, pants and jackets changes with the seasons, men can look forward to making a new statement every time new arrivals hit the store. Owner Tim Snell and buyer Bob Petrash say that their mandate is to provide quality clothing

and superior services. The business has built its reputation on knowing what well-dressed men like to wear and providing that extra touch, from tailoring to delivery, that earns customer loyalty. A policy of no charge for alterations on regular-priced merchandise exemplifies the friendly approach at Rob Rae Clothiers. Try this pillar of the Red Deer business community on for style.

#101-4807 50 Avenue,
Red Deer AB
(403) 343-1477

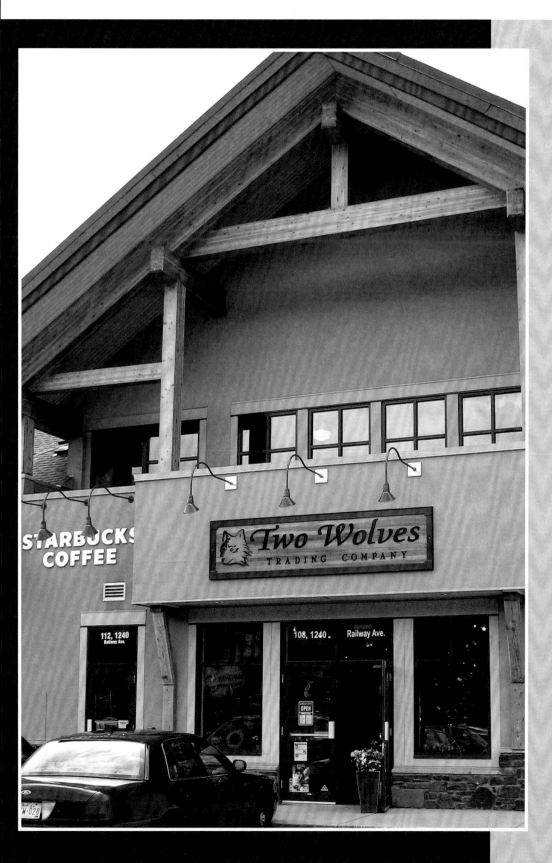

Two Wolves Trading Company

In 2004, Andrea Rankin and Michelle Oruski, two friends, thought to pool their talents and resources in a business that would allow them more time with their families. The result is Two Wolves Trading Company, a casual art gallery masquerading as a home décor shop. Two Wolves Trading Company features an array of furniture and accessories for the home created by Canadian artists. No matter where you look when you enter, form meets function in a vivid array of colors and textures. Renowned local artist Fraser McGurk not only contributes limited-edition giclee prints, but remarkable paintings on wood that employ intense pigments and paints. Influenced by artists such as Lawren Harris and Bill Weber, McGurk has yet developed a style all his own. In addition to McGurk's work and a broad selection of country furnishings, Two Wolves also stocks a large collection of handmade giftware and house ware items, such as vases, dishware, candle holders and picture frames. Andrea and Michelle take great pride in the store and in offering personalized service to all of their customers. They have established a wedding gift registry and offer gift wrapping services. Discover a treasure trove of Canadian treasures at Two Wolves Trading Company.

108-1240 Railway Avenue, Canmore AB
(403) 678-9791
www.twowolves.net

Audrey's Books

Writers and book lovers meet at Audrey's Books for book signings, book launches, readings and other literary events arranged by owners Steve and Sharon Budnarchuck. The Edmonton bookstore hosts more than 50 such events each year as a service to authors and readers. The selection will enchant any book lover and the store thrives on offering unusual books, making it a practical alternative to national retailers. The history section will interest amateur and professional history buffs and the large business collection will help you succeed in any enterprise. Steve handles administrative matters, and Sharon handles merchandising and marketing. For the Budnarchucks, who bought the store in 1988, interaction with community leaders is one of the most rewarding parts of business ownership. Sharon is chair of the city's LitFest, which brings together an international coterie of writers in Canada's only creative nonfiction literary festival. The couple won an award from the mayor for Sustained Support of the Arts. Audrey's was incorporated in 1975 and traces its beginnings to a bookstore opened by Mel Hurtig in 1956, which grew into one of Canada's largest retail operations. Canada's best known economic nationalist sold his stores in 1972 to concentrate on publishing such Canadian classics as *The Canadian Encyclopedia*. For a book environment that supports Canadian writers and enhances the local literary experience, Indulge your Passion for Books at Audrey's Books.

10702 Jasper Avenue, Edmonton AB (780) 423-3487 or (800) 661-3640

Jacques Cartier Clothier/Quviuk Boutique

Canada's latest gift to the fashion world is the wool of the Canadian Arctic musk ox called qiviuk. Heralded as the world's softest, rarest and most luxurious fibre, it has yet to gain the recognition of, say, cashmere, though Fernando Alvarez, CEO of Jacques Cartier Clothiers, is working hard to change that. Through a partnership he forged with the Inuvialuit of the Arctic, who are the harvesters of qiviuk, JCC processes most of the qiviuk in the world. From this the company creates cardigan sweaters, shawls, mittens and other clothing that is admired for its beauty and considered eight times as warm as sheep's wool. Everybody who wears qiviuk loves it, especially those in colder climes. Fans include fashion magazine editors, Hollywood stars and Christina Oxenburg, daughter of Princess Elizabeth of Yugoslavia, who is so enthusiastic that she represents the JCC line in New York. Mr. Alvarez keeps letters from Queen Elizabeth that thank him for the gorgeous sweater and shawl that he sent her the last time she visited Canada. You can find qiviuk clothing at the Jacques Cartier Clothiers store in Banff. The Qiviuk Boutique also carries a fine selection at its locations in the Banff Springs Hotel and Chateau Lake Louise. Make a distinctively Canadian fashion statement by dressing in qiviuk from Jacques Cartier Clothiers.

131A Banff Avenue, Banff AB
(403) 762-5445
www.qiviuk.com

Jupiter Cannabis Shop

You'll find beautiful glass pipes, glass water pipes and smoking commodities at the Jupiter Cannabis Shop, where glass artists Tom and Denyse Doran sell their exclusive products. Federally incorporated on April 20, 1982, the Dorans have enjoyed a lifetime of creativity. Their offerings include Jupiter Crystal Collectibles and a Swarovski line of crystal figurines. As the demographic of Edmonton began to turn toward a younger, hipper crowd, the Jupiter Cannabis shop was so successful that the Dorans opened a large shop in Toronto, specializing in original art glass leisure devices. Always a family business, Tom Jr. is now one of the owners and Sara is the manager of the Edmonton shop. Jupiter carries a divine line of original art glass water pipes, hand pipes and bubblers. Necessary props, such as grinders, scales, cleansing products, books and more than 300 varieties of rolling papers are available. Visit the Jupiter Cannabis Shop to experience their legendary customer service and impressive selection of everything 420.

10408 Whyte Avenue, Edmonton AB
(780) 433-1967
www.jupitergrass.ca

Call the Kettle Black

Whether you are a novice, a gourmet chef or just appreciate quality cooking implements, you will love Call the Kettle Black. The shop proudly specializes in mid to high-end kitchen gear. Every artist knows that having the right tools makes the difference, and this is the place for the culinary artist or enthusiast. Popular cookware lines include Calphalon, All-Clad and Le Creuset. The colourful Emile Henry bakeware is perfect for featuring your next masterfully baked dish.

For a flawless dinner party, adorn your table with Spiegelau stemware, Wedgwood dinnerware and Henckels flatware. Premium knives in stock come from a range of quality makers. You can chop, dice, brew, blend, mix and melt anything with the wide range of counter top appliances. Call the Kettle Black has a gift registry, so the shop is the perfect place to buy wedding, birthday and anniversary gifts. The right accessories make cooking that much more fun. Since taking over the original 102 Avenue location a decade ago, owner Darcy Kaser has expanded into a second location at Riverbend Square. You'll find every gadget you could possibly need at Call the Kettle Black

12523 102 Avenue, Edmonton AB (Downtown)
(780) 448-2861
444 Riverbend Square, Edmonton AB (Riverbend)
(780) 434-1622
www.callthekettleblack.com

Photo courtesy of Ellis Brothers Photography

Ultra Violet Floral Studio Inc.

Sometimes you just have to break all the rules to bring your highest creativity to life. Co-founders Janet Waldon and Bernard Gauvreau are anything but ordinary and when these former ice-dancing partners conspired to open their own flower shop there was no doubt it would be fantastic. The shop is an open-concept studio, where customers can watch as their arrangements are artfully created using exceptional and exotic flowers. The trademark personal service and artistry is also extended to wedding consultations and custom events. Every flower for every occasion is chosen with care. Even before Ultra Violet opened, there was something special about this studio and the way it operates. When overbooked contractors could not arrive for the renovation to the building, friends and family stepped in and worked around the clock for eight

weeks to make the dream come true. What has transpired is a burgeoning business that stands on its own and justifies the efforts of its supporters. Ultra Violet conscientiously contributes to the community by sponsoring floral arrangements for several local theatre and art galleries. When you want more than just another bunch of flowers, visit Ultra Violet Floral Studio and pick up an ephemeral work of art.

12234 107 Avenue, Edmonton AB
(780) 454 9990
www.uvfloral.ca

Frozen Ocean

Frozen Ocean is a recreational clothing and lifestyle store for folks who don't just live life but reach out and grab it by the horns. This thoroughly original shop was founded by Robert and Roberta Sternloff, who first began by making clothes for board sports from home. Demand for their high-quality, stylish fashion clothing soared quickly, and in 1992 the couple opened in Canmore. Since then, Frozen Ocean has been able to expand to four more Alberta communities—see the web site for details. The shop caters to the skateboard, snowboard and surfing culture. Its array of specialty items is designed for those adrenalin junkies who are always searching for the next thrill. Comfortable, rugged clothing helps you enjoy the ride. The shop's collection is designed for boarders of all shapes and sizes. There are long-sleeves, hoodies and T-shirts for guys and gals, as well as beanies and caps with embroidered logos. The store carries a choice inventory of jeans, cargos and shorts made with the highest quality hemp and cotton. It also has a near-endless selection of silk screened prints to enhance the boarding lifestyle. Frozen Ocean's Calgary and Halifax stores have a surfboard line created by Volcanic Surf Boards and carry an array of surf accessories, such as leashes, wax and board bags. Grab your board and jump into the fray in grand style and comfort with lifestyle fashions from Frozen Ocean.

830 Main Street, Canmore AB
(403) 678-8853
www.frozenocean.ca

Artifacts Custom Furniture & Restorations

Making your imagination a reality is the specialty of the woodworkers at Artifacts Custom Furniture & Restorations. Terry and Cindi Armstrong opened Artifacts to share their passion and talent for woodwork with all of Alberta. Their creations reference the past, often using reclaimed wood and imported reproduction antique hardware, such as knobs and pulls. Some of the challenges they enjoy include matching newly created pieces to vintage pieces. Terry showed an interest in antiques at an early age. He dragged his first piece home when he was 11 years old. In the following years, he perfected his craft, finding his niche when he and Cindi launched Artifacts. They now provide custom wood work for homes, individuals and businesses. Terry's experience in wood carving encompasses dimensional animals and the kind of detailed designs and motifs so necessary to performing accurate, quality furniture restorations. He has built custom furniture for antique dealers, customer referrals and interior designers, giving him a strong background for specific requests. Services include hand-built mantles, kitchen islands, tables and expert antique refinishing and upholstery. The shop inspires an impressive level of confidence, with the result that many customers refer their friends to Artifacts. If it's made out of wood, Artifacts can do whatever needs to be done. To see the work, stop by the shop in Nanton or browse the fine pieces displayed and the hardware catalogue available on the website.

Nanton AB
(403) 646-2705
www.artifactsfurniture.com

Tribal Connection Market

When you enter the Tribal Connection Market in Okotoks, you'll feel like you've stepped out of southern Alberta and into another country. It's just a matter of deciding which one. This diverse shop carries home décor, jewelry, food and coffee from all over the globe. Although it's located on a main street in a quaint bedroom community, you can purchase treasures from places as exotic as Peru, Uganda, Guatemala and India. Owner Adele Henderson conceived of the import market as a Fair Trade venue for international farmers and artisans to sell their wares. "I want to sell food and giftware that we can take pride in," Henderson says. "If we know someone is getting a fair price for the work they are doing, we feel good about selling that product in our store. And we know our customers are happy about being able to buy it." Take home some Fair Trade coffee or stop for a latte in the market café. You'll find fresh soups, panini and cinnamon buns to keep you fueled up for a long browse. Don't miss the amazing collection of jewelry and crystals from all over the world. There's something for everyone, ranging from wooden earrings made in Indonesia to shimmering amber rings from Poland. Expect proficient service from the knowledgeable staff. You'll also find beautiful imported furniture, such as coffee and end tables and a fun selection of musical instruments. Take a tour of world cultures and handiwork via Okotoks at the Tribal Connection Market.

41 McRae Street, Okotoks AB
(403) 995-1898

The Sugar Pine Company, Ltd.

Explore a world of creativity at The Sugar Pine Company. With its massive selection of fabrics, gifts and quilting supplies, the Sugar Pine Company has attracted a worldwide quilting circle of fans. In 2005, the Canmore store was featured in *Better Homes and Gardens Quilt Sampler Magazine,* profiling North America's favourite quilt shops. That recognition joined numerous local accolades, including the Outstanding Achievement Award from Husqvarna Viking and the Business of the Year Award from the Canmore-Kananaskis Chamber of Commerce. The greatest reward for owners Leah Murphy and Claire Bank, though, is the enthusiastic support of customers, who return again and again to answer all their quilting needs. The 5,000-square-foot store stocks more than 8,000 bolts of designer fabrics on its second floor; you'll find more than 700 bolts of flannel alone. In addition to quilting fabrics, you'll find fabrics suitable for clothing and home decorating. The store also stocks a large variety of quilting patterns and kits, with many portraying landscape and wildlife themes. The main floor features a variety of gifts, knitting and needlework supplies, and Rocky Mountain souvenirs, as well as a classroom that is often full of eager pupils of all skill levels. The Sugar Pine hosts an annual quilting event, the Canadian Rockies Quilt Art Canmore Conference, drawing people from all over the globe to learn from the world's foremost quilting instructors. You will find everything you need to keep yourself in stitches at The Sugar Pine Company.

737 10 Street #1, Canmore AB
(403) 678-9603
www.thesugarpine.com

Timeworn Charm

Timeworn Charm presents home décor with vintage flair. Owner Jodie Folkerts is often seen busily stocking the shelves and decorating with newly arrived, vintage-inspired home décor and gifts throughout the store. Whether it is country and cottage accents or the ever-popular shabby-chic style you are searching for, Timeworn Charm has items to complement your home. Favorites include tin advertising signs, quilts and chandeliers. Accessorize your garden with outdoor treasures or expand your collections with antique wares. Timeworn Charm also offers a good selection of jewellery. As many customers are aware, much of the merchandise is one-of-a-kind and sells quickly, so it's always a good idea to visit often. The staff is helpful and knowledgeable about decorating issues. Their friendly service is a hallmark of the shop. Accentuate your home or garden with the lure of the classic from Timeworn Charm.

5105 50 Avenue, Lacombe AB
(403) 782-6747

The Primrose

Besides a cute, flowering plant, the Primrose is also a darling clothing boutique. This Lacombe shop has been owned by Joyce Spears for the last seven years. Although her two associates, Brenda Riep and Mavis Prevost, are responsible for maintaining the store's atmosphere and displays, Joyce is always around to assist customers in finding just the right outfit. With a large selection of fashion apparel, customers at the Primrose come from far and wide to check out the newly arrived seasonal pieces. Frank Lyman, Eric Alexander and Jag Jeans are just a few

of the many designers and brands you'll find when you examine the boutique's merchandise. Dresses, suits and even a special lingerie line grace the shop's racks. Egyptian cotton nightgowns and a specialty bra line called Tab are some of the most popular items. When you've decided on your new outfit, don't forget to complete your look with a matching purse, necklace or other accessory. In addition to women's wear, the Primrose carries an assortment of clothing for babies and young children. Joyce Spears has built her boutique on the principals of stylish attire and impeccable service. The ladies at the Primrose invite you to drop by their shop to find your perfect new look.

5008 50 Street, Lacombe AB
(403) 782-2820

Touchstones

The ammolite in the jewellery at Touchstones comes from Alberta, the jade from British Columbia. The diamonds, set in 14 or 18-karat gold, are also mined in Canada. Indeed, Touchstones does its homeland proud with its extensive selection of Canadian-made jewellery,

in styles that bridge the gap between the classic and the contemporary. A customer favorite is the featured line of Elle jewellery, which sets the finest quality semi-precious and precious stones in sterling silver. Gaze into the display cases and see blue topaz, green peridot and purple amethyst dance before your eyes. Let the friendly staff help you find a ring, necklace or pendant that suits your style —and a pair of earrings to match. This shop is also known around Banff for its fine selection of Swarovski crystal figurines. Drop by Touchstones in the heart of downtown Banff and leave wearing something beautiful that celebrates the bounty of Canada.

117 Banff Avenue, Banff AB
(403) 762-3938

Edelweiss Imports

In the heart of northwest Calgary, a European treasure awaits your discovery. Immerse yourself in the sights, sounds and smells of Europe the moment you step inside Edelweiss Village. You are invited to explore the European delicatessen and import store, and pause to indulge in a scrumptious ethnic lunch. The delicious German baking is all created in the Edelweiss kitchen using the finest ingredients. A large variety of imported German, Dutch, Polish and Scandinavian favorites fill the food aisles. You won't want to miss the authentic gifts and household items direct from Europe in the ever-changing gift boutique. At Edelweiss Imports you will find a truly European shopping experience.

1921 20 Avenue NW, Calgary AB (403) 282-6600
www.edelweissimports.com

The Tin Box—Edmonton

Whatever you are trying to accessorize—your home, your garden or your person—the Tin Box aims to give you stylish choices. The 3,000-square-foot Edmonton boutique store turns browsing for a gift or decoration into an inspirational journey of discovery. The shop suits every budget and stays open seven days a week. You will find kitchenware, body care products from the Thymes and Rocky Mountain Soap Company, and fashion accessories, including leather handbags from Derek Alexander. One department is devoted to items for children; another specializes in garden decoration. Locally designed jewellery is always in demand. Everything about the Tin Box is fun, fashionable and out-of-the-ordinary, eliciting a wow response from all visitors, whether they live nearby or stop by on their travels. You could try coming in for just a minute, but then the store's sensational merchandise captures your imagination, and next thing you know you've passed an enjoyable hour wrapped up in forward-thinking products. The Tin Box is a family concern, opened in 2005 by the husband and wife team David and Treasure Richardson. The store follows in the footsteps of its sister store in Canmore, opened in 1994 by David's sister Kari Meggs and her husband, Sean. You can visit often, because the Tin Box renews its inventory frequently. Browse to your heart's content at the Tin Box, where the trendy extras in life are as fun to find as they are to own.

10512–82 Avenue (Whyte Avenue), Edmonton AB (780) 436-2006 *www.thetinbox.ca*

Deanna Berry—Personal Shopper

Before you take on the trendy shops of Calgary, let Deanna Berry's keen fashion sense and local experience guide you to the hot spots of the Alberta fashion scene. Deanna owned a clothing boutique in Calgary for over four years. Her experience in the fashion industry extends beyond the realm of personal shopping into the fast-paced world of fashion shows, design and consulting. In addition to being available for personal consultations, Deanna travels from store to store to help Canadian designers and shop owners showcase their newest items. If you're walking past a boutique in downtown Calgary and happen to see a fashion show, it's likely Deanna is involved. With an eye for styles ranging from professional to funky-modern, Deanna can help you find the outfit perfectly suited to your specific needs. Looking for something formal? Let Deanna scout out the hard-to-find shops to find you a stunning gown. If you're not sure what you're looking for, but want to explore the latest style developments, Deanna can direct you to some of the up-and-coming boutiques. After a consultation with Deanna, be prepared to answer questions about your new eye for style. Deanna travels the world in search of the hottest new designers and often comes back with ideas to accelerate the Calgary apparel scene. Are you ready to create some fashion buzz? Let Deanna Berry, personal shopper and fashion consultant, help you do it.

Calgary, AB
(403) 861-8655

Boca Loca

With a mission to bring the authentic taste of Mexico to Calgary, Boca Loca has been serving classic Mexican dishes to discerning customers since 2000. Renette Kurz and her staff serve wonderful tamales, tostadas and burritos, as well as daily soups such as Pozole Rojo. The popular chicken burritos are so delicious that it's actually a good idea to pre-order one. Don't leave without trying the Mexican coffee or hot chocolate. Both are spiced with soft Mexican cinnamon. Dedicated, experienced cooks provide authenticity and flavor that comes through in every meal. The service is swift and attentive and the selection is comprehensive. Boca Loca is much more than a Mexican restaurant. It offers hard-to-find Mexican foods and groceries, festival supplies and party accessories. Fresh produce and fresh tortillas, spices, salsa and Mexican candies are all on hand. The business offers a full menu of catering services. Boca Loca also hosts a variety of cooking classes. You can find cookbooks and kitchenware—everything you'll need to re-create the tasty fare that's made here. Boca Loca is salvation itself for Calgary's Texan-American oil patch families. A visit to either Boca Loca location is second only to a visit to Mexico, so be sure to stop by soon.

1512 11 Street SW, Calgary AB
(403) 802-4600
777 Northmount Drive NW, Calgary AB
(403) 289-2202
www.bocalocacalgary.com

Crossroads Market

It's crowded, it's chaotic and it's full of fun, especially if you love a bargain. We're talking about the Crossroads Market, a year-round weekend destination for thousands of Calgarians. Crossroads Market is home to a flea market, international food fair, antique market, art gallery, and farmers market all located in a trendy 100,000 square foot building in historic Inglewood. Why does shopping at malls and grocery stores feel like such a chore, while shopping at the Crossroads Market feels like an event? Maybe it's the good feeling you get when you buy fruits and vegetables directly from the producer. Maybe it's the energy that carries you from one stall to another, past bins of tomatoes, carrots and peaches. Maybe it's the thrill of the hunt to find that one-of-a-kind gift, or seeing antiques and collectibles reminiscent of your childhood. Crossroads is a gathering place where cultures meet, so deals go down in many languages. Impromptu music fills the air when South American Pan Flute Bands show up and put on a show. Head here with a friend or two and see which of you can claim the most interesting combination of purchases at the end of the day. Do a crock pot, two jars of honey and a 10-pound case of hot chile peppers beat an antique tea kettle, pewter dragon and a bag of giant carrots? For shopping in an exciting atmosphere, hurry to the Crossroads Market.

1235 26 Avenue SE, Calgary AB (403) 291-5208
www.crossroadsmarket.ca

Forobosco Building/ Lucia's Gems & Gifts/ Bearberry Photo & Canadiana

Long after that t-shirt declaring that you have been to Jasper has faded, the rainbow colors in your ammolite ring will still be as dazzling as the day you bought it at Lucia's Gems & Gifts. This long-established business strives to be a souvenir shop for people who wish to take home something special and a little different from their trip. Lucia's Gems & Gifts carries a whimsical line of boxer shorts, nightshirts and aprons in addition to jewelry. The ammolite used in its beautiful pieces comes from the Korite ammolite mine in Alberta, the only commercial mine of its kind in the world. In addition to ammolite, Lucia's features jade, soapstone and polar ice diamonds in its rings, pendants and earrings. Bearberry Photo & Canadiana is Lucia's co-tenant in the Forobosco Building, part full-service camera store and part arts and crafts showcase. Bearberry offers pottery, raku, jade inukshuks and other handcrafted Canadian items. Other gifts include luxurious Deborah Murray blankets and souvenir hiking socks. Find gifts and souvenirs to be cherished for years at Lucia's Gems & Gifts and Bearberry Photo & Canadiana.

612 Connaught Drive, Jasper AB
(780) 852-3980 (Lucia's Gems & Gifts)
(780) 852-1112 (Bearberry Photo & Canadiana)

Saffron Artistic Expressions

Saffron, situated in the heart of Cochrane, is a bright and colourful contemporary gallery with a unique collection of artistic expressions created by artists from across Canada. It is a gallery with spice. Saffron has an eclectic collection of painting, jewellery, handblown glassware, handbags, pottery and a variety of other beautifully designed wares. Tara Torr, Saffron's owner and operator, is widely supported by more than 80 different artists and designers, all of them Canadian and handpicked to suit Saffron's contemporary style. You can meet local artists at the galley several times a week, or take a pottery class for adults or for children. Dominating the collection are local artists from the west coast. Within Alberta, Edmonton provides calendars and other illustrations from valérydesignwrks, textile bags from Lines Designs and Lemonade, jewellery from Handmade on Venus and fine wall art. Artists such as Marianne Jespersen from the Calgary area constitute the majority of colorful fine wall art displayed in Saffron. From British Columbia come the necklaces and earrings of Gingerly Designs and stylish bags from Kairos Designs. Whether your search is for fine art paintings, gifts or funky fashion accessories, Saffron promotes individuality and flair in all of the their talented Canadian artists and artisans. Tara and all of the staff at Saffron invite you to visit and see the best that Canada has to offer.

Bay 3, 320 1 Street W, Cochrane AB
(403) 932-7040
www.saffronstudios.ca

The Jim and Pat Real Estate Team

Real estate is a family tradition for Jim and Pat. Jim started his real estate career in 1979 and Pat brought his marketing background to the team in 2000. Since that time, no other agent has sold more real estate in central Alberta than the Jim and Pat Real Estate Team. Over the last few years the team has grown to include administrative members and selling partners. This expansion allows team members to specialize in a few small areas so each element of the home-selling process is handled efficiently. It is not uncommon to hear clients rave about the quality care they received. "We used them again because, for us, it was comfort level," said Mark and Nicole Boulaine, who have used the team to sell three of their homes. "We knew that not only did they have the experience, but all the tools necessary to sell our home for top dollar, fast and with no hassles. Dealing with the Jim and Pat Real Estate Team was a no-brainer." Jim and Pat are both long-time Sylvan Lakers and are an integral part of the community. Whether it is through coaching minor sports, volunteering, town development committees or sponsoring events, they are actively involved. Their goal is to make the process as hassle-free as possible, and accomplish this through consistent communication and integrity driven decisions. Jim and Pat combine their extensive knowledge of the area with sensible advice and cutting-edge technology, dramatically increasing your chances of finding your dream home or attracting potential buyers. Whether you are new to town or a local, consider putting the Jim and Pat Real Estate Team to work for you.

#1, 4914–50 Avenue, Sylvan Lake AB (403) 887-8579 *www.jimandpatteam.com*

The Galleria Arts & Crafts

Susan Copley is inspired by Canadian artists and she wants you to be captivated by them as well. Her store, the Galleria Arts & Crafts, is the largest independently owned retail and handcrafted arts store in Canada. The two-story Calgary store represents as many as 500 artists and craftspeople who work in dozens of mediums and share one important trait—they are all Canadian. Are you in the market for dinnerware? The functional pottery found here has many distinct glazes and will be the talk of your next dinner party. You can warm up a wall with a woven wall hanging, enjoy the dazzle of stained glass or delight the children in your life with handcrafted wooden toys and the kids clothing is in a class by itself. Look for Nova Scotia pewter or real Canadian maple leaves encrusted in bronze. The original artwork celebrates landscapes, animals and city scenes from throughout Canada. Mouth-blown, moulded, recycled and kiln-fired glass can add interest and colour to any room. Jewellery runs the gamut from funky bead necklaces and brooches made of handmade paper to sterling silver. Many of the pieces in the Galleria are one-of-a-kind or collectibles, such as the hand-carved wooden moose, reproduction Inukshuks made by Inuit artisans, or sculptured aluminum figurines. If you want to know the story behind any of the handmade arts and crafts, an easygoing and knowledgeable staff is there when you need them. Plan on plenty of time to browse through the gifts and exclusive offerings at the Galleria Arts & Crafts.

1141 Kensington Road NW, Calgary AB
(403) 270-3612
www.calgarycraftedgifts.com

Ammonite Factory & Gallery

The Ammonite Factory & Gallery offers the best in ammolite jewellery, including necklaces, earrings, bracelets, rings and cuff links. Free-standing pieces attract art enthusiasts, while polished and capped gemstones appeal to gem collectors. Today's stunning ammolite jewellery comes to you from prehistoric fossilized organisms. More than 70 million years ago, snail-like creatures known as ammonites flourished in a tropical seabed that is now Alberta. As the seabed receded, the shells of the ocean-dwelling creatures were crushed by vegetation and silt and eventually fossilized during a glacial age. Ammonites that were crushed even further and *concreted* became what is now known as ammolite. Today, gem-grade ammolite is mined exclusively in the Bearspaw formation in southeastern Alberta. It has been named Alberta's official gemstone. Since 1987, owner Richard Morgen has personally gathered the precious stones, which are recovered by open pit mining. Take a factory tour with manager Claire Jones and learn about the mining and manufacturing process. When selecting ammolite, notice the color. High grades have shades of at least three colours, while lower grades display one or two dominant colours. Blackfoot tribe legend tells us that ammolite symbolizes wealth, abundance and good luck. You'll find a hardy dose of each when you visit the Ammonite Factory & Gallery.

106 Bow Meadows Crescent, Canmore AB
(403) 678-1786
www.ammonitefactory.ca

Penelope Designs, Inc.

Penelope Designs is for women who know what they want in fashion. Penelope is the place to go for shoes, clothing and accessories, both timeless classics and funky trends. You'll see pops of color and style that are appropriate to the workplace but never dowdy. Owned and operated by Penny Main, Penelope Designs stocks the work of more than 15 designers and appeals to professional women from 20 to 60. Main prides herself on superior service. If you find a style you like but would prefer a different color or size not in stock, she'll order it for you and give you a call when it comes in. Savvy shoppers can also place order through her snappy website and receive the same attentive service. Inspired in part by her years spent living abroad and traveling the world, Main stocks designers from Europe, Canada and the United States. Her worldliness is reflected in her selection of high-fashion work-wear. Whether Penelope's loyal clients yearn for a promotion or already rule the boardroom at a big firm, they'll find just what they're looking for at this boutique: beautiful, chic clothing, jewelry and accessories for the professional *and* fashionable woman. To find wardrobe inspiration for the modern woman, take a shopping excursion to Penelope Designs.

1419A-9 Avenue SE, Calgary AB
(403) 235-3153
www.penelopedesigns.ca

Angel Scent Lavender

Angel Scent Lavender is a special gift shop situated in one of Cochrane's most prestigious historical homes. Built in 1910, it has been transformed into a beautiful and tranquil setting. Owner Cindy Murray has cultivated her passion for lavender to create an assortment of her own bath and beauty products, culinary delights, cleaning necessities and essential oils all from the lavender on her farm. Lavender has a wealth of therapeutic properties, as well as its calming and soothing attributes. Angel Scent Lavender was named 2006 Business of the Year in Cochrane, which is evident once you embark upon your journey, whether it is the storefront, taking a leisurely walk in the lavender gardens or relaxing with a glass of lavender iced tea on the porch. For a truly remarkable experience, Cindy invites you to discover how all things lavender will enhance your life.

308-3 Street W, Cochrane AB
(403) 851-0405
www.angelscentlavender.com

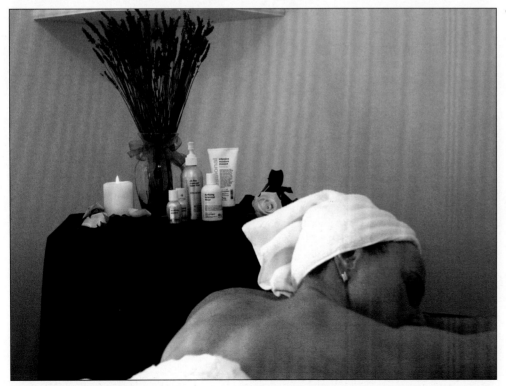

The Lavender House Esthetics & Day Spa

Lavender is the reigning color, fragrance and overall inspiration for The Lavender House. Cochrane's only day spa offers an abundance of aesthetic treatments and services. In the warmer months, it offers hot stone massage outdoors among the fresh lavender gardens. Lavender is traditionally known as a natural remedy believed to relieve anxiety, depression and notably enhance relaxation. Indulge in an array of treatments, while basking in the surroundings of an original 1910 Victorian home. Conclude your journey with a stroll through the lavender gardens and sense the warmth and tranquility of lavender. Candy Pente and Sue Garland are the gracious hosts who will assure your stay at The Lavender House is a first class experience. Candy and Sue invite you to walk through their doors and unwind in the serene surroundings exclusively known as The Lavender House.

308 3 Street W, Cochrane AB
(403) 932-6811

From the Ground Up Design Ltd.

The Asian and Middle Eastern furnishings at From the Ground Up Design Ltd. delight customers with unusual details and fine workmanship. Co-owners Gale LeBlanc and Jane Mackay teamed up to form the business in 2003 and moved the shop to its present Inglewood location in 2004. They purchase hand-carved wood and stone directly from families in small villages. They also hire master carpenters to turn reclaimed teak into modern furniture in styles ranging from rustic to urban contemporary. The store offers a blend of international influences to lend individual character to your home. Look for statuettes, carved furniture, upholstered and leather-wrapped pieces and many adornments. You might find an antique, a reproduction or something entirely fresh in this extraordinary shop, where products are both chic and eco-friendly. Gale holds a bachelor's degree in interior design, while Jane spent 12 years in Asia as a geologist involved in mineral exploration. Her deep attachments to the people of Indonesia caused her to reach out to help survivors by adopting an Indonesian village. From the Ground Up Design Ltd. operates out of the old and recently renovated Garry Theatre. Chris Morrison is the very capable store manager. The original hardwood floors and architectural details of the theatre add character to the shop and provide a fitting backdrop for the furniture collection. For pieces that bring the earthy calm of the outdoors into your home, visit From the Ground Up Design Ltd.

1229 9 Avenue SE, Calgary AB
(403) 252-0990
www.thegroundup.ca

Antique Junction

Get ready to spend some time before entering Antique Junction. The 3,200-square-foot showroom offers an eclectic mix of items that you won't want to miss. Whether you're decorating a spacious new home or just adding flair to your 30-year-old country cabin, you'll find accent pieces to captivate and charm. Vintage skis, snowshoes and sleighs provide an outdoorsy look. Paddles and fishing rods create a feeling that sports enthusiasts will love. History buffs will go for the Old West décor, complete with horse-related items. Samplings of vintage posters and collectables are available, too. Intermingled with antiques, you'll find sofas, comfy chairs and luxurious leather furniture—all new and waiting to beautify your surroundings. Pick up a trendy corduroy, denim or down-filled pillow for that extra pizzazz. Co-owners Mike Gordon and Tim Nokes joined together to create a showroom filled with new, antique, consignment and auction items. Plan a visit to Antique Junction, where every aisle offers treasures from the past and delightful décor for the future.

112-1160 Railway Avenue, Canmore AB
(403) 609-0244

Ginger Laurier

Donita Beaulieu went into business nearly 20 years ago selling Birkenstock sandals from her home. "My customers were like friends," she says. "They'd sit in my living room and I'd haul shoes up and down the stairs to the basement." She was certainly nervous when she first opened her boutique, Ginger Laurier. "For the first time, I had overhead." She needn't have worried. Customers lined up at the door. The store has expanded to over 1,800 square feet.

Ginger Laurier sells fabulous footwear, special couture from Canadian, European and American designers. Finish off your outfit with accessories and jewelry from around the world. Of course, you can still buy Birkenstocks here. Donita loves helping people and her goal is to make a difference in your shopping experience. Her team of caring staff shares her philosophy. Visit Ginger Laurier. You'll love what you find.

52 McRae Street, Okotoks AB
(403) 938-6146

Rumpled Quilt Skins

Whether you're an expert quilter or haven't picked up a needle and thread for years, Rumpled Quilt Skins will give you a reason to dust off that old sewing machine and put it to good use. Owned by Linda and Gil Freund, this quaint quilt shop stands out amongst the wealth of specialty shops in Olde Towne Okotoks. Inside the doors of this recently rejuvenated one-hundred-year-old general store lies a full-service sewer's paradise. You'll discover a wide array of fabrics and sewing machines as well as a heaping dose of old-fashioned charm and friendliness. The Freund family is pleased to offer inspirational classes where customers can learn all kinds of techniques, from piecing and machine embroidery to software lessons. Although you can find the most advanced sewing technology at Rumpled Quilt Skins, quality is never compromised and vintage techniques are treasured. The shop's knowledgeable instructors have been widely

acknowledged for their expertise and are committed to equipping you with the skills necessary for your current and future projects. Their dedication and hands-on guidance have helped the shop develop its loyal clientele. The guestbook at the shop's front door proves that Rumpled Quilt Skins not only has a high reputation in the local community but is also a destination for people around the world. Don't forget to add your signature on the way out.

64 N Railway Street, Okotoks AB
(403) 938-6269
www.rumpledquiltskins.ca

Eye on Design

Since 1999, Eye on Design has been bringing refreshing and creative fashion alternatives to Calgary. Located in historical downtown Inglewood, this boutique is one of the city's best kept shopping secrets. Owners Joanne Ford and Anne Wood, along with Jocelyne and Marla, recognize the value of expressing individuality with dramatic yet functional clothing. When you step into the boutique, you instantly feel as if it is all about you. With their focus on personal attention they ensure that you leave feeling and looking fabulous. Eye on Design views clothing as an art, and their passionate approach to fashion means you will find local and European clothing and accessory lines ranging from the elegant to the eclectic– the latest in fashion from designers not widely available. If you need some guidance, take advantage of a personal shopping appointment and let them help you create a look that is all your own. This shop is for the confident woman who seeks clothes that are fun, funky, and edgy. Whether you are searching for a wardrobe for work, casual wear or something for a special occasion, come in to Eye on Design for a shopping experience like no other.

1219 A 9 Avenue SE, Calgary AB
(403) 266-4750
www.eyeondesign.ca

Stonewaters Home Elements

Stonewaters Home Elements makes it possible for you to furnish your home in a way that says you feel a connection to the land. Owners Mike Gordon and Tim Nokes conceived the business in 1999 out of the desire to help clients reflect an authentic Canadian mountain lifestyle. Expect to find high-end products crafted from wood and natural leather as well as slate and steel. Lamps, lampshades and pieces of furniture adorned with alpine images exemplify the Stonewaters style of understated elegance with a rustic feel. Items are either Canadian-made or else purchased from the finest importers. You'll also find decorations and antiques rich with character. Whether your goal is make over your home like a mountain lodge or to add just a touch of Stonewaters to a room, Mike and Tom have ideas. The custom design center offers hundreds of fabric choices to help you create the space that you see in your dreams. In keeping with the owners' belief that service is an integral part of being in business on the Main Street of a small town, the Stonewaters staff is knowledgeable and accommodating. For furniture and home accessories inspired by the majestic Rocky Mountains, see Stonewaters Home Elements.

638 Main Street, Canmore AB **(403) 609-4477** www.stonewaters.com

Iris Sikina RE/MAX West Real Estate

Thinking of buying a piece of property or selling your home? Call Iris Sikina, a top-notch realtor at RE/MAX West Real Estate. With over 12 years of experience, Iris does urban and rural homes, land, commercial, retail, business or development property. Services include virtual tours, specialty marketing pieces and top placement in the market with advertising and her website. Iris is committed to putting her experience to work for you. She is a member of the RE/MAX Platinum Club, RE/MAX Hall Of Fame member and a repeat recipient of the prestigious MLS Million Dollar Club. Iris is passionate about keeping up with the current market trends. View all listings on her website. The City of Cochrane is a bustling heritage town nestled in the foothills of the Rocky Mountains and just 10 minutes from Calgary, giving you a small town lifestyle with the resources of the city. Historic Main Street and the surrounding community offer a mix of residential, commercial and industrial interests and serve a population base of over 20,000, with projections of future growth to 50,000 in the next 10 years. With solid school systems and recreational opportunities, Cochrane is a great place to raise a family. From festivals, farmers markets and walking paths along the Bow River, Jumping Pound and Big Hill Creek, to hang gliding, fishing and golfing, there is always something to do. Less than an hour west of town enjoy skiing, camping and cultural events. Nearby Calgary provides an international airport, theatre, the Calgary Stampede, hockey, mega shopping and more. Iris Sikina can help you sell your home or relocate to centre of it all in the prettiest valley in Big Hill Country.

120 5 Avenue W, Cochrane AB
(403) 390-SOLD (7653)
www.isellcochrane.com

Unique Canadian Alps Gift Shop

The Unique Canadian Alps Gift Shop does indeed carry quite unusual gift items, ranging from German cuckoo clocks to hand-carved walking sticks. Located in the heart of downtown Banff, this lovely shop employs a multilingual people-oriented staff, all of them quite knowledgeable. The cuckoo clocks are magnificent. The shop has clocks with hand-spliced shingle roofs, hand-painted dancing figures, rotating waterwheels and automatic night shut-off, among many other features. You'll find pewter-topped, hand-painted German ceramic beer steins in a variety of beautiful and detailed designs. The shop's selection includes native crafts, such as exquisite jade animal carvings, dream catchers and pewter art. Other delightful items include hand-painted Russian nesting doll sets, Nutcracker figures and Christmas ornaments. You'll see German hunting knives, along with a full line-up of Swiss Army knives that feature up to 33 functions. This shop produces T-shirts and sweatshirts under its own label. Other souvenir items include Canadian maple syrup in fancy bottles. As a direct importer, prices are very reasonable. Though Canada-based, the shop's German roots are in a Nuremberg shop opened in 1865, called *Der Töpferladen*. For a different gift shop experience, visit the Unique Canadian Alps Gift Shop.

109 Banff Avenue, Banff AB
(403) 762-9340
www.toepferladen.com/home_can.php

Spirit of the Earth

Lynn Doyle is the Soul Proprietor of Spirit of the Earth. Located in downtown Canmore, Spirit of the Earth offers a relaxed and nurturing atmosphere that serves an eclectic clientele world-wide. Lynn's shop specializes in gifts and medicines from the earth—rocks, gems, crystal, jewellery, sweetgrass, smudges and herbs—as well as books and cards. You'll find mind and body enhancing music, candles, salt lamps, bath products, aromatherapy and oils. It's apparent that Lynn has taken great care in providing a wholesome and natural selection of quality items. For those seeking guidance and support upon their life's path, Lynn also provides

spiritual coaching, readings, crystal healings and shamanic journies. Lynn grew up on a farm overlooking Georgian Bay in Ontario and has always had a deep connection with Mother Earth. After many years in the corporate world she wanted to do something that not only nurtured her soul but brought support to others, so six years ago she opened Spirit of the Earth. Come in and experience it for yourself. Your soul will thank you.

633 Main Street, Canmore AB
(403) 609-4456

Glacier's Edge

No matter how loudly parents complain, they may never stop their kids from splashing in puddles. Fortunately, adults can dress their children for the occasion with clothing from Glacier's Edge. This store enjoys a strong reputation that extends far beyond Canmore, with customers coming from as far away as Calgary and Edmonton to dress their kids from head to toe. They discover a large selection of footwear and outerwear for hiking, skiing, school and all that zany fun that comes with childhood. Owner Karen Beringer used to have trouble

finding clothing for her two sons when they would vacation in Canmore. When she moved to town permanently in 1999, she decided to fix that. Her sons taught her well that kids want stuff that's cool, not just practical. Glacier's Edge meets that demand with stylish, cutting edge lines from Columbia, Point Zero, Ocean Pacific and many other leading brands. Karen moved the business to its present location in 2005, allowing her to offer more merchandise and to provide customers with more room to browse. Find clothing for puddle splashers and other active kids at Glacier's Edge.

100-737 Main Street, Canmore AB
(403) 678-4779
www.glaciersedge.com

Andrews Diamonds

Diamonds may be a girl's best friend, but for Verage Shimoon, they're his passion and life's work. Verage fell in love with diamonds and fine jewelry at an early age. He was just 15 when he began a seven-year apprenticeship to learn the jewelry trade. He's been in the fine jewelry business since 1975. Verage opened Andrews Diamonds with Sylvia Andrews two years ago. He believes they are on the road to becoming the largest retailer of Canadian and non-Canadian diamonds in central Alberta. Their growth is spurred by a high degree of customer service that draws customers from all over Alberta and the surrounding provinces, even as far away as British Columbia and Saskatchewan. Whether its an individual looking for a special gift or a couple seeking the perfect engagement ring, customers enjoy one-on-one consultations with Verage to design their ideal piece. Verage prides himself on the quality of his diamonds and workmanship of each piece. The store has an exquisite variety of diamonds in all sizes and grades, which means there's something for every budget. Come to Andrews Diamonds, where Verage Shimoon turns diamonds into works of art just for you.

3B–2250-50 Avenue, Red Deer AB
(403) 346-9249

The Tin Box—Canmore

The Tin Box contains a trendy mix of home furnishings and personal accessories from around the world. You will find 3,000 non-traditional greeting cards with artsy, funny and raunchy themes. The jewellery selection ranges from casual to formal with pieces for kids and adults in prices for all budgets. The Tin Box is a good place to find a new handbag or wallet. It also offers home accent pieces in clean designs, suitable for urban settings as well as mountain lodges. The store opened in 1994. It quickly became a top Canadian retailer and was nominated for Retailer of the Year in 1999. Owners Kari and Sean Meggs have expanded the store three times in response to the popularity of the shop and their vision of creating a store reminiscent of the Kitsilano area in Vancouver. At buying shows, they keep their eyes open for purveyors of cool who can deliver the WOW factor they are looking for. Manager Kelly Tindill and her staff operate much like a family, taking an active role in shaping the store, which changes one third of its contents with each new season. In partnership with their in-laws Treasure and Dave Richardson, they opened a second location in Edmonton in 2004 they describe as "the Canmore store on steroids." Come see what's fun and new at both stores.

#3, 837 8 Street, Canmore AB
(403) 678-9666
10512 82 Avenue, Edmonton AB
(780) 436-2006

Cozy Cottage Interiors

Cozy Cottage Interiors began with a compliment or two. When guests visited owner Laura Budd's country home, they admired her impeccable taste in decorating. With a passion to help others achieve their decorating dreams, Budd opened Cozy Cottage Interiors eight years ago. This quaint shop specializes in cottage and country décor, and is overflowing with birdhouses, shabby-chic furniture, braided rugs, antiques and everything charming. Splashes of plaids and ginghams catch your eye as you stroll through the well-stocked aisles. With more than 6,000 feet of showroom space, the store provides one-stop shopping for the country-cottage enthusiast. Choose your living and dining room pieces and then move on to the garden shop where you'll find just the right accents to cozy up your patio. Personal items such as bath and body products or aromatherapy candles complete the cottage-look picture. Budd travels extensively buying the quality products her customers have come to expect. Stop by Cozy Cottage Interiors and see for yourself.

162-8228 MacLeod Trail SE, Calgary AL
(403) 238-2767

Hi Jinx Toy Shop

Hi Jinx Toy Shop is like a fairy tale, so magical that it delights both young and old. Kids feel like princes and princesses when they find that everything here is devoted to making them smile. Adults feel like kids again, because the entire place is like one big invitation to play. Ravensburger puzzles, Folkmanis puppets and a wide selection of games, including such classics as chess, cribbage and backgammon, beckon guests of the shop. Lego, Schleich and Playmobil are some of the featured lines. Owner Sonja Jovanovic, who has a background in speech pathology, emphasizes educational games and toys and is particularly committed to items appealing to special-needs children. Before owning the business, she was a regular customer who shopped at the store for things that she could use in her therapy sessions. She is proud that Hi Jinx Toy Shop is a destination stop for folks from all over who appreciate the quality of her hard-to-find merchandise. Expect reasonable prices and quick gift wrapping when you experience the magic of the Hi Jinx Toy shop.

712B Main Street, Canmore AB
(403) 678-2068

Memento's

Chocolate—mmm, good. Meander on over to Memento's, a quaint little shop located in the heart of beautiful downtown Canmore. Showcasing Belgian chocolate and MacKay's ice cream, a long-time community favorite, Memento's is adorned with local art, handcrafted collectibles and limited edition photography complimented with lovingly quilted scenes of the Canadian Rockies. Expect this great selection, plus a splash of jewelry, supple lotions and a variety of good books that can all be savoured in the shade or the sun outside when you relax on one of Memento's comfy patio settees. Memento's—gifts for all occasions.

101-822 Main Street, Canmore AB
(403) 609-3170

Cupid's Corner

Undergarments may go mostly unseen, but as every woman knows, they can completely change the way you feel about yourself. With this in mind, Yoshiko Hara and Carla Wizniak launched

Cupid's Corner six years ago. This Canmore shop specializes in intimate apparel and the kind of accessories saved for the most private moments. Life is sure to feel just a bit more interesting with a lace camisole or a pretty matching bra and panties. A satin dressing gown and some delicate slippers might even add some spice to your love life. Beyond upscale lingerie, Cupid's Corner carries romantic toys and oils along with an array of items offering sensual appeal. "Clothing shouldn't be boring," says Yoshiko, who enjoys helping people feel more confident about themselves. Carla and Yoshiko have had many years to get to know the interests of their Canmore neighbors. Carla hails from Hudson Bay, but has been a Bow Valley resident for 17 years. Yoshiko, originally from Chiba, Japan, has lived in the Bow Valley 12 years. Find something silky and sexy to put next to your skin with a visit to Cupid's Corner.

830 Main Street #105, Canmore AB
(403) 609-9979

Tumbleweedz Fashion Gallery

Laurel Garvin's Tumbleweedz Fashion Gallery delivers fashion heaven to her discerning patrons. The whimsical tumbleweed, free of spirit, inspired the name of her boutique. Tumbleweedz offers exclusive items you just won't find in department stores. Linda Lundström's La Parka concept line allows you to choose fabrics for a custom coat, which you can then accessorize with coordinating muffs and gloves. Sarah Pacini, Crea, Sandwich and Zaffiri are just some of the designer labels you'll find at this shop. Simon Chang's designs are also prominent. Clothing sizes range from four to 20 and plus size lines are available. Among the fine undergarments offered, you'll find Hanky Panky, arguably the most comfortable lace thong you'll ever wear. Cindy Crawford and Kate Hudson are just two celebrities who agree. Shoes include Anne Klein, Bandolino, Nine West and Kenneth Cole. Hats, handbags, scarves and distinctive costume jewellery ensure you'll be well dressed for any occasion. Whether you're looking for a well-put-together casual outfit or sophisticated eveningwear, Laurel's knowledgeable staff can help you select a knockout costume. A former model, Laurel wisely advises, "The fashions you wear should express your own style and spirit." Sign up for the VIP list on the website or in the shop so you won't miss out on special sales, new arrivals and fashion events. Stop in at the Tumbleweedz Fashion Gallery and browse the superb collections brought together just for you.

#2–505 1 Street W, Cochrane AB (403) 932-0781 *www.tumbleweedz.com*

Photos courtesy of Tumbleweedz Fashion Gallery

Banff Candle Company

With a broad assortment of locally made goods, Banff Candle Company carries much more than just candles. A brother and sister duo, Eagle and Vincy Ling, saw great potential in the Banff Candle Company and decided to buy the shop in 2003. The two make a point to stay on top of local and tourist demand for their products and are always expanding and diversifying the shop's product lines. Customers travel from all over to explore the huge variety of Canadian-made candles and candleholders. Besides candles, Banff Candle Company carries a selection of other fine gifts such as purses, brooches and souvenirs. Friendly staff members look forward to servicing both locals and tourists every day, and they are committed to helping their customers find that perfect gift or memento. Most of the shop's jewelry and fashionable trinkets are handcrafted by local Canadian artisans, both established and up-and-coming. At Banff Candle Company, the abundance of handmade decorative gifts and excellent selection of Canadian-made candles ensure you'll find just the thing you're looking for.

Shop C, 117 Banff Avenue, Banff AB
(403) 760-2721

Banff Original Gifts

Before you return home from your holiday, don't forget to pick up souvenirs for all your family and friends. If you're looking for a one-stop souvenir shop, Banff Original Gifts is just that. Whatever your heart desires, you are guaranteed to find it. Jackets, sweaters, and woolly socks will keep you warm long after you've left the Canadian mountains. With 200 T-shirt designs starting at only 10 dollars each, there's no excuse but to pick one up for everyone in your

family. Owner Vincy Ling moved to Canada in 2000. Five years later, she partnered with her brother Eagle to open Banff Original Gifts, one of Banff's most successful stores. The shop is filled with an enormous selection of trinkets, from thimbles to stuffed children's toys, and all at affordable prices. If you're in search of an authentic piece of Canada, the shop also carries beautiful jade and copper jewelry handcrafted by local artists. Fill your suitcase with souvenirs from Banff Original Gifts and bring a piece of Banff home to your entire family.

127 Banff Avenue, Banff AB
(403) 760-8622

Sgt. Preston's Outpost

Sgt. Preston's Outpost is the place to shop for Royal Canadian Mounted Police memorabilia and gift items. This Canadian owned store's concept is based on the popular radio and television show of the 1950s and 1960s, Sergeant Preston of the Yukon. Assisted by his trusty dog, Yukon King, Sergeant Preston always got his man. You may remember some of his famous lines, such as "On, you huskies" and "Well, King, this case is closed". The shop carries on the tradition

Photo by Tara Hunt

of the valiant Mounties with a large stock of R.C.M.P. products. Staff members are happy to relate the history of the organization. You can even have your photo taken with a Mountie mannequin. You'll find gift and souvenir items, including teddy bears, dogs, dolls and Mountie figurines, along with official pins and a selection of hats. An assortment of clothing items such as official T-shirts and sweatshirts are as popular as they are plentiful. Crests on the T-shirts are emblazoned with the Queen's crown, with six maple leaves on each side, representing Canada's 10 provinces and two territories. The motto reads, *maintiens le droit*, which translates as defending the law. A royalty is collected on items with the R.C.M.P. symbols and logos that supports R.C.M.P. community policing programs. Be sure to stop at Sgt. Preston's Outpost for a little history and a lot of fun.

Clock Tower Mall, 108 Banff Avenue, Banff AB
(403) 762-5335

The Cowboy Trail

The Cowboy Trail Tourism Association

Take a trip back to the Old West on Alberta's Cowboy Trail. The trail is a 700-kilometre stretch that extends all the way from Cardston to Mayerthorpe. Winding along the foothills of the Alberta Rocky Mountains, the Cowboy Trail meanders through a narrow band of mixed forests and grasslands and is known for its moderate climate and wide variety of wildlife. First Nations people settled the area thousands of years ago, with ranching families bringing cattle in the 1880s. The Old West lives on in the art, history, food and culture of the region. This is a road suitable for both a lazy Sunday drive and a cattle drive—and you'll see both here, along with families out riding horses. Want to saddle up and explore the region on horseback? Outfitters can get you all the gear and guides you'll need to explore this beautiful country the same way the cowboys did. The cowboy is celebrated in these parts, with a variety of cowboy-themed events, including rodeos and parades. Those looking for the real cowboy experience will delight in the chance to stay at a guest ranch or working ranch in the area. Native cultures are also celebrated here, with powwows and many other events. After all this activity, you may just be looking for a place to relax, and the Cowboy Trail leads you there too, with luxurious bed-and-breakfasts where you'll be treated like family. Bring a bit of the Old West home with you at one of the western craft and antique stores of the region. Let the Cowboy Trail Tourism Association lead you on an Old West adventure with the friendly folks of the region.

High River AB
(403) 652-7010 or (866) 627-3051
www.thecowboytrail.com

Sierra West Cabins and Ranch Vacations

There are still cowboys living the life immortalized in Western legends from bygone days. Guests at Sierra West Cabins and Ranch Vacations, a division of the Lonesome Pine cattle ranch, can experience that life for themselves while staying here. Bring your own horse or rent one and join the gang on a cattle drive or pack trip. You can do your own riding and roping, or if a beginner, the ranch hands will teach you. Nearby fresh water streams, rivers and lakes will lure the fishermen. Close proximity to historic sites, provincial parks and forest reserves allow for plenty of exploration by the adventurers. Three log cabins on the banks of Todd Creek provide the lodging. Two of the cabins are newer additions, but the third was the original homestead, built in 1905. The Sundowner and Homesteader cabins have corrals and horse shelters. Enjoy the comradeship of fellow horsemen as you saddle up and join the Sierra West Frontier Cattle Drive. You'll ride the open ranges, drive cattle and indulge in some down-home country cooking. The High Sierra Pack Trip takes you through the scenic foothills and the Livingstone Mountain Range to the Gap, where Old Man River carved a path through the mountains centuries ago. Evening campfires and cowboy poetry on the four day trip serve to blur the lines of time between now and long years past, when fur traders travelled the river. Owners Randy and Ginny Donahue invite you to participate in the life they know best. Explore scenic Southwest Alberta during your stay at Sierra West Cabins and Ranch Vacations.

Lundbreck AB
(403) 628-2431
www.sierrawest-777.com

Great Canadian Barn Dance

The Great Canadian Barn Dance (GCBD) is one of the few businesses that specifically caters to families. This family-owned, full-service resort is located near the Waterton-Glacier International Peace Park. On-site campgrounds keep you close to the entertainment, offer a view of the Rocky Mountains and provide a base from which to explore the area. Accommodation choices include the 90-site family campground, Bed & Breakfast Lodge, three bedroom cottage, teepee or full-service RV camp. There are canoes and rowboats, horseshoe pits, a sports field and playgrounds available for guests. The dinner and dances and are offered every weekend from spring to fall and during the Christmas season. They take place in a 94-year-old barn and feature the live music of the Kunkel Family Band. The dance includes a dinner of tender Alberta Triple-A beef, delicious baked beans, homemade buns, coleslaw and potatoes, plus fine baked goods for dessert. The GCBD also hosts reservation-only Western Legends Dinner Shows and several summer festivals. Lloyd Kunkel started the operation in 1985 and made the decision to make the events alcohol-free. This decision set the course for the future, making the GCBD a family destination, fun for all ages. Trevor Kunkel is currently taking over the reigns of the operation and staying true to the family traditions. Make your reservation and bring your family to join in the great food and good-time festivities at Great Canadian Barn Dance.

#1 Hill Spring, Hill Spring AB
(403) 626-3407 or (866) 626-3407
www.greatcanadianbarndance.com

Anchor D Guiding & Outfitting

Tapping your pencil on the desk, listening to the rush of traffic outside, the thought of getting out of the city and reconnecting with nature seems like a far off dream. It is easier than you might think, with a horseback riding vacation from Anchor D Guiding & Outfitting. Owners Dewy and Jan Matthews started the business 22 years ago to give visitors the opportunity to experience the stunning beauty of the Canadian Rockies from the back of a gentle steed matched to your level of expertise. You can bring a group of friends for a fun day on the trails and finish with a steak dinner back at the ranch. Longer trips, ranging from four to seven days, take you into the breathtaking high country. Teams of draft horses pulling covered wagons carry food and gear to the campsites. After a day of riding, enjoy the wholesome dinner prepared for you, kick back by the fire and then sleep in the comfort of a walled canvas tent. With a maximum of 12 guests per trip, you're ensured the personal attention you need. If roughing it is not your style, make your home base at Grandpa's Cabin, a two bedroom luxury getaway with a full kitchen and all of the comforts of home. From there, ride the trails, go for a hike or enjoy one of the many nearby recreational opportunities. A true Western adventure is waiting for you at Anchor D Guiding & Outfitting.

Highway 546, 15 km W of Turner Valley AB
(403) 933-2867
www.anchord.com

Longview Jerky Shop

While riding on the Cowboy Trail, you should always have some jerky tucked away in your saddle. Longview Jerky Shop off Highway 22 has a jerky for most any palate, from its popular original style to pioneer style, which is chewier. All the jerky is made from 100 percent Alberta beef. You can find fancy flavors such as Szechwan, Rough Neck and ginger beef, or for those who like it hot, Prairie Fire Jerky. For people who like a softer treat, jerky stix is just the ticket. There's even a chew-like jerky for old timers, available in pocket size containers. Longview offers personalized gift boxes, gourmet sauces and a variety of fresh sausage. Owners Lenard and Ann Kirk started Longview as a butcher shop 30 years ago, and since then it has gained the added distinction of a jerky lover's paradise. Len's son, Tom, to whom Len has passed all of his secrets and Tom's wife, Shannon now own the jerky shop. The third generation of Kirks are in the business, with Tom and Shannon's four children lending a hand and making the delicious snacks. The Kirks are proud of their jerky, a nutritional snack packed with protein that's always vacuum-sealed for freshness, making it the perfect snack for traveling. In fact, climbers took strips of Longview jerky up Mt. Everest with them on two separate climbs. Longview jerky was also featured in the Winter 2005 edition of *Motorcycle Escape* and won the Reader's Choice Awards for Best Kept Secret of the Foothills. Whether you're planning to climb a mountain or just surf the Internet, Longview Jerky Shop is a great place to stock up on your favorite hearty snack.

148 Morrison Road, Longview AB
(403) 558-3960
www.longviewjerkyshop.com

Iris Sikina RE/MAX West Real Estate

Thinking of buying a piece of property or selling your home? Call Iris Sikina, a top-notch realtor at RE/MAX West Real Estate. With over 12 years of experience, Iris does urban and rural homes, land, commercial, retail, business or development property. Services include virtual tours, specialty marketing pieces and top placement in the market with advertising and her website. Iris is committed to putting her experience to work for you. She is a member of the RE/MAX Platinum Club, RE/MAX Hall Of Fame member and a repeat recipient of the prestigious MLS Million Dollar Club. Iris is passionate about keeping up with the current market trends. View all listings on her website. The City of Cochrane is a bustling heritage town nestled in the foothills of the Rocky Mountains and just 10 minutes from Calgary, giving you a small town lifestyle with the resources of the city. Historic Main Street and the surrounding community offer a mix of residential, commercial and industrial interests and serve a population base of over 20,000, with projections of future growth to 50,000 in the next 10 years. With solid school systems and recreational opportunities, Cochrane is a great place to raise a family. From festivals, farmers markets and walking paths along the Bow River, Jumping Pound and Big Hill Creek, to hang gliding, fishing and golfing, there is always something to do. Less than an hour west of town enjoy skiing, camping and cultural events. Nearby Calgary provides an international airport, theatre, the Calgary Stampede, hockey, mega shopping and more. Iris Sikina can help you sell your home or relocate to centre of it all in the prettiest valley in Big Hill Country.

120 5 Avenue W, Cochrane AB
(403) 390-SOLD (7653)
www.isellcochrane.com

Lone Pine Ranch

Judging by Sylvia Martinetz' guest book, the dream
of living on a ranch must have worldwide appeal.
She has hosted folks from as far away as Europe,
China and Australia at her Lone Pine Ranch Bed &
Breakfast & Bale. Sylvia invites everyone to take part
in chores and activities on the 139-acre spread, or to
relax and enjoy the peace and quiet. There is always
something that needs to be done, if you choose join in,
because the ranch is home to cows, sheep and lambs,
plus a few horses, donkeys and llamas—more than 50
animals in all, counting dogs and cats. Large enough
to accommodate a family, each of the six poplar log
cabins on the property features two queen beds, a
hide-a-bed couch, sitting area and private bath. The
cabins do not come with television or telephone, but
there is a beaver pond right outside that often puts on
a better show than any cable channel. Other wildlife
that thrives on the ranch and at nearby Chip Lake
includes deer, elk and a variety of waterfowl. Even
bear and cougar are occasionally spotted. Sylvia gets
guests ready for the day with a hearty and plentiful
breakfast. Horses are welcome on the ranch, hence
her claim that she offers bale in addition to breakfast.
Sylvia maintains ties to her native Germany by
hosting an exchange program with German kids
at the ranch. Come from your corner of the world
to experience the good life at Lone Pine Ranch.

102 Range Road, Wildwood AB
(780) 325-3817
www.lonepineranch.ca

Trail Riders of the Canadian Rockies

The Trail Riders of the Canadian Rockies (TRCR) is a non-profit club that has been organizing horseback trail rides in the Canadian Rockies since 1923. The club is unique in that each summer it switches riding areas to explore different valleys and high mountain passes during 10 six-day rides from a back-country base camp. Horses, tack, meals and accommodations are all provided. In the beginning, outfitter Walter Nixon led a group of travellers through the Canadian Rockies. It was an experience that inspired all members of the party, including Reginald Townsend, editor of *Country Life in America*, H.B. Clow, president of the Rand McNally map makers, R.H. Palenske, Chicago artist, Dr. J. Murray Gibbon, publicity agent of the Canadian Pacific Railway (CPR), and Byron Harmon, official photographer of the Alpine Club of Canada. These men, who wanted to share these incredible vistas and experiences with others, had an influential hand in the subsequent development of the Order of the Trail Riders of the Canadian Rockies, with the CPR serving as the sponsor 'till 1961. The first official ride implemented the Teepee Town back-country accommodations and Trip Recognition Achievement pins that have become two of the group's many traditions. Palenske created the pin designs. In 1929, Townsend gave the club a beautiful large silver trophy on which has been inscribed the names of the winners of the annual amateur photography contest for pictures taken on the ride. The first teepees were painted by Chief Walking-in-the-Road and two assistants from the Stoney band. Current paintings on the teepees stay true to their traditional roots. Since 1961, TRCR has been operating as a non-profit association run by a volunteer executive. TRCR is an open-membership club for novice to experienced riders ages eight to 80. Join a tradition that has endured for more than 80 years when you ride with the Trail Riders of the Canadian Rockies.

Calgary AB *www.trail-rides.ca*

Homeplace Ranch

Mac McKenny and his family know what it means to live close to nature. At Homeplace Ranch, Mac, his wife, Jayne and young daughter Jessica share their simple ranch life with up to 14 guests at a time. The ranch is open during the working season, from April to October, for stays ranging from four days to two weeks. During the winter, families sometimes rent the lodge as a private retreat. A typical day at the ranch begins with a hearty breakfast featuring home-baked breads. Then the wranglers will match you up with one of 42 horses. Soon you'll be saddling up your own horse and helping to fence and feed the livestock. You might choose to go fishing or on an all-day guided ride into 7,000 acres of valleys, streams and foothills. Some

guests choose to golf or raft for a day and return to the ranch at night. A satisfying supper completes your day. You'll enjoy a private room and bath and the easygoing charms of the lodge, its owners and hands. Mac grew up in the outfitting business and purchased Homeplace in 1978. His dedicated wrangler, Brad, has been trail boss for 14 years. Dive into the ranch life of southern Alberta with a visit to Homeplace Ranch.

Site 2, Box 6, RR#1, Priddis AB
(403) 931-3245 or (877) 921-3245
www.homeplaceranch.com

Bragg Creek Trading Post

Owners Robb and Barbara Teghtmeyer and their sons, Jonn and Karl, operate the Bragg Creek Trading Post, a family business for 75 years. Approaching the entrance, you may see deer ambling on the grounds, smell the fragrance of native pines or season permitting, view freshly fallen snow. The chilly traveler is greeted with the welcoming blaze of a 1920s wood-burning stove, amidst the lively conversation of locals and the earthy fragrance of freshly tanned hides. You'll soon be at ease in the camaraderie, while gaining an insider's view into the tradition and history of the area. Next to the post is the famed Stoney Trail, which winds through the foothills in a north-to-south route used by local tribespeople for centuries. During the early 1930s, the

trading post established a trading relationship with these Native American travelers which continues today, with native artisans trading artwork and crafts at the post. You'll find beautifully crafted leather moccasins, mukluks and many one-of-a-kind beaded items. The Teghtmeyers also offer just-picked local tomatoes and succulent bison t-bones for your dinner menu. In fact, you could say it is a truly distinct shopping experience for everything you need in the smallest possible space. The Teghtmeyer family invites you and your family to visit their spectacular corner of Alberta.

117 White Avenue, Bragg Creek AB
(403) 949-3737